The War in the Air
Volume 2

The War in the Air
Volume 2
A History of the RFC & RNAS During the Dardanelles Campaign, the Battles of Loos & the Somme, and Home Waters 1915-16

H. A. Jones

The War in the Air
Volume 2
A History of the RFC & RNAS During the Dardanelles Campaign, the Battles of Loos & the Somme, and Home Waters 1915-16
by H. A. Jones

First published under the title
The War in the Air Volume 2

Leonaur is an imprint of Oakpast Ltd
Copyright in this form © 2018 Oakpast Ltd

ISBN: 978-1-78282-716-0 (hardcover)
ISBN: 978-1-78282-717-7 (softcover)

http://www.leonaur.com

Publisher's Notes

The views expressed in this book are not necessarily those of the publisher.

Contents

Preface	7
The Dardanelles Campaign	9
The Western Front to the Battle of Loos	78
The Months Before the Somme Struggle	141
The Battles of the Somme, 1916	191
The Battles of the Somme, 1916 (continued)	254
The Royal Naval Air Service in Home Waters (1915)	312
The Royal Naval Air Service in Home Waters (1916)	350
Appendix 1	414
Appendix 2	416
Appendix 3	418
Appendix 4	420
Appendix 5	423
Appendix 6	424
Appendix 7	429
Appendix 8	439
Appendix 9	441

Preface

This second volume of the History of the part played in the war by the British air forces tells the air story of the Dardanelles Campaign, of the Western Front from the winter of 1914-15 to the end of the Somme Battles in November 1916, and of the naval operations in Home Waters down to the end of 1916. It includes, also, the naval air operations from Dunkirk in 1915 and 1916 and the bombing operations from Luxeuil in the latter part of 1916.

Sir Walter Raleigh, after he had finished correcting the proofs of the first volume, set out on a flying tour of the Middle East. At Mosul he fell sick of a fever and came home to die. The late Dr. D. G. Hogarth was appointed to the task of carrying on the history, but he was compelled, through ill-health and pressure of other work, to give it up.

In planning this volume, the present author has kept in mind the general ideas which prompted Sir Walter Raleigh when he wrote Volume 1. The air story has been superimposed on a framework of the naval and military operations. These operations are, of necessity, strictly summarized, and only such of them as affect the air story are included.

Under the hard hammer of war, the air services expanded rapidly. The causes and ideas which influenced the direction of that expansion are no less important than the operations themselves. The reader will find, therefore, a general narrative of development running through the history.

The work of the air services was, in an unusual degree, individualistic. To give a representative picture of that work, incidents chosen from the varied activities that grew up are quoted. Many other incidents, no less striking or courageous, have been omitted. The statement in the preface to the first volume must be repeated, that the heroes of this story are only samples. Officers who took part in the events described in the text are given the rank they held at the time.

Where they are referred to more generally they are given the rank they held when the book was written.

In the preparation of the volume the author has been enormously helped by the staff of the Air Historical Branch to whom he pays willing tribute. Particularly must he mention Mr. J. C. Nerney. To all those officers who have talked to him of the events in which they played a part he is deeply grateful. Their help has added colour and accuracy to the narrative. He is indebted, also, to Professor D. Nichol Smith who kindly read the proofs and made many suggestions, and to the Director of the German *Reichsarchiv*, Potsdam, for willing answers to numerous questions. The published books on the war which have been used are acknowledged in the text. The author would mention two others which he has occasionally consulted: *A History of the Great War*, by Colonel John Buchan, and *Battlefields of the World War*, by Douglas W. Johnson.

The author must make one final acknowledgement. He was privileged to work in close touch with Sir Walter Raleigh on the first volume. To be with him was an education. Those who knew Sir Walter best may find many traces of his influence throughout this book.

H. A. Jones.

Abbreviations

A.M. = Air Mechanic	Fr. = French
B. = Battleship	Ger. = German
B.Cr. = Battle Cruiser	L.Cr. = Light Cruiser
Br. = British	Ldg. Mech. = Leading Mechanic
Cmdre. = Commodore	Mon. = Monitor
Comnr. = Commander	P.O. = Petty Officer
C.P.O. = Chief Petty Officer	Sqdn. = Squadron
Cr. = Cruiser	S/M. = Submarine
Flt. = Flight	T.B.D. = Destroyer

W/T. = Wireless Telegraphy

CHAPTER 1

The Dardanelles Campaign

From ten thousand feet above Achi Baba, in the clear light of an Eastern morning, an observer may look down and see, spread below him, the whole savage Gallipoli Peninsula. Savage, because to the eye which can read the ground from the air the shadow-pattern beneath reveals deep scrub-covered ravines and rugged broken hills, and the lack of road and hamlet tells of the inhospitable nature of the country.

But from high above the harshness appears softened. The peninsula lies outstretched in the setting of a jewelled sea. To the far northeast, some thirty miles away, the ancient and once flourishing town of Gallipoli slopes, a compact cluster of houses, to the sea. A few miles beyond, the land narrows to the Isthmus fortified in 1854 by British and French engineers with earthworks still standing as the Bulair lines. That part of the coast which lies along the Gulf of Xeros from the Isthmus to Cape Suvla is revealed, from the deep shadow cast by the morning sun along the sea, as a line of cliffs offering little or no chance of a foothold to an invader, but about Suvla, and southwards to Gaba Tepe, the heights are broken by flat stretches of beach.

The barrier begins again at Gaba Tepe and continues to Cape Helles, with slight occasional breaks. Here and there a narrow strip of sand fringes the base of a cliff but, in the main, except in the neighbourhood of Cape Helles itself, the coast would appear to be unclimbable by infantry. The dominating features in the southern part of the peninsula are the hill-mass of Sari Bair, with its culminating peak nearly 1,000 feet above the level of the sea; the Kilid Bahr plateau, 700 feet high; and Achi Baba, a bare, lonely lump, 600 feet high, commanding the extreme south of the peninsula, near Cape Helles. Each of these main features rises above a stretch of difficult country with a confusion of *nullahs* which will require many hours of study from the

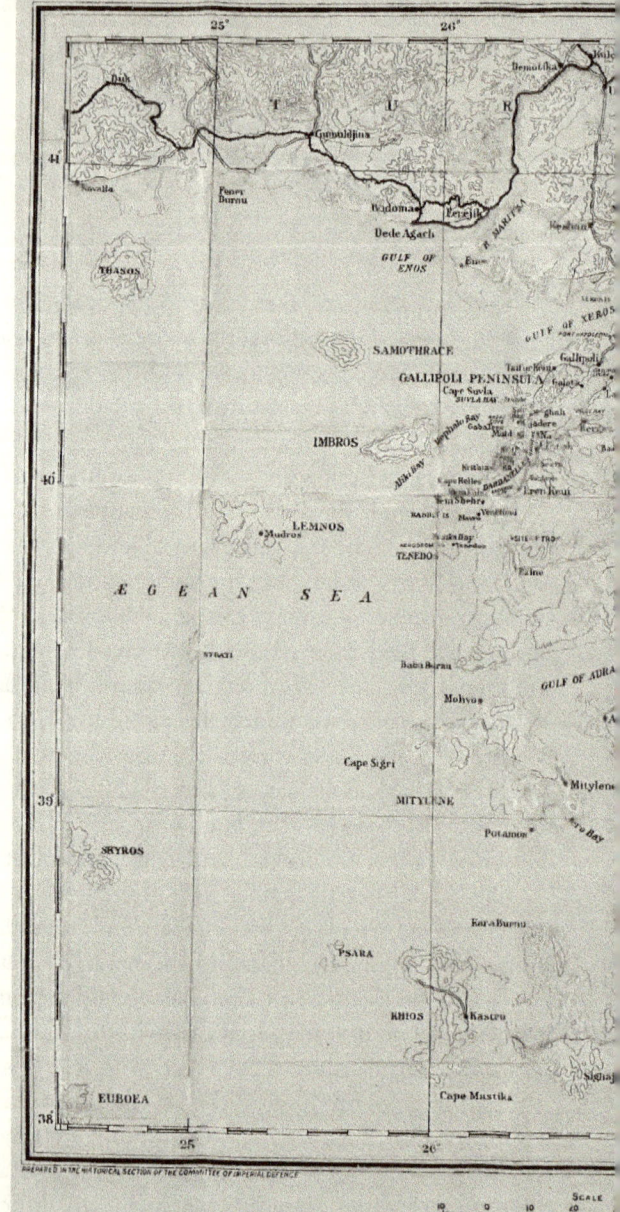

OPERATIONS IN
EGEAN.
15.

air before any human being may come above them with a pretence at picking out one gully from another. The ground leading to these heights is of the most difficult type which any infantry may fight over. The heights themselves, skilfully defended, may hold off the most stubborn and repeated efforts to take them. So much is obvious to the trained eye above.

The straits of the Dardanelles, the former Hellespont, bridged by Xerxes and Alexander, stretch for forty-seven miles in a north-easterly direction. On the Asiatic side of this great strategic highway the land shows up a fresher green, watered by many streams which lose themselves like tortuous silver ribbons in the mists of the mountainous distance. At the entrance to the straits the country on the Asiatic side is low, but rises gradually, through a broad undulating plain, to the village of Eren Keui, about 600 feet above the level of the sea. North-east of Eren Keui high ground approaches the coast, but beyond Kephez as far as Chanak there is a flat belt broken only by the western spur of Bairak Tepe mountain. From Chanak the ground rises slightly to a plateau which stretches to Nagara. Much of the country along the whole Asiatic coast is wooded and offers good concealment for artillery.

If the observer in the air were studying the peninsula from the only maps which the Allied forces possessed in the early days of the campaign, he would soon be aware that, although the main features might be correctly shown, the multitudinous folds in the ground, and the rivers too, were given at best approximately, and often incorrectly. Some important features were omitted altogether. For example, the vast Gully Ravine, fifty to a hundred yards wide and extending some three miles, with precipitous banks a hundred feet high, was not even indicated. And this ravine was to prove one of the vital tactical features in the campaign. The complete unreliability of the maps was, for long, a serious handicap to the airmen who were called upon to reconnoitre and to report the effect of the fire.

Far south, on the Asiatic side, is seen the coast of Mitylene; some fifteen miles from Cape Helles the island of Tenedos lies in the sparkling sea; out to the west, still nearer, is Imbros; further west, and bearing slightly south, is the blurred outline of Lemnos; north-west, faintly pencilled, far beyond the coast of Imbros, stands snow-capped Samothrace. These are the islands from which the bases for a campaign might be chosen.

In the year 1906 the British General Staff had reviewed the problem of the taking of the Gallipoli Peninsula by combined naval and military action. After careful deliberation they were not prepared to recommend the attempt. They said:

> The successful conclusion of a military operation against the Gallipoli Peninsula must hinge upon the ability of the fleet, not only to dominate the Turkish defences with gunfire, and to crush their field troops during that period of helplessness which exists while an army is in actual process of disembarkation, but also to cover the advance of troops once ashore, until they could gain a firm foothold, and establish themselves upon the high ground in rear of the coast defences of the Dardanelles.

They went on to express a doubt whether the co-operating fleet would be able to give this absolute guarantee. The Director of Naval Intelligence, recognising the great risks involved, was in general agreement with this view, but thought the army had underrated the value of the assistance which the fleet might give. The General Staff further stated that:

> Military opinion, looking at the question from the point of view of coast defence, will be in entire agreement with the naval view that unaided action by the Fleet, bearing in mind the risks involved, is much to be deprecated.

So was the problem left, and these memoranda of the experts gathered the dust. (Sir Ian Hamilton did not know of their existence until he returned to England at the end of the campaign.)

On the 2nd of August 1914, before Great Britain and Germany were yet at war, a formal treaty between the German and Turkish Governments was drafted and signed in Constantinople. (*Deutsche Dokumente zum Kriegsausbruch*, No, 733). The Turkish signatories, including Enver Pasha, Minister for War, and Talaat Bey, Minister of the Interior, undertook to do all they could to bring the Ottoman Empire into line with the Central Powers. The first sign of the influence of the pro-German Turks came on the 10th of August, when the German cruisers, *Goeben* and *Breslau*, were allowed to pass, unhindered, up the straits to Constantinople where they were purchased, on paper, by the Ottoman Government. In reply to Allied protests, the Turkish Government gave assurances that the German crews would be sent back to their country and replaced by Turkish personnel, but, in fact, the German crews were reinforced. Other acts of unfriendliness followed.

It was not long before the British naval mission was relieved of executive power; on the 1st of October the Capitulations, by which foreigners were granted immunity from the civil or criminal jurisdiction of the Turkish state, were abolished; about the same time the Turks began to assemble large forces in Palestine, whence they threatened the Suez Canal and Egypt; and there was a continuous propaganda in the Turkish press directed against Great Britain. Consequently, a British fleet was kept at Tenedos, where it was on the 27th of October when the Turkish fleet steamed into the Black Sea to attack Russia. Two days later the Turkish warships were bombarding Russian ports. On the 30th an Allied ultimatum was presented at Constantinople, and the diplomats were collecting their passports. Next day the British Government issued orders for hostilities against Turkey to begin.

On the 3rd of November the fleet from Tenedos bombarded the outer forts of the Dardanelles for ten minutes, partly as a demonstration, and partly to test the effective range of the Turkish guns. This action, which, according to General Djevad Pasha, the Turkish commander, caused more damage than any subsequent naval bombardment, was, it must be confessed, unfortunate, since, by directing the Turkish mind in the first flush of war to the peninsula, it prejudiced the chances of any future serious attempt to force the straits. The fleet, after their ten-minute interlude, drew off, but the Turk sat back alert, quietly took stock of his position, and accelerated his previously considered defensive programme. General Djevad Pasha says:

> The bombardment of November, 1914 warned me, and I spent the rest of my time developing the defences.'

At a meeting of the War Council on November the 25th 1914, Mr. Winston Churchill, the First Lord of the Admiralty, gave his view that the best way to defend Egypt was to attack some part of Turkey's Asiatic coast, and, as an extension of the idea, he suggested an attack on the Gallipoli Peninsula. He seemed not to underrate the difficulty or magnitude of the task. Lord Kitchener, the Secretary of State for War, who was thinking in terms of a 'diversion on the Turkish communications', did not consider the moment for action had arrived. Although the matter was not pressed to any conclusion, the Admiralty, as opportunity offered, sent transport to Alexandria:

> In case the War Office should, at a later stage, wish to undertake a joint naval and military operation in the Eastern Mediterranean.

A telegram from Russia brought the question to a head. This came from the British Ambassador, Sir George Buchanan, on the 2nd of January 1915, and after stating that the Russians were being pressed in the Caucasus, expressed a hope on behalf of the Russian Government that, to relieve this pressure, a demonstration against the Turks might be made in some other quarter. On the following day the War Office drafted a reply, which was sent through the Foreign Office, that a demonstration would be made. This reply did not define the time or place.

Lord Kitchener, when he read the Russian telegram, sat down and wrote to Mr. Churchill, saying that:

> The only place that a demonstration might have some effect in stopping reinforcements going East would be the Dardanelles.

He went on to point out that the army had no troops to land anywhere, and that they 'would not be ready for anything big for some months'.

That the Admiralty were thinking of something stronger than a demonstration, is to be seen from the telegram sent by the First Lord on the 3rd of January to Vice-Admiral S. H. Carden, commanding the Eastern Mediterranean Squadron, who would be in charge of whatever operations were decided upon. 'Do you consider', he asked, 'the forcing of the Dardanelles by ships alone, a practical operation?' He added that the importance of the results would justify severe losses.

On the 5th the eagerly awaited reply came back:

> I do not consider the Dardanelles can be rushed. They might be forced by extended operations, with a large number of ships.

The admiral in a telegram on the 11th showed that, by extended operations, he had in mind a systematic progressive destruction of the forts, the fleet feeling its way, as it were, step by step through to the Narrows and the sea of Marmara. The time required was estimated at about one month. On the 13th of January, following a long discussion by the War Council, the Government decided that:

> The Admiralty should prepare for a naval expedition in February to bombard and take the Gallipoli Peninsula, with Constantinople as its objective.

The die was cast for an unaided naval attack. What were the new factors in 1915 which were not present in 1906 when the experts had pronounced against the attempt? One of the chief was the new air weapon. The effectiveness of naval bombardment, it was held by some, was enormously increased by this new power of observation, especially by indirect laying. Naval ordnance, too, had greatly developed since 1906. What modern artillery could do against permanent works had been well illustrated at Liege and Namur where supposedly impregnable fortresses collapsed after a few days' attack.

The development of naval power had culminated in the production of the *Queen Elizabeth* which could fire fifteen-inch shells of tremendous destructive force. This battleship was to be used against the straits defences and would, it was expected, revolutionize all previous ideas of the effect of naval bombardment. Another weapon, the submarine, could now be expected to get through to the sea of Marmara and play havoc with the Turkish communications. Since 1906, too, there had been wars in the Balkans which had seriously damaged the military prestige of Turkey.

It may be said at once that some of these new factors were overrated. The event was to prove that the reorganised Turkish army could defend with a tenacity second only to the incomparable spirit with which the attackers went to their more formidable task. But perhaps most serious of all was the lack of appreciation of the differences between field attacks on fortresses and naval bombardment. The easy disasters to the Belgian fortresses had, indeed, come with a shock of surprise, but these works were overwhelmed by howitzer fire, that is to say, by heavy projectiles with a steep angle of descent which dropped from the blue in the vulnerable heart of the forts.

They were fired, further, from a fixed platform, air observers were able to report the general fire effect, and infantry were at once at hand to attack when the forts were silenced. Although the gun is a more accurate weapon, and has greater penetrative powers than the howitzer, guns, as mounted on board ship, cannot be given elevation sufficient for high-angle fire comparable with that of the howitzers. In a word, shells from guns knock at the front door, which may be made indefinitely thick, whereas howitzer shells come in at the roof.

It was not, however, the permanent forts which mattered most; they could, at least, be pounded into silence. It was the concealed forts and the mobile batteries, many of which were placed on the dead slopes of the ravines. Within range of the naval guns but often out of their reach, they were able to bring a deadly fire to bear, not only in protection of the mine-fields, but, later in the campaign, against the attacking infantry.

Yet it has been conceded by the Turkish General Staff that the Dardanelles might have been taken at the outset of hostilities by naval action alone on a larger scale than was eventually tried; that they might have been taken, but at greater cost, when the naval attack was made, had the Allies been prepared to go on after the 18th of March in the determined expectation of sacrificing many more vessels as the price of the prize; or, lastly, that they would have fallen, had the combined military and naval attempt been made with a military force at least one and a half times as great as that used for the first landings. (*A Short History of Turkish Operations in the World War*, vol. i., by the Historical Section, Turkish General Staff).

But when Turkey came into the war a hundred anxieties were pressing on the directing minds at home, and no matter how dazzling the Gallipoli adventure might appear, it could not be allowed to blind the eyes to the vital facts that the line in France must be held and that the German fleet must be contained. There had, as yet, been a bare three months in which to organise and develop our resources.

At the Dardanelles, naval strength was to be largely spent before military strength was spared. Military strength itself was developed in stages, and again was to be largely spent before the air service was in a position to give adequate support. Conquest of the straits offered brilliant, possibly decisive, results. In January 1915 the navy alone had the resources to make the effort. The naval commander on the spot had given his opinion that the straits might be taken by a series of progressive attacks. To those at home his plan seemed to offer the minimum of risk and had the further advantage that, if necessary, the action might be broken off at any time.

THE NAVAL ATTACKS.

The British fleet for the attack, consisting chiefly of older classes of battleships, was drawn from all parts of the world. Admiral Carden was anxious not to begin until the whole force was assembled, but political and other considerations were pressing, and on February the 19th the bombardment was opened by the British and French ships. Other vessels were already on their way to join the attacking fleet. They were coming from home waters, from the Suez Canal, from the south-east coast of America, the East Indies, and from off the Tagus. On March the 12th the cruiser *Askold* arrived to represent the Imperial Russian Navy.

One tiny unit of this vast array was something new in the history of naval bombardment. For the first time a seaplane carrier took up her position with a fleet which had set out to conquer a hostile coast. The *Ark Royal*, which bore the name of the flagship that sailed out to challenge the Spanish Armada, was the first vessel to be fitted out exclusively as a seaplane carrier for fleet service. It is an old point of naval teaching that England's frontiers are the enemy's coasts, so that when aircraft came to add to the navy's weapons, attention was naturally directed to the question of taking the aircraft with the fleet to what might be almost any part of the world. Few of the many naval developments of recent years have given rise to more novel and delicate problems. The technical difficulties often appeared beyond solution, but time and again naval pilots offered themselves for flying experiments when nothing but experiments, often involving great risks, would tell the designers and constructors what they wished to know.

So far back as 1911, a Short biplane had been flown off a specially built trackway on the forecastle of H.M.S. *Africa*, moored to a buoy in Sheerness Harbour. Two other aeroplane flights off the forecastles of ships steaming up to twelve knots were made in 1912, and during 1913 many flights with an eighty horse-power Caudron seaplane were made from a trackway built on the forecastle of the old cruiser *Hermes*. These experiments promised success, but little progress followed for the reason that the length of platform which was necessary was so great as to interfere with the ship's guns. It may be seen at once that naval flying opinion would in those days favour seaplanes because of their power to rise from or alight on the surface of the water, and the Admiralty took up the question of a special seaplane carrier.

Towards the end of 1913 there was, in frame, in the shipbuilding yard of the Blyth Company, a suitable tramp steamer. The vessel had a length of some three hundred and fifty-two feet, an extreme breadth of fifty feet, and a mean draught of eighteen feet; her speed was given as eleven knots, and displacement as 7,450 tons. The Admiralty decided to convert this tramp into a carrier. She had to be entirely redesigned. The machinery was placed right aft and the bridge as far aft as possible. To provide for the possible use of aeroplanes, the sheer of the vessel was cut down to give a straight flying-off deck 130 feet long. The hold was made into a single hangar, 150 feet long, 45 feet wide, and 15 feet high, capable of accommodating ten seaplanes. Steam cranes were installed for hoisting.

There were large workshops equipped for the testing and repairing of engines and machines. The *Ark Royal,* a wonder ship in her day, was launched in September 1914, was rapidly completed, and was commissioned for service by Commander R. H. Clark-Hall on December the 9th. On the 13th of January 1915, the day of the Government decision that the navy prepare for an attack on the Dardanelles, she was at Harwich, and orders were at once given that she be ready to put to sea at the end of the month. On Monday, the 1st of February, at midnight, she slipped from her buoy and picked her way out of Sheerness Harbour, on her first adventure. She proved very steady despite heavy gales in the Channel and the Bay of Biscay and arrived at Tenedos on the 17th of February, two days before the opening of the bombardment.

Unfortunately, the aircraft that came out of the *Ark Royal* were, with one exception, sadly inefficient for the work they would be called upon to do. They were one Short and two Wight two-seater seaplanes, each fitted with a 200 horse-power Canton Unné engine; three Sopwith two-seater seaplanes fitted with 100 horse-power Monosoupape engines; and two Sopwith Tabloid single-seater aeroplanes fitted with eighty horse-power Gnome engines. The exception was the Short. Of the others, the Sopwith and Wight seaplanes were found to be most difficult or even impossible to get off the choppy sea, whipped up on most days by the prevailing westerly winds of early spring. When the sea was quiet, there was often a flat calm which made it, perhaps, even more difficult to get the machines off the water.

Furthermore, none of the seaplanes could go high enough for efficient spotting even if the engines were developing their full power. If the engines were running badly—and, partly because they had always to be run full out, they were often running badly—the seaplanes were subjected to undue risk of damage from gun and rifle fire from the ground. So that in good weather the fleet had only six machines for its all work, and in bad weather, one. On the 5th of March, when a Sopwith seaplane crashed, the six fair-weather machines were reduced to five. The two aeroplanes could not be used at first, as on the whole island of Tenedos there was no ground that could be cleared to form an aerodrome without considerable expenditure of time and labour.

Even had the seaplanes possessed all the virtues of their kind, they would still have suffered one drawback. They were to be used for flying over the land on reconnaissance and spotting work, whereas they could only safely alight, in the event of a forced descent, on the sea. And since the engines of *Ark Royal's* seaplanes were unreliable, the pilot had often to fly with one eye on the water, keeping within gliding distance, unless the object of his flight was of the importance to justify the fullest risk of his craft.

In view of the disadvantages under which the carrier worked, her achievement was a remarkable one. The low 'ceiling' of the seaplanes, although dangerous, did not militate against detailed reconnaissance. An Admiralty letter of the 15th of February, referring to the outer defences which had been bombarded in November, said:

> It is possible none of these defences may have been reduced, and also that the defences have been supplemented by concealed batteries and howitzers. To discover these, thorough aerial reconnaissances should be carried out before commencing operations.

The *Ark Royal* got to work at once on the day of her arrival, and it was well she did, since that day was one of the only three until the end of the month on which flying was possible. The other days were the 19th and 26th of February.

Four flights were attempted on the 17th, but three failed, two through engine trouble, and one because the seaplane refused to leave the slight sea. The successful flight was made on one of the Wights by Flight Lieutenant G. R. Bromet and Flight Commander H. A. Williamson, who left at 5.30 p.m. in dull weather, and, from about 4,000 feet, examined the forts of the outer defences and searched for batteries along the coast for three or four miles up the straits. They were back at 6.45 with seven bullet holes in their seaplane, and a report which confirmed the information about the entrance forts that the vice-admiral already possessed, and showed, in addition, that many new trenches had been dug round Cape Tekke on the peninsula, and south and inland of Orkanie (Fort 4) on the Asiatic coast. A twenty-pound bomb which was dropped from the seaplane on Kum Kale hit the wall of one of the forts.

The morning of the 19th of February saw the sun come up over the heights of Asia, and flood with its brilliance the quiet sea and the sleeping hills. At half-past seven *Ark Royal* weighed and steamed to the tiny island of Mavro, south of which she anchored at ten minutes past nine. Before she left Tenedos, she had hoisted out the Short for Flight Commander C. F. Kilner and Sub-Lieutenant W. Park to reconnoitre the coast from Besika Bay, eight miles south of the entrance, to Gaba Tepe, twelve miles north of it. The officers were back at Mavro with their report at 9.15 a.m., which told the admiral the exact position of the barracks and fort at Helles (No. 1), and that the guns at Cape Tekke could not fire northward of north-west, and so would be unable to disturb the *Triumph* in the position from which she was to attack the Helles fort.

Owing to ground mist, observation was not good, but, after careful searching, the officers reported they could find no batteries near Yeni Keui nor between Cape Tekke and Gaba Tepe. At 11.2 a.m. Williamson and Bromet, on a Wight, left to spot on to Orkanie for *Cornwallis*, which had fired the first shot of the day at 9.51 a.m. Visibility from the air was now perfect and the guns in the fort could be seen in clear detail. Nothing, it seemed, could save them from rapid destruction. The seaplane's wireless tapped out the signal to begin. Not a shot was fired. For an hour the pilot flew backwards and forwards between the ship and the target, but *Cornwallis* remained silent. The reason was a defective capstan which prevented her from complying with an order of the admiral who, to improve the shooting, had instructed the bombarding ships to anchor. She therefore gave place to *Vengeance*.

There is little question that had *Cornwallis* been in action for the full time that the seaplane was able to stay up to observe for her, the guns in Orkanie must have suffered considerable damage. Meanwhile the officers in the seaplane, unaware of the reason for the lack of response to their signals but realising that further attempts to co-operate with *Cornwallis* were useless, flew over the various forts to make an examination of the damage done by the morning's bombardment. Their report showed that the guns were still intact in Orkanie, Kum Kale (No. 6), and Sedd el Bahr (No. 3).

The admiral, however, well satisfied with the better shooting after the ships had anchored, decided that the long-range bombardment had been effective enough for the fleet to close, and at 2.0 p.m. he made the signal for the second stage of the operation to begin. This stage was to be an overwhelming of the forts by a close bombardment, and a sweeping of the channel towards the entrance of the straits.

A curious inactivity in the afternoon led to the belief that the outer forts had been silenced, but that the position was still pretty much as Williamson and Bromet had reported at midday was apparent at 4.40 p.m., when the *Suffren* was near enough to Orkanie to see that the armament was intact. She was about to pound the fort when she misread a signal from Vice-Admiral Carden and began to haul off. Almost at the same time *Vengeance*, which had been ordered to 'cease fire and examine forts', came suddenly under stinging attack from both Helles and Orkanie as she was steaming at good speed for the centre of the entrance. The forts, indeed, gave the best possible proof that they were little the worse for the bombardment.

In the meantime, two seaplanes were over Helles trying to spot *Inflexible* on to the fort, but were both having trouble with their wireless. On one the aerial was jammed beyond yielding, in the other the wireless set had short-circuited. But so many ships were firing at the same target that spotting would have been impossible. The guns of No. 1 Fort were reported to be intact about thirty yards from the cliff's edge, but nothing could be seen of what had happened at Sedd el Bahr or Kum Kale, since at the time when the seaplanes were over these forts the guns were shrouded in smoke.

At 5.30 p.m. the bombarding fleet withdrew. At 7.5 p.m. *Ark Royal* hoisted in her seaplanes and returned to her anchorage south of Tenedos. That one day had been enough to show that to put a gun out of action a direct hit on the gun itself or on its mounting, or else the blowing up of its magazine, was necessary, and the seaplanes had given little promise that they could do their part in directing the ships' guns on to the vital part of their target.

A word of explanation is due here on the subject of air spotting for the ships and of the early wireless sets with which the seaplanes were equipped. Before the war naval aircraft wireless had been developed chiefly to provide a rapid means for communicating information which might be gained by patrolling air-observers. Its possible use for the control of ships' gun-fire had excited little interest in the navy. Consequently, at the beginning of the Dardanelles Campaign the ships were without previous experience of air fire-control or of signalling to aircraft by searchlight.

Nor was there yet any agreed code. The receiving sets in the ships had, for the most part, to be improvised, some of them being made by the telegraphist ratings. The *Ark Royal* took out two Sterling sets, but no officer expert in aircraft wireless. The Sterling set, at that early time, was hardly out of its experimental stage, and, in fact, had been served out to the seaplanes before it had been put into war service in France.

******

The Sterling set was first made by the Sterling Telephone Company from the designs and rough model set got out, in October 1914, by Lieutenant B. Binyon, R.N.V.R., a Naval Air Service wireless officer at Eastchurch.

✶✶✶✶✶✶

The event was to show that the installation was too lightly made, that the accumulators were unsatisfactory, and that their capacity gave little or no margin unless the cells were in fairly good condition and well charged. No facilities existed for testing the state of charging, so that machines often went up with the cells only partially charged. The absence, too, of expert technical staff prevented a proper examination of the wireless apparatus before each flight, a defect which was accentuated when the sets had been transferred from one seaplane to another.

The weather, which had been so brilliant on the opening day of the bombardment, broke during the night, and for five days no operations were possible. But on the 25th the bombardment, in which *Queen Elizabeth* and *Agamemnon* took part, met with more success. The experience of the opening day had shown that it was essential for the ships to be at anchor. The long-range bombardment from the anchored battleships on the 25th put the only four long-range Turkish guns out of action. The short-range forts suffered less, but they were abandoned probably because they were now looked upon as death-traps by their defenders. The Turks still fired away with howitzers concealed in the hills; they even tried a few sporting but harmless shots at *Ark Royal*, which had, unhappily, not been able to take any part in the day's work. Although many efforts were made to get off the water, the sea proved too choppy for the seaplanes, and the spotting for the bombarding ships was done by other vessels. Where, as for instance at Helles or Orkanie, these could get observation at right angles to the line of fire, this form of spotting was fairly satisfactory, but there could be few occasions when spotting from vessels would be effective.

The problem now was to destroy the guns of the shortrange outer forts which had, at the moment, only been abandoned by the Turk. It was decided to do this by landing demolition parties on both sides of the straits. Parties were accordingly put ashore in the afternoon of February the 26th at Sedd el Bahr and Kum Kale. Kilner and Park, who had gone up in the Short seaplane in the morning, had reported that three guns along the south-east front of the fort at Sedd el Bahr, three along the north-west front at Kum Kale, and the southern gun at Helles, appeared to be in place, but that all other guns in these forts, as well as those at Orkanie, appeared out of place, although not necessarily destroyed.

The Sedd el Bahr landing-party found that actually four of the six guns of the fort were undamaged; these they rapidly destroyed, as well as two 12-pounder field guns near the fort. The Kum Kale party, whose ambitious programme included the guns in the Orkanie battery and anti-aircraft guns at Achilles Tomb nearby, went to Orkanie first. They found one 9.4-inch gun remaining in the fort and destroyed it, as well as two 4-inch anti-aircraft guns. The party were ordered to return on board at dusk before they were able to destroy the guns in Kum Kale. Both landing parties had met with opposition, but did their work with great courage and efficiency.

They had not had time, however, to do all that was necessary, and, next day. *Irresistible* landed a second party at Sedd el Bahr which destroyed, by gun-cotton, six modern 6-inch howitzers on the cliffs to the east of the fort, and on March the 1st, under the same gallant leader. Lieutenant F. H. Sandford, a demolition party was landed at Kum Kale, where they found only one of the nine guns of the fort unserviceable and seven entirely untouched. All these they destroyed as well as six 12-pounders to the westward, and, on the way home, four Nordenfeldt guns and a motor searchlight.

So, went the outer forts, but the campaign was only beginning; when the November bombardment took place, no more than the regular batteries and a few field guns allotted to them existed, but by the end of 1914 not only had the regular forts been strengthened, but twenty mobile 6-inch howitzers had been concealed about Eren Keui and twelve more on the European side. During January and February four more were added as well as twenty-four 8-inch or 6-inch mortars. The Turks had placed this artillery to prevent the Allied ships from bombarding the Narrows, and they proposed to do this by keeping up a barrage on those areas from which the ships were best able to tackle the inner forts grouped around Kilid Bahr on the European shore, and around Chanak—the more formidable group—on the Asiatic side.

In addition, all available field guns were brought up and placed in positions covering the mine-fields. The field batteries could hardly have been knocked out by the low trajectory fire of the Allied ships, even were they located from the air. It came to be realised, in fact, so soon as the 1st of March, that the navy might be unable to break through without using troops to clear the land. That the enemy was stiffening his land defences was obvious from a report from an observer who, on the 1st of March, flew as far as Dardanos and saw entrenchments and gun positions along the whole coast. Although no guns were located, what appeared to be parked artillery was seen.

On the 4th came further evidence. Landing parties which were sent to Sedd el Bahr and Orkanie to make certain that these positions were demolished, met with stout resistance and could do nothing, and seaplanes which flew over the forts in connexion with these landings were heavily fired on, one receiving eight bullets, another twenty-eight.

The bombardment of the inner defences began on the 5th of March, and *Queen Elizabeth* was expected to take the leading part in their destruction. The spotting for her was to be done both by seaplanes and by battleships inside the straits. The ships could not anchor, and no less than three had to be told off for the task, to run up in succession, at twelve minutes' interval, to within ten thousand yards of Kephez Point before turning. This, for the ships, meant spotting from a distance of from seven to eight miles, as well as a continuous change of spotting officer.

Here, then, was a great chance for the seaplanes; could they rise to the occasion? The *Queen Elizabeth* was anchored two and a half miles south-west of Gaba Tepe, and sent her first shells over the peninsula at noon. The *Ark Royal* had closed the battleship at 10.00 a.m. and sent a Sopwith away at 11.14, carrying Flight Lieutenant W. H. S. Garnett and Flight Commander Williamson. Ill luck began at once. The seaplane was climbing well and the weather conditions were perfect. Suddenly, when the seaplane had got to 3,000 feet, the propeller burst. The craft got out of control and crashed in the sea where it was completely wrecked. Both occupants, picked up by the *Usk*, were found to be severely shaken, and Williamson had received injuries which kept him in hospital for some weeks.

Another Sopwith, piloted by Flight Lieutenant N. S. Douglas with Flight Sub-Lieutenant E. H. Dunning as observer, went off at 12.14. All promised well; the seaplane got up to 3,000 feet over the peninsula, and the observer tested the wireless which was working well, but as he was about to signal, the pilot was hit in the leg by a rifle bullet. There was nothing for it but to go home at once for a change of pilot. Flight Lieutenant R. H. Kershaw took the control lever and the Sopwith went away again at 2.10, and Dunning signalled a few observations before *Queen Elizabeth* ceased fire owing to the bad light. She had herself been subjected to the inconvenience of seventeen hits by mobile guns, and although she had put many shells into the forts, no guns, as was afterwards learned, had actually been damaged.

The *Queen Elizabeth* tried again on the 6th of March, but no seaplanes could get off, and the one spotting vessel inside the straits had difficulty in signalling owing to enemy wireless jamming. The indirect fire of the great battleship had failed, and the failure was due to the lack of air observation. There is little doubt that she could, with efficient spotting from above, have done great damage to the forts, and she might, with a sufficient expenditure of ammunition, have smashed every gun. Without observation of her fire she could achieve only moral effect, which was of little use unless followed up at once with an attempted break through by the fleet. It was decided to have another try from inside the straits. On the 7th no flying was possible, and on the 8th a seaplane which went up, in squally weather, to spot for *Queen Elizabeth* could see nothing because of low-lying clouds. The fleet made little impression on this day, and drew off to make no further important daylight bombardment until the great attack on the 18th of March.

Meanwhile *Ark Royal* went on the move. From the 10th to the 12th of March she was at Xeros island in connexion with operations at the Bulair lines. The weather was bad, but two flights were made, one on the 10th which reported Kavak bridge still intact in spite of the attempts which had been made to destroy it, the other on the 12th which showed that the Bulair lines had been considerably strengthened and that not much damage had been done either to Fort Sultan or to Fort Napoleon, both of which had been bombarded.

In the evening of the 12th the carrier went back to Tenedos, and on the following five days many useful reconnaissance flights were made by her seaplanes over the Dardanelles. Gun emplacements on both shores were located and information as to camps, etc. given, but the most important work, for much depended on it, was the observation of the straits for mines. Mine-field reconnaissances were made on each day from the 13th to the 17th of March inclusive, and none of these flights reported mines much west of Kephez Bay, but between that area and the Narrows many were seen.

It is now known that the serious losses which the fleet suffered on the 18th were caused by a mine-field parallel to the shore in Eren Keui bay, that is to say in an area which had often been swept and which, up to the 17th, had been clear according to the air reports. To test the visibility from the air, mines had been sunk near *Ark Royal* and examined from 1,000, 1,500, and 3,000 feet at depths of five, ten, and eighteen feet for each observation. They were seen each time quite clearly; before going off on each mine reconnaissance, the airmen flew over the experimentally sunk mines to test the visibility for each varying time and day.

It is, of course, one thing to detect mines which you know to be at some particular spot and another, and very different thing, to be reliably certain that there are none over a wide stretch of sea, especially in waters, such as the straits, disturbed by swift-moving currents. Such an absolute negative is beyond the capacity of any air observer. All the same it may be asserted, with some confidence, that a regularly laid mine-field in Eren Keui bay, flown over on five successive days, stood a good chance of being discovered. It has been stated that the field was laid on the night of the 8th of March and that the mines, which were to have such a definite effect on the course of the campaign, lay unsuspected for ten days.

We may accept the statement that the field was first laid on the 8th of March, but some of the mines were definitely destroyed by the sweepers and some, possibly, broke away, since on the two nights before the attack the Area was swept again without any mines being encountered. It is now known, in fact, that a group of new mines was put into position some time during the night which preceded the attack. the account published by the Turkish General Staff says:

> Actually, it was owing to the heroic determination of our brave naval officers on the night of 17th/18th March, that this bay was sown afresh with mines, and it is they who were responsible for the failure of the Allied Fleet.

The object of the great naval attack on the 18th was to silence the Narrows defences and the mine-field batteries to allow the trawlers to sweep a passage through the formidable Kephez mine-field by day, all sweeping attempts by night having failed. The operations were now in charge of Vice-Admiral J. M. de Robeck who had taken over the command on the previous day, following the sudden illness of Admiral Carden. The *Ark Royal* was to send up a seaplane every hour to report the effect of the bombardment. The day broke fine and cloudless, ideal for air observation. The sweepers early reported all clear in the area in which the fleet was to work and *Agamemnon* led the first division into the straits at 10.30 a.m.; an hour later the ships were in position and fire was opened. Meanwhile the Turks worked their scattered guns and howitzers from the shore with good effect and most of the ships were hit many times.

At half-past twelve Flight Lieutenant R. Whitehead with Lieutenant L. H. Strain went out on a Wight to ascertain the progress of the ships' fire. They reported that Medjidieh (13), Hamidieh II (16), Namazieh (17), and Hamidieh I (19) were all manned and firing rapidly, but that Chemenlik (20) was not manned. They saw also that 13, 17, and 19 were being repeatedly hit, although, owing to the thick smoke, they found it impossible to estimate the damage. The forts at Mount Dardanos and at Kephez Point were not manned, but there were many field guns in the vicinity. A line of boats was seen above the Narrows lying broadside to the stream, engaged possibly in mine-laying. Many other active guns were reported.

The information, as it was observed, was at once sent back by wireless. Before the Wight had landed, Flight Lieutenant Douglas with Petty Officer B. J. Brady had got off on a Sopwith. They found by the time they were over the forts that only Hamidieh I, south of Chanak, was firing with any determination. All her guns were still in action, and the shells from *Vengeance* which were falling into her were exploding in the centre of the fort but doing little or no damage to the guns. Chemenlik, it was confirmed, was not manned, and two of the guns were pointing at a sharp upward angle.

A little after this, the troublesome Hamidieh I concentrated with salvoes on *Irresistible* which soon developed a slight list. At 4.15 *Irresistible* struck a mine and had to be abandoned. At five minutes past six *Ocean*, in the act of withdrawing, struck a mine; she, too, was abandoned. The *Inflexible* had been mined soon after 4, but, although badly crippled, had got to Tenedos. Nor was this all. The French battleship *Bouvet* which had been the first vessel to fall a victim had gone down rapidly with a loss of over 600 lives. In addition, the *Gaulois* and *Suffren* were badly damaged.

As soon as it became evident that the area had been insufficiently swept, the engagement was broken off. Notwithstanding the comparatively favourable second air report, very little permanent damage had indeed been done to the forts. The Turks have since stated that they had to cease firing for considerable periods to clean the dirt and grit from the guns due to hits on the parapets of the forts. The day had ended in a very serious setback, and the whole plan of operations had to be reconsidered.

Preparations for the Landings.

Whilst the naval bombardments were being directed against the Dardanelles, there was liveliness at home. Even before the opening attack the Government were making arrangements to concentrate a considerable military force in the Mediterranean. On the 15th of February Vice-Admiral Sir Henry Jackson, of the Admiralty War Staff, in a memorandum to Vice-Admiral S. H. Carden said:

> The provision of the necessary military forces to enable the fruits of this heavy naval undertaking to be gathered must never be lost sight of.... It is considered ... that the full advantage of the undertaking would only be obtained by the occupation of the Peninsula...

On the 16th of February an important, informal, meeting of ministers decided that a large force be massed in the Eastern Mediterranean 'to be available in case of necessity to support the naval attack on the Dardanelles' and Major-General Sir William Birdwood was, later, sent out to report on their employment. On the 5th of March he wired to Lord Kitchener:

> I am very doubtful if the navy can force the passage unassisted.

On the 11th of March it was decided to appoint General Sir Ian Hamilton to the military command. He was told of the appointment on the 12th and informed that the fleet had undertaken to force the passage of the Dardanelles and that:

> The employment of military forces on any large scale for land operations at this juncture is only contemplated in the event of the Fleet failing to get through after every effort has been exhausted....

It is clear that, at this time. Lord Kitchener still thought the navy would force the straits, and Sir Ian Hamilton went out to his task under that impression. On the 17th of March he had arrived and was conferring with Admiral de Robeck on board his flagship. On the 18th, whilst the disastrous attack on the Narrows was being made. Sir Ian made a personal reconnaissance in the *Phaeton* of the whole coast. His conversations and what he saw brought home to him the difficulty which the fleet had to face from mobile guns, and the fact that these could only be dealt with by landing troops in strength.

He also realised the delicate problems that landing must now involve, and that neither his own troops nor the French under General d'Amade were as yet in a position to undertake it. On the 19th of March he telegraphed to Lord Kitchener:

..I am being most reluctantly driven towards the conclusion that the Dardanelles are less likely to be forced by battleships than at one time seemed probable. ...The Army's share will not be a case of landing parties for the destruction of forts, etc., but rather a case of a deliberate and progressive military operation carried out in force in order to make good the passage of the Navy.

Lord Kitchener at once replied in a telegram which Sir Ian rightly interpreted as instructions that he was to take the peninsula. At a conference with the military on March the 22nd Admiral de Robeck became convinced that the object of the campaign could only be attained by the continuous co-operation of the two services, and he learned that General Hamilton would help with his whole force, but that the army could not be ready for something like a month. Mudros offered no facilities for reorganising, and all the troops, except the 3rd Australian Brigade and the Marines, would have to go to Egypt to get ready. The date of the new combined attack would therefore be about the middle of April.

During this time of waiting, the forces at the Dardanelles were not idle. It is, in fact, during the periods of preparation for battle that the air service does some of its most important work; and the service was now in a better position for doing it. The main role of the navy now was reconnaissance in preparation for the landing of the army, and for the air part of this work the admiral had been reinforced by No. 3 Aeroplane Squadron of the Naval Air Service, which came to the Dardanelles with some of the most adventurous and best trained pilots in the service, and, although the war was still young, came, too, with a tradition.

The squadron was the first naval aeroplane unit to go overseas, when on August the 27th, 1914, under Wing Commander C. R. Samson, it flew to Ostend to work with the brigade of marines who were to occupy the town. On the 1st of September 1914 it was withdrawn to Dunkirk with a view to defending England against Zeppelin attacks. On October the 8th Flight Lieutenant R. L. G. Marix of the squadron had raided Düsseldorf, where he destroyed a new Zeppelin in her hangar, and on the same day Squadron Commander Spenser D. A. Grey attacked Cologne where, unable on account of mist to locate the Zeppelin sheds, he bombed the main railway station.

From its base at Dunkirk, in the strenuous fluctuating early days of the war, the squadron had many adventures both in aeroplanes and armoured cars. When the cry for aeroplanes came from the Dardanelles, the squadron was withdrawn from Dunkirk to Dover, and, now called No. 3, made ready for the Mediterranean. The personnel and aeroplanes were sent away in batches. On the 24th of March 1915 the advance party arrived at Tenedos, but, owing to a gale, the machines could not be got off until the 26th and 27th. Some days later the balance of personnel and equipment arrived. The squadron now consisted of eleven pilots, three observers, two doctors, an engineer officer, an armament officer, and 100 men.

The aeroplanes numbered eighteen, but they were of six varieties. There were eight Henri Farmans, two B.E.2c's, two B.E.2's, two Sopwith Tabloids, one Breguet, and three Maurice Farmans. Of this illassorted collection, the Henri Farmans proved useful only for singleseater photographic work; they were underpowered, slow, and quickly got out of truth. The B.E.2c's would not often take a passenger high enough for spotting purposes. The Tabloids, owing to limited vision, were useful chiefly for single-seater fighting, and there was to be little opportunity for them to do the only thing they could do.

The Breguet was an experimental type intended for long-distance bombing, but her engine gave much trouble, and only three flights on her were actually made. When these were eliminated there remained, for all the spotting and reconnaissance and bombing required, the three Maurice Farmans and the two B.E.2's. Of the Maurices, two were fitted with 100 horse-power Renault engines, and the other, which had already flown for about 120 hours in France, with a 140 horse-power Canton Unné engine. The B.E.'s, one old and one new, had 70 horse-power Renaults.

The aerodrome which No. 3 Squadron used was situated on the north coast of the island, about three and a half miles from Tenedos town, with which it was connected by a rough unmetalled road. When the area was chosen, it was a vineyard, filled with flourishing trees. Commander Clark Hall mustered a band of Greek labourers and directed them in the work of clearing the site, and an excellent aerodrome, some 600 yards by 300 yards, resulted. A rough road was made down to the water's edge.

The business of landing the aeroplanes was a tedious one, and is worthy of mention as showing the difficulties which attended each small step of the campaign. The transport *Abda*, in which were the first aeroplanes to arrive, was placed alongside *Ark Royal* which, with her main derrick, hoisted the heavy aeroplane cases off the *Abda* on to a 47-foot launch and a sailing pinnace lent by *Vengeance*. The Maurice Farman aeroplanes, which had been packed in cases of fragile construction, 47 feet long and weighing two tons, were particularly troublesome to unload. The ships' boats were eventually, with their load, hauled as far ashore as they would go, and the cases got off over planks and rollers; thence they were pushed on rollers along the roughly improvised road by Greek labourers patiently exhorted by the sailors. The eleven aeroplanes in the *Abda* were landed, without damage, in two days; the packing cases served later to house some of the men. From the aerodrome the yellow gleaming peninsula could be seen towards the north-east. Helles was some seventeen and a half miles away, and the cove, soon to be identified as Anzac, thirty-one miles, formidable distances for aeroplanes unprovided with any means of riding the waves.

Those of the aeroplanes brought out which were fit for their job were used continuously, three or more flights being made by each on every flying day. One of them, at least, deserves more than a passing mention. The old B.E. had already done an amount of work which would have justified her retirement to less active service. Built by Messrs. Hewlett and Blondeau, she was first flown at Eastchurch in January 1914, and continuously to the outbreak of war she was flown by Commander Samson and most of the other naval pilots, who came to look upon her as ageless. At the Spithead review in July 1914, Samson flew her from Eastchurch and manoeuvred over the ships. He flew her, too, to war in August, and she never failed any of her pilots during the next five months on a multitude of jobs.

Squadron Commander E. L. Gerrard took her to bomb Düsseldorf in September 1914, but was frustrated by thick mists. Commander Samson used her for bombing Ostend and Zeebrugge. On the 27th of February, when orders came to go home, Samson flew her, through a heavy fog, to Dover where she arrived first of the squadron's aeroplanes. The only rest she got was on her journey to Tenedos. She was flown throughout the remainder of the Dardanelles campaign until, in January 1916, when the squadron returned to England, she was considered unfit to travel, and was broken up. Air Commodore Samson says:

> At the last, I must say I only flew her occasionally simply for old acquaintance sake.

She has earned her mention in any history of the war in the air.

The vice-admiral had decided to use the aeroplanes for reconnaissances of the straits and their neighbourhood, and to send *Ark Royal*, with her seaplanes, to distances from Tenedos which made the use of land-machines undesirable. So, the carrier, reaping the advantages of sea-power, went wandering off, as shall be told hereafter, to distant coasts, to the Gulf of Adramyti, to Smyrna, Enos, and to Bulair. Before she went away she was able to pass over to Commander Samson the knowledge that the seaplane observers had laboriously collected. She passed on, too, the information obtained as a result of two reconnaissances made since the last naval attack.

The first, on the 26th of March, by Flight Lieutenant Bromet and Sub-Lieutenant Park on a Wight, was sent out to discover what damage the bombardment of the 18th had done to the forts. Their detailed report showed that although at Medjidieh and at Hamidieh II the barracks were destroyed, the forts otherwise appeared intact; that two new emplacements south of Kephez Point each contained six guns or howitzers; that at Hamidieh I, where many shells had fallen in the centre of the fort without damaging the guns, large bodies of men were working feverishly; and that other parties were working south of Kephez Point. The other flight, on the 28th, was made by Flight Sub-Lieutenant Dunning alone in a Sopwith over Orkanie. He saw no signs of life either in the fort or in the whole district west of In Tepe. During his flight he spotted for the *Majestic* on to Orkanie, and, telling the battleship to change to Yeni Shehr, he spotted for her again on to the village. This was but one of many fine attempts at single-seater spotting made by this pilot.

The first aeroplane flight was made on this same day, but before the work of No. 3 Squadron is touched on, one or two extracts from Wing Commander Samson's standing orders will serve to light up the conditions under which his squadron worked. From a comprehensive list of thirty-two the following are chosen:

> Pilots always to be armed with a revolver or pistol; to carry binoculars; some safety device, either waistcoat, patent life-belt or petrol can.
>
> Observers always to carry rifle; proper charts for journey (in addition small scale chart of whole Peninsula); binoculars; life-saving device or petrol can; watch if not fitted to the aeroplane.
>
> At all times the pilot should carry out independent observa-

tions and note down what he sees (noting the times). Nail a pad of paper on the instrument board for this purpose. Particular attention being paid to shipping in the straits.

Pilots and observers are to familiarise themselves with the photographs of Turkish men-of-war described in *The World's Fighting Ships*. This book is in the office.

On the return from a flight, pilot and observer to immediately report to me, or, in my absence, to the senior officer present. The observer is to telephone the important part of his report to Headquarters and then make out his report. The report is to be made out immediately after the return from a flight.

Don't make wild statements... A small accurate report is worth pages of rhetoric giving no real information.

If an enemy aeroplane is sighted, attack it, reporting you are doing so, if spotting.

Don't try to do what is termed by some people as 'Stunt Flying.' This is not wanted for war, and is not conduct required of an officer.

The orders referring to the procedure to be followed if compelled to alight on enemy territory included:

If you have any bombs or grenades in the aeroplane, and you have any time, place them clear of the aeroplane, unwind the fans, and hope they will detonate on being handled.

Between the day of the first aeroplane flight, March the 28th, and the day of the landings by the army, April the 25th, the aeroplanes of No. 3 Squadron were over the peninsula at every opportunity which the trying weather afforded. Systematically the officers plotted the enemy positions; they controlled a part of the ships' fire against enemy batteries, especially those in the difficult country on the Asiatic side; they procured some crude but useful photographs of the landing beaches and the ground in their immediate neighbourhood, and they wrote descriptions of the beaches as they appeared from the air; they corrected the inaccurate maps; and they dropped bombs on batteries and camps.

All the information that was brought in was passed on to headquarters at once, but the squadron commander kept also a map which was supplemented and brought up to date from the air reports, from day to day, and this map was handed to Sir Ian Hamilton before the landings.

Most of the early photography, which was of an experimental kind, was done by one officer. Flight Lieutenant C. H. Butler, who began on the 4th of April with a small folding Goertz-Anschutz camera. A better camera was later borrowed from the French squadron, which under Captain Cesari had come out in May, and Butler fixed this alongside his seat outside the nacelle. Until the end of June, when he was badly wounded, he exposed in all some 700 plates, piecing groups together to form maps of each important area, and these maps, from time to time, were passed to army headquarters. It was not until the end of August that a regular photographic section was organised; thereafter the progress of aerial photography was rapid.

Before the landing, spotting flights were made by the aeroplanes for *the London, Majestic, Swiftsure, Prince George, Triumph, Talbot, Agamemnon,* and *Albion.* A report of *Prince George,* dated April the 9th, says:

> An aeroplane spotted for us and gave us a fine object lesson in what can be done in this respect. It was about 6000 feet above the battery, flying in figure of eight, but at that distance looked as if it were stationary over the target. It sent the result of each shot by W/T immediately it fell, and the rapidity with which it spotted and transmitted was quite a revelation to most of us.

The method used, at that time, to signal the fall of the shots was for the air observer, when over the target, to send the call on his wireless to open fire, and afterwards to give firstly the distance at which the shell had exploded beyond or short of the target, and secondly the distance right or left. Thus, the wireless signal S. 100, L. 50 meant that the shot had pitched one hundred yards short and fifty yards to the left, looking from the ship towards the target. At first, the ship used to repeat, on her searchlight, each correction sent by the aeroplane, but this was soon discontinued as it wasted time, and took the observer's mind off the target.

In the early days the pilots used to spot, using the observer as a signaller, but as inexperienced observers were trained all, except a few pilots of great experience, left the spotting entirely to them. The new observers were chiefly light-weight midshipmen who, following a request from Wing Commander Samson, had been selected, on April the 10th, from scores of volunteers from the fleet. By this time two army observers had arrived from Egypt, and the Vice-Admiral was able to report to the Admiralty that his immediate air requirements were fully provided for, and that he would only want drafts to replace casualties.

The two new weapons of war which operated, the one from the clouds, the other from under the sea, will often be linked together in this history, for the submarine had no greater enemy than aircraft, and, sometimes, no greater friend. Had these two weapons been on the spot, in sufficient numbers to attack decisively the precarious Turkish communications to the peninsula, the enemy could not have stood his ground. Inadequate as they were, they nearly did prove decisive, as shall be seen later when the aircraft bombing attacks are reviewed.

The episode which calls for mention here is one of co-operation between the two arms, which ended unhappily for the under-water craft. On the 12th of April Lieutenant Commander T. S. Brodie, of the submarine E.15, was taken up for a flight to Kephez Point to look at the lie of the land and the Narrows, in particular, through which he was to take his craft, and, as the aeroplane turned over the Point, he had a good view of the spot, south of the Kephez Light, where disaster was to overtake him. In the dark hours of the 17th he began his attempt.

At dawn an aeroplane left with a load of bombs which it was proposed to drop to divert the eyes of the Turkish defenders from the water during the critical period when the submarine would be passing through the Narrows. A second aeroplane left at 7.30 a.m. carrying as passenger Lieutenant Commander C. G. Brodie, one of Admiral de Robeck's staff officers and a brother of the submarine commander. When this aeroplane, flying at 6,000 feet, approached Kephez the fact that the adventure had ended in disaster was made clear. Captain C. G. Brodie, R.N. says:

> At this height E.15, even well out as she was, was not easily recognisable, but I caught the glint of her bow hydro-planes awash and knew her and her fate at a glance. We altered course to get rid of our bombs at Chanak and get back to report. A small vessel, possibly a torpedo boat, went alongside E.15 while we had her in sight.

Long afterwards it was known that the submarine, on rising to fix position, had been caught in the treacherous current and driven hard aground. The commanding officer as he went into the conning tower to get a better view was killed by a Turkish shell. After some hasty pre-arranged measures of destruction, the crew took to the water.

There five were killed by shells, now falling fast, but the remainder were swept inshore by the current and rescued, the more exhausted of them being helped along by Turkish soldiers who did not hesitate to plunge into the sea.

It was most important that the submarine should not be salved by the enemy, and an aeroplane bombing raid was made in the afternoon. The bombs did not hit their target, but fell near enough to cause a destroyer, which was attempting to haul the E.15 off, to move away. Meanwhile Admiral de Robeck was making plans for the submarine's destruction. This was not easy of accomplishment. She lay under the guns of Fort Dardanos, and the Turks hurried also a number of other guns to the spot to cover their salvage operations. Two submarine attacks were tried, and failed. Then *Triumph* and *Majestic*, spotted for by aeroplanes, tried but found they could not reach her with their guns, on account of the fierce fire which met their efforts.

Undaunted, these ships provided two boats, fitted with dropping gear for 14-inch torpedoes, and during the impenetrable darkness of the night of the 18th of April, these boats, led by Lieutenant Commander E. G. Robinson, went in to attack. They were picked up by the searchlights and fiercely fired at, but the lights momentarily revealed the E.15, and a torpedo was fired at her by *Majestic's* boat, which was itself hit, just as the torpedo exploded in the distance.

The *Triumph's* boat got off its shot, rushed to the rescue of its companions in the adventure, and, doubly loaded, got back with the loss of only one man. Whether their gallant effort had been rewarded, they did not know, since the result of the explosion was not observed. Next morning, however, aeroplane observers who flew over the spot, saw that the torpedo had got home, leaving the submarine completely heeled over, derelict and helpless.

On the 15th of April an enemy aerodrome was located at Chanak, and, on the 18th, six 100-lb. bombs dropped on it, destroyed the main hangar, with a German machine that was inside. Not until July was enemy air activity in this theatre of war of much account. Before that month two or three aeroplanes and one seaplane—all of German manufacture, with German pilots and, usually, Turkish observers—were in service. Later in the campaign two Turkish pilots were also flying on this front.

In July new machines arrived from Germany, but even after this the average number of aeroplanes in use during the last half of 1915 was only eight, and of seaplanes, one. Not until the evacuation of Helles did a German machine court combat, and because on the whole the German aeroplanes were faster, the British found it most difficult to bring them to a fight.

Whilst the aeroplane observers were watching the enemy in the southern half of the peninsula, the seaplanes were helping to distract the minds of the Turks to other possible landing-places. On the 31st of March *Ark Royal* accompanied a small Allied squadron to Mitylene, whence her seaplanes examined the whole northern coast of the Gulf of Adramyti. No troops or gun emplacements were observed, but the object was rather to be seen than to see, to mislead the enemy to a belief that a landing might be made there. The carrier returned to Mudros to oil and to take on a new Wight, and on April the 4th, Easter Sunday, she was back outside the Gulf of Smyrna, over which two flights were made, mapping the defences and noting shipping in the harbour.

The seaplanes were fired on by shore guns, anti-aircraft guns, and by torpedo-boats. Their crews retaliated by dropping bombs, of which four exploded in the middle of a working party. The *Ark Royal* returned at once to Tenedos, and on the 6th of April she was away again north to the Gulf of Enos. On the 7th a reconnaissance flight over the town of Enos reported no troops or guns, nor any movement in the town, and parties from *Swiftsure* and *Majestic* thereupon got into cutters and made a feint landing. On the following day the carrier went to Mudros where she took on board two Sopwith Schneider Cup seaplanes in exchange for her Tabloids. They were of the type on which Mr. C. Howard Pixton had won the international race for the Schneider Trophy, at Monaco, in April 1914. (He covered the 28 laps of the 150-nautical-mile course in 2 hours $13^{2/5}$ seconds). They were single-seaters, and would therefore be of restricted use.

One of the old type Sopwiths was transferred to Minerva, for patrolling the Gulf of Smyrna. This seaplane made eight successful flights over the town and harbour, but by the 20th, through exposure, it was out of truth and was handed back to *Ark Royal* at Mudros for repair. In the meantime, the carrier had made a trip to the Gulf of Xeros, where she arrived on the 12th to reconnoitre the town of Gallipoli and to help the fleet to destroy the magazine at Taifur Keui. A section of the magazine was blown up, with seaplane spotting, by *Lord Nelson* on the 16th, and on the same day Gallipoli was reconnoitred by two Sopwiths which dropped bombs on the Turkish battleship, *Turgud Reis*, which they found anchored in Gallipoli Liman. On the 17th of April

Ark Royal returned to Mudros, and no further flying was done by her seaplanes over the peninsula before the day of the landings.

By this time the air service had been augmented by a curious craft. She was the *Manica*, the first vessel to be converted for use as a kite-balloon ship. She was a single-screw steamer of 3,500 tons, capable of a speed of eleven knots. On the 4th of March General Birdwood had telegraphed to Lord Kitchener that a man-lifting kite or captive balloon would be of great use to the navy not only for spotting long-range fire, but also for detecting the concealed batteries which were causing so much trouble. When this request was placed before the Board of Admiralty immediate action followed, and the tramp steamer *Manica*, which was at the time engaged in the useful but prosaic task of unloading manure in the Manchester ship canal, was acquired and hurriedly prepared to take a balloon of the Drachen type of 28,000 cubic feet capacity.

As it was considered that successful operations at Gallipoli might necessitate the balloon working on land, mechanical transport was stowed in the after hold of the ship so that when she went away on the 27th of March she was ready to provide a kite balloon for service ashore or afloat. She had accommodation for six kite-balloon officers, eighty-three ratings, 200 hydrogen cylinders, and, in addition, gas plant and other fittings. At that time only thirty trained airship ratings could be spared, and the section had been completed by volunteers from the home anti-aircraft corps. The ship arrived in Mudros harbour on April the 9th. A successful trial flight of the balloon had been made on the way from Malta, and another in co-operation with the cruiser *Bacchante* was carried out off Mudros on April the 15th. Next day Squadron Commander J. D. Mackworth, who was in charge of the section, reported:

> I consider that the results obtainable from the very rough and ready apparatus in the *Manica*, warrant the question of properly designed kite balloon ships being taken up. The observation is in many respects not inferior to that obtained from aeroplanes, the communications are incomparably better and more reliable, and the chances of a breakdown very much less.

When the *Manica* was fitted out kite balloons were almost unknown in England, and Squadron Commander Mackworth was the only trained observer in the section. It was not until some months later that relief observers, hurriedly trained at Roehampton, began to arrive at the Dardanelles. A naval gunnery officer was lent to the ship on her arrival to instruct observers in fire-observation and in methods of transmission of information to the firing ship. This officer was retained for several months.

The kite balloon had many advantages over any other form of observation. It could remain up all day and, since the observer was in uninterrupted communication with the firing ship, fire-control was as nearly perfect as it could be. In addition, the observer could devote his whole attention to the work of spotting. On the other hand, the parent ship would drift occasionally, taking the balloon out of the view of the target. Soon, too,—a tribute to the effectiveness of fire when controlled by the balloon,—the enemy brought up guns to the shore and began to shell the balloon with shrapnel, compelling *Manica* to go further off, and this, combined with the low heights from which the early balloons had to work, gave the observer a much foreshortened view and made many objectives difficult to identify. Balloons throughout the war were a vulnerable target for aeroplanes, but *Manica's* balloon survived many attacks. In spite of its disadvantages the balloon worked so well, especially in the weeks following its arrival, that the Admiralty approved the fitting out of six additional ships. The *Manica* did her first successful spotting for *Bacchante* on the 19th of April. The commander of the section gives a vivid picture of this day's work:

'The enemy were not aware of the presence of a balloon-ship, and had taken no special precautions against being overlooked. The consequence was that when *Manica* put up her balloon, the first sight which greeted the observers was a sleeping camp, neatly arranged in a dip in the ground, out of sight of *Bacchante* but within easy range of her guns. Through their excellent field-glasses they could see an occasional dot moving about, but for the most part the camp was not yet astir. If there were sentries, they doubtless regarded the distant balloon hanging in the sky as a harmless form of amusement for the jaded British, and saw no connection between it and the long guns of the *Bacchante* which were nuzzling round toward them.

But the boom of the cruiser's forward turret opened their eyes, and a rude awakening followed when the top of a hillock some hundred yards beyond the camp was hurled into the air. No reveille ever blown commanded so instant a response. Every tent burst into life, and the ground was soon swarming with running specks. A second shot burst on the northernmost fringe of the camp, and a third right in the midst of the tents. *Bacchante* had the range to a nicety, and began to fire salvoes of 6-inch. A scene of indescribable confusion followed. Tents were rent to pieces and flung into the air, dust spouted in huge fans and columns, and brightly through the reek could be seen the flashes of the bursting shells. Like ants from an overturned nest, the little brown dots swarmed and scattered. Across the plain galloped a few terrified mules, and in an incredibly short time the wreckage was complete. Of the once orderly camp nothing remained but torn earth and twisted canvas, and when the smoke cleared away, no movement was to be seen. The trial was simple but convincing. *Manica* signalled Cease fire and lumbered home behind her consort, metaphorically wagging her tail.' (*Blackwood's Magazine*, April 1927, 'The First Naval Kite Balloon', by John Mackworth).

The battleships indeed knew the value of the sting which the balloon had added to their fire, and when, a few weeks later, *Triumph* reported that *Manica* was being attacked by a submarine, every ship in sight, with a fierce protective feeling, was at once firing. It detracts nothing from their feeling that the submarine was an inverted tin bath.

The Landings at Helles and Anzac,

For the adventure of landing, the army was ready at its bases about the third week in April awaiting a spell of fine weather. It may be well to restate here that Sir Ian Hamilton's object was to reduce the forts at the Narrows so that the fleet might pass through the straits. For reasons which he has set out fully in his dispatches, the general decided to land the whole of his army in the southern half of the peninsula and to concentrate on the capture of Kilid Bahr. The places chosen for the landings were: a group of four small beaches in the toe about Cape Helles (lettered from east to west 'S', 'V', 'W', and 'X'); a broken cliff some three miles up the Aegean coast from the toe (lettered 'Y') which seemed to offer a pivotal point from which the Turkish line of retreat from 'S', 'V', 'W', and 'X' beaches could be cut, and Achi Baba turned; and a beach (Anzac) of fair extent, north of Gaba Tepe, whence, it was hoped, the force might strike at the whole of the enemy communications with the Narrows at their most vital point. Coincident with these landings there was to be a temporary landing of French troops on the Asiatic side at Kum Kale and feint landings near Bulair and in Besika Bay.

There were in Mudros harbour, being fitted into the scheme for the landing, three units of the Royal Naval Air Service whose duty was, not in the air, but on the ground. They were Nos. 3 and 4 Armoured Car Squadrons, and No. 10 Motor Cycle Machine-Gun Squadron. These squadrons had come into being as part of the Naval Air Service organisation as a result of the success which had attended Commander Samson's motorcar operations in the early days in Belgium before the war of movement ceased. Once the western front became stabilized, few opportunities could present themselves for the useful employment of armoured cars in France, and they were therefore available for any less stagnant sphere of operations.

When the Gallipoli landings were decided upon, these squadrons were sent to the Mediterranean to give a helping hand to the army. Part of them arrived at Lemnos in the *Inkosi* at the end of March, and the remainder, after a brief diversion in Egypt, in the *Inkonka* in the middle of April. Sir Ian Hamilton, whilst he hoped that the opportunity for using the armoured cars and motorcycles might come after the landings had been made good, saw a ready and immediate use for the machine-guns and their trained crews. He therefore ordered Lieutenant-Commander J. C. Wedgwood of No. 3 Armoured Car Squadron to report to Commander Edward Unwin, who was preparing the *River Clyde* for her famous beaching exploit at Sedd el Bahr. The strip of sand under Sedd el Bahr, known as 'V' beach, was a defender's paradise.

Between the bluff on which the village was built and the opposite bluff crowned by No. 1 Fort, the ground forms a slightly concave amphitheatre. The buildings on the bluffs, crumbled by the fleet's bombardment, afforded good cover to the Turkish riflemen. Between the beach and the terraced defenders were lines of barbed-wire entanglements. In face of such a defensive position, some special means for landing the covering party had to be devised. It was ultimately arranged that the advance party at this beach as elsewhere should be landed from open boats in tows, but that the bulk of the covering party should be run ashore at Sedd el Bahr in the collier *River Clyde*, into the side of which large ports had been cut to give egress to lighters which were to form a bridge to the beach. To give immediate protection to these troops Commander Unwin arranged with Lieutenant-Commander Wedgwood that he should mount and man eleven of his maxim guns on the forecastle of the collier.

Under the direction of the latter officer, steel-plate and sandbag protection was hurriedly fitted up, not only for the machine-gun positions, but along the whole of the upper deck and bridges, a precaution which, Sir Ian Hamilton has stated, proved to be the salvation of the force when troops were compelled later to move about the deck under the eyes of the Turkish riflemen. At noon on the 22nd of April the *River Clyde*, with four officers, a surgeon, and seventy-two men of No. 3 Armoured Car Squadron amongst those on board, left Lemnos for Tenedos to take in, westward of ancient Troy, her human freight of some two thousand infantry.

Meanwhile No. 4 Armoured Car Squadron, under the command of Squadron Commander C. E. Risk, was ordered to Skyros to join the Royal Naval Division for their diversion at Bulair. No. 10 Squadron, under Lieutenant-Commander A. E. Whalley, remained on board the *Inkosi* to be at hand to take their place on shore at Helles once the landing had been secured.

At noon on the 23rd of April the long-awaited spell of fine weather, so essential to the success of the enterprise, seemed to have set in, and Admiral de Robeck at once gave orders that the preliminary movements should begin at sundown. When darkness fell on the 24th the British sections had reached, or were nearing, their rendezvous. But darkness brought anxiety. A wet moon cast its subdued light on the assembled ships, and a keen wind was ruffling the sea. Any break in the weather must mean postponement. The weather, however, withdrew its threat and the sea gradually died to perfect calm. The moon, freed of its halo, flooded the Aegean night, passed over the ships, and set behind those off Gaba Tepe, outlining them in sharp silhouette. At three the moon had dipped, and the word was given to carry on. The Turk had long been preparing for invasion: renowned for his defensive qualities, he was reinforced in spirit by a confidence in the impregnability of his positions.

The Helles landings were made by the 29th Division and by three battalions of the Royal Naval Division, supported later by the rest of the Royal Naval and the French divisions. At 'S' beach the landing party were ashore about 7.30 a.m., and ten minutes later had secured, with little loss, the ridge overlooking the eastern end of the bay. At 'V' beach the direct landing from the tows was attempted at 6.53 a.m. and, about the same hour, the *River Clyde* was run aground. When the tows were within twenty yards of the shore the sea began to hiss with Turkish bullets. Few boats survived this twenty yards, and then but a handful of their occupants got through the unbroken entanglements under a murderous fire to the shelter of the low sandy escarpment which backed the foreshore. The rest, dead or wounded, drifted helplessly in their open boats.

The men in the *River Clyde* fared little better. Her commander, unperturbed by a rain of shells from the Asiatic batteries, had run his ship on the pre-arranged spot on the eastern end of the beach, but the shore proved to shelve more gently than had been expected and the hopper grounded before she was high enough for the flying gangway to reach the shore. To add to the misfortune, one of the connecting lighters swung away, leaving a further gap between the hopper and the *River Clyde*. Commander Unwin at once took a party into the water and toiled in the bullet-swept sea in an attempt to get the lighters into some sort of position.

Meanwhile, the armoured car machine-gun detachment in the bows of the collier averted a complete disaster. They raked the Turkish trenches and machine-gun posts with such accuracy and persistence that the naval party in the water were able to continue their work for a full hour until, once again, they had got the hopper into position. Their fire prevented any attempts to rush the few survivors who were hanging on to their position on shore. At eight o'clock, with the hopper once more in place, a party of the Munsters was led out from the *River Clyde*, but the whole Turkish fire was concentrated on them and all the fire of the maxims proved insufficient to cover their journey to the beach.

So complete indeed was the mastery of the defenders that, until their fire could be subdued, it was obvious no landing was possible. At 8.10 a.m. *Queen Elizabeth* arrived to reinforce the fire of the supporting ship, *Albion*. A little later *Cornwallis* joined them from Morto Bay, but nothing that these battleships could do was enough, and, by 11.30, it was recognised that there would be no progress until darkness should come to blind the eyes of the Turkish defenders. All day the machine-gunners in the *River Clyde* kept up their duel with the enemy marksmen; not a gun went out of action although in at least one casemate every man of the gun's crew was wounded. Commander Unwin, suffering from slight wounds and exposure as a result of two long sojourns in the water, had pushed off alone from the collier in a lifeboat at 9.30 a.m. to bring in wounded who were lying on a spit of rock near the beach. His progress was anxiously watched by those on board the collier.

Petty Officer J. H. Russell of No. 3 Armoured Car Squadron, seeing that the rescuer, single-handed as he was, was experiencing great difficulty in getting the wounded into the boat, dived overboard without waiting to get permission and swam to help. He got to the boat, but was quickly shot through the abdomen. When Commander Unwin could do no more through exhaustion, the boat was hauled back to the ship with the two rescuers clinging to the sheltered side. At half-past ten a further attempt to bring in wounded was made in a boat manned by three men, including Petty Officer G. C. P. Rumming of the armoured car squadron. By the time the boat was loaded up with its wounded, Rumming's two companions had been hit, and the tow-line to the boat had been cut in half. Undaunted, Petty Officer Rumming took the line and manoeuvred the boat back to the ship.

When at last the sun dipped on that flawless Sunday evening, the bridge to the beach was finally completed and the surviving soldiers in the *River Clyde* were able to get ashore. The machine-gunners remained on board the collier for the time being, but could do little in the dark to help the infantry who fought all night. They refused to accept a rest. For three hours Lieutenant-Commander Wedgwood and Petty Officer Rumming worked waist deep in water to assist the wounded back to safety. Other officers and men moved among the wounded for nearly a mile along the beach, often close to the Turkish lines, giving what comfort they could. Surgeon P. B. Kelly of the armoured car squadron had been hit in the foot early on the morning of the 25th; but although he was unable to walk, he received a ceaseless stream of wounded until the morning of the 27th, by which time he had attended to seven hundred and fifty casualties.

At 5.40 on the morning of April the 26th the *Albion* opened fire and quickly knocked out a machine-gun which from Sedd el Bahr castle had been taking heavy toll of the troops. *Cornwallis* then joined *Albion*, and the bombardment which the two ships kept up together, with the covering machine-gun fire from the *River Clyde*, enabled our men on shore to go forward and to get a footing in Sedd el Bahr village by ten o'clock, and on the hill crest, three-quarters of a mile inland, by two in the afternoon. At half-past two Lieutenant-Commander Wedgwood received orders to land four of his machine-guns. These were pushed forward to the northern fringe of Sedd el Bahr village where they stood their ground all night against counter-attacks.

Meanwhile the troops on the left at 'V' beach had made connexion with 'W' beach to their westward. The men at this beach had had almost as hard a time. Those who got ashore on the morning of the 25th found that the ships' bombardment had done no damage to the lines of wire on land, but by half-past eleven they had fought through their obstacles so well that they had taken the important Hill 35 and had made junction with the 'X' landing which had been made good with few losses. At 'Y' beach, although the subsidiary flank landing was not maintained, the stand which the landing party made for twenty-nine hours diverted enemy troops from the extreme southern beaches where their presence might have turned the balance in the first critical hours.

The Anzac landing was not expected to meet with serious opposition for the reason that the coast was so difficult the Turk could hardly suppose it would be chosen for a descent. As it happened, the tows, probably because of the inshore current, did not keep direction, and they came to a beach a mile and a half north of the one which had been chosen and memorized. This accident had advantage and disadvantage. The advantage was that the beach originally selected was defended by a system of trenches, which were missed, and that the new beach was better defiladed from shell-fire. The disadvantage was an immediate one. The new beach was more closely overhung by cliffs rising to two or three hundred feet, cut into a tangle of precipices and ravines and clothed with almost impenetrable scrub. In the approach, furthermore, tows, and in consequence units, had become mixed.

But these formidable disadvantages did not disturb the men. They fixed their bayonets, scrambled their way up the cliffs, and were soon on the top, with the Turkish defenders on the run. They had begun to land soon after four in the morning and, by half-past eight, advanced troops were entrenching about a mile inland until the main body should be landed. Bombs dropped by five aeroplanes on Maidos on the 23rd of April had been so effective as to cause the Turks to transfer the two reserve battalions that were in the town to a camp which, unfortunately, was some miles nearer to the Anzac beach, and these battalions moved, at the first warning, to meet the invaders.

They were, even as the Australians began to entrench, within striking distance, and soon the diggers had to pause to beat off the first of a series of continuous attacks. By two o'clock in the afternoon the whole of the infantry of the Australian division (12,000 men) and two batteries of Indian Mountain Artillery were ashore, and a semi-circular position had been occupied with its right about a mile north of Gaba Tepe, and its left on the high ground by Fisherman's Hut. Within another hour, two piers, one a barrel pier supplemented by pontoons, the other a boat pier, had been erected, and landing facilities vastly improved. During the afternoon and night, the Australian and New Zealand division, except one regiment, were landed, as well as a few guns and howitzers.

Thus, a total of 20,000 men with guns, stores and water had, in twenty-four hours, been passed, under continuous fire, through the strip of cliff-bound beach, whilst in the opposite direction a stream of wounded was being passed back to the ships. And the casualties were heavy. Indeed, so severe was the pressure that on the evening of the 25th Sir William Birdwood feared it would be necessary to withdraw. But Sir Ian Hamilton directed him to maintain his position at all costs, and, though the cost was great, he continued to hang on. At one point on the right this hanging on took a literal form. The New Zealanders had been compelled to dig in not a half-dozen yards from the cliff's edge. Day and night, they withstood attempts to push them over the edge; they had been ordered to maintain their position, and they did not fail.

On the 28th of April some of the sorely tried Anzac troops were relieved in the front line by two brigades of the Royal Naval Division. During the night a detachment of No. 4 Armoured Car Squadron, under Squadron Commander C. E. Risk, was landed with four machine-guns and went into the line with the Marine Brigade, where they suffered many casualties, including their commander wounded and the officer who took over from him, Lieutenant-Commander J. R. Boothby, killed. The detachment received orders to re-embark for Helles on the morning of the 2nd of May, but two of the guns under Lieutenant T. D. Hallam were in a critical forward position from which it proved impossible to move them until the night of the 4th. For six days and nights these guns were worked continuously, withstanding many attempts to rush their positions. When at last Hallam was able to get his guns away, they had both been shot out of action.

The full story of the landings is for another historian. Only enough has been summarised here to show how the army came to get on the peninsula at all, so that the work of the airmen over them may be intelligible. And no summary, it may be said at once, can do justice to a feat which is full of the stuff of wonder. The Dardanelles struggle is long since ended. We may lament this or that decision, or ring the changes with many an 'if' or 'and'. In the wisdom which time brings to the judgement of events which are past, we may more profitably, perhaps, draw comfort from the knowledge that throughout the campaign the commander's great faith in his troops never went unanswered. At no time did they fall below all that flesh and blood might be expected to stand. At times they reached heights hardly measurable by any human standard. Those peaceful idealists who look forward to a future Utopia may well find material for their hopes here. The searching mind of posterity, as it plays about the battlefields, cannot fail to respond with all that is best in its own heart.

The aeroplanes co-operated with the landings at Helles, and the seaplanes and the kite balloon at Anzac, in weather which was ideal for flying. The aeroplanes were up, without a break, throughout the day of the 25th of April, one, relieved at intervals, over the Asiatic coast, another over the Helles area. Each pilot of the squadron made three long flights. The first aeroplanes were over the coast at dawn, with orders to spot for the ships covering the landing on any Turkish batteries that were firing. As soon as the Turks opened fire the aeroplane observers had no difficulty in picking up targets, and their wireless soon began to buzz with urgent signals. But the ships paid no attention to them, and the reason is not far to seek. Enough has already been said to show that the amount of fire necessary to reduce the Turkish positions had not yet been realised, and the overworked covering ships had a sufficiency of targets staring them in the face.

The aeroplanes, at last, were in a position to give efficient spotting help, but adequate supporting fire was not there. The day of low-flying aeroplanes attacking with machine-guns was not yet. Wing-Commander Samson said:

> It was rotten, seeing the soldiers get hell at the landing places. Knowing the defences, I did not believe they would be able to get ashore.

But they did get ashore, exhausting themselves in overcoming the initial opposition, and since there were no reinforcements the scheme for a rapid advance to the inner defences was frustrated. Once the troops were actually established the ships had more leisure to attend to aircraft signals, and the aeroplanes were in constant demand. They spotted also for shore artillery with Very lights, as the batteries, in the beginning, were unable to take in wireless messages. The effectiveness of their fire-control was apparent before the week following the landings had ended, when there was a marked decrease in the Turkish fire, especially from the Asiatic side. The aeroplanes also bombed guns, camps, and troops, took photographs of the important inland positions, and reconnoitred the whole peninsula as far as Bulair, as well as the Asiatic coast. Their reports gave Sir Ian Hamilton some indication of the rapid movements of the Turkish troops to counter him.

The seaplanes and *Manica's* balloon which watched the Anzac area were handicapped by the difficulty of the country. The balloon observer from his basket could see a deep scrub-covered ravine running inland in a north-easterly direction from the south end of the beach, and a small steep gully at right angles to the beach at the north end. Beyond the cliffs which stretch between these two indentations he saw the country broken by a bewildering confusion of deep ravines, scrub-covered or sandy cliffed, stretching upwards through the tumbled minor peaks of Sari Bair to the principal mass of the mountain itself with its disarray of satellite spurs—a district frowned upon by nature and left by man to its own brooding.

The Narrows and part of the sea of Marmara were within view. The balloon with two observers had gone up on the landing day at 5.21 a.m., and fourteen minutes later, when already the advanced troops were scrambling over the cliff tops below, one of the observers discovered the battleship *Turgud Reis* in the Narrows. He reported her to *Triumph*, which opened fire, chasing her out of sight.

Soon after nine she was again in view and *Triumph* once more got on her, causing her to get under way, when *Turgud Reis* began, in her turn, to bombard the Anzac transports as the main body were taking to the boats. The transports moved out of range with consequent delay, but *Triumph*, spotted for by the balloon observer, soon compelled *Turgud Reis* to move off and the disembarkation went on again. An American officer, who was on a visit to the Dardanelles from Constantinople at the time, reported watching the Turkish battleship come under fire, he said:

> The first salvo struck at least 1,000 yards from her, the second about 500 yards, the third passed through her rigging striking the water not more than 50 feet beyond her. She then had to stop firing and move out of range.

The Turkish battleship gave no further trouble until the afternoon, when the balloon observers saw her return to the Narrows and again got *Triumph* to move her. The first ascent of the balloon lasted from 5.21 a.m. until 2.5 p.m., and for nearly nine hours the same observers were on constant duty on their unsteady platform watching the Anzac's right flank and spotting on the Turkish positions in that area in close and effective co-operation with the *Triumph*.

The seaplane observers had the greatest difficulty in finding the Turkish batteries, well concealed in the scrub, and so jealous were battery commanders to keep the secret of their positions that, when aircraft were near them, they held back their fire. General Birdwood was quick to take advantage of their sensitiveness, and asked that as far as possible the seaplanes should keep in the area of the lines, especially while movements of troops were being made. This was done and the volume of fire kept down, thus easing to some small extent the pressure on the infantry.

In the early morning of the 27th *Turgud Reis* suddenly began to drop 11-inch shells near the *Ark Royal* off Gaba Tepe, causing the carrier to move off hurriedly. Dunning and Park went up on the Short to spot *Triumph* on the enemy battleship, but she steamed out of range. The airmen flew back to look for batteries about the lines. They found one, well concealed, and went down to 2,500 feet to have a closer look. Their temerity was rewarded by a burst of bullets which narrowly missed both officers and shot through a chassis strut, which was subsequently broken on alighting. The Turks had done better than they knew. Old 136 was nearly finished. The strut was mended, but on her next attempt to get off the water both her struts buckled, and the engine which was submerged never ran well again.

Although 136 tried a few more jobs, she fades from the picture. Delivered by Messrs. Short to Isle of Grain in September 1914, she had carried Flight Commander Kilner and Lieutenant Erskine Childers to Cuxhaven on Christmas Day of 1914, when those officers reported on the German fleet in the Schillig roads. Commander Clark-Hall had written from the *Ark Royal* that she was the most valuable and only rough-weather seaplane on board the ship. She was one of the earliest of the Shorts to be fitted with folding wings. When she folded her wings for the last time she could do so in peace, for she had done her bit.

The *Ark Royal* continued her work over the Anzac beaches from off Gaba Tepe until the threat of submarine attacks drove her into Kephalo Bay at Imbros. She had lent a seaplane to the light cruiser *Doris* which took part in the Bulair diversion. This machine made two flights over the Bulair lines and the northern shore of the Gulf of Xeros on the 25th of April, and reported no movements in the area. On the 26th the *Doris* came south, and her Sopwith on the 27th searched for a submarine which had been reported near Gaba Tepe. The seaplane also reconnoitred the coast from Gaba Tepe to Sedd el Bahr. By the 30th the shock of the firing from the *Doris's* after 6-inch guns had shaken the seaplane and stripped the fuselage of its fabric; it was exchanged for one of the Schneider Cup Sopwiths, which went south with *Doris* and did a number of important reconnaissance flights over Smyrna.

The *Manica's* balloon made seven ascents on the 26th of April to spot for the *Triumph* and *Queen Elizabeth*; the latter ship, when directed on to Kojadere, blew up a magazine in the afternoon. On the following day the balloon observer saw Turkish transports below Nagara apparently making for Maidos or Kilia Liman. He put *Queen Elizabeth* on to the largest of them, signalling the first shot fifty yards short and the second fifty yards over. After the third shot, to the listening ears of Vice-Admiral de Robeck came the message 'O.K.'

'What do they mean by O.K.?' he shouted down the telephone. 'Have we hit her?'

The question was signalled across to the *Manica* and back came the reply: 'Yes, she's sinking by the stern and I am putting you on another.'

The ship so quickly hit at a range of seven miles was the *Scutari*, an old British steamer detained on the outbreak of war; she went down in a few minutes, but her crew, except one officer and two men, were saved. The transports, when they were discovered by the balloon observer, were on their way from Constantinople, to be used afterwards to bring reinforcements to the peninsula from the Asiatic side. As it happened, the *Scutari* was the only one of the group without a load of troops; the remaining ships were diverted to Ak Bashi Liman, where they would be screened by the intervening hills from the balloon observer.

The German general, Liman von Sanders, was himself at Maidos, an eyewitness of the danger which threatened the proposed ferry service from which he had hoped so much. The work of the balloon after this is a long catalogue of batteries hit or silenced, and entrenchments, camps, and stores damaged or destroyed. So great was its success at this stage, when, as yet, the enemy batteries did not keep the parent ship at extreme ranges, that the vice-admiral telegraphed for two more balloons. In the meantime, an old military spherical balloon which had seen service in South Africa was fitted on board the tug *Rescue*, but, after a few days of unrewarded experiment, its use was discontinued.

The cost which we had had to pay to get a footing on the peninsula had been great. So urgent was it, however, that time should not be given to the enemy to recover that Sir Ian Hamilton ordered a general attack towards Achi Baba to be made on the morning of the 28th of April by the 29th Division, supported on their right by the French, who had landed at 'V' beach on the evening of the 26th. In this attack No. 3 Armoured Car Squadron played a conspicuous part. At 7 a.m. on the 27th they had been relieved in their posts on the outskirts of Sedd el Bahr by the French. On the morning of the 28th, acting on his own initiative, Commander Wedgwood took his guns along the Krithia road and got into position at the junction of the British and French fronts. There he was at 1 p.m. when he was ordered to move forward along a *nullah* on the left of the road into Krithia, towards which the 29th Division had made early progress.

Through the heat of the afternoon the men toiled with their guns over the rough ground. By three o'clock they found themselves pushing through exhausted troops who were retiring as a result of determined Turkish counter-attacks made with the bayonet. The position was critical. Lieutenant-Commander Wedgwood, assisted by Sub-Lieutenant C. H. Parkes and Chief Petty Officer John Little, rallied some six hundred of the men and stemmed the retirement on his sector. Chief Petty Officer Little exposed himself recklessly in his successful efforts to put new fighting spirit into the stragglers. With the troops thus rallied Lieutenant-Commander Wedgwood advanced a hundred yards and dug a line of trenches and also posts for his machine-guns. In the evening a retirement was ordered to a position a mile in rear.

Here the machine-gun detachment came under the orders of the 88th Infantry Brigade and continued to fight in the front line. They did yeoman service on the 1st of May when, at the rising of the moon, the Turks, in a series of desperate attacks, broke through the line on both their flanks, but found the centre, manned by the maxims, unshakable. When after a long night of confused and bloody fighting the dawn broke red over Achi Baba, ranks of motionless forms in front of the trenches told of the full execution of the machine-guns, and Turks silhouetted in retirement against the sky-line on the flanks revealed the failure of the enemy to maintain the break through.

On the 5th of May the remainder of the squadron were landed from the *Inkosi*, and on the same day No. 4 Armoured Car Squadron arrived in the *Inkonka* from the Anzac area. In addition, there were, working with the troops on Helles, two further sections from No. 10 Motor Cycle Squadron. The first of these sections had been landed on the 28th of April and the second a few days later. All the Naval Air Service machine-guns fought in the fierce Allied attacks from the 6th to the 8th of May. Machine-guns in these early days were precious beyond price, and these sections became, in effect, travelling units over the Helles area, moving wherever the need was greatest.

Although the attacks on the 6th of May and the two following days were pressed with great determination, they resulted in the gain of only a few hundred yards of ground, and it became clear that Sir Ian Hamilton would require strong reinforcements before he could hope to take Achi Baba and clear the defences which dominated the straits. He was promised considerable reinforcements, but was told that they could not begin to arrive until the middle of July.

On the 18th of May No. 3 Armoured Car Squadron was withdrawn from the line. By that time the commanding officer had been wounded and the unit was considerably weakened by other casualties, sickness, and exhaustion. Three days later it was decided to withdraw also No. 4 Squadron. A section from each squadron was kept on the peninsula, to be equipped with four armoured ears each as soon as the cars could be disembarked with a view to using them in the next Allied attack. The remaining sections of the two squadrons were ordered to hand over, temporarily, their maxims to the East Lancashire Division and to proceed to Mudros. To take their place at Helles the remainder of No. 10 Motor Cycle Squadron were landed. This squadron was reorganised into three sections of six guns each, which were allotted respectively to the 29th Division, the East Lancashire Division, and the Royal Naval Division.

It was Sir Ian Hamilton's intention, whilst awaiting the promised reinforcements which would enable him to resume the offensive on a big scale, to keep up minor attacks in the Helles area which offered better shooting for the ships' guns than the more difficult Anzac country. The Turk, however, did not quietly acquiesce in this policy. On the night of the 18th/19th of May he made a determined attempt to push the Anzac defenders into the sea. Happily, the aeroplane squadron had been prompt in spotting the preparations for this attack. Flight Commander R. L. G. Marix, whilst patrolling on the look-out for enemy aircraft on the morning of the 17th of May, had been struck by the unusual activity at the port of Ak Bashi Liman, where four transports and several smaller craft were unloading stores and troops, and by a large new camp, inland from the port, already filled with soldiers.

When Flight Commander Marix came back with this information which pointed to the arrival of a fresh division, (the 2nd Division from Constantinople), a bomb raid on the camps was planned for the afternoon. Marix loaded one 100-lb. and fourteen 20-lb. bombs on the Breguet and went up with Commander Samson in the observer's seat. This was the first bomb raid on the port and it was highly successful, creating something like panic amongst the dock hands and killing or wounding fifty-seven soldiers. The officers then made a reconnaissance of the shipping in the straits and of the eastern coast of the peninsula, and their observations confirmed the strength of the new reinforcements. When these air reports were received at General Headquarters it was concluded that an early attack on the Anzac position was likely, and General Birdwood was so informed.

In the afternoon of the 18th of May he warned all his subordinate commanders that the attack would probably come during the night. His warning was received in the trenches at 10. 0 p.m., and as the Turkish soldiers, in the deep darkness which preceded the dawn, crept to the assault, they were awaited in perfect readiness. The Turkish attack was pressed relentlessly, almost fanatically, but the air had robbed the assault of surprise, the defenders could not be shaken, and, by the 24th of May, so thick lay the Turkish dead, killed during the five days' series of assaults, that an armistice had to be granted to the enemy for their burial. There is, perhaps, no better example, than is offered by the story of this action, of the far-reaching effect of a simple and timely piece of observation from the air.

Towards the end of May the Allied position was profoundly affected by the arrival of the first German submarine. (This was the U.21, under Lieutenant-Commander Hersing, which had left the Ems on April 25th, journeying via the Orkneys and Cattaro). Disaster followed in its wake. First the *Triumph* was torpedoed on the 25th, and then the *Majestic* two days later. The passing of these two well-known ships had an immediate and tonic effect on the spirits of the Turkish troops. The British destroyers had now to take on the job of giving the army its fire support, and the position was not remedied until the end of July when monitors and 'blister' ships arrived and made large-calibre fire from stationary platforms again possible.

With the submarines came, too, a new responsibility for the air, together with a new menace. The *Ark Royal* was not considered fast enough to operate in unprotected waters and was kept in Kephalo Bay, Imbros, where she became, in effect, a depot ship for all the aircraft which came to be settled on the island. Her seaplanes, from a base in the sheltered Aliki Bay, continued to do the routine of spotting, photography and reconnaissance.

Sir Ian Hamilton planned the second of his attacks in the Helles area for the 4th of June. The aeroplanes of No. 3 Squadron spent the days preceding the attack on reconnaissance and artillery work. Flight Lieutenant Butler got some useful photographs of the complicated Turkish entrenchments south of Krithia, from which maps were made up and delivered by air to advanced General Headquarters at Helles. Pilots of the squadron used these photographic maps, also, to help in the direction of the artillery fire.

Early in May a rough aerodrome had been made on Helles to enable observers to land and report urgent information to corps headquarters without loss of time, and to allow aeroplanes to be available during daylight for emergency flying. The aerodrome, however, had disadvantages. It was cramped, the approaches were bad, and it was under observation from the Turks on Achi Baba, with the result that it was heavily shelled when aeroplanes were on it for any length of time. The dust raised by the aeroplanes, too, as they landed on the sandy surface, got into the engines. However, the aerodrome economised valuable time especially before and during the advance on the 4th of June.

******

The Helles aerodrome was given up, except for emergency landings, on the 29th of June. By that time three aeroplanes had been wrecked on the landing ground by Turkish shell-fire. A dummy aeroplane erected on the aerodrome in October induced the enemy to waste 650 shells in three days.

******

It was in this attack that the air service armoured cars were used for the first time on Gallipoli. Four cars had been landed on the 26th of May and four more on the 3rd of June, and were housed in specially prepared deep dug-outs. The cars were manned by the two sections of Nos. 3 and 4 Squadrons which had been retained on the peninsula, and their operations were directed by Lieutenant-Commander R. B. B. Colmore, who had taken over general command of the armoured car units in the Mediterranean on the 11th of May. There were two roads and a track towards Krithia along which it was deemed possible that the cars could usefully work, but these roads were cut across by many lines of trenches.

Before they could be used much bridging work had to be done, whilst, along the track, night parties had to go out to cut down the tangled heather and undergrowth to make it possible for the cars to pass. It was essential that the crew of each car should know every feature and obstacle in front of them, and Lieutenant-Commander Colmore, with his officers, mapped the area as far as the Turkish front-line wire by personal reconnaissance made by day and night.

The bombardment of the Turkish trenches opened at eight on the morning of the 4th. From dawn an aeroplane of No. 3 Squadron had patrolled continuously over the trenches to keep enemy airmen from observing our movements. Once the bombardment began, other aeroplanes went up to send corrections to our batteries and to watch the enemy lines of communication. At noon the infantry went forward on a front stretching from Kereves Dere in a northerly direction to the sea.

Along most of the front the attack was immediately successful, but at two vital points little progress could be made. On the British right the French were forced back to their original line by counter-attacks, thus compelling the British troops in this sector to swing back in conformity. On the British left it was found that the bombardment had failed to destroy the Turkish front-line wire and no progress was made. In the centre, however, an advance of from two hundred to four hundred yards was maintained on a three mile front. The eight armoured cars moved off along the three roads under heavy shell-fire as the infantry assaulted.

On the left track the two cars were held up at the firing line by an unbridged trench and eventually returned to the main road. On this road, also, it proved impossible to get across the bridge over the front line. Two of the cars in attempting to do so were partly ditched and were at once shelled. It was only on the right road that the cars reached the Turkish front line, but here again they were held by a high stone-faced parapet. When it became clear that the cars could do nothing to help the advance, they were withdrawn. Three officers, including Lieutenant-Commander Colmore, and a petty officer, (Chief Petty Officer G. C. P. Rumming who died of his wounds in November 1917), had been wounded and the cars had suffered minor damage from shell-fire.

They had done what they could, but the conditions were against them, and Sir Ian Hamilton decided that as long as trench warfare persisted there could be no further use for armoured cars on the peninsula. Three officers and thirty-four men of No. 3 Squadron with four machine-guns were attached to the VIII Corps, and the remaining personnel of this squadron and the section of No. 4 Squadron were ordered to await transport to Alexandria, whence their units had gone from Mudros.

The part played by the armoured cars had been disappointing, but the dismounted machine-guns of No. 10 Motor Cycle Squadron did great work in the forefront of the battle, fighting side by side with the assaulting infantry. Of the ten guns which the squadron manned, one with its crew was blown up by a direct hit, another with most of its crew disabled was lost to a Turkish bayonet attack, but was retaken almost at once, two others fell into the hands of the enemy because their crews were dead or wounded and there was no one to bring the guns back when the Royal Naval Division were forced to retire, and one other was put out of action by an exploding shell. Owing to the heavy losses of the squadron, it became necessary to reorganise it into two sections of six guns each.

Whilst the infantry attack was in progress, one of the aeroplane pilots landed on the aerodrome at Helles with the information that he had seen a German submarine near the Rabbit Islands. Commander Samson, who was on the aerodrome, had a 100-lb. bomb put under his aeroplane and went off at once. After some searching he found the enemy underwater craft totally submerged, but showing up plainly in the entrance to the straits, making towards a French cruiser which, with her fire, was supporting the right flank of the attack. He dived and released his bomb, which was fitted with a direct-action fuse and exploded on the surface of the water. When the disturbance caused by the burst of the bomb subsided, Commander Samson was chagrined to see the submarine pass, apparently unharmed, underneath the cruiser. She was not seen again until the evening, by which time she had got through to Ak Bashi Liman, where Commander Samson saw her on the surface as he was returning from a long reconnaissance. He had no bombs, but gave her a few rounds from his rifle.

On the 22nd of June a German aeroplane was shot down, near Achi Baba, by Flight Commander C, H. Collet and Major R. E. T. Hogg. They were on a Voisin and fought the German with a rifle for twenty minutes, hitting the engine. The officers went home for bombs with which to finish the German aeroplane, but found, when they returned, that it had been moved. The French air service located it later, and called up its own artillery who blew it up with a direct hit.

On the 28th of June a second attack at Helles was made by the British against the Turkish right, the objective being the lines of trenches which rested on the coast. In this attack the armoured car squadrons had eight machineguns in action. The advance went well, and the five lines of captured trenches were won and held.

Thirty-one hours' flying during the day were recorded by the aeroplanes, during which many small bombs were dropped on Turkish troops and batteries taking part in the action, and infantry and ammunition columns were reported from the air and engaged and scattered by our 60-pounder batteries. Some of the aeroplane flying was made over the Anzac area, where there took place a subsidiary attack to draw off Turkish reinforcements from the southern sector.

Aeroplane observers, on the 28th, saw considerable movements of enemy troops in front of the Anzac positions and Turks assembling in the second-line trenches. This concentration heralded the heavy counter-attacks made on the night of the 29th/30th of June, which met with no success. This proved to be the last serious effort of the Turks against the Anzac position.

When the *Ark Royal* was driven into Kephalo Bay by the submarine threat she made way at sea for a faster carrier, *Ben-my-Chree*, which, under Squadron Commander C. J. L'Estrange Malone, arrived at Iero Bay, Mitylene, on the 12th of June. Before being converted as a carrier, this ship was engaged in the passenger service between Liverpool and the Isle of Man. She had, since April, been on active service in the North Sea. Her maximum speed was about twenty-two knots, and she had accommodation for three Short and two scout-type seaplanes ready for service. Her Shorts, which were adapted to launch torpedoes, were more powerfully engined than anything in the *Ark Royal*. She was fitted with a large upper-deck hangar aft, and a trackway forward, and had an efficient testing and repair workshop. The seaplanes were hoisted by a derrick on the mainmast worked by steam winches.

The *Ben-my-Chree* proved a great addition to the air strength in the Eastern Mediterranean. She provided, indeed, a highly mobile, self-contained air unit and proved her value in a diversity of ways. Her seaplanes were, at various times, used for bombing, torpedo attacks, spotting for ships' gun-fire, reconnaissance by day and night, low-flying attacks on troops, and antisubmarine patrols, and their sphere of operations extended over the peninsula, the Asiatic side of the straits, the Bulgarian coast, Smyrna, and the Greek islands as far west as Milo. (She proved her value as a ship on the 2nd of September 1915, when, in answer to an S.O.S., she rescued 694 troops and 121 crew from the transport *Southland*, torpedoed thirty miles off Mudros.)

Soon after the arrival of the reinforcement represented by *Ben-my-*

Chree, the whole air service in the Eastern Mediterranean was closely inspected, and reported on, by a senior officer of wide military air experience. Colonel F. H. Sykes, who had served continuously in France from the beginning of the war, had returned to England in May 1915, and the Admiralty at once applied for his services, so that they might send him to the Dardanelles. Colonel Sykes arrived and was conferring with Vice-Admiral de Robeck and Sir Ian Hamilton on the 24th of June. He went on to visit all the air units and to discuss the conditions with the flying officers and the naval and military staffs. He drew up a closely reasoned report which was dispatched to the Admiralty on the 9th of July. On the same day he sent a cablegram summarising his recommendations. The problem as it presented itself to him was, firstly, one of organisation, and secondly, of reinforcement.

The various air units were widely separated from one another, and from the staffs and ships with which they were working. His first recommendation, therefore, was that all the naval air units be more centrally grouped, and that a closer channel of communication be established between them and the naval and military headquarters. This could best be done by a concentration of the flying units, under a central headquarters, at Kephalo, on Imbros, where there was now an aerodrome. He further recommended the supply of aeroplanes of a standard type for three squadrons (thirty-six with eighteen in reserve and eighteen spare engines). The aeroplanes asked for were eighteen B.E.2c's fitted with R.A.F. engines, and eighteen Maurice Farmans fitted with 100 horse-power Renaults, together with their reserves and spares.

In addition, six air cameras with personnel to form a photographic section, twenty-four Lewis or Vickers guns with mountings for B.E.'s or Maurice Farmans, and a supply of standard wireless sets, and daylight signalling lamps, would be wanted. For the increased demands for anti-submarine work, he asked for eight 'S.S.' airships, and six two-seater and two single-seater seaplanes; also, if it could be sent out at once, a further complete kite-balloon section for fleet-spotting. Hangars and sheds to hold thirty-six machines would be necessary. Colonel Sykes proposed that a unit to train observers should be formed and equipped with aircraft that were considered unsuitable for flying over the enemy.

These wide proposals were agreed to by the Admiralty, and Colonel Sykes was appointed, with the rank of Wing Captain, on the 24th of July to command the Royal Naval Air Service units in the Eastern Mediterranean. By this time a second kite-balloon ship, *Hector*, had come to reinforce the *Manica*. She was a cargo vessel of some 4,660 tons and had been hurriedly fitted out in a similar way to the *Manica*. She arrived on the 9th of July and at once got to work to help in the spotting for the ships. Colonel Sykes proceeded to concentrate his aeroplanes on Imbros at an aerodrome on the east side of Kephalo harbour; by the end of July the French air service was left in undisputed possession of the landing ground on Tenedos.

The Battle of Suvla Bay

By this time Sir Ian Hamilton's preparations were nearing completion for what was to prove the last great offensive action on the peninsula. The supreme object of the new attack was the capture of the dominating feature of the formidable Sari Bair Ridge, following which it was hoped that an advance to the Narrows defences would be possible. For this operation, which would, if successful, grip the waist of the peninsula from Gaba Tepe to Maidos, the commander-in-chief proposed to reinforce the Anzac front and to make a new landing in Suvla Bay. Surprise was essential, and the night of the 6th of August was fixed for the attack, since it was preceded by some nights when there would be little or no moon to illuminate the putting ashore of the reinforcements at Anzac Cove.

To divert the attention of the enemy from the peninsula, and in the hope that he might be led to suspect an attempted landing near Smyrna, a somewhat elaborate bombardment was staged, on August the 3rd, of the port of Sighajik lying across the neck of land some twenty miles south-west of Smyrna. A feint landing was made at dusk. The *Ben-my-Chree* had been put under the orders of the French Admiral for this diversion and reconnaissance flights were made by two of her seaplanes.

The aeroplane unit, from its new aerodrome on Imbros, was well situated for the new offensive. The economy in flying time effected by the change from Tenedos was the more important since none of the reinforcements asked for by Colonel Sykes had yet arrived. The air reconnaissances of the Suvla area, so urgently needed, had to be made in such a way as not to arouse the suspicions of the Turk. The aeroplanes therefore flew at a high altitude and stayed over the peninsula only for brief periods. On the 4th of August all the existing trenches and gun emplacements were carefully noted by Captain A. A. Walser, and a sketch of the position, which he made from the air, was handed to General Headquarters. He reported that most of the gun emplacements were not occupied, an observation which was confirmed on the following day by Second Lieutenant the Hon. M. H. R. Knatchbull-Hugessen, who stated further that the group of trenches north of Salt Lake was unmanned. Some detailed photographs were procured of the defences on Chocolate Hill, which was to be one of the first objectives of the new landing-force. During the 6th the only enemy troops that were seen were moving away from the area. The conditions indeed, as reported by the aeroplane observers, were full of promise.

The Suvla landing was made through the black night of the 6th/7th of August. Twenty thousand men were quietly put ashore, and soon demonstrated the truth of the aeroplane reports that the enemy was wholly unready to resist their advance. There were against them, in fact, no more than two thousand men, mostly of the Gallipoli *Gendarmerie*, backed up by only a few scattered guns. Unhappily, an initial delay in the advance, owing to disorganisation which followed the landing, held up the attack on Chocolate Hill, planned for the morning of the 7th, until 5.30 p.m., and not until darkness fell was the hill wholly captured. By this time, too, our men on the left had pushed along the coast ridge to its highest point at Kiretch Tepe Sirt.

But the day's advance was lamentably short of what had been hoped would be achieved in the few hours which followed the landing. It had been planned that the troops should, on the first day, seize the ridge east of Chocolate Hill, and with it the pastoral country on which the army was to rely for its water supply. The failure to do this was calamitous, and the necessity of getting water up to the troops, laboriously from the beaches, led to confusion and delay. Even so the position might have been remedied on the next day by a determined move forward. But throughout the precious hours of Sunday the 8th, when the remnants of the scattered *Gendarmerie* were ready to evacuate their positions, and when, according to the Turkish authorities, there was not a single soldier along the whole stretch of ground from Kiretch Tepe Sirt to 'W' Hill, no advance was attempted.

An observer flying over this area in the early morning of the 8th was puzzled by the complete quiet. He had expected to find the battle in full swing and was led, by the inactivity below him, to the conclusion that our men must have pushed far beyond their objectives although he could nowhere locate them. Any doubt of the unhappy consequences of the delay in pressing the advance was dispelled by the reports of the observers who reconnoitred the Turkish lines of communication. In the afternoon of the 7th Second Lieutenant Knatchbull-Hugessen, piloted by Squadron Commander R. Bell Davies, had reported no movement towards the new landing beach, but large encampments in the neighbourhood of Bulair and numerous smaller ones dotted along the important Uzun Keupri road.

On the morning of the 8th observers came back with the news that troops were pouring down from the camps about Bulair and that some of them had already reached the villages immediately behind the Suvla front. When, at dawn on the 9th, the Suvla attack was resumed, the Turkish reinforcements were in position. Although the British attacks, in the sweltering summer heat, were now valiantly pressed, no prodigies of self-sacrifice could make up for the precious wasted hours of the two days which followed the landing. There is, perhaps, no sadder illustration in modern war of the price that has to be paid for failure to exploit surprise, at the right moment, to the utmost limit of the endurance of the troops.

On the 9th a new air service maxim squadron went into action on the Suvla front. This squadron. No. 11, under Lieutenant-Commander J. W. Stocks, had arrived at Mudros together with No. 9 Armoured Car Squadron (Lieutenant-Commander A. D. Borton) at the end of July. No. 9 Squadron was also sent to Suvla, where it was landed on the morning of the 16th and went into position with its machine-guns along the front of the 10th Division.

Meanwhile the main Anzac attack, which had begun at 9.30 p.m. on August the 6th, was being pressed with skill and determination. It lasted four days, cost 12,000 men, and failed in the end owing, in part, to the enormous difficulty of night marching through the rough country, but in the main to the failure of the help which the Suvla force had been expected to give.

On the 11th two Turkish transports were seen from the air to be disembarking troops and stores at Ak Bashi Liman, and on the following morning the activity about this port was intense, and observers brought back news of movements both from Ak Bashi and Kilia Liman towards the Suvla and Anzac fronts. These and other observations on the following days left no doubt that the enemy was bringing further reinforcements through Chanak on the Asiatic shore. To impede the transference of these troops across the straits and to harass movements of troops down the peninsula, *Ben-my-Chree* and a monitor operated for some days in the Gulf of Xeros. The seaplanes kept close watch and directed the fire of the monitor on Turkish formations which were seen on the roads while other seaplanes attacked the troops with bombs. Furthermore, it was from *Ben-my-Chree* at this time, as shall be told later, that the historic seaplane-torpedo attacks were made on enemy transports.

With initial failure of the new operations came a lull. On the 21st the Suvla force tried but failed again to take 'W' Hill, one of its original objectives. Once more the demand went home for more men, but Sir Ian Hamilton was told there were none for him. On the 27th, with the capture of Hill 60, the Suvla force made its last serious effort. From that date the supply of munitions and reinforcements began to fall away.

Towards the end of August, the last reinforcement reached the armoured car squadrons. The new unit, No. 12 Squadron, under Lieutenant-Commander H. E. Taylor, arrived with only three machine-guns and no armoured cars, and was used to relieve No. 10 Squadron which had been continuously in action at Helles since the days following the first landings.

Meanwhile the new board of Admiralty, formed on the resignation of Mr. Winston Churchill at the end of May, had arranged to transfer to the army all the semi-military ground services which had grown up as part of the Royal Naval Air Service. In this category were the armoured car squadrons, and the War Office agreed, in August, to take all these over. When this decision was communicated to Sir Ian Hamilton, he wired at once urging that the air service machine-gun squadrons should be allowed to remain undisturbed. They were, he said, one of the most valuable assets in his force, and if they were broken up important posts along the firing line would be seriously weakened.

In the result it was agreed that the armoured cars and all stores, including those at Alexandria, should be handed over, at once, but that the Naval Air Service personnel should remain to train military machine-gunners; all further reinforcements were to be supplied by the army. Not before December 1915 had the naval squadrons on the peninsula handed over the last of their maxims to the infantry. Many officers and men went over with their guns. The remainder, especially those with technical knowledge, were attached to the aeroplane units or were sent home for flying duties.

In the last days of August, the overworked aeroplane wing, (for the change of nomenclature to Wings see chapter 6, 'Destruction of the Naval Zeppelin L.12), struggling against sickness in the summer heat, received welcome help with the arrival of No. 2 Wing, under the command of Wing Commander E. L. Gerrard. By this time a new aerodrome, constructed by Turkish prisoners, to accommodate both wings, was nearing completion at Kephalo Point on Imbros. The aerodrome originally occupied by No. 3 Wing, on the east side of Kephalo harbour, had proved unsatisfactory. It was bordered on three sides by high cliffs and on the fourth by sand dunes, and eddies set up by the wind often made landing or taking off a difficult feat.

On August the 19th Flight Commander C. H. Collet, a very gallant and experienced pilot, had been caught, with engine failure, in a bad *remous*. His aeroplane crashed and caught fire and, in spite of the self-sacrifice of Chief Petty Officer M. S. Keogh who rushed into the intense heat and dragged the pilot nearly clear before he himself was overcome, Captain Collet had died of his injuries. The new aerodrome offered no such disadvantages and was used continuously by Nos. 2 and 3 Wings until the evacuation. No. 2 Wing brought out sixteen pilots, 200 men, twenty-two aeroplanes, and a good supply of hangars, workshop lorries, and spare engines. The aeroplanes were not of the type which Colonel Sykes had asked for. They were six Morane Parasol two-seater monoplanes, fitted with 80 horse-power le Rhone engines; six B.E.2c biplanes, fitted with 75 horse-power Renaults; six Caudron biplanes, and four Bristol Scout single-seater biplanes, all fitted with 80 horse-power Gnomes.

Of these, the Caudrons were not used for active service, and the Moranes, which required very skilful handling, gave trouble because their rotary engines picked up the fine sand in embarrassing quantities. Commander Samson handed to the wing two of his Voisin biplanes fitted with 140 horse-power Canton Unné engines. It took time for the new pilots to get to know the peninsula, but, by the autumn, the whole air service was in full flight.

An additional kite-balloon ship, *Canning*, arrived on the 2nd of October to take the place of *Manica* which had gone home to be refitted in the middle of September. The *Canning*, of 5,375 tons, was fitted with many improved devices prompted by the experience gained in the *Manica*. A large hold space had been cleared forward so that the balloon could be carried already inflated. These reinforcements added greatly to the assistance which the air service was able to give to the fleet, especially in their bombardments of the Turkish lines of communication. Further, the service had now the first real opportunity to strike, by bombing, its own direct blow at the enemy.

The Air attacks on the Turkish Communications

Nothing, perhaps, caused the Turkish command more uneasiness than the possibility of the communications to the peninsula being so attacked as to have the effect of a victory on the actual front. From Constantinople, the main base, supplies and reinforcements might go by sea through the Marmara or by the Thracian railway to Uzun Keupri, and thence by road through Keshan and Bulair. The sea route, more direct and more comfortable, was virtually closed after April by the daring of the British submarines, and but rarely did the Turk try to move transports across. And when he did he found a new menace.

A 5,000-ton supply ship earned fame, on the 12th of August, as the first vessel in history to be torpedoed from the air. The *Ben-my-Chree*, from the Gulf of Xeros, sent a Short, piloted by Flight Commander C. H. K. Edmonds, across the Isthmus to attack shipping. The seaplane carried a 14-inch torpedo slung longitudinally under its fuselage. Off Injeh Burnu Edmonds spotted a large steamer and, gliding to within fifteen feet of the water, he released his torpedo at a range of 300 yards. The missile exploded abreast the mainmast, sending columns of water and debris high in the air, and the pilot, as he flew away, saw the steamer settling down by the stern. When, however, reports from the British submarines came to be studied, it was found that his victim had already been torpedoed and shelled four days previously and left by the submarine E.14 beached in shallow water. Although, as it happened, Edmonds had only completed the work of the underwater craft, his feat was no less of a portent, and if any doubt of its meaning still existed in the Turkish mind, it was soon to be dispelled.

On the 17th of August he repeated his brilliant exploit against the shipping which was bringing stores and reinforcements into Ak Bashi Liman from the Asiatic coast to meet the new menace at Suvla. His torpedo, released from fifteen to twenty feet, and at about 800 yards' range, hit the middle one of three steamers, which was set on fire, gutted, and eventually taken to Constantinople. Whilst this was happening Flight Lieutenant G. B. Dacre, who was also on his way to Ak Bashi Liman, was having trouble with his engine, and had to land in the straits about five miles south-west of Galata, close to an enemy hospital ship. A wave of the hand was enough to convince those in the ship that he was friendly.

When the hospital ship was gone, Dacre looked for a target for his torpedo, and soon saw, in False Bay on the Asiatic coast, what he was seeking. His engine was now running better, so he taxied across the Straits and fired his shot at a large steam tug. He had time to see the tug give a violent lurch as he taxied out of the bay again under rifle fire. After a run of two miles he was able to take the seaplane off the water and to get within gliding distance of *Ben-my-Chree* in Xeros Bay before the engine gave out again. The small steamer which he had attacked was sunk by the explosion.

These revolutionary successes seriously affected the morale of the crews of the. Turkish ships, and helped to complete the work of the submarines. Unhappily, the torpedo-loaded Short seaplane could only be made to get off the water and fly under ideal conditions. A calm sea with a slight breeze was essential and the engine had to be running perfectly. Further, the weight of the torpedo so restricted the amount of petrol which could be carried that a flight of much more than three-quarters of an hour was not possible. So, it came about that while a number of torpedo-attacks from the air were attempted, only three were successfully concluded. There were, however, many aircraft attacks with bombs. In all, during 1915, seventy such attacks were made by aeroplanes and seaplanes on enemy war vessels, transports, tugs, lighters, and sailing craft; two large steamers and one tug were hit and damaged, and one lighter and six *dhows* were wrecked.

The enemy was thus compelled by the threat of submarine and aircraft attack to rely almost entirely on his overland route by Uzun Keupri and Bulair. The road between these two places was kept in good repair, and it is estimated that between May and December 1915 some hundred thousand pack-animals and two hundred thousand troops passed over it. The road itself was bombed on several occasions by aeroplanes, but although large craters were often made they were soon filled in, and the resultant surface offered no great obstacle to the pack-animals or bullock-carts which formed the bulk of the transport.

When Bulgaria came into the war, in October, the railway between that country and Turkey became of strategic importance, and the problem of bombing it was considered. The objective which offered best results to the air was Ferejik junction where the Salonika-Constantinople railway is joined by the branch line from Dede Agach. But before the air command was ready to do this bombing the Bulgarians had overrun Serbia and had thus freed the Berlin-Constantinople railway, an ominous fact which meant that Turkey would at last be able to get the munitions she so badly needed. This railway, however, had a vulnerable link within aircraft range at a point, south of Kellee Burgas, where the line bridges the River Maritza. The destruction of this bridge, urged by an Admiralty telegram on the 5th of November, would not only cut the Berlin route, but also the Salonika line which branches off near the western end of the bridge.

On the 8th of November the first attacks were made by an aeroplane from Imbros fitted with an extra petrol tank, and by two of *Ben-my-Chree*, Short seaplanes starting from near Enos. This meant for the aeroplane a total distance of over one hundred and eighty miles, of which sixty were over the sea, and for the seaplanes more than one hundred and twenty miles, of which all but ten were over the land. Each machine carried two 112-lb. bombs. The aeroplane, a Maurice Farman piloted by Commander Samson with Captain I. A. E. Edwards as observer, flew over the target at 800 feet. The two bombs were aimed at the centre of the bridge, but fell together about five yards to the south of it, causing enough strain to one of the piers to delay traffic for forty-eight hours. The observer brought back a full reconnaissance report of the area covered by the flight.

The seaplane pilots, Flight Commander Edmonds and Flight Lieutenant Dacre, attacked the bridge from 500 feet and 1,000 feet, respectively: they failed to hit the bridge, but their bombs damaged the permanent way. Other aeroplane attacks were made on the 10th, 13th, 16th, 18th, and 24th of November. A night-attack was tried on the 13th of November by Flight Commander J. R. W. Smyth-Pigott of No. 2 Wing on a B.E.2c. In the faint moonlight he located the bridge, but his bombs failed to hit. Although on no occasion was there thus a direct hit to reward the pilots' efforts, damage was caused to the embankments, to the permanent way, and to Uzun Keupri station. Following the first of the attacks, the Turk, alarmed, had rushed a number of anti-aircraft guns to the bridge, and their fire was enough to rob the bombs of their final accuracy.

Ferejik was bombed by flights of from two to six aeroplanes on the 13th, 16th, 18th, and 19th of November, and on the 1st of December. In all, seventeen 112-lb. and twenty-four 20-lb. bombs were dropped, and destroyed the main buildings of the south station, and damaged rolling stock and sections of the permanent way. It was during the attack on the 19th of November that Squadron Commander R. Bell Davies on a single-seater Nieuport won the Victoria Cross. One of the bombing aeroplanes, a Henri Farman, piloted by Flight Sub-Lieutenant G. F. Smylie, was badly damaged over the station by rifle fire.

Smylie, who still had one bomb left, was forced to land; a group of enemy soldiers came hot foot in his direction; he set fire to his aeroplane, relying on the bomb to wreck it as the flames did their work. But he saw that Bell Davies was landing, so he exploded the bomb with his pistol, ran to where Davies was now waiting for him, and, crouching in discomfort under the petrol tank, was taken into the air. Bell Davies, who had judged and faced his risks with great coolness, carried his burden safely home with the same skill. His report on the effects of his bombing dismisses this episode with the words:

> Returning saw H.5 burning in marshes. Picked up pilot.

In addition to Ferejik, other vulnerable points were Dede Agach and Bodoma junction, but both were within range of the ships' guns, and *Ben-my-Chreeh's* seaplanes therefore confined their action to reporting the ships' fire. They also by reconnaissance, spotting, and photography assisted on October the 21st in a feint landing at Fener Point.

Aircraft bombing attacks on the Turkish troops, once they got to the peninsula, were more intensive than those made against distant points. The troops moved by sea were attacked at their landing-places, of which the principal ones were Maidos, Ak Bashi Liman, Kilia Liman, and Gallipoli. Ak Bashi Liman received closest attention. The first raid on the port on the 17th of May by the Breguet, as has been told, killed or wounded fifty-seven soldiers, whilst the dock-hands, seized with panic, ran from their work and could not be induced to return for several hours, a routine which they repeated each time afterwards when aircraft appeared overhead.

This port, too, suffered much from ships' fire directed by aircraft. One typical example, which took place on the 30th of August, may be quoted. Wing Commander Samson (observer. Captain A. H. Keith-Jopp) spotted for the monitor M.15 which stood off the Anzac coast. The range worked out at 18,000 yards. Air Commodore Samson says:

> In Ak Bashi Liman, were lying two steamers alongside each other, both about 200 feet long, three or four tugs and about twenty *dhows* busily unloading. I got up to 6,000 feet where I could get a good view both of M.15 and Ak Bashi Liman. I took care to keep about four miles away from Ak Bashi in order not to arouse their suspicions. When ready I ordered fire. The first shot fell about 800 yards short fortunately behind the hills so that no notice was taken by the Turks. The next shot fell on the beach and killed some Turks. The third shot fell into the sea. We now had got the range. A terrible panic occurred. The tugs that had got *dhows* in tow cut them off and steamed for the Asiatic shore. The gangs on the beach who were by now well used to aeroplane bombs, dropped everything and fled to the

hills. I was trying to get a hit on the two steamers which were still at anchor. The eighth shot hit one.

Jopp said, "What correction must I signal?"

"I said, "Report O.K." (hit).

The ninth shell hit the second steamer. When it is remembered that these two ships were lying alongside each other, the range was 18,000 yards, that hills 800 to 1,000 feet were intervening, and that M.I 5 was just lying with her bows up against a little mark buoy and rolling in the swell, this shooting is really wonderful. One steamer sank and the other got on fire. Whether she finally sank or not I couldn't say.

So crowded was the port that the many air bomb-raids seldom failed to inflict casualties. A Turkish staff officer, who took the precaution to move his headquarters two miles outside the town, has stated that daylight work had to be abandoned except on important occasions, and, even at night, orders were given to the working parties that only hand-lanterns might be used. A party at Kilia Liman, working with a flare on the pier during the night of September the 19th, attracted a 112-lb. bomb, which hastened the general usage of hand-lanterns. The attack on Maidos by five aeroplanes on the 23rd of April, already referred to, killed twenty soldiers, wounded others, and started many fires, causing the Turks to move the 72nd Regiment out of the town, and to issue orders that transport and other traffic must be suspended in future during daylight.

At Gallipoli the flour mills, which largely supplied the Turkish Army, were frequently bombed, but situated in a crowded area, they formed a difficult target. One 112-lb. bomb hit a flour store, completely wrecking it and killing two soldiers. Seaplane and aeroplane observers, too, spotted on to the mills for ships and monitors, and although they were never put out of action, some of the buildings were damaged and milling machinery wrecked.

A midshipman observer attached to No. 3 Wing had the satisfaction on the 3rd of October, when spotting for the M.I 5 on this target, of seeing a stray shot from the monitor blow up, in the harbour, a tug loaded with ammunition, and, a little later, two other shots sink a *dhow* and two sailing vessels which were too slow to follow the other shipping which fled across the straits. Chanak and Kilia Liman were repeatedly attacked from the air; the coal depot at Nagara was hit on two occasions; and on other occasions the piers at Bergaz Liman and

Kilia Liman were damaged.

The Turkish troops, once encamped, were not allowed to rest. At first, they used white tents, but soon learnt caution. A large part of Jissoi camp was wrecked on the 23rd of April, and of Boghali camp on the 30th of April. The Turks began then to camouflage the tents and to go into bivouacs and dug-outs, but the attacks continued, especially all over the southern part of the peninsula, and the effect on the troops' morale was considerable, as has been affirmed by many Turkish witnesses. The rest camp in the Soghanli Dere suffered as much as any. This camp housed, in dug-outs and caves on the hill-sides, the reserves for the Achi Baba Army, who were a target not only for the indirect fire of the ships and the British bombs, but also for the remorseless attention of the French aeroplane squadron.

Apart from the organised bombing attacks, reconnaissance pilots usually carried a bomb or two with which to annoy the enemy. The routine dawn reconnaissance, for instance, took the pilot over the peninsula at the moment when the mens' breakfasts were being got ready. The valleys, in which troops were in reserve, would be full of little fires, and it was always easy to pick out the places where the soldiers were most concentrated. A casual bomb was enough to induce the Turkish cooks, for miles around, to extinguish their fires, with the annoying result that many breakfasts were spoiled. The effect of these petty annoyances was cumulative.

When they were on the move about the peninsula, the troops were still a target. No. 3 Wing alone made thirty-five bombing attacks on convoys in 1915. In the danger zone, from Ak Bashi Liman to the southward, the aeroplane attacks, which were made not only with bombs but also, later in the campaign, with machine-gun fire from a low height, forced the enemy to split up his columns into sections of five carts or twenty pack-animals, marching at intervals of a mile apart, with orders to halt and take cover whenever an aeroplane was seen. But even this did not suffice, and movements by day soon came to be made only when absolutely necessary. In the less dangerous area, north of Ak Bashi, the Turk was not so cautious, and many convoys were found by the aeroplanes and destroyed or scattered.

A bomb dropped by Wing Commander Samson in the middle of September might have affected the future history of the Ottoman empire. This officer, flying his Nieuport single-seater on general reconnaissance behind Anzac, saw a motorcar near Turshun Keui. This means of transport was rare enough to suggest that it was only used by highly-placed officials and, as Wing Commander Samson had two bombs, he dived to attack. His first bomb exploded behind the car, which stopped, the occupants rushing for the cover of a ditch. Samson flew off, but when, from a distance, he saw the car on the move again, he returned and released his second bomb, which was near enough for fragments to hit the car without, however, wounding the passengers. One of those passengers, according to information given by a Turkish staff officer after the war, was Mustapha Kemal, destined to make history as his country's leader.

The order of importance given by Turkish authorities to the methods of attack on their communications is submarine, aircraft, and bombardment by the ships. The sea route, as has been seen, was virtually closed, and the alternative land route, with its 160 miles of railway and 100 miles of road was, at best, a tedious and precarious one. It took some time to organise the transport which this long route demanded, and at one time, in June, the Turkish Fifth Army, owing to the failure of its supplies, was reduced to 160 rounds of ammunition per man. Had it been possible to close the road, especially at night, by aircraft attack, and ships' fire, the Turks on the peninsula must quickly have exhausted their stocks and could hardly have withstood Sir Ian Hamilton's attacks.

It was out of the question that the few aeroplanes could achieve this absolute effect, but that, by a bold use of their limited material, the air commanders did much to harass the Turkish troops cannot be denied. The Turkish air raids, on the other hand, were severely restricted by the action of the Naval Air Service officers. Less than two hundred bombs, and those mostly of 15-lb. weight, were dropped by enemy airmen. The total casualties caused by these bombs, so far as can be traced, were five killed and eight wounded. (During the whole Dardanelles operations our own aeroplanes and seaplanes dropped 1,155 bombs of a total approximate weight of 27 tons).

All the British bombing activity had to be undertaken in face of the extra work put on the Naval Air Service by the enemy submarine threat. In addition to anti-submarine patrols by seaplanes, and even aeroplanes from time to time, there were, from the middle of September, patrols by an airship of the 'S.S.' or submarine scout type, known in flying dialect as *Blimps*. Colonel Sykes had suggested that a force of eight of these invaluable hybrids should be sent out to the Eastern Mediterranean, but only one was put into use. Owing to difficulties of handling and housing, and because one Blimp sufficed to cover the danger area, two others which reached the Dardanelles, were not inflated. The airship survived many bombing attacks made against its shed on Imbros until the 21st of October when the 'S.S.' section was transferred to Mudros.

THE EVACUATION OF THE PENINSULA.

There is, perhaps, something of pathos in the fact that the air service, as the year wore on, became so strong that it was able to deny to the enemy any sight of an intention to withdraw from the peninsula. A word on some of the aeroplanes with which the service was reinforced throughout the year will help to explain this fact. The first batch of aeroplanes to arrive, in May, when reinforcements were so badly needed, had been no accretion to the strength. They were six Henri Farmans, fitted with 80 horse-power Gnomes, a type that had already proved useless for active service over the peninsula. They were therefore sent back to England, as they arrived, in their packing cases, since they would have their uses at home as school machines.

In June came five Voisins with 140 horse-power Canton Unné engines. The engines had to be run full out to take the Voisins to a useful height, and they lasted an average of twenty flying hours only. The Voisins, however, did good work before their early ends; three of them were lost by falling in the sea, and two were wrecked by shellfire at Helles aerodrome. But there came still better machines to replace the Voisins in July. They were two invaluable Maurice Farmans (no horse-power Renaults) and six Nieuports (80 horse-power le Rhones).

At the end of July, too, there came four Henri Farmans, each fitted with the 140 horse-power Canton Unné engine, and these aeroplanes were good enough for reconnaissance, bombing, and fire-control work. Of all these, the Maurice Farman stood alone as an all-round machine. The Nieuport came next in efficiency, especially for fighting, single-seater reconnaissance, and light bombing: although constantly left exposed to the weather, it maintained its performance and shape.

Early in October the 10th Division and the French troops left the peninsula, unostentatiously, for Salonika. To this new centre of activity, also, *Ark Royal* was ordered to move hurriedly on the 7th of November. For five months the carrier had been settled in Kephalo Bay, Imbros, whilst her seaplanes, from their base in Aliki Bay, had given continuous help to the bombarding ships and had kept up a network of submarine patrols. The spotting for the ships, which had been vague and inaccurate at first, improved to the point when it was rapid and reliable. Panoramic and vertical photographs were first taken of the targets on which spotting observation by the seaplanes was required. With the panoramic view before him, any observer could pick up the target without waste of time.

Over his vertical photograph he had a transparent scale showing the actual distances on the ground, and, by first flying over the ship and setting the scale to the line of fire, the observer could, on the photograph, identify the fall of each shell and read, on the scale, the error in range and deflection. Most of the flying from Aliki Bay was done for the ships guarding the Helles left flank and for those operating off the Anzac area. For more distant work sea-planes from the base were lent from time to time to the monitors. In September a Short was placed on board the monitor *Roberts*, which operated off the Rabbit Islands, with the help of its seaplane, against batteries on the Asiatic coast.

Another Short, lent to the monitor *Raglan*, worked, in October, from the Gulf of Xeros, and directed the fire of the monitor on the Gallipoli flour mills, and the fire of the cruiser *Theseus* on military camps in the northern part of the peninsula. On the 1st of November *Ark Royal* moved to Mudros whence, after taking in stores, she went on to Iero Bay, Mitylene. From that base her seaplanes made a number of reconnaissance and photographic flights over Smyrna before the orders came to move to Salonika. With her arrival at the latter port on the 8th of November, the *Ark Royal* passes from the Dardanelles story. Much had been asked of her, the first of her kind. If she disappointed expectations, she had, at least, given invaluable help, and her very failures formed material for the architecture of future successes.

Meanwhile, General Sir Charles Monro had arrived at the Dardanelles on the 27th of October, in the place of Sir Ian Hamilton who had gone home ten days before. In forty-eight hours Sir Charles had reported in favour of evacuation. The Turkish forces were growing stronger, and winter was coming on. What winter might mean was brought home on the 27th of November, when twenty-four hours of torrential rain were suddenly followed by three days of snow blizzard. Many on both sides were drowned or frozen. In the Anzac area the river-beds suddenly filled with torrential water which rushed debris and frozen Turks through the Anzac lines to the sea.

On December the 7th the Government decided to withdraw from Suvla and Anzac, and at dawn on Monday the 20th the evacuation was complete. By constant patrol, the two aeroplane wings prevented any hostile aircraft from flying over these two beaches during the whole week which preceded our coming away. Observers over the area on the morning after the evacuation saw excited Turkish troops gathered about the burning British dumps. Three days after Christmas Sir Charles Monro was ordered to evacuate also the Helles area, and by the 9th of January 1916 the last man had stepped off. Throughout this operation the aeroplanes were on patrol and again allowed no enemy to pass. A recent arrival of six Bristol Scouts, fitted with Lewis guns, had put a weapon in their hands which ensured their ability to do this last service for those below.

The pilots and observers eased their spirits by a continuous bombing of the Turkish troops. They did not work without losses. On January the 6th Flight Commander H. A. Busk went off to bomb, but was never heard of again. He probably came down somewhere in the sea, on which his aeroplane would be unable to stay for any length of time. Two days later Flight Sub-Lieutenant S. A. Black was killed in an accident at Imbros. On the 11th. Flight Sub-Lieutenant C. H. Brinsmead and Lieutenant N. H. Boles of the Dorset Regiment were brought down and killed off Helles by two enemy aeroplanes, and on the following day Flight Sub-Lieutenant J. S. Bolas and Midshipman D. M. Branson, R.N., were shot down in the same locality.

Bolas was killed, but his companion, wounded, was made prisoner. It is a point of some interest that the last days of the campaign should be reserved for the only flying losses which the enemy air service inflicted, and that coincidence should give ominous distinction to the second letter of the alphabet. (These enemy successes coincided with the arrival in the area of three Fokker fighting monoplanes).

When the units of the army had gone their various ways, the navy still had the responsibility of keeping the mouth of the straits, and they required a strong air contingent to help them. A majority of the air units stayed on, but what they did afterwards must be told later in this history.

The Gallipoli adventure has a unique place in the history of war. For the first time a campaign was conducted by combined forces on, under, and over the sea, and on and over the land. Never again in the war were seaplanes compelled to work so much over the land, nor aeroplanes so much over the sea. Too soon the young service had to bear on its wings a load of responsibility on which at times depended the fortunes of the enterprise. If at first the means fell short of what was indispensable to success, the spirit of the personnel never did. The difficulties which the service had to overcome to keep its machines in the air called forth every ounce of ingenuity and patience of which the ground personnel were capable. Sand and dust, often driven along in clouds by a hot stinging wind, choked the engines and added enormously to the task of the mechanics whose job it was to keep them in running order. The summer heat warped and weakened the woodwork of the aeroplanes and seaplanes.

That the aeroplanes had to operate from an island base robbed their all too short effective working life of many hours. It was calculated that an average of half an hour was so wasted on every flight. It added, too, an almost certain risk of loss of the aeroplane if the pilot were compelled to alight on the sea. New aircraft coming out to reinforce the front were often delayed or damaged on their long journey from home. Pilots and observers had to learn, as they went along, the novel and intricate business of spotting for the ships on to land targets completely hidden from those who fired the guns.

Young midshipmen stepped into the observer's cockpit and coolly directed the fire of a battleship. Army officers left their comrades on the peninsula to help the air service in its responsibility of observing and harassing the movements of the Turkish troops. The Dardanelles formed a section of a vast front, every stretch of which cried out for the new air weapon. That enough material was found to ensure continuous air superiority over the peninsula was, perhaps, even more than might have been hoped.

The evacuation of Gallipoli was as fine a feat of arms as history may show. Yet it was a retreat. Positions which had been won and held with a great outpouring of life were quietly relinquished. We may freely give our admiration to the enemy for the grim, resourceful, and, at the last, successful, brilliance of his defence. As the British transports drew away from Gallipoli, the troops, their minds clouded with memories, strained their eyes eastwards until the peninsula blended with the distant mists. They were never again, so long as the war endured, to look upon those familiar heights consecrated with their dead.

With the airmen it was different. They did not cease to fly over the old battle-grounds, keeping a more lonely vigil than in the days of the conflict. The beaches and battle-scarred hills below were silent now and immortal as the plain of Troy across the straits. When controversy on the inception and possibilities of the campaign is ended, the Dardanelles struggle will be celebrated, so long as men remember, for what it was, a bold enterprise prosecuted, on the spot, with a courage and a self-sacrifice beyond the touch of failure.

THE DARDANELLES.

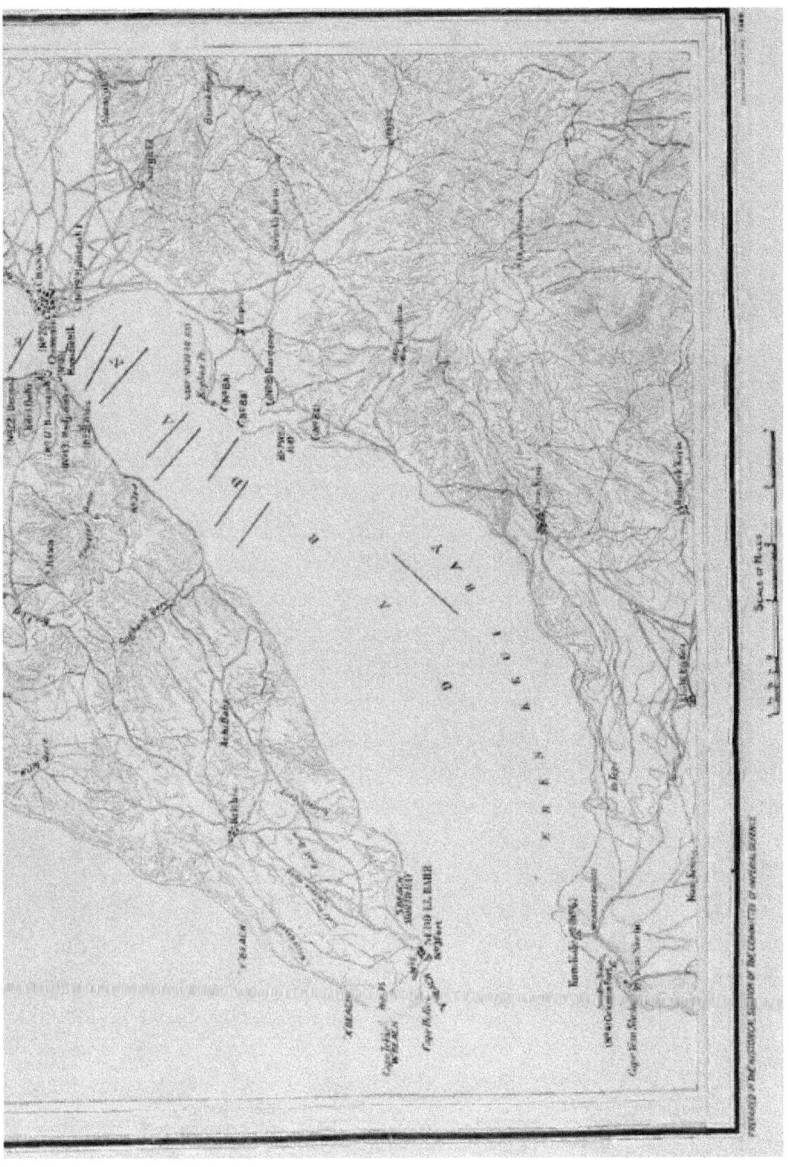

CHAPTER 2

The Western Front to the Battle of Loos

When the German thrust for the Channel ports failed before Ypres in the autumn of 1914, Germany temporarily acquiesced in a state of siege warfare in the west. The first phase of the struggle had given her the greater part of Belgium and the rich industrial districts of north-eastern France. She was already well organised to sustain a long campaign, and, with these additions, her rulers were able to frame a programme of munition production which was to give them a dominant superiority almost to the end of the war. In England, in that first winter, the people looked forward to a speedy decision in the following summer. It was wise, they thought, that Lord Kitchener should prepare for a period of three years, but that his preparations might even be inadequate was beyond the imagination of a people uninstructed in military problems.

Sir John French, whose splendid confidence had brought the expeditionary force through the first critical months, thought that the German line in France might be broken in the following year, but his optimism was not shared by some members of the Government. (*1914* by Sir John French, the early campaigns of the Great War by the British Commander, is also published by Leonaur). To these, who saw deadlock in the west, the Dardanelles offered all the advantages of a vulnerable flank. But the offensive in France must be maintained, and on the day the fleet opened the bombardment against the outer forts of the Straits, plans for the Battle of Neuve Chapelle had been sanctioned. The Russian armies, it seemed to many, had gradually advanced to a position in the south whence they would soon overrun the Hungarian plains. In the north they were now holding the attacks of Hindenburg, and since German troops were being diverted from the west to the east, an attack in the west would be opportune and should prove of great service to our Russian Allies. But spring and summer were to bring disillusion.

The problems which confronted the air command in that first winter were many. As yet reconnaissance was the only real help which the airmen were able to give to the army, but it was clear to the searching mind of Major-General Sir David Henderson, the commander of the Royal Flying Corps, that the airmen must, in addition, be the eyes of the artillery and must extend the range of the artillery by carrying bombs to objectives beyond the limit of the guns. And he knew, too, that the time would come when the flying men would be compelled to fight for the freedom to do their job. He was ably supported by Lieutenant-Colonel W. S. Brancker at the War Office, who used his driving power to procure the men, aeroplanes, and equipment which the corps would need.

Towards the end of November 1914, Henderson, satisfied that the force which he had done so much to create and had been privileged to command during its first days in war, was on the road to a progressive future, turned his eyes to the trenches where the infantry were bearing the tedium of the struggle. He came of mixed highland and lowland stock. He had the quiet, patient tenacity of the lowlands, but at times the highlands played on his mind and brought him a call to adventure. The highlands had sent him into the air to become the oldest pilot in the world, and the highlands, as the line grew thinner at Ypres, called him to the trenches.

On the 22nd of November he was given command of the 1st Division, but his stay with them was to be brief. Lord Kitchener, when he came to hear of it, would have none of it. Henderson had been his head of intelligence in South Africa; Kitchener knew his worth, and knew, too, that the Flying Corps would need him to carry through the great air expansion which he was planning. Accordingly, on the 20th of December, General Henderson was back again in command of the Royal Flying Corps.

Before Henderson went to the infantry he had suggested a decentralisation of the air service whereby squadrons would be grouped together in wings. When he got back, this reorganisation had been carried out by Colonel F. H. Sykes, who had commanded the corps during General Henderson's absence. On the 29th of November 1914 Nos. 2 and 3 Squadrons had been grouped to form the First Wing, and Nos. 5 and 6 Squadrons to form the Second Wing. No. 4 Squadron, with a wireless unit and the advanced base of the Aircraft Park, remained at the Flying Corps headquarters at St. Omer. The First Wing was commanded by Lieutenant-Colonel H. M. Trenchard, who had arrived from England on the 18th of November, and the Second Wing by Lieutenant-Colonel C. J. Burke.

When, on Christmas Day, the expeditionary force was reorganised into two armies, the First Wing was attached to the First Army under Sir Douglas Haig, and the Second Wing to the Second Army under Sir Horace Smith-Dorrien. The new wings suffered a set-back on December the 28th, when a violent storm which raged along the whole line wrecked thirty aeroplanes, sixteen of them beyond repair, a serious loss to the small force of those early days.

Air reconnaissance was now in the nature of a routine insurance against surprise. Broadly speaking, it settled to two kinds—tactical and strategical. Tactical reconnaissance may be said to be confined to the immediate battle area to locate and examine trenches, gun emplacements, reserves, and rail-heads, chiefly to satisfy the corps or divisional commanders who wish to know what there is on their immediate front, as well as the changes that take place from day to day, so that they may make their local dispositions to the best purpose. Strategical reconnaissance, which begins where tactical leaves off, helps the commander of an army to know his opponent's mind, and to deduce his plan of campaign.

A good air observer must possess many virtues. He must be physically fit and temperamentally cool, and he must report only on what he sees. He cannot have too extensive a knowledge of military matters. Unless he is imaginative, he may not know what to look for, but he must shun any temptation to make conjectures. Some sudden insight which he gets of the enemy's intention may have far-reaching consequences, but false observation may do great harm. The best qualified observer will see little when he first flies. Until his eye gets accustomed to scouring a large stretch of country so that objects of military importance are at once distinguished and recognised, his reports will be of little value.

Before the infantry came to learn in France something of the peculiarities of air observation, they sometimes complained that German airmen were up at dawn to search for our troops, whereas the Flying Corps were much later astir and were most active in the evening; but the blame is with the sun which rises in the east. In the early morning the German airmen were often in the best position to see, whereas the visibility into the sun, always limited, might be too poor for any observation of value to the British airmen. A word or two on what the airman can see will help to illustrate the value of reconnaissance. Digging cannot effectively be concealed. Tracks show up clearly: a track which might be passed over on the ground and not noticed, will be plain thousands of feet up. One man walking along a road may be clearly visible, but men moving across country, unless they are in close formation, can hardly be seen above three thousand feet.

There are some who think that if they look up from the ground their white faces will be visible, but this is only true if the face of the observer be distinguishable also as he looks over the side of his aeroplane. Objects or men, concealed in the shadow cast by some other object, are most difficult to detect. On the other hand, moving objects, on a sunny day, will often be first revealed by their moving shadows. Men may remain unseen in a wood or in a village if they do not reveal themselves by movement, by smoke from their fires, or, for instance, by firing at the aeroplane. One of the most tell-tale things which an observer may see, in stationary warfare, is rolling-stock at the rail-heads behind the enemy front.

Important movements cannot be made without concentrations of road or rail transport, and the airmen, by keeping the enemy's rail and military centres under regular observation, especially at daybreak and sundown, may surprise movements which anticipate the night or which have been overtaken by the dawn. Routine reconnaissance will have disclosed the normal amount of rolling-stock to be seen at the various important rail-centres so that any considerable increase or decrease becomes apparent. A large increase in the evening may indicate that troops and guns are about to move away from the neighbourhood, whereas an increase in the morning may show that reinforcements have come in during the night. There are other features which tell much.

The construction of new roads or bridges or railway sidings, the pushing forward of rail-heads, the building of new hutments in back areas, the pulling down of hutments in other areas, the establishment of dumps or new aerodromes, all are material for knowledge of the enemy's intentions. The army intelligence staff working on the reports brought in throughout the day, examining, comparing, assessing, gradually piece together the story of the enemy: the effect of their deductions appears in the orders which the army commander issues to his troops. Reconnaissance work is not spectacular. A flying officer has compared it with the routine of going to the office daily, the aeroplane being substituted for the suburban train. The officer does his daily job and goes home; the board sit in debate over the profit and loss account.

The most important problem of all was that of air cooperation with the artillery. The growing depth and strength of defences made artillery preparation and support essential to successful infantry attack. And it came to be realised—although slowly at first by many artillery officers—that the artillery, increasing in calibre and range, must look to the air for much of the observation on which its efficiency depends. It was now a question of how to provide the means, elaborate the process, and train both the air and artillery units in the new art.

The first difficulty in co-operation between the two arms was one of communication. Experience had already shown that of the three main methods of signalling from the air, namely, coloured Very lights, electric lamps, and wireless, the last was easily the most effective. The early wireless sets, however, had the great drawback that they were clumsy and heavy. They weighed about seventy-five pounds, and the two-seater aeroplanes in which they were first installed could carry no observer, the apparatus filling the observer's cockpit, even overflowing into the pilot's compartment. Thus, Very lights and signalling lamps were being used side by side with wireless well into 1915. There was a widely held idea, at that time, that the set must be powerful.

Many officers considered that aircraft wireless must have a reasonably long range to transmit reconnaissance information from the air when the armies were on the move again. They did not foresee that the main use of air wireless would be to facilitate co-operation with the artillery, and that the weaker the set consistent with the range of the guns the better. This fact was, however, fully realised at Flying Corps headquarters, and the quest for a light and compact apparatus went on ceaselessly. The reward came in the autumn of 1915 when the Sterling set, greatly improved in the field, was reduced to a weight of less than twenty pounds and could be so disposed as to offer no obstruction to pilot or observer.

As wireless co-operation grew in importance, the wireless unit expanded. On the 8th of December 1914 it became No. 9 Squadron, charged with the duty of supplying wireless aeroplanes on detachment as required by the army corps. But the demands became so insistent that, before the year ended, flights from the squadron were allotted to each of the two wings as nuclei of wing wireless squadrons. The headquarters of No. 9 Squadron at St. Omer continued to handle all wireless equipment, to act as guardian to the wireless flights, and to train new personnel not only for the squadrons but also for the wireless with the artillery units.

Towards the end of January 1915, Captain B. E. Smythies, a former Royal Engineer officer of wireless experience, arrived at St. Omer to help the headquarters wireless unit. he says:

> At headquarters the wireless organisation appeared primitive; two operators and a few instrument repairers worked under canvas in a gravel pit, tools and power were supplied from a workshop lorry which was frequently out of order, while the men, thirty miles from the line, slept in a barn on straw *palliasses*.

His immediate concern was to set up an organisation for the training of men in the handling of wireless equipment and to extend the workshops. Every endeavour was made to get hold of men with technical experience, not only by direct enlistment at home, but also from other army units. By the beginning of March, the wireless unit was further strengthened by the arrival of two technical officers. These were Second Lieutenants T. Vincent Smith and S. C. Callaghan, the first civilian experts to be commissioned direct in the Royal Flying Corps for wireless duties. (On the 18th of March 1915 these officers were posted respectively to No. 3 Squadron—First Wing—and to No. 5 Squadron—Second Wing—they were, therefore, the first of the specialist squadron wireless officers).

The idea that the detached flights of No. 9 Squadron should expand into wing wireless squadrons was soon abandoned. It was now realised that wireless must play its part in the routine work of every squadron. In February, therefore, the two wing wireless flights were transferred to Nos. 2 and 6 Squadrons. (The flights from Nos. 2 and 6 Squadrons thus set free were sent to St. Omer to form a new squadron—No. 16—under the command of Captain F.V. Holt, on the 10th of February. The squadron was completed by a flight similarly set free from No. 5 Squadron on the 1st of March).

Thereafter a wireless flight was gradually incorporated in each squadron. By the beginning of April, the wireless flights were working smoothly in their new squadrons, and No. 9 Squadron, now reduced to a headquarters, was disbanded. Captain Smythies's unit was absorbed by the Aircraft Park, the gipsy encampment moving from the gravel pit to a workshop on the aerodrome at St. Omer.

From now onwards the supply of material from England became increasingly regular. A small wireless operators' school was formed to give complete training to men transferred from the army; operators coming from England were also put through a finishing course at the school before being posted to the squadrons and to batteries. Captain H. C. T. Dowding, in command of No. 9 Squadron when it was disbanded, returned to England with about six of the technical personnel and formed at Brooklands, on the 1st of April 1915, a new No. 9 Squadron which became, in effect, the first home wireless school of the Royal Flying Corps.

The difficulties which had to be overcome before effective co-operation with the artillery was possible, were not only those of the wireless apparatus. A great need was a means of describing the positions of targets simply and accurately. This need was met by the squared map, and the story of the introduction of that map, in use throughout the war and familiar to every officer, is of historic interest. It came to be used by all arms, but it was the outcome of the earliest efforts at aeroplane wireless cooperation with the artillery. The reader may be reminded that the recognised British military system of identifying a point was to describe it with reference to a specified letter in the name of some place on the map, as for example, 'under the P in COMPIEGNE.' This system was too cumbersome and too indefinite for wireless signalling.

When, therefore, in September 1914, Lieutenant D. S. Lewis had carried out his first memorable wireless attempt to control artillery fire from the air, he had laboriously squared maps in ink for his own and the battery commander's use. These maps cannot be found, but presumably the squares were lettered and numbered, somewhat on the principle of the squared ordnance survey map, in such a way that the battery commander could be referred, by a simple wireless message, to the vicinity of any point on the map. Lieutenant Lewis showed his map to Major W. G. H. Salmond, then a staff officer at Flying Corps headquarters.

Major Salmond, a former artillery officer, was quick to grasp the value of the squared map for all air wireless work and the necessity for supplying similar maps to all flying and artillery units. He went at once to see Major E. M. Jack, the officer in charge of the topographical section at G.H.Q. This officer took up the idea with enthusiasm and, in consultation with the Flying Corps and with the help of artillery officers, produced a specimen sheet so lettered and numbered that any point on the ground could be defined, quite simply, within a few yards. The process of so describing an object was known as pinpointing. Squared maps were first used by the Flying Corps in co-operation with the artillery on the I Corps front in October 1914. The success of the principle was immediate, and the I Corps clamoured for a supply of the maps for the use of all arms. Soon the whole battle area was covered by a series of contiguous sheets, and the first great obstacle to the rapid communication of information from the wireless aeroplane to the ground had disappeared. (For an example of a squared map, see chapter 4, 'The Second Phase.')

The next step forward was the simplification of the wireless code by which the fall of the shells was signalled to the artillery from the air. This took place in January 1915, and in this once again Lewis played a conspicuous part. At a conference attended by the chief artillery officers and representatives of the Flying Corps, at which the gunner officers were in favour of keeping the old method of signalling 'left' and 'right', 'short', and 'over', and so forth. Captain B. T. James had suggested that the infantry method of indicating points by the hour positions on the clock was more suitable. Captain Lewis, prompted by this suggestion, addressed, on January the 25th 1915, a pencilled memorandum to Major J. M. Salmond, his squadron commander, he says:

> I have evolved a more elaborate system of ranging, applicable chiefly to heavy siege howitzers where economy of ammunition is most important. I have a celluloid disc, with circles inserted at 25, 100, 200, 300, 400 yards radius according to the scale of the map. Outside are painted the figures of a clock. The circles are lettered A to E. The disc is pinned with its centre on the target and its XII-VI diameter towards the battery firing. Shots are then signalled down according to their position on the map, C9, B2, etc. This will eliminate all error except that of map reading and I think it well worth trying. I intend to try it the next time I range the 9.2.

After some trials, this method was adopted with the modification that the XII-VI line was always to be true north and south instead of from the target to the battery, and that the circles imagined to circumscribe the target were taken as at 50, 100, 200, 300, 400, and 500 yards, and lettered, A, B, C, D, E, and F, respectively. After some experience it was found desirable, for greater accuracy, to add two further circles at ten and twenty-five yards radius from the target. These circles were lettered Y and Z. By putting the XII-VI line true north-south it was possible to use the clock-code method to range any battery whether the observer knew its position or not. The clock-code, simple in its application, was first used in battle at Neuve Chapelle and proved efficient and time-saving. It was adopted by the Flying Corps on all fronts and is still in use, a tribute to the memory of two zealous officers.

Whilst the squadrons went about their daily jobs of reconnaissance and artillery co-operation, enthusiasts were working at the problem of air photography which was to revolutionise the science of military intelligence. The desire for knowledge of the enemy is unlimited, whereas the powers of the air observers cannot be adequate for the fulfilment of all the demands made upon them. They cannot, with their eyes, cover the whole ground to bring back a complete picture, nor can they cover it sufficiently often to keep the picture up to date. They pass rapidly on their way and have little time for detailed inspection.

But these deficiencies of the human eye were remedied by the camera. The camera pictures only what is there, omits nothing, provides a record which can be easily duplicated, and supplies a means for recording, with relentless precision, the multitudinous changes that take place within the restless area of an army at war. This is not to say that personal reconnaissance ended with the coming of air photography. It was often a personal observation that suggested useful subjects for the camera, and it was only by personal reconnaissance, too, that doubtful objects on a photograph could be elucidated.

In September 1914, during the Battle of the Aisne, No. 3 Squadron, which, under the keen guidance of Major H. R. M. Brooke-Popham, had experimented successfully with air photography in the days before the war, had procured some photographs of the enemy trenches. The pictures, however, were indistinct and the army staff were not impressed. Nevertheless, the Flying Corps persevered with their experiments, and by the end of 1914 were being rewarded with clearer photographs. (*1914: the Marne and the Aisne* by H. W. Carless-Davis and A. Neville Hilditch is also published by Leonaur). The French air service, however, were at this time getting better results than our own air service, and Colonel Sykes sent for Major W. G. H. Salmond and showed him a map, reduced by our Ally, on which the German trenches had been outlined from information derived from air photographs.

He was anxious that the Flying Corps should similarly assist the army, and he instructed Major Salmond to study the French photographic organisation. This officer visited a French corps headquarters and found that whereas our own skilled photographic personnel were few and were distributed amongst the squadrons, the French were more generously supplied with technical talent, whilst their organisation was highly centralised. In his report he advocated the concentration of all photographic personnel into sections, one for each flying wing.

Sir David Henderson at once formed an experimental section which he sent, in the middle of January 1915, to First Wing headquarters. The section consisted of Lieutenants J. T. C. Moore-Brabazon and C. D. M. Campbell, Flight Sergeant F. C. V. Laws and 2nd Air Mechanic W. D. Corse. They were instructed to report, after experience in the wings, on the best form of organisation and camera for air photography. Colonel Trenchard, firmly impressed with the military possibilities of photography, gave his new section every encouragement, and they were soon busy on the design of a new-type air camera. From these small beginnings, indeed, grew the whole overseas photographic organisation.

The experiences of two flying officers will help to illustrate the position of air photography at this time. Lieutenant C. C. Darley of No. 3 Squadron had fixed up a dark room in the recesses of a stable of the *château* in which he was billeted. He bought his chemicals in Bethune and developed his own plates. He was usually able to identify the photographs, but the staff officers who were to use them were not always so successful, and Darley often went to corps or divisional headquarters to explain his pictures. Towards the end of January, he had collected enough plates to make up a map showing the German and British trench system along the whole front covered by his squadron. His chief thought in doing this was to have something for his own use when observing over the area, but Major J. M. Salmond, his squadron commander, took the map to corps headquarters where it created some stir as showing how the information on the photographs could be reproduced in a form intelligible to all officers.

Early in February photography played its first important part in an infantry attack. This was a brilliant action by British and French troops, which resulted, on the 6th, in the capture of some troublesome brick stacks south of the La Bassée Canal. No. 3 Squadron was ordered to photograph these stacks before the attack, and Lieutenant Darley went up with Lieutenant V. H. N. Wadham, in very clear weather, and got the best results which the Flying Corps had yet achieved. He was taken by Colonel Trenchard to a conference of British and French

87

generals. The photographs were produced and revealed a new long German sap, hitherto unknown to the French, and, as a result of this new information, the plan of attack was modified. A study of the photographs, too, made it possible to arrange in advance what should be the precise junction, during the attack, between the Allied troops. General Joffre was so impressed that he sent a request that copies of the Flying Corps photographs might be supplied to him.

Wing Commander W. S. Douglas, then an observer in No. 2 Squadron, tells how he was appointed air photographer to his unit because he had had a camera as a boy. He cut a rectangular hole in the bottom of his cockpit in a B.E.2a, and his practice, when the area to be photographed nearly filled the aperture, was to push his camera through the hole and take his snapshot, he says:

> This procedure, was not too easy in the cramped space available, especially as the weather was cold and bulky flying kit a necessity. Each plate had to be changed by hand, and I spoilt many plates by clumsy handling with frozen fingers. A proportion of the photographs, however, were successful.

The camera here referred to was of the folding type with bellows, but something better was on its way. In February Lieutenants Moore-Brabazon and Campbell, in co-operation with the Thornton-Pickard Manufacturing Company, had produced their new box-type camera—the first successful British camera specially designed for photography from the air. It was known as the 'A' camera and made use of the Mackenzie-Wishart 5x4 slide and envelope. It took the form of a conical box, built to withstand rough usage, with the lens in a recessed front at a fixed distance from the plate. The observer gripped the camera through straps or brass handles as he leaned over the side of the aeroplane to take his photographs.

The chief objection to the camera was that the first exposure called for eleven distinct operations and each subsequent exposure, ten. This was no small demand to make on an observer, already keyed to high tension, who had to lean from his cockpit into a gale of wind and fumble through thick gloves or with fingers numbed by cold.

******

It was quickly found that, to ensure verticality in the photographs for mapping purposes, the camera must be fixed to the aeroplane. As soon as this was done, the task of the observer was eased. The next step in development came in the summer of

1915 when a semi-automatic plate-changing mechanism was fitted. The improved apparatus was known as the 'C' camera, (For a survey of the war development of air cameras the reader may refer to a paper 'On Some Photographic Apparatus used in Aerial Photography', by Major Charles W. Gamble in the *Transactions of the Optical Society*, March 1919).

★★★★★★

In spite of its drawbacks the new camera gave excellent results, and contracts for its manufacture were placed. It was first used over the enemy trenches by No. 3 Squadron on the 2nd of March. Lieutenants Moore-Brabazon and Campbell, in a comprehensive report, confirmed the desirability of setting up a photographic section at each wing headquarters to develop all plates exposed by the squadron observers and to print and distribute all photographs. The scheme was adopted and the original section at First Wing was called upon to organise the photographic sections in the other wings.

THE BATTLE OF NEUVE CHAPELLE
(Order of Battle, Royal Flying Corps, Appendix 1)

These photographic successes were timely because the plans for the spring offensive were under discussion. Since he was short of guns and ammunition, Sir John French had to confine his thoughts to some part of the line where we were at a tactical advantage, or where, if the attack went well, the enemy's retirement must of necessity be to a less favourable position. The army commanders, early in February 1915, had been asked to go into the question, and, on the 19th, the plan submitted by Sir Douglas Haig had been adopted. This plan had for its immediate object the capture of the village of Neuve Chapelle which formed a salient exposed to assault from two sides. If the attack met with success, the distant Aubers ridge might become an objective with a promise of far-reaching results.

The pioneer photography work of Nos. 2 and 3 Squadrons had given Sir Douglas Haig a picture of much of the Neuve Chapelle area, and this picture was completed, before the end of February, to cover the whole German trench system in front of the First Army to a depth of from 700 to 1,500 yards. The entrenchments, which the photographs recorded, were then carefully traced on skeleton maps of a scale of one in eight thousand, and on these maps the details of the plan of attack were based. Orders for the artillery were drawn up after a study of the positions of the various defended points as revealed by

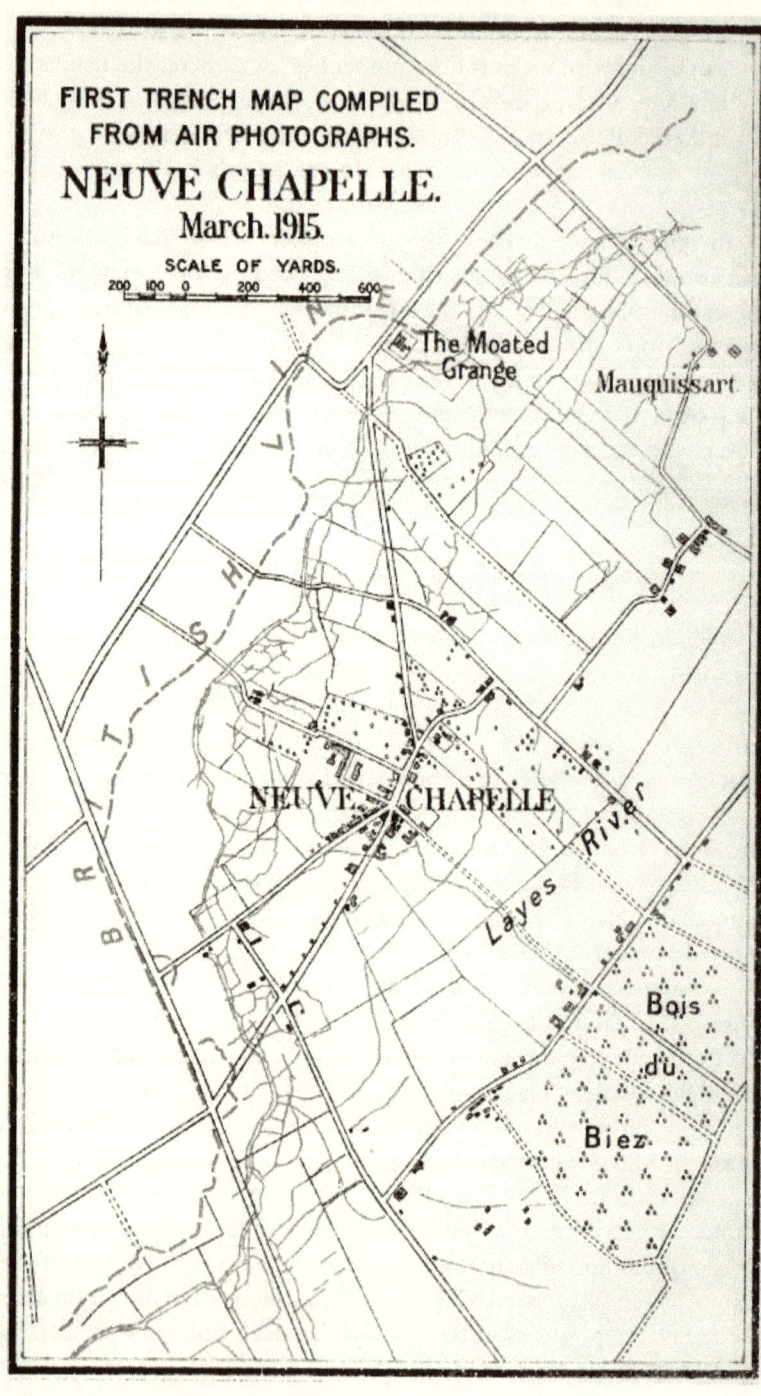

the air photographs, and, furthermore, it was possible to deduce, from the direction of the communication trenches, what the main line of approach of the enemy would be. Some fifteen hundred copies of the map were issued to each of the army corps before the attack, so that, for the first time in its history, the British Army went into action with a picture of the hidden intricacies of the enemy defences, and, after the first assault, bombing parties were able to make their way, without loss of time, to their separate objectives.

The three days' battle was opened by the First Army at 7.30 a.m. on the 10th of March in weather which began badly and got rapidly worse as the operation progressed. From five thousand feet above the battlefield on that morning the whole village of Neuve Chapelle could be seen in detail, the red roofs and red bricks of its houses pleasantly patched against the green fields, for the day of bombardments so intense as to alter the face of the earth had not yet arrived. The bombardment which preceded the assault had the appearance, from above, of a solid line of cotton wool stretching from the Moated Grange in the north to Richebourg l'Avoué in the south, and ending abruptly at both ends.

The German troops could be seen at places grouped in their front-line trenches, but at other points they appeared as black dots, edged away from the cotton wool, waiting for the bombardment to cease. Major L. V. S. Blacker who, as an observer, was flying over the area in the morning, tells of his surprise at seeing the British infantry moving across country to the attack looking like 'ants walking across a billiard table', and not, as he had expected, 'like masses coming from a football contest'. The attack, indeed, looked extraordinarily thin from above, but it was strong enough to meet with splendid initial success; before noon the whole village of Neuve Chapelle and the roads leading northward and south-westward from the eastern end of the village were gained, and the position was being consolidated.

Further advance was barred by enemy strong points chiefly at the tree-screened north-west corner of the Bois du Biez; a small hummock in front of the bridge over the Layes River; a hummock in front of a group of houses south of Mauquissart; and another point in front of Mauquissart. These strong points formed, in fact, the keystone of the enemy's resistance and, after the battle, the new German line was built along them. It was not possible to infer from the map which had been made up from the air photographs that any of these positions was strong enough to hold up the advance, nor were they positions which would be obvious on the ground. They were not, in fact, manned at all before the attack began. Had the weather held, the air might have been able to give the artillery sufficient assistance to dominate them and there would then have been a different tale to tell.

As the main attack was made by the First Army, the bulk of the air work fell to the First Wing and, for closer liaison. Colonel Trenchard had established an advanced wing headquarters at the First Army Report Centre at Merville. He split up his squadrons into detachments to work directly with the First Army headquarters, the two heavy artillery groups, and with the attacking corps. From Merville a detachment worked for the Army headquarters, for the IV Corps, and for the northern or No. 2 Group of the artillery; from Hinges for the southern or No. 1 Group; and from Chocques for the 1st and Indian Corps. A further detachment was held in reserve at Aire.

One of the main features of the artillery work was the countering of the hostile batteries. To destroy the enemy guns is the ideal, but this, which requires a considerable volume of deliberate and carefully directed heavy fire, has to give place, during an attack, to the silencing, or neutralizing, of as many enemy batteries as possible. Although the squally days of early March had limited co-operation with the guns, most of the known enemy batteries and strong points had already been registered, and on the opening day of the attack observers were able to bring fire to bear on many of the enemy guns which they saw to be active.

The war diary of No. 1 Group refers to the air work as follows:

> In fulfilling their mission as counter batteries, the Group artillery received the utmost assistance from the section of wireless aeroplanes under the command of Captain Lewis, D.S.O. These aeroplanes were invaluable in sending information as to the positions of hostile batteries which were active. As regards the observation and correction of fire by the wireless aeroplanes the observers stated that very little correction was necessary on any of the targets, and that the shooting of the Group appeared to be very effective. Most of the German batteries had been previously registered.

Two units of the Royal Naval Air Service gave the army a helping hand in the day's fighting. They were No. 2 Armoured Car Squadron under Lieutenant-Commander the Duke of Westminster and the armoured train *Churchill* (one 6-inch, one 47-inch, and one 4-inch guns as well as maxims) under Commander A. Scott Littlejohns. The armoured cars and trains had played a notable part in the Antwerp operations in 1914 and, since the coming of trench warfare, had been attached to various army corps in the line. The heavy armament of the trains, (there were three, the *Churchill*, the *Jellicoe*, and the *Déguise*), had been particularly useful in the Ypres struggle of 1914.

★★★★★★

'Your command,' wrote Lieutenant-General Sir Henry Rawlinson, the Commander of the IV Corps, in November 1914, 'were always ready to take on anything and filled many a gap when we were very shorthanded.'

★★★★★★

At Neuve Chapelle, on the 10th of March, the *Churchill* was brought into action against Aubers village at 7.35 a.m. Its guns destroyed, with direct hits, the tower of the village church which was being used as an observation post, engaged hostile batteries, and swept the roads leading to the battle area with shrapnel and lyddite. Four maxim armoured cars stood by, under shell-fire, on the La Bassée-Estaires road, to co-operate with the 2nd Cavalry Division, but the expected break-through did not come.

Air reconnaissances throughout the day reported little or no movement of German reserves to the battle area. It had been estimated before the battle that the enemy could, in favourable circumstances, transfer from the Lille-Menin-Courtrai district, and from Ghent, some forty-seven battalions to the Herlies-Aubers line within thirty-seven hours of the opening of the attack. It would depend on the initial. success how many of these would be ordered to move, but it was essential that the utmost should be done to hamper the reserves as they came up, and this task was entrusted to the Flying Corps.

Bombing up to this time had been of a spasmodic nature, bombs being dropped overboard occasionally by pilots or observers who were out primarily on some other duty. There were no bomb racks, except such as could be improvised in the squadron, and there was a scarcity of bombs. But for this battle there was an attempt to choose both the place and the time to ensure that successful bombing should have the maximum effect on the general operations. Courtrai station and Menin junction were assigned to the Second Wing and the stations at Lille, Douai, and Don to the Third Wing.

★★★★★★

The Third Wing (Nos. 4 and 16 Squadrons) had been formed at

St. Omer under the command of Lieutenant-Colonel H. R. M. Brooke-Popham on the 1st of March 1915. No. 16 Squadron remained in the Wing one day only, passing to the First Wing on the 2nd of March.

✶✶✶✶✶✶

Buildings in Fournes which were supposed to house a divisional headquarters were bombed soon after six in the morning of the 10th. The attack was made by three pilots of No. 3 Squadron, led by Captain E. L. Conran with the squadron commander, Major J. M. Salmond, in the observer's seat. The two other aeroplanes which took part were flown without observers by Lieutenants W. C. K. Birch and D. R. Hanlon. The pilots attacked at three minutes' interval and were rewarded by direct hits which set fire to their objective. Captain Conran and Major Salmond three times swooped to within a hundred feet of their target before releasing their bombs. At three in the afternoon, during a lull in the infantry attack, when the troops were being organised for a second assault, the Flying Corps received orders to go ahead with their main bombing programme.

Captain G. I. Carmichael of No. 5 Squadron left at half-past three for the railway fork north of Menin. He carried a 100-lb. bomb which he dropped from a height of 120 feet, apparently blowing the rails to pieces, ten yards south of the fork. His aeroplane was considerably bumped by the force of the bomb's explosion, and it was also low enough to receive a bullet from the ground which partly disabled the engine and compelled the pilot to make the return journey at 200 feet.

Captain L. A. Strange of No. 6 Squadron did as well at Courtrai. He carried on his B.E.2c three 25-lb. French bombs. The weather was breaking again, clouds were at three thousand feet, and visibility was poor generally. Strange crossed the lines below the clouds, but an anti-aircraft shell bursting about the aeroplane sent him up into them and he navigated through them, coming out again north of Courtrai. He dived through a lower bank of clouds to the east of the town, coming down to within two hundred feet of the railway, whence he flew along the track to the station. A sentry at the end of the platform opened rifle fire on the aeroplane, but was silenced by a hand-grenade which Strange threw at him.

The pilot, now quite low, hopped the station roof and dropped his three bombs on a standing train. As he turned to watch the result of his bombing, he almost collided with a line of telegraph poles, but avoided them in time and got back safely to his aerodrome with some three dozen bullet holes in his aeroplane. A report which came through from an agent in Courtrai, a fortnight later, stated that two coaches of troops had been hit and seventy-five men killed or wounded and, further, that traffic was delayed for three days.

On the 11th of March, the second day of the battle, little further progress was made by the infantry. Visibility was now worse than on the first day. From four thousand feet, only a circular patch of ground below the aeroplane could be seen; all beyond was mist. The same positions still held up the troops, but visibility was too poor for the air service to give any adequate direction for the artillery. The bombing pilots, who were early astir, met with little better luck. Three pilots of No. 4 Squadron had gone, on the previous evening, to Bailleul to be as near as possible to their objective, the railway junction in the south-east corner of Lille. They left on B.E.2's in the dark at a quarter to five to be over Lille at daybreak.

For navigation lights each pilot carried, on his back, what in official returns is shown as a 'lamp, electric, hand' and the direction of Lille from Bailleul was indicated by electric lamps on the ground. One of the pilots, Captain R. J. F. Barton, was forced by engine failure to land soon after starting, and wrecked his aeroplane and severely shook himself in doing so. The other two officers. Lieutenants A. St. J. M. Warrand and G. W. Mapplebeck, failed to return from their venture. Warrand, it was learned, died of his injuries on the 19th of March, but Mapplebeck got back to Flying Corps headquarters in the middle of April. He had had an exciting time.

After he came down he escaped into a wood near Lille and, eluding a German search party, found help in the town from some of the inhabitants. For some time, he was concealed in Lille, and he read with mixed feelings notices offering a reward for his capture and threatening death to anyone who helped him. When the arrangements for his escape were completed, he walked to the Dutch frontier, got into Holland, and so back to duty with his old squadron in France. He continued to fly on the western front until June, when he was posted to a home squadron. He was killed in an accident to his Morane monoplane on the 24th of August, 1915.

The stormy final day was marked by violent enemy counter-attacks. The armoured train, hampered by the poor visibility, continued to sweep the enemy back areas around Aubers and Fromelles, and two 3-pounder armoured cars came into action at noon against machine-gun posts in houses in the village of Les Mottes. In the afternoon Captain G. F. Pretyman of No. 3 Squadron made two flights to locate the line of battle. He reported that the enemy still held his position between Neuve Chapelle and the Bois du Biez, but that, despite the strength of the German attacks, the British troops were maintaining their hold on the eastern edge of Neuve Chapelle village. This was an early attempt to keep the command in touch with the fluctuations of the battle-front.

Whilst the infantry struggle was going on east of the village, the bombing attacks were resumed. Captain E. R. Ludlow-Hewitt and Lieutenants E. O. Grenfell, V. A. Barrington-Kennett, and O. M. Moullin, of No. 1 Squadron, on B.E.8's, bombed the railway bridge at the north-east corner of Douai, and the junction at Don, but none of their bombs, so far as could be seen, took effect on their objectives; Ludlow-Hewitt hit the railway at Wavrin, which he mistook for Don, with a 100-lb. bomb. Moullin failed to return and was later reported a prisoner of war.

******

No. 1 Squadron, under the command of Major W. G. H. Salmond, arrived from England with four B.E.8's and eight Avros on the 7th of March, and was incorporated in the Third Wing.

******

On the aerodrome of No. 3 Squadron there was an accident to a Morane which was being loaded with French converted shells for Captain R. Cholmondeley to raid Don station. Except for a lead shearing pin, these makeshift bombs had no safety device. One of the bombs, it would seem, dropped on its nose whilst being loaded and exploded: the aeroplane went up in flames and all the people near were struck, Cholmondeley and eleven men being killed and four men seriously wounded. Wing Commander Pretyman says:

> When the flames had died down, it was discovered that all the bombs had not gone off. Major J. M. Salmond, the commanding officer of No. 3 Squadron, forbade anyone to go near the aeroplane that evening. Next morning, we found some of the wreckage had been cleared and the remaining bombs removed and buried. Major Salmond had done this himself at daybreak.

The raid on Don was made early on this same morning, the 13th, by Captain Pretyman, whose bombs blew up the centre carriages of a train in the station. At 9.0 a.m. the Duke of Westminster took two of his 3-pounder cars to the front-line trenches at Fauquissart and made excellent shooting, at 800 yards' range, against snipers and machine-gun posts in the village of Trivelet. The cars, in turn, were heavily shelled but suffered no casualties.

The opposing commands drew different lessons from the battle. Sir John French believed that what had been done here on a small scale could be repeated on a bigger scale with far-reaching results. Joffre, disinclined to sit down to a war of defence, shared this conclusion, and preparations for what, it was hoped, would prove decisive offensive action went ahead. The German command, on the other hand, concluded that their weaker armies, aided by a preponderance of artillery and munitions, could hold the Allies in the west while they turned to strike a decisive blow against Russia.

The desperate position of Austria, from which the Allies had drawn comfort, was recognised by Germany, and a combined Austro-German offensive was launched in Galicia on the 1st of May, and pushed the Russians steadily back. But Germany had greater plans. The Russian menace was to be ended once and for all, and a more ambitious offensive was opened on the 13th of July. The German armies swept past Warsaw in the first week of August, beyond Brest Litovsk by the end of the month, and, as September drew to a close, had pushed the Russians into the Pripet marshes. Russia was not out of the war as the German command had hoped, but she had, at least, suffered a severe defeat.

Germany, so heavily committed in the east, took risks in the west, but her faith was to be justified. Before the Allies were ready to attack she gave them a shock, and, once again, the shock came at Ypres. On the 1st of April the British had begun to take over a large part of the salient from the French Eighth Army, the junction of the Allied troops thus shifting from a point east of Zillebeke to where the salient crossed the Ypres-Poelcappelle road. The extension was completed by the 19th of April.

Meanwhile two new squadrons had arrived from England to reinforce the Flying Corps. No. 7, with two flights of R.E.5's and one flight of Vickers Fighters (which, however, were quickly replaced by Voisins), arrived on the 8th of April, and No. 8, the first squadron to join the expeditionary force wholly equipped with B.E.2c's, (90 h.p. R.A.F. engines), on the 15th. Both squadrons were incorporated in Colonel Brooke-Popham's Third Wing at St. Omer, and were employed on strategical reconnaissance work and on special missions for general headquarters.

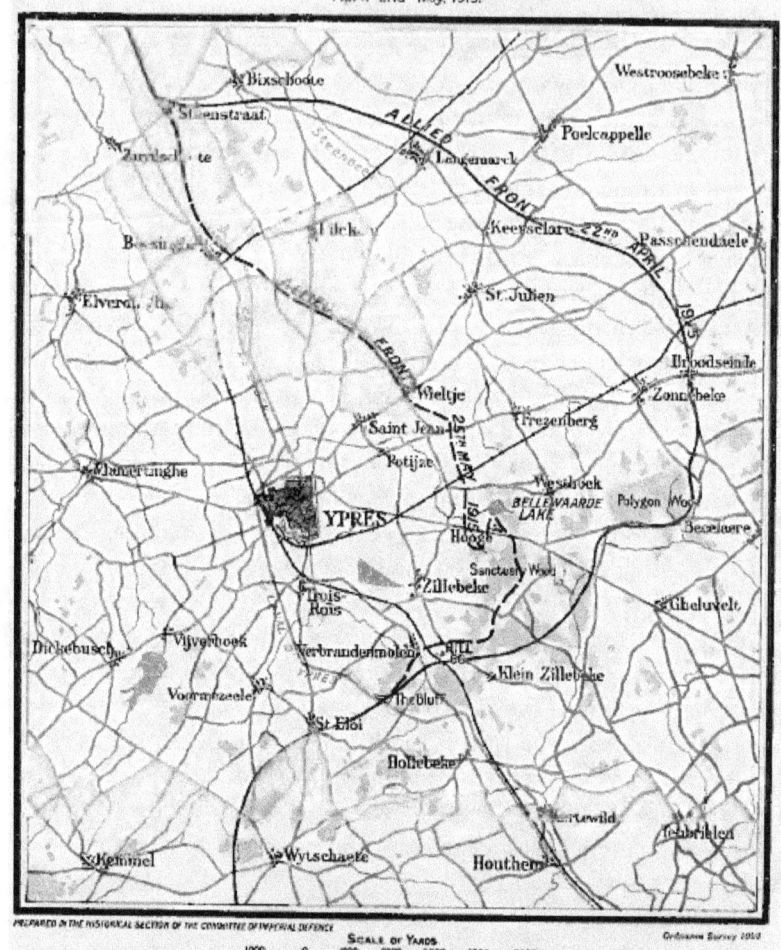

The Fighting at Hill 60

The enemy had a good view of the Ypres area, with all its important supply routes, from a hillock rising some sixty feet above the surrounding country in the south of the salient near Klein Zillebeke. This point, known as Hill 60, Sir John French decided to capture. The neighbourhood of the hill was closely reconnoitred from the air beforehand, some good photographs were obtained, and entrenchments and gun emplacements were located. On the 16th of April the guns were registered by air on the important strategic points behind the hill by which all the approaches, as well as the support trenches, were commanded.

The assault on the position was timed for 7.0 p.m. on Saturday the 17th, immediately following the explosion of the mines which had been laid under the hill. Reinforcements began to move into the line after dark on the Friday evening. It was desirable that the enemy should have no information of these reinforcements, and No. 1 Squadron was entrusted with the task of keeping German aircraft away from the hill through the daylight hours before the attack. (On the 29th of March No.1 Squadron had been detached from the Third Wing to the aerodrome at Bailleul for duty with the Second Wing). The first patrol from the squadron was sent out at 4.30 a.m. and remained up for two and a quarter hours.

A quarter of an hour before the patrol was due to return a second one started off to take its place. This arrangement continued through the day and the whole of the front from Kemmel to Ypres was covered until 7.15 p.m. No enemy aeroplanes got through, the attack came as a complete surprise, and the hill was captured at small cost to the attackers. So soon as the enemy became aware of our purpose, following the explosion of the mines, his artillery began to bombard, but the fire was to a great extent countered by our own guns, which had been previously registered from the air. In addition, Captain Ludlow-Hewitt, who was well acquainted with the German positions behind the hill, was able to pick out, by their flashes, a number of active German batteries which had by efficient camouflage hitherto escaped observation.

By the morning of the 18th of April, the British infantry had been pushed, by fierce counter-attacks, from the crest to the reverse slope of the hill. A wireless and lamp receiving station had been established at the headquarters of the 5th Division and the patrolling air observers—the first had gone up at 4.15 a.m.—made reports direct to the division of the movements of enemy troops, the positions of active batteries, and of the progress of our own artillery fire. Fighting patrols, sent out at intervals, again kept off German airmen who made many attempts to work over the area.

In the evening the crest of the hill was brilliantly retaken. Major W. G. H. Salmond, the commander of No. 1 Squadron, had been requested to make a special effort, beginning at 6.0 p.m., to note the flashes of the German guns, and he had eight aeroplanes over the hill whilst the infantry were wrestling for the summit. The observers were able to plot the positions of thirty-three active guns and, throughout the whole of the 19th, the British artillery searched the areas in which these guns had been seen on the previous night, whilst air patrols again watched the position: the enemy artillery was considerably less active.

During the 20th a German battery was reported to be dropping shells into the Hill 60 trenches. Aeroplanes of No. 1 Squadron were sent up and soon located the battery, which ceased fire. On the morning of the 21st the squadron commander was informed that Hill 60 was again being heavily shelled and that the infantry were suffering severely. He sent off a wireless aeroplane at once, and arrangements were made for all batteries with wireless receiving stations to fire in response to an air message giving the positions of the active German guns. The information sent down from this aeroplane and from a second one which relieved it in the air enabled the artillery to put down the German fire.

For some days the enemy made only minor efforts to recapture the position. At about 6.0 p.m. on the evening of the 1st of May, however, a pilot flying towards the lines saw that the hill was suffering a heavy bombardment. As soon as he arrived over the trenches the firing ceased. He flew on patrol until 7.15 p.m., when failing light compelled him to return. At once the bombardment was renewed, but the attack which followed was met with a stubborn defence and once more the enemy was driven back.

On the 5th of May the enemy came again with yet greater determination and at last retook the crest, from which counter-attacks made throughout the night failed to dislodge him. No 1 Squadron, on the 6th, were ordered to photograph the hill and its area preliminary to a new British attack on the position. The photographs were in possession of the officer commanding the attacking battalion before the action began. The enemy, however, stuck grimly to his ground, the attack proved abortive and, since no further troops could be spared, the effort to recapture the hill was abandoned.

The Battles of Ypres

But attention had been suddenly and dramatically diverted from the south to the north of the salient some days before this. A German prisoner, captured by the French before Hill 60 became a point of contention, told of an impending attack against the Salient and, bubbling over with the significance of what he knew, told, too, of secret preparations for the use of a deadly gas. As a token of good faith, he had brought with him the respirator he was to wear.

The news reached British headquarters on the 15th of April, and next day No. 6 Squadron at Poperinghe were instructed to try to test the truth of the prisoner's statements. Their reconnaissances failed to locate anything unusual; nor did flights on the following days reveal any special concentrations, except that early in the morning of the 18th increased rolling stock at Wervicq seemed to indicate the arrival of minor reinforcements. But the prisoner had stated that the attack was timed for the evening of the 15th of April, and it is a fact that the wind was unfavourable on that evening and was not blowing off the German trenches until Thursday the 22nd.

On that morning observers came back with news of considerable liveliness behind the German lines, to confirm the significance of the bombardment of Ypres which had begun on the 20th. They had seen unusual movements of trains and of men soon after 6.0 a.m. which pointed to arrivals of troops in the neighbourhood of the forest of Houthulst; as the day wore on, other reports came in from the air of an ominous stirring in the whole area.

At about five o'clock in the evening of the 22nd of April Captain L. A. Strange, of No. 6 Squadron, flying in calm and pleasant weather over the north-eastern sector of the Salient, saw a sudden bank of yellow-green cloud spring up along the German trenches and move towards the line held by the French 45th Division. On the ground, the French troops viewed its approach at first with more curiosity than alarm, but soon the gas enveloped them and passed on, leaving blue-faced dead and an open road to Ypres. The gas achieved more than had been expected of it and the enemy was not at once prepared to follow up his success.

The attack had started as a minor operation, and to convert it into a possibly decisive one, took time, which turned the scale in favour of the defence. The situation was never again so critical as on that Thursday evening, although the battles did not end until the 25th of May. An air reconnaissance at about half-past four on the morning of April the 23rd followed the line of battle between Boesinghe and St. Julien, and reported on the new line occupied by the enemy. At about half-past six signs of considerable activity on the railway at Cortemarck and on the lines leading from there to Zarren and towards Langemarck were reported. The general indication of this and other air reports was that reinforcements were moving up to the front line from rest centres in the rear. It seemed, too, from one of the reports, that the railway from Staden to the eastern edge of the forest had been extended into the forest itself to cover the detrainment of troops.

One of the first effects of the enemy advance was to bring the aerodrome at Poperinghe under shell-fire on the 24th of April, which compelled No. 6 Squadron to move back four miles to Abeele, where they were installed by the 26th. The squadron was working directly for the V Corps, whose left flank had been uncovered on the opening day of the battle by the gassing of the French. In the first few critical days before help came to them the personnel of the squadron were hard pressed to fulfil the urgent demands, particularly for tactical reconnaissance, which were made upon them.

An observer over the battle-front, between half-past four and half-past six on the morning of the 24th, reported the general line held by the enemy, and located several field works and farms which were apparently being prepared as *points d'appui*. A reconnaissance a little later reported increases of rolling stock at Ledeghem, the station serving the headquarters of the German XXVII Reserve Corps, from which it was deduced that reinforcements were reaching this corps possibly for an attack on the Salient north of the Ypres-Menin road. This attack was made at noon of the following day against the left of the 28th Division about the Broodseinde cross-roads, but was beaten off after fierce hand-to-hand fighting.

At midday there had been a break-through near St. Julien, and artillery observers saw at the same hour mounted troops and infantry moving south from Poelcappelle. An observer of No. 6 Squadron who went to inspect this area again at 5.30 p.m. reported columns of infantry and transport between Poelcappelle and Keerselare, another long column of infantry on the Poelcappelle-Langemarck road, and great train activity to and from Langemarck. At the same hour an observer saw infantry and columns of transport moving out of the forest of Houthulst towards Poelcappelle. These observations left no doubt that the enemy was making rapid movements to develop the breakthrough which he had made at St. Julien earlier in the day, and the Second Army commander was enabled to make his dispositions to counter this move.

On the 26th an observer discovered, near Langemarck, the armoured train which had been responsible for the shelling of Poperinghe. The heavy artillery was ranged on it and quickly forced it to move off, after which the shelling of the town ceased.

Reports had come in from agents that troops were being concentrated at Ghent. To interrupt their movement to the Ypres salient, bombing attacks were organised against trains on the Staden-Cortemarck-Roulers line, and on the stations at Thielt, Staden, Deynze, and Ingelmunster. During the afternoon of the 26th of April two R.E.5's of No. 7 Squadron and seven B.E.2c's of No. 8 Squadron went off from St. Omer. Five of the nine aeroplanes bombed Thielt (four 20-lb. Hales bombs), Staden (six 20-lb. bombs), Ingelmunster (twelve 20-lb. bombs), and Roulers (two 20-lb. bombs)

******

When the war began there were only two kinds of bomb in use by the British air services, the 20-lb. bomb designed by Mr. F. Marten Hale, and the 100-lb. bomb designed by the Royal Laboratory at Woolwich. Mr. Hale had patented his first rifle grenade in 1908. He first gained the interest of the naval airmen for his bomb at Eastchurch in 1913. On the outbreak of war, the 20-lb. Hales bomb was ordered in large numbers by the War Office as well as by the Admiralty. The 100-lb. Hales bomb and the 100-lb. and 112-lb. bombs, designed by the Royal Laboratory, followed and were put into early production. In October 1915 it was decided that the 112-lb. bomb was the best at about that weight, and it became the standard heavy bomb of the Royal Flying Corps until November 1916, when the 230-lb. bomb was produced.

******

The remaining four either lost their way or else their bombs failed to leave the improvised racks. The First Wing were called on to help and sent out four aeroplanes, but only two reached their objectives at Roubaix, Tourcoing, and Courtrai. The bombing of Courtrai was done by Second Lieutenant W. B. Rhodes-Moorhouse, of No. 2 Squadron, who dropped a 100-lb. bomb on the line west of the station. He was told to use his discretion as to the height from which to bomb, and he came down to 300 feet where he was met with rifle and machine-gun fire, particularly from the belfry of Courtrai church, almost on his level.

After hitting his objective, the pilot was wounded in the abdomen by a bullet; on his homeward journey he was again wounded in the thigh and in the hand, but he flew his aeroplane back to his own aerodrome at Merville, although there were nearer ones in his reach. He died of his wounds the next day, before he could learn that he was to be the first of those who were to win the Victoria Cross for work in the air. It was not inappropriate that he should head the list, for he was one of the pioneers of flying in England. He had been flying for two years before he qualified for his pilot's certificate in 1911; his faith in the air had never wavered and he had converted many to his faith.

At 5.0 p.m. on the 27th of April, General Sir H. C. O. Plumer, commanding the V Corps, was placed, in addition, in control of all the troops in the Ypres neighbourhood, his command being known as Plumer's Force. The Flying Corps squadrons in this area were again regrouped. The Second Wing was allotted entirely to the new force. No. 5 Squadron, relieved of its work for the III Corps by No. 4 Squadron which had arrived at Bailleul on the 21st of April, was moved north on the 27th to Abeele, and on the same day an advanced wing headquarters and a report centre were established at Poperinghe. The Third Wing now assumed responsibility for the air work for the Second Army, reduced temporarily to one Corps—the II—and also for the III Corps which had been withdrawn from the Second Army on the 6th of April for operations directly under G.H.Q.

The Wing incorporated, in addition to No. 4 Squadron, No. 1 Squadron which was working from Bailleul for the II Corps. To make up the strength of the Second Wing, No. 8 Squadron was transferred to Abeele on the 1st of May. The position on this day, then, was that the Second Wing had Nos. 5, 6, and 8 Squadrons all located at Abeele, whilst the Third Wing had Nos. 1 and 4 Squadrons at Bailleul, and No. 7 Squadron at St. Omer. The dividing line for close reconnaissance between the Second and Third Wings was the Ypres-Roulers railway.

On the 29th of April General Plumer had been ordered by the commander-in-chief to prepare to retire to a new line nearer Ypres. This new line was occupied on the morning of May the 4th. At 5.30 p.m. on May the 2nd, when the move was in progress, a heavy attack was made by the enemy from St. Julien and on the line to the west of it. Between six o'clock and twenty minutes past seven Captain Strange and Second Lieutenant R.V. de Halpert of No. 6 Squadron were flying over the area. At 6.50 p.m. they located a long column of troops on the St. Julien-Poelcappelle road and a massed body near the crossroads at Keerselare. The pilot came home at once and telephoned the information to Plumer's Force; the artillery got on to the enemy masses without delay and, according to prisoners' statements, made excellent shooting.

Plumer's Force was dispersed on the morning of the 7th of May, and General Plumer took over command of the Second Army from General Sir H. L. Smith-Dorrien, the V Corps, now under Lieutenant-General Sir Edmund Allenby, reverting to the Second Army. The Second Wing, once again, became responsible for the air work for the Second Army. At 7.0 a.m. on the 8th the whole of the V Corps front was heavily bombarded, and the bombardment was gradually concentrated along the sector occupied by the 28th Division. An attack which followed compelled the infantry to give way.

Between eleven o'clock and noon intense traffic behind the enemy lines was reported from the air. Most of it was towards the front, and appeared to be made up of ambulance wagons on their way to points of readiness to evacuate the wounded. In the afternoon and evening the general movement, no less intense, was away from the front. British counter-attacks through that and the following day failed to recover the lost ground.

A valuable long-distance reconnaissance by No. 7 Squadron on the 12th brought back news of a considerable stream of railway traffic moving, apparently through Valenciennes, towards Douai and Lens, and of important detrainments of troops, during the night, at Douai. This pre-occupation of the enemy, to meet an offensive in an area far south of the Salient, came as a welcome indication that the fierce pressure at Ypres might soon cease. But the respite was not yet. On the 13th a furious bombardment heralded a further attack, which was pressed through the day, but failed to gain any of the line, with the exception of a short distance lost by the 3rd Cavalry Division which had suffered heavily. In the fierce fighting on the front of this division No. 2 Armoured Car Squadron did good work.

★★★★★★

After the Battle of Neuve Chapelle No. 2 Squadron had moved to the Ypres area. In April four further armoured car squadrons (Nos. 5, 6, 8, and 15) had arrived in France, bringing the total number of cars up to thirty-six maxim and eighteen 3-pounder. Except those of Nos. 5 and 8 Squadrons which remained at Dunkirk, the light armoured cars were attached to the cavalry and the heavy (3-pounder) cars were distributed, by G.H.Q., along the front.

******

Lieutenant J. Cadman of 'B' Section of the squadron, attached to the 3rd Cavalry Division, received orders at 11.30 a.m. to bring his three maxim cars forward and co-operate in a counter-attack on the lost trenches. He moved off in advance of the attacking party, but one of the cars was quickly put out of action by shrapnel fire. The two remaining cars (*Busy* and *Bustler*) successfully negotiated the shell-pocked and tree-cumbered road. Busy getting within 100 yards of the objective trenches. As the attacking party pushed forward the Germans broke and fled, and *Busy* got off 6,500 rounds into the retreating enemy at short range. Both cars were splintered by machine-gun and shell fire, but did not retire until their mission was completed. ('The coolness and daring with which the armoured cars were handled was magnificent . . .' says a report of the G.O.C. 3rd Cavalry Division).

Desultory fighting marked the period up to May the 24th, when a fresh gas-attack against the line east of Ypres forced a breach at one point. In this attack, once again, two cars of 'B' Section of No. 2 Armoured Car Squadron worked in the front line. Sub-Lieutenants R. Cussen and R. M. Wynne-Eyton reconnoitred the Ypres-Menin road and brought their guns into action throughout the day and part of the night. Owing to the cutting of telephone lines on the 1st Cavalry Division front, and to the effects of the gas and of shell-fire, the armoured cars proved the only possible means of communication with the front-line trenches. The enemy attack necessitated a new line being taken up slightly in rear of the old one. So, did the battle end.

The Salient had been diminished in size, but the Salient was still held. The aeroplanes had kept the command in touch with the enemy's new lines, had watched the ebb and flow of movement behind the immediate front, and had flown for many hundreds of hours directing the guns. They had done much, also, to limit the activity of the German airmen, who repeatedly tried to range their own guns and to reconnoitre over the congested British area. With the cessation of the battle the calls on them did not diminish. They proceeded to the systematic photography of the area, to the plotting of the new emplacements and entrenchments which the enemy constructed, and to the routine of registration of these positions for the artillery.

AUBERS RIDGE AND FESTUBERT
(Order of Battle, Royal Flying Corps, Appendix 2)

But long before this the centre of interest had shifted south. The German attack at Ypres did not deflect the firm purpose of the Allies' spring campaign, of which the main blow was to be struck by the French in Artois. The British advance, auxiliary to the French effort, was to be made by the First Army over much of the ground covered by the battle of Neuve Chapelle, and, if successful, would give us the Aubers ridge which had been one of the greater objectives of that battle. The operation was timed to begin on the 8th of May, but on the evening of the 7th the weather was so misty as to make it doubtful whether any useful flying would be possible on the following morning.

Sir Douglas Haig, who was from the first a firm believer in the air service, was reluctant to begin without air observation, and the attack was therefore postponed until 5.0 a.m. on the morning of the 9th. The air work fell to Colonel Trenchard's First Wing, consisting of Nos. 2 and 16 Squadrons located at Merville and La Gorgue, and No. 3 Squadron at Chocques. Of these, Nos. 2 and 3 Squadrons were to work with the corps direct and No. 16 Squadron was to do the reconnaissance work for army headquarters. The whole of the enemy defence system was photographed and, as before Neuve Chapelle, maps were made on which the detailed plans of the attack were again based.

Part of the tactical work which was to be done by No. 16 Squadron for the army was of a novel kind. A disquieting feature of the Neuve Chapelle battle had been the difficulty of communication between the front and rear when the enemy's fire had cut telephone and telegraph wires. Unless some alternative method of communication could be arranged, there would always be the danger that, once an attack was launched, commanders, even at battalion headquarters, might be entirely ignorant of its progress. Where an artillery bombardment preceded the attacking infantry it was of urgent importance that the artillery commanders should be made aware of anything in the progress of the attack which might necessitate some sudden alteration of their fire.

On the third day of the Neuve Chapelle struggle a pilot, as has been told, was successful in reporting something of the progress of the battle. For the new offensive a definite scheme was drawn up to follow the battle from the air. Experiments had been made, by No. 16 Squadron at Aire, over troops in the First Army training area. In these trials the infantry were seen from 6,000 feet on certain types of ground, such as dry plough land, but on wet grass or wheat it was more difficult to find them. It was found that as the troops moved forward they could not be followed from the air with any certainty, nor could they be distinguished from their opponents.

It was, however, not possible to reproduce the actual conditions of war, and only the battle itself, it was held, would afford an adequate test. It was arranged that three Maurice Farmans of No. 16 Squadron, fitted with wireless, should, in succession, patrol the front on the day the battle opened. When the infantry reached certain pre-arranged points in their advance, they were to spread out on the ground strips of white cloth measuring seven feet by two. These strips were to be an indication to the air observer, but he was instructed to report on the infantry as he saw them and not to rely only on the strips which had the disadvantage that they might be left behind in the hurry of advance or retirement. Four ground stations were specially set aside to receive these air messages and to pass them on by telephone to wing headquarters.

Colonel Trenchard moved with his staff from Aire to Merville on the 7th, and took up his advanced headquarters in a house next to the First Army report centre, where he was in close touch with Sir Douglas Haig. To help the Flying Corps, who were unable to draw any aeroplanes away from the Ypres struggle to reinforce the First Wing for the coming attack, the French *40ᵉ Compagnie d'Aérostiers*, together with a kite balloon, were put at the disposal of Sir Douglas Haig on the 4th of May and used for artillery observation with the I Corps. This was the first kite balloon to work for the British Army on the Western front.

The battle was opened, on the 9th of May, by bombing pilots who raided enemy centres before the artillery bombardment began. The bombing, which had been planned to interrupt rail communications and to harass back areas and army headquarters, failed to achieve its object, not one of the bombs dropped, so far as could be seen, getting a direct hit on its objective. Lieutenant H. F. Glanville of No. 16 Squadron, who had left at 3.0 a.m. with two 100-lb. bombs slung under his Voisin aeroplane to attack Don, was wounded on the way, but persisted to his objective, although he failed to hit the bridge over the canal at which his bombs were aimed.

The artillery bombardment had begun at 5.0 a.m., and within half an hour the 8th Division had captured the first line about Rouges Bancs whilst detachments had seized a few points beyond. One of the

Naval Air Service 3-pounder cars took part in the operation. Its commander, Captain A. F. Wilding, R.M., the well-known tennis player, was killed by a shell. The observers of No. 16 Squadron, who watched the movements of the infantry, sent down during the day forty-two messages which came through strongly and clearly to the receiving stations. After the initial jump forward, the infantry soon discovered that the strength of the German trenches exceeded expectations, and they could make no further impression on the enemy. They did not, therefore, reach the points where it had been arranged they were to display their white strips.

Although the air observers might have had little difficulty in view of the splendid visibility in locating and reporting the strips, the actual information sent down, as the result of direct observation, was neither sufficiently detailed nor reliable enough to impress the army staff. It was not realised at that time that these drawbacks might be overcome by low flying and by patient combined training between the air observers and the infantry. Consequently, there was no immediate development of this vital method of co-operation with attacking troops.

The air co-operation with the artillery, favoured by the excellent weather, proved effective. No. 1 Group, Heavy Artillery Reserve, had to share its three aeroplanes of No. 3 Squadron with the French heavy artillery and with the 26th Heavy Battery. For the two latter a Maurice Farman attached from No. 16 Squadron was used, piloted by Lieutenant C. B. Spence who had as his observer Second Lieutenant the Hon. W. F. Rodney. These officers put the French and British guns on many German batteries, silencing their fire during the vital period of the infantry's attacks. Throughout the day they spent nearly six hours on this work, until their aeroplane was brought down by shrapnel-fire and both officers were killed. The main task of No. 1 Group was the countering of the German batteries, most of which had been previously registered.

Observers sent down, by wireless, information as to which German batteries were active. By comparing the air reports with the reports received from forward observing officers and from officers of the headquarters of divisions, telling the direction from which damaging fire appeared to be coming, it was possible to bring fire to bear on the more important targets. It was further arranged that observers could call on the 48th Heavy Battery to engage new targets which they discovered in their flight, and on any counter-battery to fire on important fleeting targets, a special signal being used. During the afternoon an observer, who saw two companies of infantry reforming in the courtyard of a farm, called up the 48th Battery, which got on to them with, according to the war diary of the Group, 'the happiest results'.

The four wireless aeroplanes of No. 2 Squadron which worked with No. 2 Group of the artillery, flew so that one aeroplane was always in the air to turn the 118th Battery on to suitable targets at the discretion of the observer. Most of these targets proved to be active batteries, but in the afternoon an observer called up the artillery to fire on an enemy battalion near Pont de Pierre; the battalion was scattered.

By the morning of the 10th of May the trenches which had been captured on the previous day had been given up. Sir Douglas Haig now proposed that all resources should be concentrated on the southern point of attack and this was approved. The new battle, identified with the village of Festubert, postponed from the 12th because of dull weather, was finally launched on the night of the 15th and continued to the 25th. The day of the 15th was bright enough for a fair amount of air work, and twenty-five targets were registered for the artillery. There were in addition two reconnaissances which brought back important information. The first, made by an observer of No. 7 Squadron, which, it will be recalled, had discovered strong enemy reinforcements moving to this front on the 12th of May, found in the early morning of the 15th considerable railway movements from east to west towards Douai and Lens.

Other movements seemed to indicate a southward transfer of troops from the Ypres salient. In the afternoon an observer of No, 16 Squadron saw a column of troops, which he estimated at about 10,000, moving west with their transport from Douai. Pilots of No. 3 Squadron sent out later to bomb these troops flew into mist and failed to locate the column.

The objective of the Festubert attack was the enemy first-line system of trenches between the Neuve Chapelle-La Bassée road and La Quinque Rue as a step on the way to the La Bassée-Lille road between the former town and Fournes. The attack was launched shortly before midnight of the 15th, but although some promising 'breaks-in' were made, on the whole there was little headway.

At dawn on the 16th Nos. 2 and 3 Squadrons were ready to bomb stations, headquarter buildings, and trains, but they were delayed by mist, and when, later in the morning, they got away, no direct hits were made on any of the objectives. The morning mist had a more serious effect on the tactical work of the four wireless aeroplanes of No. 16 Squadron; one or more of these was in the air from 4.25 a.m. to 2.0 p.m. and again from 5.0 to 6.40 in the evening, but in the early morning, when observers might have cleared up the obscurity resulting from the night-attack and the cutting of ground communications, they could see little or nothing. Most of the tactical reconnaissance and artillery observation fell to the Moranes of No. 3 Squadron, now under Major D. S. Lewis. One of these, working for No. 1 Group, came upon thirty or forty loaded omnibuses and a column of 200 men on the road from La Bassée to Violaines at about half-past twelve. The observer at once put two batteries on the target, scoring several direct hits on the column.

Late into the night of the 16th of May it was still the German intention to retake the trenches which had been lost, but reports which reached the German staff from the front showed that the position of the troops was extremely precarious, and the idea was abandoned. Instead, it was decided to hold a new line stretching roughly from Ferme du Bois to Rue d'Ouvert. Three tired battalions of the 77th Landwehr Regiment, brought down from the Ypres salient, exchanged their packs for spades and began to dig the new line at about 1.0 a.m. on the 17th. Orders were sent out by the German staff at 1.25 a.m. that after the occupation of this new line of resistance all troops still in their original trenches were to be withdrawn.

The early daylight hours were the critical hours of the battle. The hastily prepared line was far from complete and the enemy could hardly have withstood a further determined attack. But the British did not take advantage of these critical hours, and by the evening the new line was held in nearly double the strength of the original line when it was first attacked, and the precariousness of the German position was ended.

The British command did not realise until the 20th that the Germans had taken up a wholly new position. A significant air report, brought back in the early morning of the 17th by an observer of No. 16 Squadron, had revealed the construction of the extreme northern sector of the new line, but after this report was made a curtain of mist shrouded the enemy positions and prevented any flying until the 20th, so that the further progress in the digging of the line went undetected. When air observation was possible again the battle was already lost, since neither the heavy ammunition nor the troops were available for an action on a scale to overcome a position stronger than the one originally captured.

On the night of the 24th a further British attack carried a number of trenches, and Sir Douglas Haig then received orders to curtail his artillery attack and to consolidate what he had won. What he had won was an average depth of about 600 yards on a four-mile front. On the last two days of the battle, when the weather suddenly cleared, all the aeroplanes were over the lines and, by helping the artillery to knock out or silence a number of enemy batteries, brought some measure of relief to the wearied infantry. The battle, aimed to take a bite at the enemy line, had resulted in no more than a nibble.

In conjunction with the French attacks in Artois it had relieved the pressure on the Ypres salient, but more than anything it brought home to the British command the fact that there must be a far greater preparation and support with heavy artillery in any future attack. Indeed, the meagre supplies of heavy shells had been so depleted during the operations that any further important offensive was, for the time being, out of the question.

A means for extending air artillery co-operation was demonstrated during this battle. The French kite balloon working with the I Corps directed the fire of the French heavy batteries and the British armoured trains so well that Sir Douglas Haig pressed for two balloons for the First Army. Sir John French had sent home a demand for balloons so far back as March. The Admiralty were, at that time, responsible for all lighter-than-air craft. Although they had their own urgent demands to meet, they readily agreed to supply the equipment for a section if the War Office transferred personnel to the Naval Air Service for kite balloon work.

This was done, and No. 2 R.N.A.S. kite balloon section was formed at Roehampton at the end of April 1915 and sent to France, where it arrived on the 8th of May under the command of Major the Hon. C. M. P. Brabazon. It was at once allotted to the Second Army and worked for the V Corps from a position near Poperinghe, doing its first useful flight on the 25th of May when Captain W. F. MacNeece and Flight Sub-Lieutenant W. H. E. Campbell spotted for the artillery on a group of trenches. The British thus lined up in the air with the Germans, French, and Belgians.

The early work of the balloon was largely experimental and instructional, but one of its advantages was soon appreciated. To locate active batteries observers had to rely mainly on spotting the flashes when the guns fired, and the enemy soon came to give up firing as

AREA OF OPERATIONS
NORTH OF LA BASSÉE.
March – May, 1915.

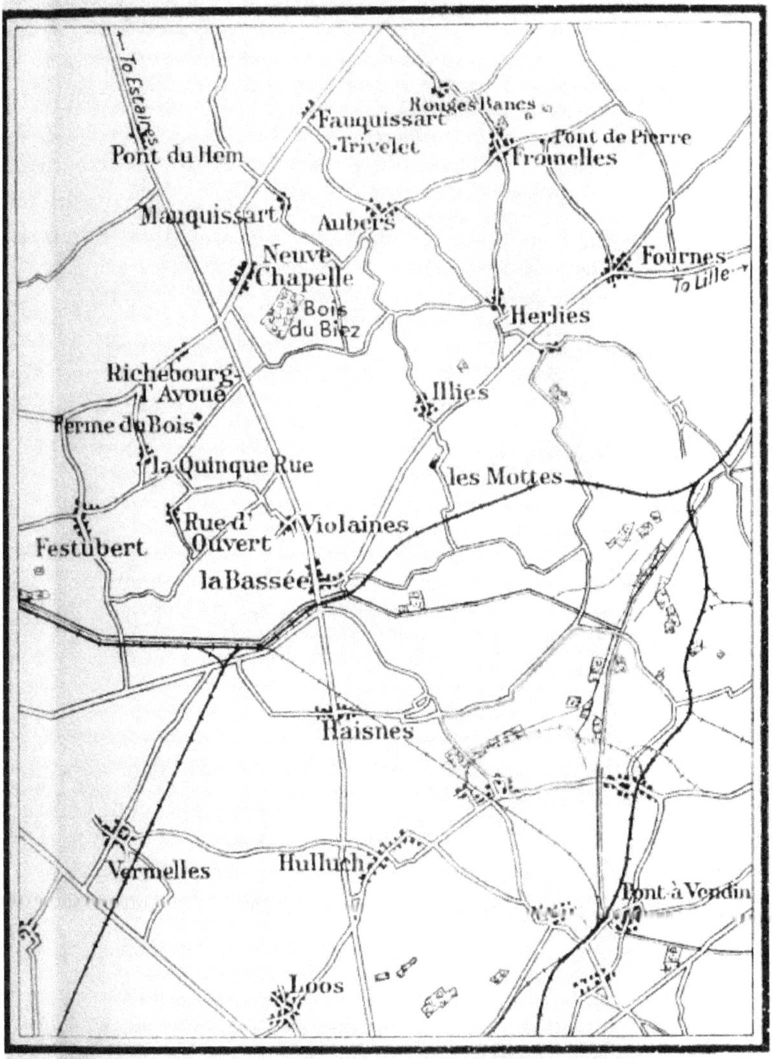

PREPARED IN THE HISTORICAL SECTION OF THE COMMITTEE OF IMPERIAL DEFENCE. Ordnance Survey 1928.

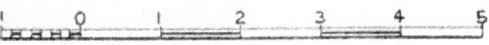

SCALE OF MILES

much as he could when aeroplanes were near him. The balloon did not suffer the disadvantage of the aeroplane that it could not stay up for any length of time. Through the daylight hours it needed to be hauled down only for a change of observer, so that if enemy batteries were going to hold back their fire for fear of being located, they would be out of action for considerable periods. This was hardly to their liking, and the balloons, therefore, came in for many attacks both from artillery and aircraft. The balloon of No. 2 Section came under fire, on the 22nd of May, from enemy artillery directed by an aeroplane, and was punctured in four places. The gas was transferred to a spare envelope and the section moved back, but enemy aircraft continued to take a keen interest in its movements and, for a time, the balloon had to be shifted to a new site every day.

An important point came up for settlement at the very beginning. It seemed to the general staff in France that, as the balloons were to work for the gunners, the artillery should have complete control of them. The only point in common between balloons and aeroplanes was that they both worked in the air, and it appeared, they said, a pity to add balloons to the responsibilities of the Flying Corps. Sir David Henderson did not share this view. Apart from their work for the artillery, the balloons would, he said, collect much information, whilst even for artillery purposes their work would be supplementary to, rather than distinct from, the work of the aeroplanes. More important perhaps was the question of supply and maintenance. Sir David Henderson said:

> I foresee very great difficulties in organising the balloon service in any other way than by utilising the resources of the Royal Flying Corps in personnel and technical knowledge, and I also think that there will be great difficulty in supplying reserves of material and in maintaining the gas supply except through the medium of the stores branch of the R.F.C.

In the result it was decided that the balloons should remain under the Flying Corps. The second balloon section to arrive was No. 4, which left England on the 26th of June and took up a position near No. 2 Section on the 1st of July.

The First Army looked with envy at the two balloons above the Second Army. On the 15th of July Sir Henry Rawlinson, commanding the IV Corps, pointed out that the Germans on his front had five or six balloons, and the fact that he had none placed him at a considerable disadvantage. The question of supply was so urgent that Sir David Henderson went to England and, at a conference at the Admiralty on the 19th of July, he proposed that the War Office should in future be responsible for the supply of balloons to the expeditionary force. The lighter-than-air contracts of the navy, however, had been placed as a whole, and the Board of Admiralty were of opinion that to ensure economy of inspection and rapidity of delivery they should continue to deal with the matter of equipment, and that Roehampton should be used as a joint training centre for all kite balloon sections. This arrangement held until the autumn of 1915, when the Flying Corps took over full responsibility for the kite balloon sections on the western front. These sections now included No. 6, which had come out on the 1oth of August and No. 8 on the 30th. The Flying Corps continued to receive balloons and equipment from the navy until July of the following year when the War Office began to place its own contracts.

The balloon problem was not the only one which appeared unsatisfactory. What the Royal Flying Corps had achieved in bombing was disappointing, and in July the whole subject was closely examined at Flying Corps headquarters. The analysis of the results of bombing by all the Allied flying units on the western front between March the 1st and June the 20th showed that, of one hundred and forty-one attempts to hinder the enemy's movements by the bombing of stations, only three had been definitely successful. Damage to the permanent way was easily repaired, whilst attacks on important railway junctions were made difficult by the increasing efficiency with which they were being defended.

On the 24th of July, therefore, it was ordered that bomb-dropping by aeroplanes, under instructions from army commanders, should be limited for the future to attacks on hostile headquarters, telephone exchanges, and munition or poison-gas factories within the army reconnaissance area. Sustained attacks with a view to interrupting the enemy's railway communications by dropping bombs on trains in motion on lines beyond the area in which troops and anti-aircraft guns were numerous, would be carried out, in conjunction with the main operations of the Allied armies, under orders to be issued by General Headquarters.

Special squadrons, said the instruction, were being trained for this purpose, but as they might have to be reinforced temporarily by detachments from the aeroplanes allotted to armies, a proportion of their pilots should still be trained in bomb-dropping. On August the 7th, at a conference between representatives of the British and French aviation services, the future bombing policy was considered. It was concluded that attacks on trains on the move afforded the best means of stopping railway traffic. A train damaged in a cutting may block a line for several days. If the train is set on fire, the rails will probably buckle so that such carriages as have not been derailed cannot be pulled or pushed along the line, which will have to be relaid as well as cleared before a train can pass.

By blocking one line in this manner one day, another on the next and so on, the whole of the enemy's railway movements may be temporarily dislocated. It was recognised that this form of air attack could only be effective if it took place on a large scale and in close co-operation with the main operations. An important result of the conference was an agreement that in the event of an attack being ordered against the enemy's railway communications the French and British aviation services would combine, and that in the meantime the two services should interchange information as to the enemy's railways, the training of pilots in bomb-dropping, and the development of bomb-sights. The policy of co-ordination between the two Allied air services in strict conjunction with ground operations was a distinct step forward, and was put into effect at the Battle of Loos, with what results shall be seen.

The first real bomb-sights were received in time to be used in the battle. If an observer in an aeroplane, flying on a straight course, releases a bomb and watches its downward path, he will see it always vertically under him. On the other hand, an observer on the ground, of bomb-proof curiosity, watching the missile, will see it fall in a curved path. The explanation, of course, is that the bomb maintains the forward speed which it shared with the aeroplane when it was attached to its carrier.

The air resistance which the bomb has to overcome causes it to trail a little behind the vertical of the aeroplane observer and affects, very slightly, the time of its fall, but the small corrections for air resistance, allowed for in the construction of bombsights, need not be considered here. There is, then, along any given course, one place in the air, and one only, from which a bomb may be released from an aeroplane with the certainty that it will hit its objective, and that place is not immediately above the target. In still air the problem would be simple of solution. The speed of the aeroplane over the ground would be the same as its speed through the air, the pilot would know his height and the rate of fall of his bomb, and so have the necessary data to construct a triangle to tell him what he wants to know, that is, the angle, in advance of the vertical, at which he must release his bomb to hit the target.

It would be a simple matter to make an instrument which could be adjusted before he went into the air to give the bomb-dropping angle for any pre-determined height. But the air is never still. The speed of the aeroplane over the ground is greater or less than its speed through the air according as it is helped or retarded by the movements of the wind. A bomb-sight to be practicable must enable the airman to find his ground speed, at any moment, and allow of a consequent simple adjustment to give the bomb-dropping angle.

On the staff of the III Corps, towards the end of 1914, was an intelligence officer, Second Lieutenant R. B. Bourdillon, whose curiosity on the subject of bombs and bomb-dropping was insatiable. Whenever he could get away to one of the aerodromes to talk over the problems with the flying officers, he went. It was not long before he had, in co-operation with Lieutenant Strange of No. 6 Squadron, evolved a simple sight, 'consisting of a couple of nails and a few lengths of wire', which was used, with crude success, by some of the bombing pilots early in 1915.

The bomb-sight problem was so important, however, that the Royal Flying Corps headquarters arranged for the transfer of Lieutenant Bourdillon and sent him home, in December 1914, to the Central Flying School at Upavon, where in the experimental flight at the school he would have facilities to work out his ideas. By the middle of 1915, in co-operation with Second Lieutenant G. M. B. Dobson, a meteorological officer at the school, Lieutenant Bourdillon had produced the famous C.F.S. (Central Flying School) bomb-sight, which was at once adopted both by the Royal Flying Corps and by the Royal Naval Air Service.

The chief novel feature of the sight was a timing scale which enabled a pilot in the air, with the help of a stop-watch, to measure his speed over the ground by two sights taken on one object. To give the correct angle for bomb-dropping, the movable foresight was then set on the timing scale to correspond with the time-interval as recorded, in seconds, on the stop-watch between the two sightings. Minor improvements were made in the original sight, and others, especially for work over the sea, were developed by the Naval Air Service, but the C.F.S. bomb-sight held pride of place on the western front until the end of 1916.

Another step forward, also to exercise its effect during the Battle of Loos, was the standardising of the system of co-operation between the air and the artillery. Progress in co-operation had been rapid, and as points of detail cropped up they had often been settled by agreement between the squadrons and the particular units with which they worked. There were two great disadvantages to this individualism. One was an unevenness of achievement, and the other was an initial loss of efficiency when squadrons were called upon to work for different formations. The question had first been raised by Major W. G. H. Salmond, following an episode during the action at Hill 60 in April 1915.

At that time his squadron—No. 1—was working with the H Corps and, in collaboration with Brigadier-General W. T. Furse, had evolved a system whereby the corps artillery could at once be called up by special signal to engage important fleeting targets. The corps front was allotted, by squares, to the batteries, and certain of these were to respond to the call from the air if it had reference to the squares within their range. The agreed signal was 'JJ' (followed by the pinpoint of the target), and it meant, in effect:

> I see a good target of the nature of a battalion, a battery on the move, or transport over a 100 yards long. All guns please engage it.

During one of the enemy attacks on Hill 60, Major Salmond had been awakened, at dawn, by a heavy cannonade to the north-east of Baillcul, and he sent up Captain Ludlow-Hewitt to find out what was happening. When this officer arrived over the lines he found a heavy attack was being launched against the V Corps front. Exceptional targets were spread out below him and he sent down message after message to the V Corps artillery. There was no response. His signals had not been properly understood. This episode showed how needful it was for all air artillery calls to be made uniform and the universal need also for some such call as the 'JJ'. Major Salmond brought the matter before Sir David Henderson, and the result was the calling of a conference, in June 1915, to thrash out the full details of co-operation with the artillery.

Major-General J. P. du Cane, the artillery adviser at G.H.Q., presided, and artillery and flying representatives attended from each of the two armies. The conference had before it a pamphlet on the co-operation of aeroplanes with other arms which had been prepared by the Flying Corps headquarter staff, and decided that all outstanding instructions on the subject should be incorporated in this pamphlet. In its amended form the pamphlet was issued in July and formed the basis of the co-operation between the air service and the army during the September offensive.

Whilst headquarters was concerning itself chiefly with questions of policy, organisation, and supplies, the wings were helping the army in the minor actions which followed the Festubert battle. At the end of May, the First Army took over from the French a stretch of line from a point south of the La Bassée Canal to the neighbourhood of Loos, and the squadrons of the First Wing were redistributed. The idea was to resume the offensive against the village of Loos, but after a study of his air reconnaissance reports Sir Douglas Haig suggested that an offensive against Chapelle St. Roch-Rue d'Ouvert offered better chances of success, and he outlined proposals for an attack on both sides of the canal. For this, however, General Headquarters reported there was insufficient ammunition, and the attack was, therefore, limited to the north of the canal and was made on the 15th of June.

As economy of ammunition was of paramount importance, particular attention was paid to air co-operation with No. I Group, Heavy Artillery Reserve. To help the First Wing two aeroplanes with pilots and observers were lent by the Naval Air Service, and continued to fly with the wing until the middle of July. On the 16th of June, the day following the assault by the First Army, the Second Army attacked with a view to taking the high ground near Bellewaarde Lake. In both actions the squadrons co-operated with tactical reconnaissance and artillery observation.

At Bellewaarde, No. 6 Squadron distinguished itself by the efficiency of its artillery co-operation. The firing throughout the day, on targets which had been registered from the air before the attack, showed a great improvement on anything previously observed, and the flying officers found so little correction was required that they had time to spare for tactical work and for the locating of new targets. Captain B. T. James in the evening located fourteen active batteries, and his wireless messages enabled the artillery to engage eleven of these at once, on to six of which he corrected the fire. This officer, who had done so much to perfect the co-operation between the air and the artillery, was brought down and killed by antiaircraft fire whilst ranging guns on the 13th of July. The loss of his experience, vision, and wholehearted enthusiasm was sadly felt by his Service.

One further example of air co-operation with the artillery on the

First Army front is worthy of mention. On the 22nd of July information came in from a French inhabitant at Douvrin, behind the German lines, that a long-range gun, responsible for the shelling of Béthune, was concealed in a factory between that town and Haisnes. The workshop in which the gun was housed had a movable roof which was replaced each time when firing ceased. Next day, although a gale was raging. Captain A. S. Barratt of No. 3 Squadron observed for the 19th Siege Battery on the emplacement and got three direct hits; the last shell, which went clean through the roof, exploded the ammunition in the shed.

In July, also, the taking over by the Third Army of the front from Gommecourt to Curlu, on the Somme, from the French Second Army, involved the redistribution of the Third Wing, now commanded by Lieutenant-Colonel J. F. A. Higgins.

★★★★★★

Lieutenant-Colonel H. R. M. Brooke-Popham succeeded Lieutenant-Colonel F. H. Sykes as G.S.O.1 at flying headquarters on the 26th of May 1915. He was in turn succeeded in command of the Third Wing by Lieutenant-Colonel Higgins on the 2nd of June.

★★★★★★

The Wing headquarters moved from St. Omer to Beauquesne on the 20th of July and was shortly followed by Nos. 4 and 8 Squadrons. On the 25th a new squadron—No. 11—arrived from England and went south to Vert Galand aerodrome to complete the wing. No. 11 Squadron was equipped with the Vickers Fighter, and was the first homogeneous fighting squadron to join the expeditionary force. Its duties, however, were not confined to fighting, but included also long reconnaissance, photography, and occasional artillery observation.

The Second Wing did good work in conjunction with the brilliant attack of the 6th Division near Hooge on the 9th of August, which not only resulted in the recapture of lost trenches, but also wrested from the enemy four hundred yards of his own trenches north of the Menin road. The greatest danger to troops attacking in this area was from enfilade artillery fire, especially from the south. The positions of the German heavy and field batteries were pretty well known, and No. 6 Squadron, before the attack, registered the artillery on all the essential points. On the morning of the 9th Nos. 1, 5, and 6 Squadrons began counter-battery work as soon as it was light, No. 6 getting its first effective fire on a German battery at two minutes past four.

The German fire was kept well under with the help of these three squadrons and the infantry got to their objectives with slight loss. A train in Langemarck station, on to which No. 5 Squadron put the 7th Siege and 31st Heavy Batteries, was cut in half, following which one of its trucks exploded and caught fire. At half-past ten the light became bad and got rapidly worse so that little air work could be done during the rest of the day, a fact of which the German batteries took full advantage, inflicting heavy casualties on the infantry in deep contrast with their earlier ineffectiveness when the Flying Corps was helping. The 6th Division, however, retained what they had won and, following this engagement, there was relative quiet along the whole British line until the autumn offensive at Loos.

The air part in that offensive was directed by a new chief. On August the 19th Colonel H. M. Trenchard took command of the Royal Flying Corps in France, and Sir David Henderson returned to the War Office to deal with the multitudinous problems of supply of men and material for the rapidly expanding air service. He took to the Army Council, of which he became a member, great personal prestige, keen technical knowledge, and war experience of the arm which he represented. He found that to meet the world-wide flood of demands which came to him, he needed the full use of the rare qualities with which he was endowed. He had often to fight for his corps in an atmosphere where there was no air tradition and where the role of the new arm was imperfectly understood.

To the end he remained unruffled and kindly in judgement of those who did not understand, but he alone knew what his serenity cost him. In one great respect that serenity was never disturbed. He knew that in its new chief in France the Flying Corps had an officer whose personality must impress itself in the difficult days ahead on a service responsive to a degree to the inspiration of its leaders.

The Battle of Loos
(Order of Battle, Royal Flying Corps, Appendix 3)

The main thrust of the autumn offensive was to be made by the French over the bare rolling downs of Champagne. To the British Army was entrusted an auxiliary attack in the neighbourhood of Loos, to be made in concert with the French Tenth Army on its right. The tension everywhere was at the extreme, for this, at last, was to be an Allied offensive on a grand scale and a breakthrough was anticipated. The British attack was to be delivered by Sir Douglas Haig's

THE BATTL
DISPOSITION OF THE FIRST

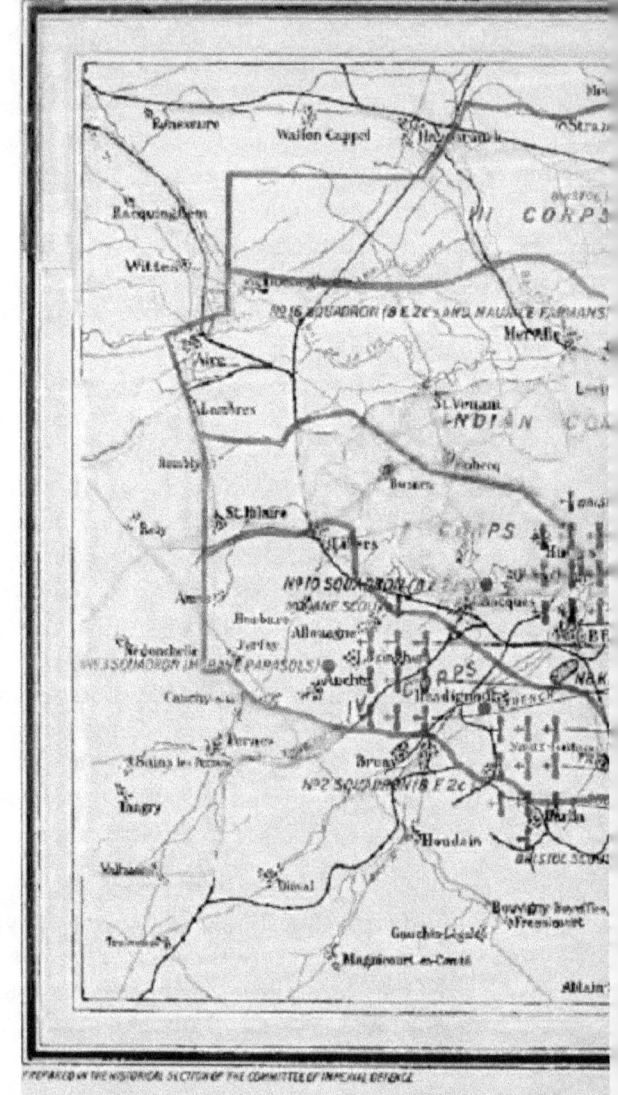

E OF LOOS.
WING, ROYAL FLYING CORPS.

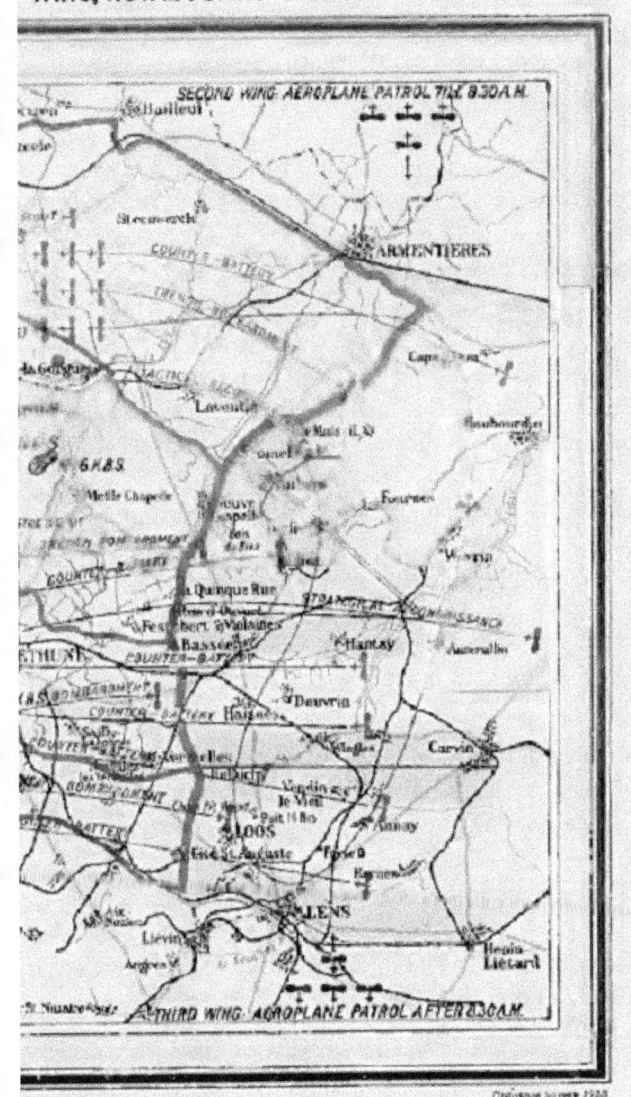

First Army which was to push forward between Lens and La Bassée towards the line Henin-Liétard-Carvin. Secondary attacks, with the object of holding the enemy to his ground, were to be made along the whole front of the Second Army and particularly by the V Corps on Bellewaarde Farm, east of Ypres.

The brunt of the flying work, except the special bombing which will be considered later, fell to the First Wing, now under Lieutenant-Colonel E. B. Ashmore and comprising squadrons 2, 3, 10, (arrived in France on the 25th of July), and 16, and kite balloon sections 6 and 8. Preparations for the battle went on steadily through the brilliant September weather. There was still a serious shortage of heavy howitzer ammunition and there could be no thorough destructive bombardment. It was therefore important that targets should be chosen which would give the greatest help to the attacking infantry, that the maximum of flying should be done to direct the fire from the air, and that frequent pictures of the results of the fire and of any new construction should be in the hands of the artillery brigade commanders, who could, at their discretion, modify their firing programmes from day to day.

These were the considerations which dominated the organisation of the First Wing for the battle. For the framing of their firing programmes the artillery commanders relied almost entirely on what they learned from the air photographs taken at frequent intervals before and during the bombardment by all squadrons, and from continuous verbal discussion with the flying officers. Except one flight of No. 10 Squadron, employed on strategical reconnaissance as far as Valenciennes for First Army headquarters, and one (wireless) flight of No. 16 Squadron, detailed for tactical reconnaissance of the army front, the whole strength of the First Wing, up to the day of the infantry attack, was employed in helping the artillery.

The front of the First Army was divided into four zones, agreeing roughly with the fronts of each army corps, and one of these zones was allotted to each squadron. No. 2 Squadron, (two flights for counter-battery work and one flight for trench bombardment), commanded by Major J. H. W. Becke, worked on the right of the line from Hesdigneul, for the divisional artillery of the IV Corps and for part of No. 1 Group (Heavy Artillery Reserve) along a front of three and a half miles; No. 3 Squadron, (*ibid* No. 2), under Major D. S. Lewis, was at Lozinghem for co-operation on a front of four and a half miles with the divisional artillery of the I Corps (including No. 5 Group,

H.A.R.) and the remainder of No. 1 Group; two flights of Major U. J. D. Bourke's No. 10 Squadron worked from Chocques for the divisional artillery of the Indian Corps and part of No. 4 Group H.A.R. on a front of four and three-quarter miles; and, finally, two flights of No. 16 Squadron at La Gorgue, under Major H. C. T. Dowding, co-operated with the divisional artillery of the III Corps and with the remainder of No. 4 Group H.A.R. along a front of six and a half miles.

This grouping ensured that the right of the line, where the main attack took place, was strongest in aeroplanes. Before the operations began the equipment for forty wireless ground stations was supplied by the Flying Corps to batteries and brigades of artillery. For counter-battery work a hard and fast line between squadrons was defined to prevent more than one observer ranging the same target.

No. 8 kite balloon section, stationed south of Bethune, co-operated with the artillery of the IV and I Corps and with No. I Group H.A.R. whilst No. 6 balloon section, near Lestrem, worked for the artillery of the Indian and III Corps and No. 4 Group H.A.R. The balloon observers had the additional task of taking continuous readings of the strength and direction of the wind for the information of the gunners.

The preliminary bombardment opened on the 21st of September, but for some weeks before this squadrons had been organised as for the battle, so that the beginning of operations brought no change in the class of work done by individual officers. For the first two days of the bombardment the weather was brilliant and the squadrons were able to work to their full artillery programmes: our batteries were registered on the first and second line trenches, gun positions, and dug-outs.

On the 23rd the weather began to break, but this did not appreciably interfere with the artillery observation. The wire entanglements in front of the enemy positions received special attention under the direction chiefly of the observers of Nos. 2 and 3 Squadrons and of the balloons. On this day the special bombing offensive was begun. Plans for this offensive, a comprehensive attack on the enemy rail communications to the battle area, had been drawn up at conferences between the French and British air services. The French bombing squadrons on the British right were to attack the junctions at Cambrai, Roisel, Tergnier, and Mézières, and French airships were to make night-raids on the junction at Busigny.

To the Royal Flying Corps was allotted the important railway triangle Lille-Douai-Valenciennes. The latter junction was to receive special attention to hamper the movement of ammunition and reinforcements from the great depots at such places as Mons and Namur. In addition, instructions had gone out to French agents to do their utmost to cut the communications at various strategic points north of the line Orchies-Valenciennes-Namur. The bombing attacks were to be continued daily during the operations.

The First Wing were fully occupied with their direct co-operation with the First Army, and the bombing, therefore, was done by the Second and Third Wings, and by No. 12 (Headquarter) Squadron which had arrived in France on the 6th of September. The orders were for pilots to follow one another at short intervals and attack any trains encountered on the lines Lille-Valenciennes-Douai, as well as the junctions and engine sheds north of Valenciennes. Outside the anti-aircraft zones at Douai and Valenciennes trains were to be attacked from about 500 feet. The results of the bombing were most encouraging.

During the day the line Douai-Valenciennes was attacked by twenty-three aeroplanes of the Third Wing, whilst Lille-Valenciennes was bombed by eight aeroplanes of the Second Wing and by three from No. 12 Squadron. A 100-lb. bomb, dropped from a height of 200 feet by Captain H. le M. Brock of No. 4 Squadron, scored a direct hit on the centre of a moving goods train near Somain. The engine and front part of the train continued east towards the junction, leaving the wrecked and rear trucks behind, but these were cleared later in the day. Other hits were reported on the track near Wallers, on the junction and on the line in front of the engine sheds north of Valenciennes, and a signal cabin near St. Amand was destroyed.

On the 24th of September, the day before the infantry attack, there was rain and mist and no bombing was possible. A number of flights over the immediate front of the First Army, however, helped the artillery to block important groups of dug-outs and to continue their wire-cutting programme.

Although during the four days' bombardment a number of new gun positions had been located from the air, the enemy artillery was, for the most part, inactive. Two extracts from the captured diary of a German battery commander throw light on this passivity. He says on the 18th of September:

> Enemy has worked hard all the morning at communication trench. The presence of hostile aeroplanes near the battery has prevented it from effectively impeding this work.

And on the 23rd, during the bombardment:

> The enemy fire on our trenches cannot be replied to immediately as enemy aeroplanes, little or not at all fired at, are flying over the battery.

The soft rain which had set in on the 24th continued through the night, and increased slightly as the troops on the morning of Saturday the 25th scrambled from their trenches to the attack. Air reconnaissances up to the previous day had reported only normal activity behind the German lines, so that any appreciable strengthening of the enemy positions was unlikely. The rain was no obstacle to the infantry. They made a brilliant jump forward in the south, where by 8.0 a.m. they had penetrated into the village of Loos. The poor visibility, however, hampered the air observers.

In addition to the observation for the artillery on pre-arranged targets, each squadron sent up two aeroplanes (No. 3 Squadron, three) to report which enemy batteries were active. Pilots flew low over the battlefield, but even then, found that the heavy smoke of the bombardment and the clouds of gas which the British had released greatly obstructed their view. At 6.15 a.m. No. 16 Squadron had reported five active batteries and proceeded to range the 14th and 118th Heavy Batteries on them. By 8.0 a.m. No. 3 Squadron had reported twenty-seven more. Ten minutes later No. 16 Squadron had discovered a further nine, and all the artillery observers were kept in constant employment helping to put these and other targets out of action.

Direct protection for the artillery aeroplanes was provided by patrols along the line La Bassée-Lens, maintained by Lieutenant-Colonel J. M. Salmond's Second Wing (Nos. 1, 5, 6, and 7 Squadrons) and by four aeroplanes of No. 11 Squadron of the Third Wing. (On the 28th of September the First Wing itself took on these patrol duties in protection of its artillery aeroplanes).

In the war diary of No. 3 Squadron, it is recorded that some of our battery commanders, owing to the conflicting information which was reaching them from the front, would not fire at the targets indicated to them from the air. This statement is illuminating. The scarcity of knowledge of what was happening along the actual front greatly influenced the fortunes of the battle. There were moments when precise information of the progress of the forward troops would have enabled the artillery commanders to rearrange their fire so as to overcome opposition which proved vital. In the late afternoon, when the British infantry, wearied with their day's fighting, came to a general line short of the Lens-La Bassée road, they began to dig in, but left a gap of more than a mile between Chalk Pit wood and the Hulluch road. Air observation of this undefended stretch of front would have been of great value.

But that was not all. What was more important was that the infantry were laboriously entrenching, unaware that in front of them between St. Auguste and Hulluch much of the German second-line position was either empty or very weakly held. Had this crucial weakness of the German position been seen and reported from the air, it might have made all the difference to the battle. With knowledge of the real position it is reasonable to assume that the infantry would have advanced the extra few hundred yards and have occupied what was, on the morrow, to prove the key-point of the enemy's resistance.

Low flying in close co-operation with attacking infantry was one of the features of the British offensive at the Somme in the following summer. At Loos, the fact that the low-flying aeroplane observer could reliably report the movements of troops who had been trained in the business of co-operation, and that flying low over an attack was not unduly hazardous was yet to be realised. All the same there were certain pre-arranged signals whereby the infantry could communicate their main line of progress to the air observers. White cloth strips were to be placed on the ground when the troops reached specified points. In at least one army corps it was laid down that the infantry were to indicate that they had gained their positions by lighting yellow smoke candles and by waving their hats on the points of their bayonets.

It was also arranged that white linen arrows were to be displayed by each battalion headquarters if their advance was held up. The arrow was to point towards the obstacle and bars were to be added to denote its distance away. The air-observer was to understand that each bar represented 200 yards and he could at once, by special signal, call for fire on the enemy target. There is no record that any of these ground strips were displayed in the battle, or, if displayed, seen from the air, nor were any smoke signals reported.

One may, perhaps, assume that the infantry, desperately occupied with the business of fighting, found little leisure for what at that time may have struck them as of academic interest to the staff rather than as a vital precaution for their own safety. Often the men told off to put out the strips were killed, and it was a novel business which would not be taken up automatically by survivors untrained to its use.

In a further attempt to keep the staff informed of the progress of the battle, Major E. W. Furse, accompanied by Flight Sergeant W. Burns of No. 3 Squadron, went out with the advancing infantry and signalled by lamp to an aeroplane which then flew back and dropped messages at advanced wing headquarters. There is a record of three messages, one on the 25th and another on the 27th, and the last on the 28th, which had reference to the attack by the Guards on Pit 14 Bis. Flight Sergeant Burns, soon after this last message was sent, was hit in the head by shrapnel and died of his wounds. Major Furse, however, carried on, but, on the 30th, he too was wounded in the head whilst making signalling arrangements from a forward position. The experience of the battle showed that a more elaborate system and considerable training and experiment would be necessary to put the subject of air co-operation with the infantry, during an attack, on a sound basis.

In spite of the unfavourable weather during the infantry attack on the 25th of September the bombing was resumed. The line Douai-Valenciennes was bombed by fourteen aeroplanes of the Second and Third Wings. Lieutenant H. R. Nicholl of No. 8 Squadron, finding a bank of fog over Valenciennes, had to go down to within 150 feet of the ground before he could see anything at all. He dropped his bombs from that height on the track and sidings. Second Lieutenant W. S. Douglas of the same squadron, again from a height of 150 feet, hit the brick supports of the bridge which carries the light railway over the main line near Wallers. The light railway was seen to be cut and the main line partly blocked with the brick debris.

Four pilots of No. 12 Squadron reported that their independent attacks had damaged one train east of Haubourdin and another between Valenciennes and Le Quesnoy, and that bombs which missed a moving train south of Seclin had broken the line in front of the train and compelled it to return the way it had come. There was a half-hearted attempt by enemy airmen to interfere with the bombing on this day. Three pilots had brief indecisive encounters in the neighbourhood of Douai, and one aeroplane of No. 8 Squadron did not return from this area.

Next morning, the 26th, the weather was worse. Thick fog shrouded the lines up to 11.0 a.m., after which the conditions improved slightly and the artillery and reconnaissance aeroplanes were able to get on with their work. The only important movements seen behind the enemy lines were at Achiet-le-Grand where a great accumulation of rolling stock was discovered. The bombing pilots again braved the weather and were brilliantly rewarded. Lieutenant M. G. Christie, of No. 7 Squadron, bombed the locomotive sheds at Valenciennes at 2.0 p.m. from a height of 4,800 feet. Ten minutes later Second Lieutenant G. G. A. Williams of No. 5 Squadron attacked the sheds again from 6,000 feet.

One 112-lb. bomb dropped by the former officer hit rolling stock outside the sheds and a similar weight bomb released from the second aeroplane burst in one of the sheds. A few minutes later a third bombing pilot who arrived over the town saw the sheds on fire. It is now known that two ammunition trains had been hit with the result that twenty trucks of shells exploded and caused a temporary cessation of all traffic at this great junction at a vital time. The attacks on moving trains in the railway triangle were continued. A train was derailed on the line Douai-Valenciennes, and another near St. Amand on the Lille route was stopped by a direct hit from a 100-lb. bomb. This train, still stationary, was hit again later in the day. These attacks were made at heights of 500 and 1,000 feet. Bombing and reconnaissance pilots reported that, as a possible result of the bombing attacks, the enemy's anti-aircraft guns were being moved back and grouped round the railway junctions.

In addition to the attacks on the Valenciennes triangle there were other attacks further south. Captain C. C. Darley, of No. 11 Squadron, had on the previous day made a reconnaissance flight to Roisel. The clouds kept him below 600 feet. He completed his reconnaissance, to the accompaniment of rainstorms and rifle fire, and came upon a considerable number of trains at Roisel and other indications of railway activity in a north-south direction. Accordingly, on the 26th, seven aeroplanes of the Third Wing were diverted to attacks on the Douai-Cambrai-Roisel lines. The pilots reported that three 100-lb. bombs had hit the rails halfway between Cambrai and Douai and that a similar weight bomb had got a direct hit on the track between Cambrai and Roisel.

In the north the Naval Air Service had been asked to co-operate in the general bombing of communications by attacking the junction at Courtrai. Two Caudrons, on the 26th, reached the town and dropped four 65-lb. bombs, but the visibility was too poor for pilots to judge of their effect.

It was the intention, next day, the 27th, to attack the accumulation of trains seen at Achiet-le-Grand, but fog and rain made this impossible. On the morning of the 28th, although the weather was little better, four pilots of No. 8 Squadron got through to Achiet and reported that one each of their four 100-lb. and twelve 20-lb. bombs, dropped from heights between 3,000 and 5,000 feet, had damaged rolling stock on the main line.

In the half-dozen rain-washed days, from the 23rd to the 28th of September, the bombing aeroplanes had dropped eighty-two 100-lb., one hundred and sixty-three 20-lb., and twenty-six small incendiary bombs, or nearly five and a half tons weight in all. Their casualties during this period were two aeroplanes missing and two pilots who returned wounded. (During the same six days two reconnaissance aeroplanes failed to return and two reconnaissance observers came back wounded). There was a further series of attacks on September the 30th on the Courtrai-Roulers-Thourout area and on the Lens-Douai sector. The only visible damage reported was, in the north, at Lichtervelde, where the track was hit and a troop train held up, and, in the south, to the line near Henin-Liétard. There were no further organised raids until the 13th of October, when the Second and Third Wings attacked the lines Lille-Valenciennes-Douai. Seven trips were made and twelve 100-lb. and eleven 20-lb. bombs were dropped with what results is not known.

The bombing attacks were made up to a distance of thirty-six miles behind the German trenches. It is difficult to assess the value of the raids owing to the lack of exact knowledge of the material and moral damage. Summarised, the carefully sifted reports of the bombers seemed to show that the railway lines had been damaged in fifteen places, that five trains had been partly wrecked, a signal cabin destroyed, and sheds at Valenciennes set on fire.

The German *Reichsarchiv*, who were kind enough to search their records for this period, gave the information that the bombing of Valenciennes on the 26th of September, blew up ammunition trains and put a stop to all traffic for some time. They state, however, that the reports of their railway authorities have been lost, so that they can give no details of the effects of the general railway bombing. They further state that although the transport of troops was probably made more difficult by the bombing attacks, all units and formations called up to reinforce the front arrived at their destinations up to time, difficulties as they occurred being overcome with comparative rapidity.

From the end of September to the middle of October the battle resolved itself into the repulse of a series of fierce enemy counter-attacks. The main fruits of the first day's advance were maintained. This advance represented, as Lord Kitchener described it, a 'substantial' victory. The larger hopes had, indeed, not been realised, but the failure of the Vimy Ridge attack on the British right, and of the main battle in Champagne, was sufficient in itself to limit the action at Loos. For its part in the battle the Flying Corps received the signal honour of a special order of the day issued by Sir John French on the 4th of October.

> The Field Marshal Commanding-in-Chief desires to express to Brigadier-General H. M. Trenchard, C.B., D.S.O., A.D.C., and all ranks of the Royal Flying Corps, his appreciation of the valuable work they have performed during the battle which commenced on the 25th of September. He recognises the extremely adverse weather conditions which entailed flying under heavy fire at very low altitudes. He desires especially to thank pilots and observers for their plucky work in co-operation with the artillery, in photography and the bomb attacks on the enemy's railways, which were of great value in interrupting his communications. Throughout these operations the Royal Flying Corps has gallantly maintained the splendid record they have achieved since the commencement of the campaign.

It was during the autumn of 1915 that the Royal Flying Corps took on a duty of a novel kind. This was the landing of secret-service agents behind the enemy lines. The first attempt, on the 13th of September, ended badly. Captain T. W. Mulcahy-Morgan of No. 6 Squadron left, on a B.E.2c, to land an agent near Courtrai. The field chosen for descent had to be near a wood so that the passenger could get quickly under cover. The only field near the selected area was small and, in landing. Captain Mulcahy-Morgan collided with a tree. Both he and his passenger were seriously injured and were ultimately made prisoners. Before the enemy arrived on the scene, however, friendly civilians had collected from the aeroplane the carrier pigeons and all papers.

There is a record of a successful attempt by Captain G. L. Cruikshank on a Morane Parasol, of No. 3 Squadron, on the 28th of September, and again by Lieutenant J. W. Woodhouse of No. 4 Squadron on the 3rd of October. On the latter occasion Lieutenant Woodhouse landed his B.E.2c at dusk, alongside a wood near Bantouzelle, about eight miles south of Cambrai. The passenger, with two baskets of pigeons, got clear into the wood, but returned when he saw that the pilot could not get his engine restarted. Woodhouse insisted that the agent return to the cover of the wood, eventually succeeded in restarting the engine alone, and scrambled into the aeroplane as it moved off. But he was not in the air long. The engine, which was over-oiled, was missing badly and he was compelled to land a second time. He ran the engine all out on the ground in short bursts to use up the surplus oil, got off again, and came down safely in the dark behind the British lines. These were the first adventures of a kind that was later to become fairly common.

The beginnings of air fighting

It was during the latter part of the battle of Loos that air fighting first began to assume a serious aspect. The air fighting from the beginning of the year to the end of Loos will here be treated as a whole, the better to illustrate the gradual changes that the air position underwent. It had, of course, been recognised, even before the war, that the machine-gun armed aeroplane would constitute a formidable weapon. It was further realised that the most effective place for the gun was a position whence it could fire ahead of the aeroplane, and since the propeller of the tractor was looked upon as a definite barrier to efficient forward fire, the pusher, in which the observer sat with a clear unobstructed view in front of him, was considered the type which must be adapted for fighting. The first aeroplanes to arrive in France definitely armed for fighting were the Maurice Farmans (pushers) flown across by 'C' Flight of No. 4 Squadron in September 1914. Each had a Lewis gun mounted on the front of the nacelle. These aeroplanes figured in a few combats, but they were too slow and too cumbersome to force a decision.

The general armament, early in 1915, was still the rifle or the pistol. The surprising thing is that these weapons were responsible for the shooting down of a number of aeroplanes. On the 22nd of January 1915, a formation of twelve German aeroplanes came in from the sea and began to bomb Dunkirk. The presence of such a formation at a time when aeroplanes on both sides usually worked singly, was a surprise and a portent. British, French, and Belgian pilots engaged the bombers and one of them, an Albatros, was shot down by a rifle bullet fired either by Captain F.V. Holt or by Lieutenant R. P. Mills of No. 4 Squadron. The bullet had put the engine out of action, but otherwise the Albatros was captured intact.

This success for the rifle was repeated on the morning of the 5th of February when a Morane of No. 3 Squadron, piloted by Second Lieutenant V. H. N. Wadham (observer. Lieutenant A. E. Borton) fought a duel with an Aviatik biplane near Merville. The German pilot opened fire with a pistol and his observer with a rifle, but the Morane did not reply until Wadham had manoeuvred to give his observer a good firing position at a range of 100 yards. The Morane proved speedier than the Aviatik and Borton kept up his rifle fire until the range had finally shortened to no more than fifty feet. At that distance he could see his bullets splintering the enemy biplane which dived away and landed two miles from its aerodrome at Lille. The Morane returned with a bullet through the propeller, another in the fuselage, and two through the planes.

That these were looked upon as isolated feats is seen from a story told by Wing Commander W. S. Douglas.

> The first time I ever encountered a German machine in the air, both the pilot (Harvey-Kelly) and myself were completely unarmed. Our machine had not been climbing well, and as I was considered somewhat heavy for an observer, Harvey-Kelly told me to leave behind all unnecessary gear. I therefore left behind my carbine and ammunition. We were taking photographs of the trench system to the north of Neuve Chapelle when I suddenly espied a German two-seater about 100 yards away and just below us. The German observer did not appear to be shooting at us. There was nothing to be done. We waved a hand to the enemy and proceeded with our task.
>
> The enemy did likewise. At the time this did not appear to me in any way ridiculous—there is a bond of sympathy between all who fly, even between enemies. But afterwards just for safety's sake I always carried a carbine with me in the air. In the ensuing two or three months I had an occasional shot at a German machine. But these encounters can hardly be dignified with the name of fights If we saw an enemy machine nearby, we would fly over towards it, and fire at it some half-a-dozen rounds. We scarcely expected to shoot the enemy down; but it was a pleasant break in the monotony of reconnaissance and artillery observation. I remember being surprised one day to hear that an observer of another squadron (his name, Lascelles, sticks in my memory to this day, though I never met him), had shot down a German machine in our lines with a rifle.

The aeroplane here referred to was an Aviatik which fell to Captain R. M. Vaughan and Second Lieutenant J. F. Lascelles on a B.E.2c of No. 4 Squadron on the 15th of April. The officers were on their way to reconnoitre as far as Bruges when they met their enemy. The observer fired twenty-four shots from an average range of eighty yards, and the Aviatik fell in the French lines near Elverdinghe. The German pilot was found to be dead, but the observer, unwounded, was made prisoner. Vaughan waited over the area long enough to watch the German aeroplane crash, and then went to Bruges.

Meanwhile single German aeroplanes were also making reconnaissance and bombing flights over the British area. It was realised that only the speediest types of aeroplane had a chance of overtaking them, and our fast aeroplanes, the so-called scouts such as the Bristol or Martinsyde, designed, but never used, for the rapid collection of information, were all tractors. There were many suggestions for using these offensively. From a position immediately over his adversary, a pilot might drop incendiary bombs or unload a shower of steel darts. There were other and more fantastic ideas. One, actually tried against the enemy by a pilot of No. 6 Squadron, was the attempted entangling of the propeller of the opposing aeroplane by a weight attached to 150 feet of cable.

This method, however, akin to the catching of birds by salting their tails, had no success. Another device, of similar character, was the trailing of a bomb fitted with hooks. The pilot was to angle his enemy and, having hooked him, was then, by means of a switch in his cockpit, to explode the bomb electrically. These various ideas had no future. But methods to fix machine-guns on the tractors to give forward fire were quickly devised. These weapons were, at that time, scarce, but gradually they were fitted to all the Scout type aeroplanes to produce, in effect, the first of the single-seater fighters. The Lewis gun was adopted rather than the Vickers for the all-important reason that it was lighter.

It was found, too, after experiment that for air work the radiator casing and cooling fins on the Lewis could be dispensed with to save weight and head resistance. Indeed, it was soon discovered that the problem in the air was not to keep the gun cool but rather to prevent the oil in the mechanism congealing in the cold temperatures at high altitudes. For a long time, this was the cause of many stoppages of the gun until research produced an efficient non-freezing oil. The earliest method of fixing the gun was on the side of the aeroplane at an angle wide enough to miss the propeller, but this had the drawback that the pilot had to manoeuvre in one direction and fight in another.

A later, and more successful, method was to fix the gun on a mounting on the top plane high enough for the bullets to clear the tips of the propeller. The pilot got on his target through sights placed in front of him and worked the gun from his cockpit by a Bowden cable. The gun had been so fixed and tested that the pilot's line of sight coincided with the line of fire at a distance in front of the aeroplane judged by the pilot to be the normal effective fighting range. A disadvantage of this method was the difficulty of changing the drum of ammunition on the gun.

Whilst the business of equipping the tractor scouts with machine-guns was proceeding, the first effective pusher fighter made its appearance. This was the Vickers Fighting biplane (F.B.5). It came to be feared by enemy aircraft during its brief reign in France and deserves a word or two. An experimental aeroplane of this type had been tried by pilots of the Royal Flying Corps at Farnborough so early as July 1914. Their reports stated that it was faster and a better climber than the Henri Farman, of which it was to some extent a development. A number were, therefore, ordered. The first Vickers Fighter, fitted with a Lewis gun in the observer's front seat, was received in France on the 5th of February 1915. Others followed and were used at first chiefly by No. 5 Squadron. They were equipped with the 100 horse-power Gnome Monosoupape engine which for a time gave much trouble. Lieutenant-Colonel Brooke-Popham wrote in April 1915:

> A case has recently been brought to my notice, where a pilot has had 22 forced landings in 30 flights in a Vickers machine.

Gradually, however, these troubles disappeared as mechanics became more learned in the idiosyncrasies of the Monosoupape engine, and the Vickers proved its superiority in many a combat.

Sir David Henderson held the view that the fighting type aeroplanes should be concentrated in one or more squadrons, but the opinion was strong in the wings that they should be distributed so that each squadron had a leavening of offensive aircraft. Henderson gave way and the fighters were split up, although it will be seen that the policy of grouping the fighters was adopted later on. Pilots in the squadrons often alternated reconnaissance or artillery work on the rifle armed two-seaters with fighting patrols on the machine-gun armed single-seater tractor or two-seater pusher. The German air service was in a similar transitional stage and fights between the two unequally armed types were not uncommon. One in which a Vickers

Fighter of No. 5 Squadron figured may be quoted. The Vickers, armed with a Lewis gun and a rifle, was piloted by Lieutenant W. H. D. Acland with 1st Air Mechanic J. N. Rogers as observer. The report of the encounter, which took place on the 10th of May, says:

> As ordered I patrolled the Ypres salient. We sighted an aeroplane not being shelled about 3 or 4 miles away to the S.E. and high up. We climbed to about 10,000' and then gave chase. He did not appear to see me and was apparently making for Lille. We caught him up and opened fire from above and behind at about 50 yards. The pilot was hit and the machine also, as I saw flakes of material flying off. They dived and we followed and the observer fired with his pistol but did little damage. I saw the observer then drop his arm as if he was hit. The machine then nose-dived from about 1500', turned on her back and fell to the ground, quite close to Lille. We came down to 2000' to look at it, the machine appeared to be completely wrecked. We then returned behind our lines and climbed to 9000' searched the Ypres salient again for German machines but could only see our own.

When machine-gun came up against machine-gun it was more difficult to force a decision. On this same day Captain Strange on a Martinsyde, armed with a machine-gun, attacked a German aeroplane at 8,000 feet over the Ypres salient. The enemy was similarly armed and turned to meet him. Both pilots fired for some time without effect and then dived away from one another to take up fresh attacking positions. Strange was in the act of changing his drum when the Martinsyde got out of control, turned upside down, threw the pilot from his seat in which he was too slackly strapped, and began to spin earthwards. Strange had a hold, with one hand, on his Lewis gun, with the other, on the rear centre strut, whilst his feet were caught up in the belt. After spinning through five thousand feet, he contrived to kick his feet free of the belt and apply them to the control lever. He was able to right the Martinsyde, regain control, and go home again to his aerodrome.

The process of equipping the two-seater tractors with machine-guns was slow owing to the shortage of these weapons, but by July 1915 distant reconnaissances were usually entrusted only to machine-gun armed aeroplanes. The early mountings for the guns were improvised and built in the squadrons. The two-seater aeroplanes working nearer the lines had to rely, in the interregnum, on the unwillingness of the enemy to press his attacks, on the probable presence of friendly fighting-type aeroplanes in the neighbourhood and, finally, on their rifles and revolvers.

The attacks on the reconnaissance aeroplanes, although still spasmodic, were now getting more determined. On the 21st of July Corporal V. Judge (observer, Second Lieutenant J. Parker) on a Voisin of No. 4 Squadron set out on a lone reconnaissance to Bapaume. Their armament was a Lewis gun and six drums of ammunition, two revolvers, and a rifle. They never came back. A note dropped by an enemy pilot over the British lines gave the news that the Voisin had been shot down in a fight, that the officer had died of his wounds and the pilot made prisoner, the note concluded:

> The German pilots have the highest praise for their opponent who died in an honourable fight.

Five days later a B.E.2c (two Lewis guns and a Mauser pistol) of the same squadron failed to return from a reconnaissance to Cambrai. It was last seen fighting a German biplane near Grandcourt and both occupants were later reported prisoners of war.

On the 31st of July Captain J. A. Liddell of No. 7 Squadron, flying an R.E.5 with Second Lieutenant R. H. Peck as his observer, was engaged on the routine morning reconnaissance near Bruges when a German pilot attacked. The R.E.5 received many hits. Captain Liddell, badly wounded in the thigh, fainted, the aeroplane fell three thousand feet in a nose dive, and then turned upside down. Liddell regained consciousness, righted the R.E.5, and at a low height, under continuous fire, took it safely to the Belgian aerodrome near Furnes where he landed half an hour after being hit. His homeward journey called for great skill, since his control wheel and throttle control had been smashed, and his landing was made difficult by the fact that one of his undercarriage struts had been broken up by bullets. Captain Liddell, who had shown indomitable pluck, was awarded the Victoria Cross. He died of his wounds a month later.

Our own fighters were taking similar toll of the enemy two-seaters. In the evening of the 25th of July Captain L. G. Hawker of No. 6 Squadron, patrolling on a Bristol Scout, attacked a German two-seater over the Ypres salient. He got off a drum of ammunition before the enemy dived steeply away. Twenty minutes later, over Houthulst forest, he found and attacked another, which went down with a damaged engine. Hawker continued his patrol and when over Hooge, at 11,000 feet, came upon a two-seater Albatros engaged in artillery observation. He approached down sun, and after a brief fight sent the Albatros down in flames, the German observer falling out as the aeroplane turned over at 10,000 feet. The wreckage fell in the British lines near Zillebeke where it continued to burn for fifteen minutes.

On the body of the dead observer was found a map on which had been pencilled the exact location of one of our batteries that had been firing at the time. On the map, also, were marked the positions of four German batteries. One of these was recognised as a battery, (identified by our own artillery as Percy), which had been persistently troublesome and had been searched for in vain by the Flying Corps for some weeks. All three German aeroplanes which Hawker had attacked were armed with machine-guns. For his exploit he was awarded the Victoria Cross. He had, at the time of his award, much distinguished service behind him. On the 19th of April he had made a daring bombing attack on the Zeppelin shed at Gontrode near Ghent, and during the critical days of the Ypres battle he had been responsible for some brilliant reconnaissance work.

Although throughout August there was a further extension of air fighting, there were few decisive combats. What is interesting is that a fighter was now occasionally ordered to escort the reconnaissance aeroplane, especially in front of the Third Army. This army, newly settling in the area from Gommecourt to the Somme, required the maximum help of its air squadrons. The whole of the new front had to be thoroughly reconnoitred and much photography had to be done. Further, to screen our own numerous movements from the eyes of enemy air observers, line patrols had to be kept up.

For some weeks after its arrival at the end of July this duty kept the Vickers Fighters of No. 11 Squadron fully employed, and during this time Nos. 4 and 8 Squadrons, in addition to their work for the Army Corps, were called on to keep Cambrai, Bapaume, Peronne, St. Quentin and the connecting railways under daily observation for the army commander. Enemy airmen in this area showed a marked determination to dispute these reconnaissances, and pilots and observers were frequently compelled to fight for their information. (By the end of September, it became necessary to provide an escort of one Vickers Fighter from No. 11 Squadron for each army reconnaissance carried out by Nos. 4 and 8 Squadrons).

That the ability to meet the army's air requirements would be conditional on the gaining of air superiority by fighting, was now beginning to emerge. It was not difficult to visualise the time when an offensive by either side would be accompanied by a clash in the air for local supremacy. Lieutenant-Colonel Brooke-Popham in a memorandum, in August, surveyed the whole problem. He called attention to the disquieting fact that the expeditionary force had expanded from four divisions to thirty, whereas the number of aeroplane squadrons had only grown from four to eleven, although many new and diverse duties had been added to their original role of reconnaissance.

> If the enemy brings troops over from the Eastern front and resumes his offensive, he will doubtless make a determined effort to prevent our discovering his movements. Then will commence the real struggle for air supremacy where numbers will be one of the essentials for success.'

Colonel Trenchard lost no time in putting forward a programme for the expansion of the Flying Corps squadrons in France. In the meantime, however, this question of supremacy was raised in an acute form by the introduction by the enemy of the fighting Fokker monoplane, the first single-seater tractor fighter fitted with a mechanism to allow of machine-gun fire through the propeller. Although the Fokker makes its first appearance in pilots' reports at the end of July 1915 and occasionally afterwards down to the end of September, it was not until October, as the Battle of Loos was dying down, that these single-seater fighters were met with in any numbers. Then began the opening phase of what was to prove a strenuous, dramatic, and fluctuating struggle for air supremacy.

CHAPTER 3

The Months Before the Somme Struggle

Three weeks before Christmas of 1915 the chiefs of the Allied armies journeyed to the pleasant village of Chantilly, there to discuss with General Joffre plans for the defeat of the enemy in the coming year. It was agreed at this conference—the first serious attempt to obtain unity of action in all theatres of war—that this might best be brought to pass by a determined and simultaneous offensive by each of the Allies. That was the position when, at noon on the 19th of December 1915, Sir Douglas Haig succeeded Sir John French as commander-in-chief of the British armies in France. A series of negotiations between Generals Haig and Joffre followed. It was recognised that the strategy which governed the fighting in 1915 would no longer hold. That strategy had aimed at the creation, by bombardment, of a breach in the enemy lines and at the rapid exploitation of the breach by the assaulting infantry.

But experience had shown that the German reserves, brought comparatively fresh to the battlefield, formed the final obstacle to success. The first object of the fighting in the new year, therefore, must be the wearing down of the enemy reserves. It was further agreed that these actions of attrition be fought by both armies in the west, but that the British should take the chief share whilst the French held themselves in reserve for the final blow. It seemed that July would be the likeliest month for the main effort, as it was desirable to allow the British command as much time as possible to receive and train its new units, and the Russian command time to re-equip its armies. This plan pre-supposed that the German Army would not attack on any big scale before the Allies were ready. That supposition, however, was to be confounded. The enemy got his blow in first, wrested the initiative from the Allies, and altered the whole aspect of the campaign in the west.

The blow fell on a front of nine miles along the banks of the Meuse, opposite Verdun, on the 21st of February 1916. As soon as the magnitude of the German offensive was realised, it became clear that the Allied plans must be greatly modified. The idea of preparatory attacks had to be given up. The French must accept the challenge and defend Verdun with their whole strength. There was no suggestion of abandoning the Allied offensive, but it was now obvious that the main thrust in France must fall to the British. General Joffre therefore asked Sir Douglas Haig to relieve the French Tenth Army in the Arras sector and to prepare an attack on as wide a front as possible north of the Somme. He promised to support the attack with an advance south of the river, the strength of which would depend on how much the French Army suffered at Verdun.

Thus, whilst the British Army was preparing to take on the bigger part, the French Army threw its whole might into the Verdun struggle. When on the 21st of May 1916 the Germans, after weeks of bitter fighting, stormed and captured Mort Homme Hill, the situation seemed so grave that General Petain pressed his commander-in-chief for an early beginning of the Somme offensive, but Joffre bade him hold on yet a little longer. Still the Germans moved forward. On the 7th of June Fort Vaux fell to them, and once again Petain prayed for relief. His request was granted. It was decided that the offensive should begin as soon as possible and it was actually launched on the 1st of July. The bombardment preliminary to the offensive opened on the 24th of June, and on that day the Germans reached the furthest point in their advance to Verdun, and although they did not abandon the struggle until the end of August, the seriousness of the threat to the great fortress was removed.

Air Reinforcements and Reorganisation.

During the greater part of the battles of the Somme the Royal Flying Corps enjoyed such a local dominance and brought home to the German command so forcibly all the fruits of that dominance, that the Germans at once set about a reorganisation of the whole of their air services and a reshaping of the policy which directed their use. The drastic nature of that reorganisation is the measure of the shock which the Flying Corps administered. This shock was made possible, as shall now be told, by the working out of an offensive policy, by the thorough and extensive training in artillery observation, photography, and co-operation with the infantry, which went on throughout the months which preceded the battle, by a conversion of the ground units to sympathy with and, to some extent, understanding of the air, and, above all, by the reinforcements of men, aeroplanes, and material which reached the Flying Corps in the field from home. At the end of the battle of Loos in October 1915 there were in France twelve air squadrons. By the 1st of July 1916 there were twenty-seven. But that was not all. The twenty-seven were better equipped, better trained, and better armed.

******

After the Battle of Loos, squadrons arrived in France as follows: No. 13 (B.E.2c's), October 19th; No. 18 (Vickers Fighters), November 19th; No. 9 (B.E.2c's), December 20th; No. 15 (B.E.2c's), December 23rd, 1915; No. 20 (F.E.2b's) and No. 21 (R.E.7's), January 23rd, 1916; No. 24 (D.H.2's), February 7th; No. 25 (F.E.2b's), February 20th; No. 27 (Martinsyde Scouts), March 1st; No. 23 (F.E.2b's), March 16th; No. 29 (D.H.2's), March 25th; No. 22 (F.E.2b's), April 1st; No. 70 (Sopwith two-seaters) one flight, May 24th, a second flight June 29th, and the third flight on the 30th of July; No. 32 (D.H.2's), and No. 60 (Moranes), May 28th.

So far as possible, the dates given are those on which the aeroplanes were flown to France, No. 60 Squadron was equipped with its machines three days after arrival in France. It received one flight each of the Morane Bullet, Biplane, and Parasol. The Parasol was quickly replaced, however, and by the middle of June the Parasol flight was entirely re-equipped with Bullets. All the above squadrons which had two-seater aeroplanes were given one or two Bristol or Martinsyde Scouts a few days after reaching France.

******

To meet the expansion of the service, actual and prospective, it became necessary, in January 1916, to organise the Royal Flying Corps into higher formations than wings. By that time the air needs of the army were divided fairly distinctly into two kinds. There was the demand for close reconnaissance, photography, and artillery co-operation on the immediate front of each army corps, and there was a demand for reconnaissance work, beyond the area covered by the corps, which had special interest for the army commander. It was natural, therefore, that the wings should be reorganised so that one or more should be responsible for the corps work and one or more for the army work.

So there came into being corps wings and army wings, and these were grouped to form brigades, one for each army. Since, too, the air work for the army headquarters called for aeroplanes of extended radius of action, those of the highest performance and most fitted to fight for their information were attached to the army wings. The formation of brigades took effect on the 30th of January 1916, when the I Brigade, commanded by Brigadier-General E. B. Ashmore, and the III Brigade, under Brigadier-General J. F. A. Higgins, came into being, comprising respectively the First and Tenth Wings, and the Third and Twelfth Wings. The II Brigade, grouping the Second and Eleventh Wings, was formed on the 10th of February by Brigadier-General J. M. Salmond. (When, on the 16th of February 1916, General Salmond was called home to reorganise flying training in England, Brigadier-General T. I. Webb-Bowen took command of the II Brigade).

Each brigade included an aircraft park and a kite balloon squadron and was, in effect, a self-sufficient air unit. The special strategical and patrol work required by G.H.Q. was the duty of two squadrons (Nos. 12 and 21) retained at Flying Corps headquarters. (The headquarter units were designated the Ninth Wing on the 14th of May 1916).

Consequent on the decentralisation of the service into brigades, it became necessary also to reorganise the headquarter staff on a higher basis. Up to this time the general supervision of the technical side of headquarter work had been an extra duty of Lieutenant-Colonel Brooke-Popham, G.S.O.1. The expansion of the squadrons however, was giving rise to a host of technical and administrative problems, and a new establishment was sanctioned which provided for the addition to the existing staff of a deputy-adjutant and quartermaster-general (D.A. & Q.M.G.). (In addition, the existing appointment of D.A.A. and Q.M.G. was raised to A.A. and Q.M.G.) Lieutenant-Colonel Brooke-Popham was appointed, with the rank of brigadier-general, to the new post on the 12th of March.

An artillery officer of considerable staff experience was brought in as G.S.O.1 to take over the operations side of the headquarter work. This was Brevet Lieutenant-Colonel Philip W. Game, who assumed duty with the Royal Flying Corps on the 19th of March. On the 30th of March the headquarter staff moved from their *château* at St. Omer (leased from its owner at a rental of twenty *francs* per day) to another *château* (at 500 *francs* per month) at St. André-aux-Bois, southeast of Montreuil, whither the British Commander-in-Chief had recently transferred his headquarters. (The St. André *château* continued to house the Flying-Corps headquarters until the end of December 1917, when an exciting and disastrous fire razed the building to the ground).

******

The staff under Major-General Trenchard now comprised: Brevet Lieutenant-Colonel P.W. Game (G.S.O.1); Major E. B. Gordon (G.S.O.2); Brigadier-General H. R. M. Brooke-Popham (D.A. & Q.M.G.); Lieutenant-Colonel F. L. Testing (A.A. and Q.M.G.); Major A. Christie (D.A.Q.M.G.); and Captain A. G. R. Garrod (Staff Captain). In addition, there were ten officers attached for special technical and liaison duties.

******

THE FOKKER SUPREMACY

Before the full effects of the expansion and reorganisation of the Royal Flying Corps in the field could be realised, the German air service had, with the fighting Fokker monoplane, made the first bid for air supremacy. It will be recalled that the influence of these fighters began to be felt towards the end of the Battle of Loos in October 1915. They fought their way to a dominant position which they held until about May 1916. Anthony Fokker, a Dutchman, had had a monoplane built to his design so far back as 1912. The first machine proved difficult to handle and Fokker, whilst flying it, was unfortunate enough to crash and kill his German officer passenger. He continued, with German backing, to improve the design, and on the outbreak of war it was considered by the German air service to be good enough for quantity production.

An outstanding feature of the Fokker monoplane, which was of clean design and good performance, was its ability to make long al most vertical dives, but what chiefly gave it its fighting superiority was the interrupter gear by which the working of the machine-gun was synchronized with the engine to allow the bullets to pass between the blades of the revolving propeller. The German pilot could take aim at his enemy in the direct line of his flight, and could keep up machine-gun fire unhampered by any necessity for a change of ammunition drums. The first of the Fokkers fitted with the interrupter gear appeared in the summer of 1915, but it was not until towards the end of that year that the number so fitted was sufficient to affect the general air position.

The tactical use of fighters was still obscure, and the Fokkers were undoubtedly robbed of their full effectiveness by being allotted, in small numbers, to various flying units, their pilots going up, without apparent co-ordination, to take on what came their way. Their method of attack drew inspiration from the hawk. The Fokker pilot would cruise at great heights over the German lines and await the passing of suitable victims. He would then swoop down from behind, coming when possible out of the sun so that his opponent might have no warning before he was startled by the rattle of a machine-gun. One long burst of fire came from the Fokker as it dived past, the dive being continued well out of range. If the British aeroplane was not shot down and persisted in its work, the German pilot would climb again and repeat his swift diving attack.

Then came the famous manoeuvre, introduced by Lieutenant Max Immelmann, which made it possible for the Fokker pilot to strike again and again with little loss of time. In the Immelmann turn the aeroplane rears up as if to loop, turns sideways over the vertical, and then comes out in the opposite direction. This manoeuvre, in which height is gained at the same time as direction is changed, took the British pilots by surprise and added to the losses which the Fokker inflicted. It may be definitely stated, however, that good as the Fokker was, and resourceful as were its pilots, its moral effect, when it was in the heyday of its superiority, was far greater than its actual success justified. The tendency to credit the monoplane with exaggerated fighting capabilities had often a cramping effect on its opponents.

The measure of the Fokker surprise and its influence on the tactical employment of our own aircraft will be clear from a brief review of the air fighting through the winter months following the Battle of Loos. As the Fokker in October 1915 begins to drive home its attacks on the long reconnaissance aeroplanes, there is a noticeable increase also in the aggressive spirit of the German artillery and other two-seater pilots. They are penetrating more and more over our lines and fight when attacked. What is anomalous, in view of the development of the fighting aeroplane, is that some of the two-seater aeroplanes, on both sides, are still crossing into enemy territory without machine-guns.

On October the 11th, for instance, the day after Immelmann claimed his fourth victim (a B.E.2c of No. 16 Squadron on photographic reconnaissance near Lille), a rifle-armed Morane of No. 3

Squadron, working over Hulluch in co-operation with the artillery, was shot down in our lines by a machine-gun armed biplane. On the same day a new Albatros on similar duty over the Loos area was attacked with machine-gun fire by three of our own artillery pilots (two B.E.2c's and one Morane). The Albatros, which proved to be entirely unarmed, landed and was captured intact. In the fights, now becoming common, over the trenches, the B.E.2c, although few claims can be advanced for its fighting capabilities, more than held its own.

One B.E.2c pilot. Second Lieutenant H. W. Medlicott, of No. 2 Squadron, showed remarkable resource in many such attacks. On October the 11th he was working with Lieutenant H. B. Russell as his observer near Vermelles, when he saw and attacked a German two-seater. He got into position under the German aeroplane to give his observer a clear field of fire from the front seat over the top of the propeller. After a sharp encounter Medlicott saw that his enemy was in trouble, and manoeuvred his B.E.2c to shepherd him towards the British lines where the German pilot eventually landed. The enemy observer, it was found, had been shot in the leg.

★★★★★★

Lieutenant Medlicott on the 10th of November 1915, with Second Lieutenant A. Whitten Brown as observer, left on his B.E.2c on reconnaissance to Valenciennes. Two other B.E.2c's from the squadron which went out to escort him ran into rain and snow and had to turn back. Medlicott went on alone but failed to return, and was later, with his observer, reported prisoner. It is in keeping with his character that on the 21st of May 1918, in a determined effort to escape from Germany he was shot and killed. His observer survived to navigate the first aeroplane to cross the Atlantic. This flight, which won the £10,000 prize offered by the London *Daily Mail*, took place on the 14th/15th of June 1919, the pilot being the late Captain Sir John Alcock.

★★★★★★

The B.E.2c pilots did not confine their fighting to the neighbourhood of the trenches. They had occasionally to escort the long reconnaissance and photographic aeroplanes and, at first, they did not always get the worst of their encounters with the Fokker. On the 22nd of October 1915 a B.E.2c, piloted by Second Lieutenant D. A. Glen (observer. Corporal E. Jones) of No. 8 Squadron, was escorting a squadron reconnaissance machine to Le Cateau. The escorting pilot who lost touch with the reconnaissance aeroplane was attacked by two Fokkers over Cambrai. An early burst from his observer's Lewis gun struck one of the Fokkers which fell in a wood; the other Fokker pilot at once gave up the fight and withdrew. It is noticeable in all the early Fokker encounters how much the success of the monoplane was dependent on the flying and shooting skill and on the determination of its pilot. There were other instances during the month when the attack was so swift and the shooting so deadly that our aeroplanes were shot almost before they caught sight of their attacker and before they had any opportunity to reply.

There was a further increase in the aggressiveness of the enemy airmen in November. On the 7th a B.E.2c reconnaissance pilot of No. 10 Squadron, escorted by a Bristol Scout, was attacked by a Fokker and an Aviatik over Douai. The Bristol pilot could not prevent the B.E.2c being shot down by the Fokker. On the same day Second Lieutenant G. S. M. Insall was patrolling the front of the Third Army on a Vickers Fighter (observer, Air Mechanic T. H. Donald) of No. 11 Squadron, when he saw an Aviatik. He gave chase, and was led by the German pilot towards a rocket battery. He saw the intention, cut off the Aviatik, and enabled his observer to fire a drum at close range which crippled the enemy's engine.

The German aeroplane went down through the clouds, closely followed by the Vickers. They came from the clouds together, the Vickers reopened fire, and the enemy landed heavily in a ploughed field. The occupants scrambled out and tried to get at their machine-gun, but Insall dived within 500 feet of the ground to give his observer a further opportunity to fire. The Germans now began to run, one helping the other who was apparently wounded. Insall turned back, dropped an incendiary bomb on the Aviatik, and left it enveloped in smoke.

On the return the Vickers, flying low, came under heavy fire; the petrol tank was pierced, the engine stopped, and the pilot was compelled to land behind a small wood 500 yards inside the French lines. The German artillery was ranged on the Vickers, but although a hundred and fifty shells were sent over none got a direct hit. In the night, behind screened lights, the damage to the Vickers was made good, and at dawn Insall flew back to his aerodrome. He was awarded the Victoria Cross and his companion the Distinguished Conduct Medal.

On the 11th of November a close reconnaissance aeroplane of No. 6 Squadron, after a fight with two enemy pilots, was shot down, and two B.E.2c's of No. 8 Squadron, flying without observers and armed only with rifles, failed to return from a bombing raid on the German aerodrome at Bellenglise, some twenty-six miles east of Albert. The plans for this raid miscarried owing to adverse weather. All available aeroplanes of Nos. 4, 8, and 13 Squadrons were to attack the aerodrome at the same time, each squadron providing its own escort.

Half the bombing aeroplanes carried an observer and a half-load of bombs, whilst the remainder flew without observers with a full bomb load. To give further protection Vickers Fighters of No. 11 Squadron were ordered to patrol the Peronne-St. Quentin area whilst the raid was in progress. But strong winds in the upper air and thick clouds over the German lines led to many pilots losing their way and a consequent disorganisation of the arrangements, with the result that two of the B.E.2c's fell victims to the enemy.

A long reconnaissance on the 14th of November attempted by a B.E.2c of No. 7 Squadron was frustrated by a German pilot who wounded the B.E.2c pilot in the leg. Dull weather with intermittent fog brought a lull in the air activity through the rest of the month. On the 30th a photographic B.E.2c of No. 16 Squadron was shot down in a fight near the German front-line trenches.

Next day, December the 1st, the same squadron lost a B. E.2C which was making the reconnaissance flight to Valenciennes. (The pilot was Lieutenant D. W. Grinnell-Milne, observer, Captain C. C. Strong. Both were taken prisoners. The pilot escaped from captivity in April 1918. See *An Escaper's Log* by Duncan Grinnell-Milne). This was caused, not by enemy action, but by the strong west wind, and it illustrates a serious difficulty which the reconnaissance—indeed all—pilots had to face. In this instance the B.E.2c developed engine trouble over Valenciennes, and the pilot had to make his way back in the teeth of a wind blowing at forty miles an hour. He got within eight miles of the trenches before the engine gave out altogether.

The prevailing westerly winds in France helped the enemy airmen in a diversity of ways. If they crossed our lines unnoticed they stood a good chance of completing their job and getting back to their lines before our fighters could climb to engage them, their escape being made easy by the extra speed which the wind gave them. Our own pilots although helped by the wind into enemy territory had to look forward to a slow return, a fact of which the German airmen and anti-aircraft gunners took every advantage. If the personnel were wounded or the aeroplane damaged, getting back was always difficulty and sometimes impossible. The German pilot, in similar predicament over our own lines, could put his nose down and often beat a hasty retreat to safety. As the war progressed and engine power developed this disadvantage, although still operative, was diminished. But in the early days it was a very real handicap.

On December the 5th two B.E.2c's of No. 13 Squadron were attacked whilst escorting a photographic aeroplane to Bellenglise and both were shot down. On the 14th a reconnaissance B.E.2c of No. 7 Squadron was met and shot down by a Fokker over Ypres, a somewhat rare event on our side of the lines. The same day Lieutenant G. S. M. Insall and his observer, Corporal T. H. Donald, were shot down, by a German two-seater, and made prisoners. (Lieutenant Insall escaped from Germany in August 1917). Next morning the long Valenciennes reconnaissance attempted by a Morane pilot of No. 3 Squadron was attacked by Lieutenant Max Immelmann. The Morane, his seventh victim, fell from a great height well over the German lines and the pilot and observer were killed.

There was a sudden burst of German activity in the air on the 19th of December, especially north of the river Lys, where a morning gas attack had been launched against a part of the Second Army front. A dead set was made against our reconnaissance aeroplanes, and the personnel were kept too busy fighting to make any detailed observations. No less than forty-six fights took place throughout the day. A B.E.2c which set out to escort a G.H.Q. reconnaissance to Bruges was shot down near Oostcamp, the pilot and observer being killed. The pilot of the reconnaissance machine extricated himself from a fight over Ypres on the way home and, although wounded in the arm and having one cylinder of his engine shot away, made a safe landing near Cassel. Two other officers came back wounded, and several aeroplanes were landed in a damaged condition. One damaged aeroplane crashed and the observer was killed.

Three Moranes of No. 3 Squadron were sent on the difficult Valenciennes reconnaissance, two of them as escort. They had fights with a Fokker and two Albatros pilots but got back safely with their information. Bad weather brought comparative quiet until the end of the month when there was again a series of determined enemy attacks. Two aeroplanes were missing on the 28th and another on the 29th. The last, a B.E.2c of No. 8 Squadron, was escorted by a similar type aeroplane to Cambrai, near which town four Fokkers appeared in the air together, but not in formation. Two attacked and at once shot down the reconnaissance aeroplane, but the escorting pilot (Lieutenant W. S. Douglas) fought his way home under repeated attacks by the four Fokkers, one of which, apparently damaged by fire from the B.E.2c, landed. Douglas was forced down, at one time, to within fifteen feet of the ground. He crossed the trenches at 800 feet and landed in a field near Arras.

The new year brought gales and rain. Although little flying was possible two aeroplanes failed to return on the 5th of January and another (a Morane of No. I Squadron on long reconnaissance for the Second Army) on the 10th. On the morning of the 12th, in a bright and clear interval, an endeavour was made to satisfy the accumulation of demands from the army. No. 1 Squadron again tried the Second Army long reconnaissance. Once more the Morane was shot down, both pilot and observer being killed. The long reconnaissance to Ghent tried by No. 12 Squadron for G.H.Q. also failed. The escorting R.E.7 pilot did not find the reconnaissance aeroplanes, which had in fact turned back owing to the bad visibility, and continued alone thinking they had gone on. The R.E.7 was shot down and both occupants killed. A Vickers Fighter which set out to escort the Cambrai reconnaissance was never seen again.

We were now paying a heavy price in the endeavour to get on with our work. It was obvious that if the long reconnaissances which the army required were to be done at all, there must, pending the arrival of the new fighting squadrons, be a revision in tactics. This was made in an order issued from Flying Corps headquarters on the 14th of January 1916 which brought about, at a stroke, one of the drastic changes in the air war—formation flying, and crystallised the effects of the whole Fokker dominance. The order reads:

> Until the Royal Flying Corps are in possession of a machine as good as or better than the German Fokker it seems that a change in the tactics employed becomes necessary. It is hoped very shortly to obtain a machine which will be able to successfully engage the Fokkers at present in use by the Germans. In the meantime, it must be laid down as a hard and fast rule that a machine proceeding on reconnaissance must be escorted by at least three other fighting machines. These machines must fly in close formation and a reconnaissance should not be continued if any of the machines become detached. This should apply to both short and distant reconnaissances. Aeroplanes proceeding on photographic duty any considerable distance east of the

line should be similarly escorted. From recent experience it seems that the Germans are now employing their aeroplanes in groups of three or four, and these numbers are frequently encountered by our aeroplanes. Flying in close formation must be practised by all pilots.

The effect of this change in tactics was equivalent to a shrinkage of the Flying Corps strength. Whilst the number of jobs required for the army did not diminish, many more aeroplanes had to be set aside for each job. As yet the tactics of formation flying and fighting were crude, but from now onward we get considerable thought and experiment devoted to this problem. Various kinds of formation were practised. In a typical one used in the Second Wing the reconnaissance pilot led with an escorting aeroplane 500 feet higher on each quarter and a rear-guard aeroplane a further 500 feet up.

On the morning of the 7th of February, a formation of this disposition set off to do the Second Army long reconnaissance, the leading pilot flying at 7,500 feet. Over Roulers the first enemy pilot appeared. Seven others closed in from various directions and took up station, in a haphazard way, behind our formation, which was well maintained. West of Thourout two Fokkers arrived. These attacked at once, one diving on the reconnaissance aeroplane and the other on an escort, but their fire was brief and inaccurate. Six more enemy aeroplanes joined the group over Cortemarck, and there were now fourteen following the four British pilots on the return journey. None of them attacked and our formation recrossed the lines safely.

Here they met two further enemy aeroplanes returning from bomb-dropping, and in a sharp encounter the pilot (Lieutenant J. Prestwich) of one of the escorting B.E.2c's was mortally wounded in the leg. There is little doubt that our aeroplanes owed their immunity during their fifty-minute flight over the German lines to the rigidity with which the pilots kept their formation. Had they been tempted, by the attacks of the two Fokkers, to split up, they would have been pounced upon, in detail, and could hardly have fought their way back against overwhelming odds.

Occasionally the number of escorting aeroplanes was doubled, two flying on either quarter and two in rear of the reconnaissance aeroplane. Formation flying, first instituted for reconnaissance purposes, was gradually adopted by the fighting patrol pilots. Experience was gained which made it possible, when the Somme battle opened, to organise a series of offensive sweeps by fighting formations far over the enemy lines.

On the 7th of February a reconnaissance of railway activity on certain of the Belgian lines was ordered by General Headquarters. No. 12 Squadron was given the task which was allocated to a B.E.2c. To escort this aeroplane three other B.E.2c's, two F.E.'s, and one Bristol Scout of the squadron were detailed as well as two F.E.'s to be supplied by the Second Wing and four R.E.'s from No. 21 Squadron. The reconnaissance was not made, but there could be no more significant tribute to the supremacy of the Fokker than is implied in this order for twelve pilots to escort one reconnaissance aeroplane.

The Fokker held.

But the Fokker was not much longer to hold pride of place in the air. Urgent demands went home for a speeding up of the production of those fighting aeroplanes already being manufactured and for further efficient fighters. The British aeroplanes which first outfought the Fokker were pushers. Of these, two types call for special notice: the F.E.2b and the de Havilland Scout (D.H.2). The first aeroplane of the F.E., or Farman Experimental, type was designed and built by Mr. Geoffrey de Havilland, and was purchased at the end of 1910 by the War Office. The design was improved by research and experiment and culminated in the aeroplane known as the F.E.2b, some of which arrived in France late in 1915.

Early in the following year the F.E.2b began to replace the Vickers Fighters. A great advantage of the F.E.2b, apart from the fact that it was fairly fast, had a reliable engine (120 h.p. Beardmore) and was easy to fly, was the wide view which the observer had from a spacious cockpit. He could stand up and move about freely and could fire his Lewis gun to the rear over the top planes. After the F.E.2b became outclassed as a day fighter it continued to work in France as a night bombing machine, and was so used with considerable success until the end of the war. The de Havilland 2, by the same designer, a single-seater fitted with a 100 horse-power Monosoupape rotary engine, had a speed of eighty-six miles per hour at 6,500 feet, could climb to 10,000 feet in twenty-five minutes, and had a ceiling of 14,000 feet.

A few single machines of both types were flying in France late in 1915, but the first complete F.E. 2b squadron to reach the Flying Corps in the field was No. 20 which arrived on the 23rd of January 1916. This squadron was called upon to do army reconnaissances and to provide escorts, and its pilots, whilst carrying out these duties, did a considerable amount of fighting. The Fokkers never hesitated to attack, but they soon found that the F.E. formations gave at least as good as they received. The first squadron equipped with the compact little D.H.2 was No. 24, which arrived on the 8th of February 1916 under the command of Major L. G. Hawker. For the first few weeks after their arrival, the pilots of this squadron patrolled the lines north of the Somme. These patrols were in the nature of training.

On the 25th of April two officers of the squadron, who were escorting the Fourth Army reconnaissance, beat off many attacks and showed that the D.H.2 could manoeuvre with great success against the Fokker. Five days later Second Lieutenant D. M. Tidmarsh of the same squadron left some F.E.2b's which he was escorting and attacked a Fokker, which dived so steeply to avoid him that it crashed on the roof of a building in Bapaume and fell to pieces before the de Havilland pilot had got close enough to fire a shot.

On the 4th of May another pilot of No. 24 Squadron, Second Lieutenant S. E. Cowan, overtook a German two-seater close to the ground near Clery, and fired a few rounds at a range of fifty yards. The German pilot tried to land, but his aeroplane hit a wire fence and broke up. Cowan climbed to 200 feet and then dived again, firing the rest of his drum. He then discovered that his thumb switch had jammed and he was forced to alight, but a bump on landing loosened the spring, and he got off again, crossing the lines under heavy fire at five hundred feet.

Meanwhile a further complete F.E.2b squadron, No. 25, had come out from England on the 20th of February, and soon found, like its companion squadron No. 20, that its aeroplanes could more than hold their own in the air.

Although it was now clear that the new British aeroplanes were a match for the best of the German fighters, the more determined of the enemy pilots still offered stubborn battle, especially on the Third Army front. This will be seen from the experience of the officers who made a reconnaissance for this army on the 31st of May. The British formation, made up of five F.E.2b's and two Martinsydes, of No. 23 Squadron, was attacked by three Fokkers over Cambrai which were first seen diving out of the sun. An F.E. was lost, the observer in another was killed, and all the aeroplanes were badly damaged by bullets. One of the attacking Fokker pilots was shot down, but his two companions followed the formation back to the lines. Although this fight was not exceptional, the last half of May showed, on the whole, a very marked decrease in the enemy's aircraft activity against the Royal Flying Corps. Sir Henry Rawlinson, the general officer commanding the Fourth Army, writing on the 23rd of May 1916, stated:

> It was about the first week in May that we sent out our reconnaissance over Bapaume escorted by the de Havilland machines. Up to that time we had been carefully training our young pilots and it was not till then that Ashmore thought them sufficiently expert to take on the Fokkers. In carrying out the reconnaissances they were attacked by the Fokkers and rendered a good account of themselves for they reported that on the first occasion they sent two Fokkers to earth in a damaged condition and on the second they destroyed another which fell in the town of Bapaume and was smashed amongst the houses. All three of these machines fell of course in the enemy's lines so we have no certain information of what actually happened to them.
>
> But the fact remains that since this occurrence we have successfully photographed the whole of the enemy's trenches in front of the Fourth Army, the first line, intermediate line, second line and third line, over a front of more than twenty miles without being once attacked by the Fokkers. This was done on the 15th, 16th, 17th, and 18th May and clearly shews that for the moment at any rate we have command of the air by day on the Fourth Army front. I cannot speak too highly of the work of these young pilots, most of whom have recently come out from England, and the de Havilland machine has unquestionably proved itself superior to the Fokker in speed, manoeuvre, climbing, and general fighting efficiency.'

While our pushers, handled with skill and determination, were subduing the Fokkers, the French produced a very effective fighting tractor. This was the small single-seater Nieuport Scout (no horse power Le Rhone engine), armed with a Lewis gun fired over the top plane by means of a Bowden cable. Its performance was superior to that of any other contemporary fighting aeroplane. It could reach 10,000 feet in ten and a half minutes and was ten miles an hour faster than the best aeroplane of the Royal Flying Corps. The first Nieuports were received by the Flying Corps in France in March 1916, and were attached to Nos. 1 and 11 Squadrons.

It was on this type of aeroplane that the first of our great fighting pilots, Albert Ball, had his early successes. His Nieuport came quickly to be feared by enemy pilots, and may be said to have been the spearhead of the achievement of the Flying Corps over the Somme. Ball was born at Nottingham on the 21st of August 1896, son of Alderman Sir Albert Ball, sometime mayor of the city. He showed an early passion for pistols which he began to collect at the age of nine years, and he spent much time in his garden firing from one end of the tennis lawn at sticks placed in the ground at the other end, so that he became a remarkable shot at an early age.

He was interested, too, in engines. When he was no more than fourteen, he appeared one day at his father's house at the head of a band of boy admirers who were propelling, on a wheelbarrow, a derelict engine which Ball had purchased. He installed the engine in his workshop and soon had it in running order.

On the outbreak of war, he joined the Sherwood Foresters, was transferred later to a cyclist corps and, whilst encamped near Ealing in the summer of 1915, took flying lessons at Hendon. His flying had to be done at dawn so that he might get back to his camp for the 6.0 a.m. parade. He was seconded to the Royal Flying Corps on January the 29th 1916, and flew overseas to join No. 13 Squadron on the 18th of February. Although his duty was chiefly artillery reconnaissance, his two-seater, in April, destroyed an enemy aeroplane and drove down two more. Ball was, however, by temperament a single-seater pilot. On May the 7th he was transferred to No. 11 Squadron to fly the new Nieuport Scout, and on the 29th he had the first of his long list of successes when he shot down two German machines.

In May, too, there arrived the first batch of tractor aeroplanes to be received by the Royal Flying Corps fitted with the so-called interrupter gear. These were the first of the famous Sopwith two-seaters (1½ Strutter), brought out from home by the Flight of No. 70 Squadron fitted with 110 h.p. Clerget engines, on the 24th of May.

******

The first aeroplane to reach the Royal Flying Corps, fitted with a synchronizing gear (Vickers), was a Bristol Scout which arrived on the 25th of March, 1916. A few other Bristols, similarly fitted, followed. It is a point of interest that the first German interrupter gear which fell into our hands was fitted on a Fokker monoplane that had a forced landing in the British lines, and was captured intact, on the 8th of April, 1916.

******

Suggestions for an interrupter gear had been put forward in England before the war but nothing came of them. The enemy, by first giving the idea practical expression on the Fokker monoplane, achieved the full effects of surprise and quickened Allied invention. The result was the appearance, early in 1916, of three British mechanical gears. The principle of these early gears was that a cam, driven by the engine and working through a series of push-rods, pressed the trigger of the gun at intervals so regulated that the revolving propeller blades were clear of the outcoming bullets. It will thus be seen that the action of these synchronizing gears was positive firing of the gun and not the interruption of its fire.

The mechanism was put into operation by a lever under the control of the pilot. The three British mechanical gears were the Vickers, the Scarff-Dibovsky, and the Arsiad, all used in conjunction with a fixed Vickers machine-gun.

★★★★★★

A French gear, designed for the Lewis gun by Sergeant-Mechanic Alkan, of the French air service, was tried experimentally about this time on a few Royal Flying Corps machines, but the arrival in France of the British gears made further trials of the Alkan unnecessary.

★★★★★★

Up to the time of the development of the synchronizing gear the Lewis was the standard machine-gun for use in aircraft. All the early experiments with interrupter gears envisaged the use of this gun, which was lighter and handier than the Vickers but suffered the disadvantage that, in comparison with the Vickers, it could only fire a few rounds (at this time, forty-seven) before it had to be recharged. (The double drum for the Lewis gun, which contained ninety-seven rounds, was first used in France in July, 1916). It was discovered, after a time, that a synchronizing gear could be more easily adapted for the Vickers than for the Lewis gun, and since synchronized fire through the propeller called for a fixed gun mounted in the fuselage the objections of unwieldiness against the Vickers disappeared. The gear which was fostered by the Royal Flying Corps was the invention and product of the Vickers firm.

The Sopwiths of the first and second Flights of No. 70 Squadron were fitted with this gear. The machines of the third Flight of the squadron, however, which arrived in France on the 30th of July, had been handed over to the Royal Flying Corps by the Admiralty, (see chapter 7, 'The Luxeuil Bombing Wing'), and had the Scarff-Dibovsky gear which had been developed by the Naval Air Service. Lieutenant-Commander V. V. Dibovsky, of the Imperial Russian Navy, had brought his scheme for machine-gun fire control to the notice of the Naval Air Service in January, 1916. Mr. F. W. Scarff, a warrant officer gunner on the staff of the Admiralty Air Department, promptly designed a mechanism to give practical embodiment to the scheme. The Scarff-Dibovsky became the standard gear for the Sopwith 1½ Strutter and was also used, towards the end of the Somme battle, by a Royal Flying Corps squadron of Nieuport two-seaters.

The only other Flying Corps squadrons which made use of interrupter gears in the Somme battle were Nos. 19 and 21. These were equipped with B.E. 12's (140 h.p. R.A.F. engines) on which the Vickers gears were fitted. (No. 19 Squadron arrived on its aerodrome on the 1st of August, 1916, and No. 21 Squadron was re-equipped with B.E. 12's towards the end of August). The Arsiad gear was designed in the field by Major A. V. Bettington, the officer commanding the Aeroplane Repair Section of No. 1 Aircraft Depot, the initials of the Section giving the gear its name. The Arsiad came well out of its trials and a few of the gears were made in England. Some of them were used in France, but they were displaced by the Vickers which became the standard mechanical gear of the Royal Flying Corps. It may be broadly stated that the synchronising gear, owing to the small number of aeroplanes equipped with it, played but a minor part in the superiority which the Royal Flying Corps achieved in the Somme battle.

The Policy of the Strategic Air Offensive.

But it was not alone the new aeroplanes which accounted for the British superiority; it was as much the policy which directed their use to ensure the maximum effect being obtained. This policy is fundamental and must be considered at some length. It is founded on nothing more than the principle of the offensive. That principle may seem to some so beautifully simple as to be almost axiomatic. But it was an axiom which the German command learned only after bitter and costly experience, and one which found highly-placed disputants on the British side.

The moral effect of aircraft attack is so great that those who are attacked from the air always call for protection. If a town is bombed there is at once a clamorous demand for aeroplanes to prevent the enemy doing such a thing again. If a bombing squadron blows up a munition dump protection for all other munition dumps is demanded.

One aeroplane flying over front line troops and attacking them with machine-gun fire may be feared by many thousands of men, and the question at once arises, Why are not our own machines on the spot to attack it as soon as it appears? There is, indeed, in time of war a constant pressure exerted from many directions for a dissipation of air power, but that pressure, if yielded to, is fatal. Aeroplanes cannot be distributed like policemen across the face of the earth. The air service must carry the war into enemy territory and keep it there. The air war becomes a test of nervous endurance. The nation which keeps a stiff upper lip, and whose air service adheres to its determined offensive, of course will, in the end, secure the greatest measure of protection from the air for all its various activities.

The policy was thrashed out in the autumn of 1915 in many conversations between General Trenchard and Commandant du Peuty, of the French air service. They talked and argued over the experiences of the two air services. They came at last to the conclusion that the corps aeroplanes could best be protected by what one might call the strategic offensive, that is, by fighting and subduing the enemy airmen far away from the aeroplanes flying in direct co-operation with the army. The experience of the French air service during the Verdun struggle confirmed the value of the strategic offensive. When that struggle began aircraft were concentrated, and, whilst their infantry were defending, the French airmen went off on the offensive.

Fighting formations attacked the German airmen whenever and wherever they were met, and the French aeroplanes generally worked and bombed far over the German lines. To counter the French the German air service undertook a series of so-called 'barrage' flights. The battle zone of the German Fifth Army was divided into four barrage zones, each of which was patrolled without interruption from dawn to sunset. The patrol pilots had instructions to let no enemy break through. The aeroplanes used for this barrage work were usually of the reconnaissance and bombing type. The first effect of this policy, therefore, was to divert these aeroplanes from their proper duties and to deny to the attacking German infantry much of the air support which they ought to have received.

But more than that the barrage flights were wholly inadequate to their task. The French pilots soon found that they could go more or less where they wished, whereas very few German aeroplanes crossed the French lines to harass the French troops at a time when they were hardly pressed and when the moral effect of aircraft would have been at a maximum. The Germans were quick to realise that something was wrong, and the first thing they did was to group their Fokker aeroplanes together. When the battle had opened the Fokkers were divided amongst the various reconnaissance flights, but as soon as it was realised that this division made them almost powerless against the French pilots, a number of Fokkers were withdrawn from other armies and allocated to the German Fifth Army, where they were formed into two special groups attached to army headquarters.

The groups were known as 'Single-seater Fighter North and South Commands' with which the personality of the German pilot Böelcke is identified. Oswald Böelcke, a keen single-hearted officer, son of a Saxon schoolmaster, had been attracted to the air in 1913 when his battalion was stationed near the flying-school at Darmstadt. He had already had considerable success as a single-seater pilot on the Fokker, in association with Lieutenant Max Immelmann, and he imbued the two new groups with his own offensive spirit.

Meanwhile, as the German airmen became more aggressive the French suffered losses, and the pilots and observers who came into the area to replace the casualties began gradually to call for direct protection for the close reconnaissance aeroplanes. The French command was induced to accede to their requests and so to adopt defensive methods. From that moment the tables were turned. The French air service began to lose its superiority and the French airmen could do very little reconnaissance, and their artillery pilots were compelled to work from inside the French lines. The French did not long acquiesce in this state of affairs. Thanks largely to the efforts made by Commandant du Peuty they went back to the offensive, regained superiority, and with it all the advantages which they had temporarily lost. General von Hoeppner, who was appointed commander of the German air service in October 1916, looking back on the Verdun operations writes:

> In the battles of attrition before Verdun, the aeroplane barrage came to be regarded as the universal panacea against the enemy Air Forces. This notion spread over the whole of the Western Front and had the most disastrous influence upon the methods of use of the airmen. The quite intelligible wish of the infantry and artillery to be rid of enemy aircraft could, it was thought, only be met by keeping German aeroplanes constantly

flying up and down the lines. It is not possible to keep down the enemy by this means. The rapidity with which the enemy aeroplanes can get away, their ability quickly to change their altitude without interfering with their observation, the difficulty of recognising an enemy in the air from a distance, all combined to prove that this kind of aerial line patrol merely meant an unlimited waste of strength to the detriment of our own reconnaissance work. "The barrage has precedence over all other work", read the instruction issued before Verdun. (Hoeppner, *Deutschlands Krieg in der Luft*).

When brigades had been formed in the Flying Corps in the beginning of 1916, General Trenchard had allocated the squadrons which were best able to protect themselves, to the army wings. Now that fighting was becoming specialized and profiting by the lessons of Verdun, he decided that these wings should take over all the fighting aeroplanes. Accordingly, towards the end of April, he assembled his brigade commanders and explained that it would soon be necessary to take all scout-type aeroplanes from the corps squadrons and to concentrate them in the army wings. This, in fact, was gradually done, so that by the middle of August 1916 no corps squadron had fighters on its strength, and the principle of differentiating offensive fighting and corps work was definitely established, and was not departed from throughout the remainder of the war.

THE DEVELOPMENT OF THE ANTI-AIRCRAFT ARTILLERY.

In the above broad consideration of the see-saw of air fighting on the western front, no mention has been made of the part played by anti-aircraft artillery. This was not a Royal Flying Corps responsibility, but it was so intimately bound up with the employment of aeroplanes that the air story will not be intelligible without some account of the organisation which grew up to the help of the air service. The anti-aircraft shell may be likened to a fighting aeroplane which reaches its opponent in seconds rather than minutes.

It had not, of course, the same certainty, but its moral effect was great. It tended to keep enemy pilots high up, harassed them in their work, had a heartening effect on the men on the ground to whom it gave visible protection, and, incidentally, signalled the whereabouts of hostile aircraft to friendly pilots who might be near. But most important of all, from the Flying Corps point of view, was the fact that good ground defences reduced the demands made on the aeroplanes for protection and so released them for their more urgent primary duties.

When war began, no British anti-aircraft gun, even moderately efficient, was in existence. The army in the field had to content itself in the first months with what protection a few one-pounder pom-poms could give it. If a pom-pom shell hit its mark it might be as effective as any other missile, but it failed to exert any moral effect as it did not burst in the air, and a hostile pilot might fly peacefully on his way oblivious of the efforts being made to bring him down.

The pom-pom need not be taken seriously. It did something towards filling a gap whilst a more effective gun was being adapted. This was the Royal Horse Artillery thirteen-pounder (six hundredweight) gun, which was mounted on a motor chassis and fired high explosive or shrapnel. By January of 1915 it had proved its efficiency and an establishment was drawn up for mobile sections of two guns, the intention being to supply one section to each division. The six hundredweight thirteen-pounder did yeoman service until 1916, but the efficiency of the gun was seriously curtailed, from the summer of 1915, by the banning of the use of its high explosive shell which had proved highly dangerous, occasionally blowing up its gun. The position was not remedied until April 1916, when the shell was improved to the point of safety and was again taken into service.

The value of each type of shell demands a word or two. Shrapnel was considered more effective against the occupants of an unarmoured machine, but unless the shell got a direct hit, it did not spell much danger to the aeroplane. The high explosive shell broke up into splinters which might easily suffice to wreck a machine or kill its personnel. Above all, it had an unpleasant effect which shrapnel shells failed to produce. The noise of an aeroplane's engine cuts out the droning sound which accompanies the flight of a shell, and the explosion is what the crew first hear. The sudden vicious bark of high explosive startles the nerves, whereas the more subdued fizzing of shrapnel is apt, unless unpleasantly close, to create but mild distraction. One advantage of the shrapnel shell, however, was the facility it gave for putting a barrage about a balloon to defeat aeroplane attacks.

The relative positions of the German and British armies in anti-aircraft equipment in the middle of 1915 caused Sir John French some anxiety. His demand for one section for each division had not been met. At the end of July 1915 there were twenty-eight divisions in France and only thirteen anti-aircraft sections. Those sections, too, were handicapped, for the time being, by the ban on their high explosive shells. The German artillery observers from just over their own lines did their work little troubled by gunfire, and enemy pilots who ventured along the lines of communication reconnoitring the railheads and dumps went almost unmolested from the ground. Even when they were fired at their great height usually kept them beyond reach of the shells.

On the other hand, British aeroplanes at that time suffered far more from gunfire than from enemy aircraft. Rarely did an aeroplane come back from a job over the lines undamaged by shell splinters, and the repair or replacement of damaged parts often kept a machine out of work for several days. Sir John, therefore, drew the attention of the Army Council to the urgency of his need for more guns and, at the same time, pressed for a better weapon. The War Office replied that new types were under trial, and that they had every hope of producing a more suitable gun before the supply of the converted Horse Artillery thirteen-pounder had been exhausted. The type that came triumphant from its trials was the eighteen-pounder field gun, bored out to a calibre of three inches and known as the thirteen-pounder nine hundredweight gun. It was highly mobile and could send its shells to a maximum height of 19,000 feet. Throughout 1916 this gun gradually replaced the lighter type. It remained, to the end, the standard mobile gun in forward battle areas.

To protect his back areas Sir John French had asked for fifteen sections over and above the number required with the divisions. For this purpose performance could be improved at the expense of mobility and the more powerful, semi-mobile, three-inch (twenty hundredweight) and twelve-pounder (twelve hundredweight) guns were produced.

As the anti-aircraft sections arrived in France they were attached to the headquarters of the Royal Flying Corps for a brief preliminary training in the recognition and characteristics of contemporary aircraft. In June 1915 No. 14 Anti-Aircraft Section became a school of instruction through which new sections passed after their first day or two with the Flying Corps. An improvement in organisation took place in November 1915 when the anti-aircraft sections were grouped into four-gun batteries, which were placed, for tactical purposes, under the army artillery commander. This grouping ensured unity of action and closer co-operation between the guns of each battery, and facilitated the interchange of information and experience between all the anti-aircraft units along the front.

By the beginning of 1916 the anti-aircraft position was greatly improved, but the deficiency in the number of guns in France was still serious. In February Sir Douglas Haig wrote to the War Office that the supply of his divisions and lines of communication on the agreed scale required one hundred and twelve guns, whereas he had at his disposal no more than sixty-seven. Furthermore, the French were pressing for greater help in the protection of bases such as Calais, Boulogne, Abbeville, and Rouen, where British military interests were rapidly expanding, and unless more guns were forthcoming this request could only be met by denuding the already sparsely protected front line. He also asked for searchlights for use in conjunction with the guns at the more important depots as the enemy was now bombing at night.

The War Office had to reconcile the demands from France with the widespread requests which came in from every threatened point at home. The gigantic task of turning a highly organised nation over to war production and, at the same time, of finding protection for congested and vital areas against Zeppelin raids, called for ingenuity and anxious judgement. The great need of Sir Douglas Haig was fully appreciated. The guns were on order but difficulties arose on all sides which confounded the manufacturers' estimates of times of delivery. The harassed authorities at home made every effort to speed up deliveries. By the 22nd of April 1916 Sir Douglas Haig had received an additional thirteen guns bringing his total, without counting his reserves, to eighty.

In addition, he had twelve two-pounder pom-poms manned by the Royal Marine Artillery. On the 1st of July 1916, when the Somme battle opened, the total number of anti-aircraft guns with the British armies, excluding the twelve two-pounder pom-poms, was one hundred and thirteen, of which no less than seventy were of the new thirteen-pounder nine hundredweight type. Eighteen guns were along the lines of communication, eight were attached to General Headquarters, and eighty-seven were distributed among the four armies in the line. The Second Army had twenty-three and six others on their way to join them, the First, eighteen, the Third, sixteen, and the Fourth Army, along the battle front, twenty-four.

******

On the 18th of November 1916, when the battle ended, the total number of anti-aircraft guns had reached one hundred and sixty-nine, which, with a few exceptions, were of the thirteen-pounder nine hundredweight type. Twenty-six were on the lines of communication, six were attached to General Headquarters, thirty-five to the Second Army, twenty to the First, twenty-four to the Third, twenty to the Fifth, and thirty to the Fourth Army.

✶✶✶✶✶✶

EXPANSION OF THE WORK OF THE CORPS SQUADRONS.

The change which came over the air position on the western front in the months before the Somme has been outlined. We have seen the ground defences growing against the enemy. We have seen how the fighting aeroplanes lost and regained superiority. It is well to emphasise that air fighting was waged to win freedom of movement for the reconnaissance, photographic, bombing, and artillery aeroplanes in their essential task of helping the army to overcome their enemy, and to deny similar freedom to the opposing air service. It remains now to consider how the fruits of the fighting policy fell to the corps squadrons.

The development of the air help for the artillery is perhaps most important. The German *Reichsarchiv* has set it on record that the initial British infantry successes in the Somme battle were due to the unquestionable superiority over the Germans of the British air co-operation with the artillery. That is a wide statement, but a study of the patient, painstaking work of the artillery aeroplanes shows that success came because it was worked for with a firm will, which prompted the flying officers and the gunners to meet and to overcome the many technical and organisation difficulties and to learn something from every failure. What made the air and artillery cooperation so important during the battle was that the undulating uplands of the Somme shielded hosts of important targets, even near the front-line trenches, from any observation from the ground.

Foremost of the targets for the artillery were the enemy's batteries. Just as the air service had to fight before it could get on with its real work, so the guns had to fight one another for the power to help the infantry. A pamphlet issued by the general staff in the field in January 1916 stated:

> Counter-battery work is in many ways the most important, as it is certainly the most difficult, of the tasks of the artillery under present conditions. It has been steadily growing in importance and is now recognised as an essential element both in offensive operations and in the work of "holding the line".

General Hindenburg, writing later in the year on the experience of the Verdun fighting, is even more emphatic:

> To engage the enemy's artillery (with the help of aeroplane observers) is the principal and most effective means of fighting a defensive battle to a successful conclusion. Should this succeed, the enemy's attack is absolutely paralysed.

The first task is to find your enemy's guns. No one knew better the value of concealment than the battery commander. He took every advantage which the country offered for hiding his positions, and often so camouflaged his whereabouts that, unless he was actually seen to fire, he might remain undetected although aeroplanes flew over the area again and again. Even when a flash was seen, it was not conclusive evidence of a gun position. An imitation of the flash from a gun was often staged from a dummy pit, or guns were run temporarily into a dummy position, fired, and pulled out again when it was thought the air-observer had been sufficiently deceived.

Once the batteries were located, the real task began. Heavy guns and ammunition still had to be husbanded, but in the comparative quiet between offensive operations, systematic registration and destruction of hostile batteries went on steadily. It was held that however carefully thought out the purely artillery arrangements might be, final success depended on the air-observers. The closest co-operation between the artillery and the Flying Corps was therefore essential. It was laid down that artillery programmes must be prepared by the officer in command of the counter-battery group in consultation with the commander of the squadron working for him, and air-observers were instructed to talk over every aspect of the day's work with the battery commander when they got back from the lines.

★★★★★★

From the beginning of 1916 batteries detailed for counter-battery work were grouped by areas into separate commands. At each counterbattery headquarters all intelligence on the subject of the enemy's batteries was centralized and recorded, a fact which greatly facilitated the co-operation with the air.

★★★★★★

Throughout the period, then, of holding the line the air-observers acquired practice and efficiency, and goodwill was built up between them and the gunners. The expansion of the Royal Flying Corps, however, had not kept pace with the great increase in the artillery.

There were, further, serious technical difficulties of signalling to the gunners which had still to be overcome. Sir Henry Rawlinson at a conference in the middle of April 1916 summed up the position:

> Much more practice is still required with aircraft and artillery. There has been improvement, but not yet enough.

One great improvement, however, was at hand. A drawback to wireless signalling from aircraft was its susceptibility to jamming, either intentionally by the enemy, or by messages sent out from other friendly aircraft working near. This limited the number of aeroplanes which could work for the artillery along any given front. There was the added difficulty that wireless aeroplanes would now be required, during an attack, to work in co-operation with the infantry. Either jamming must be overcome technically or the number of artillery aeroplanes on the front during the battle must be further reduced—a serious contingency.

The difficulty was overcome partly by a tightening up of the organisation and by the reduction of signals to the minimum, but chiefly by a simple device which originated in the Third Wing. With this device, known as the 'clapper-break', it was possible to vary the pitch or tone of the note sent out by the aeroplane observer. A ground operator could by the pitch of the signals distinguish one aeroplane from another working on the same wave length. The Sterling transmitter without the clapper-break gave a high note. The clapper-break when fitted could be tuned to give either a low or a medium note. Two flights of each corps squadron, therefore, were equipped with clapper-breaks, one to give a low and one a medium note, whilst the third flight used the normal Sterling set.

On the low note the transmitter had an increased range, so that the low note flight was usually used for long range work and the high note flight was allocated to trench reconnaissance and contact patrol. There may be little of the stuff of romance in the story of the clapper-break, but that simple instrument made it possible to use double the number of aeroplanes at the same time over any given area, and so, in the end, added enormously to the help which the air service could give to the soldiers in the trenches. An experiment made by the Third Wing in April 1916 showed that one wireless aeroplane for about every 2,000 yards of trench line was the efficient maximum that could be employed. Although the clapper-break continued in use until the end of the war on the same basis as when it was first introduced, wireless apparatus and the skill of the observers and ground operators improved so greatly that at the time of the armistice one wireless aeroplane along every 400 yards of front could be used in battle without fear of undue jamming.

Another great step forward was a new method of calling on the artillery to engage sudden targets. The Somme offensive, it was hoped, would lead to some measure of open warfare. Once the batteries moved forward they would be confronted with new and unknown targets, and there might be little or no opportunity for pre-arrangement with the corps squadrons. Under the new system the whole battle area was divided into zones. It was an elaboration of the method of co-operation devised in the spring of 1915 by No. 1 Squadron in conjunction with the artillery of the II Corps. When Major E. R. Ludlow-Hewitt, who had worked the system with No. 1 Squadron, took command of No. 3 Squadron in the beginning of November 1915, he gave much attention to the perfection of the details of the system.

It emerged in June 1916 as a general instruction. The zones were based on the lettered squares of the 1/40,000 map. Each of those squares was divided into four zones, lettered, for example. A, B, C, and D. Each zone, covering an area 3,000 yards square, had a two-letter call made up of the map square letter, followed by the zone letter. The aeroplane observer sent down information of troops or active batteries which he saw, prefacing his message with the call of the particular zone in which the target was seen. The wireless operators with batteries would take in, normally, only those calls on to zones within which their guns could fire.

The group artillery commander might arrange beforehand for certain batteries to fire on receipt of calls applicable to their zones, or he might keep the control in his own hands, giving instructions direct to particular battery commanders immediately he received the air messages. Once fire was opened the observer could signal its effect in the ordinary way. The zone call was limited, at first, to artillery up to and including six-inch guns and howitzers. It could, of course, be used for heavier types, but it was held that even in open warfare the entry of the heavier types into action would be deliberate so that spotting for them could generally be pre-arranged.

Stated simply, the effect of the zone call system was this. It ensured that at any given moment every sector of the possible battle area was the concern of definite battery commanders and it enabled the air-observers, without knowing the positions of the batteries or, indeed, anything about them, to give the battery commanders their targets and to correct their fire in the ordinary way. It reduced the necessity for personal liaison between the flying officers and the gunners to the minimum, and so eliminated the confusion which might otherwise arise from difficulty of communication when the armies were moving.

Closely bound up with the development of artillery co-operation was the advance made in air photography and in the art of reading the photographs. Reports on the photographic work of the French air service at Verdun showed how vital that work was even during actual attacks. The French set up developing stations at the corps headquarters where pilots landed and handed over their plates. Some hundred prints, made at top speed, were distributed direct to batteries and companies.

As many as 5,000 prints were made at a forward developing station in one day, and it often happened that the corps commander had prints in his hands within one hour of the exposure of the plates over the enemy lines. More than for anything else the photographs proved valuable for judging the effects of the artillery bombardment, on which, indeed, during much of the fighting, they were the principal source of information. Whilst General Mangin was attacking Fort Douaumont on the 22nd of May, aeroplanes were sent out at intervals to photograph the area of the fighting. The plates were rapidly developed and prints were then taken by air and dropped on General Mangin's advanced headquarters. The aeroplanes, in fact, were the advanced eyes of the general throughout the attack.

Air photography had already made enormous strides in the British air service. The arrangement whereby the plates were developed and the prints made at the wing headquarters had brought many advantages. The concentration of the technical side had co-ordinated progress. But, by the spring of 1916, the demands for photographs were becoming so enormous that the wing sections were getting overburdened and there were unavoidable delays in the delivery of prints. There were occasions when prints reached the units too late for full advantage to be taken of the new information they revealed.

This was especially the case with the artillery who, for accuracy of shooting, constantly needed up to date photographs to supplement their maps. To speed up the delivery of prints it was now deemed essential to establish a small photographic section in each corps squadron, and in each army reconnaissance squadron. This decentralisation of photography to squadrons took place in the middle of April 1916.

(It was laid down that the squadron photographic section should consist of one non-commissioned officer and three men). Under the new arrangement the army corps staff gave orders direct to the commander of the attached squadron for all photographs within five miles of their corps front. Beyond this area photography was the responsibility of the army wing.

Experience in the reading of air photographs had shown that they might be made to reveal considerably more than the positions of trenches and strong points. An air picture of a part of the battle area must be closely studied. With a map of the area in front of him the expert first of all visualises the configuration and nature of the ground. He then notes the direction of light at the time when the photograph was taken. Shadows play an important part in the interpretation, and when the direction of light is known it can be seen at once whether any particular point under observation is convex or concave, and the length of the shadow will tell its relative height or depth. The important military features he looks for are battery positions, trench mortar and machine-gun emplacements, snipers' posts, tracks, trolley-lines, headquarters, telephone exchanges, wire, and so forth.

Cable trenches which give a valuable clue to the positions of headquarters and important centres can be distinguished, when open, by their comparatively straight course and narrow construction, and even when closed they are well defined. Tracks and ammunition trolley-lines form a valuable guide to the enemy's movements. Nothing gives a fuller insight into the daily life of the troops than tracks for they are almost impossible of concealment. From them can be deduced which are the principal and which the secondary lines of traffic, and the routes by which, in an attack, men and ammunition will be brought up to eject the intruders. Trolley-lines can usually be distinguished for what they are owing to their straightness and comparative narrowness.

Trolleys are not easily made to take sharp bends, and nature has endowed men who make use of a trolley track with an instinct for walking between the rails and so keeping the track narrow. These are no light matters. A vigilant artillery or machine-gun commander could bring devastating fire to bear, especially at night, on points indicated by the position of the tracks and trolley-lines on the photographs. These are examples only, and are given to show that, apart from the larger strategic schemes based on the air photography, the business of deducing all manner of information and of acting in a tactical way on what was learned was widespread and continuous.

Air Co-operation with Attacking Infantry
(Contact Patrol)

During this restless time of preparation there was developed, too, what was to prove one of the most important roles of aircraft—co-operation with attacking infantry. The attempts made at Aubers Ridge in 1915 had brought out the main difficulty which was how to distinguish friend from foe. Trials were therefore made in May 1915 to see whether daylight smoke signals of various colours, lighted by troops, would suffice to reveal their positions. The results were promising. In the middle of July 1915, 300 Brock flares had been ordered for further experiment, and towards the end of August, observers of No. 1 Squadron, working with troops of the Second Army, found that they could easily distinguish the yellow smoke of these flares, even at a height of 6,000 feet. A number were therefore issued to the armies in November 1915 to be used when the opportunity should arise.

During the French attacks in Champagne in the autumn of 1915 their infantry had used signalling lamps, flares, and strips of cloth, the positions of which observers plotted on to maps which they dropped from time to time at pre-arranged report centres. During the Battle of Verdun, the French concentrated observers specially qualified for this work, and as a result of the experience gained General Joffre, on the 17th of April 1916, issued general instructions laying down the details of co-operation between the air and the infantry.

On this memorandum was based the British contact patrol organisation which was put into effect at the Somme. At the time when General Joffre's memorandum was sent out the Flying Corps were again experimenting, this time on a wider scale. Aeroplanes of the IV Brigade co-operated with troops of the Fourth Army in their training area west of Albert. The infantry advanced to definite lines from which they signalled to the aircraft with flares and lamps. The aeroplanes noted their positions and dropped or sent back messages by wireless. Co-operation with the infantry had at last reached a practical stage.

The British provisional instructions for contact work which were issued on the 26th of May 1916 stated that aeroplanes bearing distinctive marks were to have the sole duty of tactical observation of the battlefield, reporting direct to the formation for which they were working, usually the army corps headquarters. The infantry were to indicate their progress by lighting flares on the initiative of the company or section commander; in reply to the question from the aeroplane 'Where are you?'; at certain hours previously specified in orders;

and on reaching pre-arranged positions. At the same time a percentage of the attacking troops were to carry on their backs metal mirrors, the flashes from which, in suitable light, would it was hoped enable the air-observers to follow the main line of advance. (It was stated that 320 flares and 80 mirrors would be issued to each attacking battalion. Actually, owing to the failure of contracts, the supply of flares, in the early days of the battle, fell considerably short of the authorised scale).

The aeroplanes were to receive messages from battalion and brigade headquarters by means of ground signals or lamps. The observer, in addition to transmitting the information signalled from the ground, was instructed to keep the command informed of enemy movements during the preliminary bombardment, the progress of the attack once it was launched, the movements of reserves to the battle, and the staging of counterattacks.

A code was laid down for communication between the aeroplane and the ground. To make its signals to the aeroplane each headquarters had a signalling panel, at this time a large Louvre shutter of six or eight laths painted white on one side and a neutral tint on the other. The laths were connected by tapes and the ground operator could work his tapes so as to expose the white side of the laths to spell out messages in Morse: it was found by experiment that the messages could be read up to a height of from five to six thousand feet.

The French at Verdun had received some useful tactical information from their balloons and, to train British balloon observers in this work, a school was set up at St. Riquier near Abbeville on the 23rd of May. Experience at the school showed that a column *en route*, or artillery and extended formations, could be followed from a balloon up to a distance of from eleven to twelve thousand yards. Halted troops were difficult to locate and, if they were discovered, it was not easy to say what they were. Flares were seen up to six or seven thousand yards. The results which were obtained at the school were so encouraging that three kite balloon sections were specially attached to the Fourth Army for tactical work during the first attack on the Somme.

Changes in Bombing Tactics.

The area behind the lines opposite to the British front received constant attention from bombing aeroplanes. In November and December 1915, the Third Wing continuously bombed and left little standing of a group of new military buildings near Achiet-le-Grand. For one of these raids, on the 25th of November, nine aeroplanes of

No. 13 Squadron collected over Beauquesne and flew together, causing confusion among the German antiaircraft batteries whose shooting was exceptionally bad. Thus, was exploded the idea that to fly in groups was to offer an exaggerated target to the enemy gunners.

Miraumont and Le Sars, centres for the accumulation of material and of great rail activity, were also bombed by this wing. During a raid on Le Sars, on the 17th of January 1916, it is stated that:

> Considerable difficulty was experienced by some pilots in flying over the target owing to the number of machines in the air, and it appears that in attacks by a large number of machines better results would be obtained if an interval was maintained between squadrons.

The feature of these raids was the concentration of all the available aeroplanes of the wing to bomb one single objective together. The raids, indeed, mark a definite change of bombing tactics. Attacks (except on trains in motion) by small detachments on many objectives now give place to the mass bombing of single targets. It was considered that if the objective was not distant more than thirty miles from the line the bombers would be adequately protected by fighting aeroplanes cruising between the bombing aeroplanes and enemy aerodromes. The bombers could then be flown without observers or any need of close escort. For more distant objectives two out of every ten bombing aeroplanes would carry, instead of a load of bombs, an observer with an extra Lewis gun. (An interesting memorandum, reviewing bombing principles and methods of attack at this time, issued by R.F.C.H.Q. on the 21st of December 1915, is given as Appendix 6). The bombing groups increased in size from fourteen or twenty aeroplanes in December to thirty-one (twenty-three bombers and eight escorts) in a raid on Carvin on the 9th of March.

Meanwhile, as the reader will recall, flying in formation had been introduced into the Royal Flying Corps in January 1916, and from that time the bombing groups or masses became definite formations. The systems of formation varied in the different brigades, but all had this in common, that they aimed at compactness.

The policy to govern bombing was laid down in a headquarters instruction in the middle of February 1916 as follows:

> No bombing should be done at a distance greater than a few miles from our front line unless the results obtained and the object in view are commensurate with the possible losses in

pilots and machines. The bombing of such objectives as munition depots, headquarters of formations, &c., which have been definitely located and of railway stations and bridges, should be reserved until it can be carried out in connexion with definite operations of an important nature. Depots at headquarters might be moved or given special protection if prematurely bombed and might then be unlocated or too well protected to be attacked with success at the time when bombing would be of particular value.

Damage to railways can be so quickly repaired that no appreciable results are gained by attacking them unless such enterprises are undertaken at the right moment, *i.e.* at a time when even a temporary interruption to traffic on these railways would interfere with important operations then in progress. Raids on enemy aerodromes should only be undertaken when specially recommended by the R.F.C. and then they should be carried out on a sufficient scale to give a reasonable prospect of success. Bombing of aerodromes on a small scale produces little result and is not worth the risk involved. There is no objection to bombing raids against objectives such as billets close to our lines intended to destroy or harass enemy personnel.

In February, also, permission was obtained from the commander-in-chief for the night bombing of points up to a distance of five or six miles over the lines. Until further experience had been gained the number of aeroplanes was limited to two in one night from an army. General Trenchard had asked for this permission as the enemy was already bombing at night, and he was anxious that they should not get ahead of the Flying Corps in experience of night flying. He was anxious to learn, too, what value we might be able to get from night reconnaissance work. Night flying had been done with some success before the war, and was tried at odd intervals in 1915, particularly by the naval air unit at Dunkirk.

Following the request of General Trenchard orders were issued on the 21st of February to all brigades that they should take every opportunity to bomb at night. These orders followed the success of the first attempt which was made on Cambrai aerodrome at full moon on the night of the 19th/20th of February, by Captains E. D. Horsfall and J. E. Tennant of No. 4 Squadron, each flying in a B.E.2c, without an observer. Tennant dropped his seven 20-lb. Hales bombs into the sheds from thirty feet; the planes of his aeroplane were rent by splinters from his own bombs. Horsfall carried two 112-lb. bombs; they failed to leave the rack over the German aerodrome, but did so finally when the pilot was nearly home again. This night attempt, however, was to stand alone for the time being. The weather was unfavourable, but more important the severe shortage of pilots at this time limited Flying Corps work to what was essential.

No night bombing was in fact done in March and April, but this did not mean that pilots were denied experience of night flying. General Trenchard on the 8th of April directed that practice in night flying should be made on the British side of the lines; during these flights reconnaissance reports were to be made out and checked afterwards as far as possible. These night practices were made on every favourable occasion. On the 16th/17th of May there were twenty-four ascents, one of which was an attempt to range for a siege battery, but the shells exploded without any flash, and the effort failed. Reconnaissances were now being made over the enemy lines, but visibility was never good enough for other than rough and spasmodic observation.

Aerodromes and the Housing of Aeroplanes,

Attendant upon the growth of the Royal Flying Corps in France and the widening of its work for the army came problems of housing and supply. A word or two on the finding and fitting up of suitable landing grounds for the new squadrons will illustrate the difficulties which had to be overcome before an aeroplane could be got into the air. The first question was a practical one. A clear field, preferably in open country, measuring about three hundred yards square and close to a road good enough for heavy motor transport, was essential. Aeroplanes must take off or alight up wind, a variable element which precludes the use of any site that is not fairly level. The best surface for a landing ground is short grass or stubble. It must not be soft or the aeroplane may tip up.

Few undercarriages, too, will survive a passage over rough ground, especially if broken up by ridges. Ideal sites are always rare, and in the battle area the shortage was made more acute by keen competition for desirable sites from other units of the army. Once the site was found the task of getting possession of a foreign field was begun. The flying officer having made his choice would, with his French liaison companion, pay a tactful visit to the owner of the land. If terms could not be arranged amicably the ground was requisitioned.

The register at the *Mairie* was consulted so that the amount to be paid as rent should be in accordance with local values. French law allows of the occupation of land for bivouacs without payment, but indemnifies owners against damage done by the occupying troops. A fixed percentage therefore was always added to the normal rent of the aerodrome to cover depreciation. The taking over of land met, as is to be expected, with objections and bargaining. It reduced the area of cultivation at a time when there was an urgent demand for foodstuffs and it inflicted hardship on those who lived by the soil.

These considerations imposed the strictest economy in the lay-out of aerodromes. If it was possible a partial use of the land was allowed to the farmers. Cattle, for instance, continued to graze on the big aerodrome at Clairmarais, unmindful of the mild excitement which they gave to pilots who were called on to avoid them. Not that all aerodromes had a surplus of herbage. Seed of the fast growing Italian rye grass was imported for sowing on many bare patches.

To house the aeroplanes portable hangars of service design sufficed until the beginning of 1915. The type which gave most satisfaction was the R.E.7 tent built by the Royal Aircraft Factory. Three of these tents, which weighed sixteen hundredweight each, could be packed on a three-ton lorry. The tent was originally designed to accommodate one R.E.7 (two-seater), but, later, with careful stowing it could house as many as three single-seater fighter aeroplanes. The R.E.7 tent became the standard model of light portable field service hangars and, when the war ended, more than six hundred were in use in France.

It had the disadvantage, common to all light hangars, that it could not be relied upon to withstand high winds or severe weather, and it had, further, a tendency to sag and so bear down on the top wings of the aeroplanes which it housed.

Another factory designed hangar, which offered similar accommodation but was more satisfactory in bad weather, was known as the R.A.F. heavy portable. It weighed two and three-quarter tons and required the whole of one lorry for its transport. A number of these hangars were in use in France to the end of the war. As aerodromes became established more or less permanently, fixed wooden sheds, which had many advantages over the somewhat fragile tents, were constructed by the Royal Engineers. The first was erected on Bailleul aerodrome in February 1915, and by the end of the year similar shelters were common on all aerodromes, although enough portable hangars to ensure mobility were always kept in use.

Late in 1915 the Royal Engineers improved on their design and began to erect sheds of steel construction. These were of two types. Type 'A' was fifty-two feet by forty-two feet, and type 'B' was sixty feet by seventy-five feet. In the middle of 1916, owing to scarcity of labour, it was found difficult to get armies to erect these sheds, and they were therefore given up for squadron aerodromes. Type 'B' however, was used until the end of the war, in depots, to house both aeroplanes and stores.

A shed that offered most of the advantages of the Royal Engineer structures, but was at the same time portable, had appeared in the beginning of 1915. This was the famous Bessonneau hangar that took its name from its French designer. The early type, about sixty-five feet square, was a light detachable wooden framework covered with canvas. It could house four to six two-seater aeroplanes, weighed eight and a half tons, and required five or six lorries for its transport. The first Bessonneau arrived at St. Omer in January 1915, and by the end of July six more had been delivered. A slightly larger type measuring some sixty-six feet by seventy-nine feet was now being built, and twenty of these were taken into use by the Royal Flying Corps before the end of 1915.

In addition, a few small workshop Bessonneaux had been bought in August. At the beginning of 1916, a serious position was created when the Bessonneau firm informed the Royal Flying Corps that, owing to an acute shortage of cotton, they were unable to accept any further orders for hangars. The question of supplying our Ally with this raw material was referred to the authorities at home, and at the same time steps were taken to organise the building of Bessonneau hangars in England. This was no easy task.

Many trades were concerned and the whole country had to be searched before anyone could be found to produce some of the special fittings. Indeed, at first, a small ship-chandling firm in the east end of London was the only source of supply for the metal fittings for the wire ropes which braced the framework, and for a time the capacity of this firm governed the whole Bessonneau output of the British Empire. Whilst the difficulties of manufacture at home were being overcome, another source of supply was found in France. The design of a hangar similar to the Bessonneau was submitted in February 1916 by Major Matrat of the French Army, who stated that his firm could satisfy moderate demands. Twenty-five Matrat hangars were thereupon ordered, all of which were in use along the front by the end of the year.

The Matrat filled a gap but did not prove wholly satisfactory. During the Somme battles the hangar position would have given cause for anxiety had not the French come further to our help. Firstly, on three aerodromes which were taken over from the French air service for the battle, nine Bessonneaux were left standing, and secondly, the cotton shortage of our Ally having been remedied, the Bessonneau firm were able, in July 1916, to resume delivery of their hangars to the Royal Flying Corps. Included among the new hangars was the super-Bessonneau which could house as many as a dozen single-seater fighters. It measured eighty-five feet by ninety feet, weighed thirty-five tons, and spread itself over eighteen lorries when it was moved.

Before the end of the battle the position was greatly improved by the first arrivals of British built Bessonneaux of high grade material and workmanship. Now that adequate supplies were assured from home our dependence on the French manufacturers was ended. Their aid had been invaluable. They had given us unstintingly of their material and of their experience. The former enabled us to carry on in France; the latter helped us to organise the manufacture of hangars at home.

★★★★★★

The squadrons were responsible for the erection of their own portable hangars, but the privately designed hangars were, at first, put up under the direction of civilian experts from the French makers. Later, Royal Flying Corps tent parties were trained and became highly skilled in the rapid building or dismantling of every type of hangar.

★★★★★

The Development of the Aircraft Parks and Depots

As the aerodromes spread, so the organisation for supplying the multitudinous demands from the squadrons expanded. The original Aircraft Park was a mobile unit consisting of a stores section and a workshop section. Essential parts of it could pack up and move off completely in twenty-four hours. But as new activities were developed in the squadrons, calling for additional complicated equipment, the Park commander soon found that his unit at St. Omer was acquiring the permanency and immobility of a gigantic factory and emporium. His shops were repairing aeroplanes, mechanical transport, wireless, armament, navigation and photographic equipment. His stores officers were daily issuing anything from the smallest spare parts to complete aeroplanes.

The requisitions which they dealt with included items so various as special boxes of matches for the firing of aeroplanes which settled on the wrong side of the lines, and horserakes or lawn-mowers for keeping aerodromes trim. By July of 1915 the Park had become too unwieldy to cope with the increasing demands made on it, and a second Aircraft Park had then been formed at Candas to cater for the flying units working with the recently formed Third Army. This Park was designated No. 3 to identify it with the army which it supplied. A new difficulty arose. The railhead for this Park was at Doullens, whereas all aircraft stores from England were being landed at the port depot at Boulogne whence no supply trains ran direct to Doullens. It became necessary, therefore, to form a direct port depot at Rouen for No. 3 Aircraft Park.

The idea was that each army should have its own aircraft park. It was evident, however, that the parks would still be immobile unless they were relieved of much of their heavy repair work, and unless they carried the minimum of supplies consistent with keeping their squadrons efficient.

The whole question of the reorganisation of the Flying Corps was being debated at this time, and as soon as the decision to form brigades for each army was made, the supply question was put on a sound basis by converting the original aircraft parks into fixed supply and repair depots and by forming new mobile parks with each brigade. The new parks came into being on the 15th of December 1915, as follows: No. 1 Army Aircraft Park at Aire, No. 2 at Hazebrouck, and No. 3 at Beauval. The original Park at St. Omer was rechristened No. I Aircraft Depot, and the park at Candas became No. 2 Aircraft Depot. These two depots grew in size, but sufficed for the remainder of the war to feed the whole Flying Corps in the west.

The depots maintained three months' supply of aeronautical and transport stores, received all new aircraft from England or France, keeping always a reserve in their hangars, manufactured experimental fittings, and overhauled and reconstructed aeroplanes, balloons, transport, and all flying accessories. The parks drew their supplies from the depots for all the squadrons in their army. They kept on hand from a fortnight to one month's supply of aeronautical stores, and on no account, were they permitted to impair their mobility by exceeding their maximum allowance. They had facilities for minor repairs to aeroplanes, but were first and foremost issuing centres. The main supply organisation outlined above proved so flexible that it was able to meet all the demands arising from the subsequent expansion of the service, throwing off sections from time to time which came to spread their network behind the whole length of the battle front.

The vital problem of the overhaul and repair of engines remained the duty of the shops which had been started at Pont de L'Arche near Rouen as a branch of the original Aircraft Park. They became known under the new organisation as the Engine Repair Shops and, until the war ended, most of the invalid engines on the western front passed through their vast mechanical hospital.

To assist wing and squadron commanders to formulate their technical requirements, to keep a check on their intricate stores, and to supervise the transport, workshops, and so forth, equipment officers had been introduced into the service in the beginning of 1915. In June, officers for wireless were established in wings and, in the following month, in squadrons, and were given the new grade. Later this grading embraced all those non-flying officers whose specialist knowledge made smooth the working of so highly technical a service. Although much of the detailed technical work involved in the running of a squadron was taken off the commander's shoulders by his equipment officers, the keeping of records in the squadron office grew and multiplied until the time came to appoint a special officer to relieve the commander of much of this paper work. In June 1916 provision was made for a recording officer, who became responsible for keeping the day to day records of the squadron's work.

Minor Actions between Loos and the Somme.

The British Army in the west fought no great action after Loos until the Somme battle opened in July 1916, but there was continuous and often fierce local fighting along the line. The Ypres salient, where all the higher ground was held by the enemy, was the centre of much of this activity. Partly to distract attention from the preparations for the Verdun offensive the Germans opened a vigorous bombardment against the Salient on the 8th of February 1916, and followed this, in the early morning of the 12th, with infantry attacks against the British left, north of Ypres; these attacks were repulsed. Next day a concentrated bombardment blotted out our front trenches in the south of the Salient near Hooge, and, on the 14th, after further shelling and the explosion of mines, there was an attack on Hooge and the collection of stumps known as Sanctuary Wood.

These attacks were also held. But the enemy had greater success at an important point farther south, on the north bank of the Ypres-Comines Canal. The excavation for the canal had left heaped at this point a narrow, tree-covered mound rising about thirty feet above the plain. The eastern part of this mound, known as The Bluff, was held by the British; its loss would give the enemy an observation post for enfilade fire of the British positions. On the 14th of February our trenches on The Bluff were almost obliterated by bombardment and the position was then captured by a sudden rush of infantry. It was held for seventeen days until a final British counter-attack, taking the Germans by surprise, captured all that had been lost and a bit more.

The main air work in connexion with these attacks fell to No. 6 Squadron, and has added interest as a special emergency artillery scheme was put into practice. This scheme had been worked out between the Second Army and the Second Wing early in February 1916, to allow squadrons to switch over from routine work to special work in defence or attack. On receipt of the message. *General Artillery Action*, squadrons were immediately to send their aeroplanes to work to a pre-arranged programme of artillery co-operation, and reconnaissances of the corps and army areas. On receipt of the message, *Situation Normal*, routine work was to be resumed.

The attack on the left of the Ypres salient on the 12th of February provided the first occasion for the trial of the new scheme. The message for general action was received by No. 6 Squadron in failing light at 4.35 p.m., but aeroplanes went away at once, and a number of active German batteries were reported before darkness compelled the pilots to return. The next general action message came at 7.45 a.m. on the 15th of February in connexion with British counter-attacks against The Bluff, but the miserable weather kept the aeroplanes on the ground until early in the afternoon, when they went off and reported sixteen active German batteries, before Situation Normal was received at 3.15 p.m. No. 6 Squadron continued to observe for the artillery and reconnoitre up to half past five. Special action was not ordered again until the day of the recapture of The Bluff—March the 2nd.

In the meantime, enemy airmen were more aggressive than they had been for some time past, and they made many day and night bombing raids into the British area. The recapture of The Bluff was preceded by some days of preliminary bombardment. On the afternoon before the attack, observers of the II Brigade, flying over the snow-covered plain, discovered thirty-three enemy batteries, many of them firing from new positions and, according to the artillery war diaries, the information proved of great value for counter battery work once the attack was launched. The V Corps artillery commander pays tribute in his report of the operations to the help of the Flying Corps:

> The 6th Squadron R.F.C. were indefatigable during the whole period of the operations. Notwithstanding the very unsuitable weather—wind, clouds and mist—they were constantly in the air, and through their exertions all the howitzer batteries were satisfactorily registered on their final objectives, the firing, support, reserve and communication trenches were most seriously damaged, many fresh batteries were located, and generally speaking the hostile aeroplanes were kept clear of our lines whilst our batteries were engaged.

This squadron lived up to its reputation again at the end of the month when the British began an attack to straighten out a small salient which had been dented into the line at St. Eloi. The operation was begun on the 27th of March by the firing of six large mines under the enemy trenches, followed half a minute later by a rush of infantry. One of the mine craters was occupied by the Germans but, on the 3rd of April, the enemy infantry were pushed out of this and the capture of the original objective was completed.

During the first two days. *General Artillery Action* was in force for Nos. 1 and 6 Squadrons who reported, and observed fire on, many German batteries. At 9.0 a.m. on the 27th of March No. 5 Squadron had taken some clear photographs of the new mine craters. Until the 6th of April No. 6 Squadron did good counterbattery work in bad weather conditions. Fighting around the craters continued throughout April, the men waging war often waist-deep in mud and with mud-choked rifles and machine-guns. By the end of the month the craters were judged untenable, exposed as they were to the full weight of the enemy's artillery, and our troops were back once again in the positions held before the attack was launched. All the time this desultory fighting was in progress the flying squadrons were mainly occupied in helping the artillery.

In May there was a German attack on the Vimy Ridge, and in June a more important attack on the Ypres Salient. The Vimy attack, made on the 21st of May, opened with a bombardment at a quarter past four in the afternoon, and with air activity over Lens and Vimy. The attack was borne by the IV Corps and the air work fell chiefly to the squadron—No. 18—working with this corps, and to No. 10 Kite Balloon Section. The balloon went up at 4.43 p.m., and was up all night except that it was twice hauled down for a few minutes, to relieve the personnel. The balloon observers watched the enemy bombardment, reporting its culmination at about 9.0 p.m., its lifting when the enemy attacked, and its subsequent spasmodic movements. Artillery aeroplanes of No. 18 Squadron were out soon after four in the morning of the 22nd of May, but there was little enemy activity.

In the afternoon Souchez came in for heavy shelling and, at about 5.30 p.m., the bombardment was intensified at Givenchy with the help of German aeroplane observation. The patrol of No. 18 Squadron was doubled and Nos. 25 and 10 Squadrons co-operated. No. 10 Squadron later reported that shelling was increasing in intensity, and another wireless aeroplane was sent out, bringing the number up to the maximum that could be worked along the flight front. All observers located active guns. Fighting patrols were maintained over the area through the day and enemy pilots approaching the lines were consistently attacked. A tactical reconnaissance of the German positions was made in the late afternoon.

Observation was too hazy for the balloon in the morning; at midday, however, it went up but found the haze was still pronounced, and the observers saw little activity. On the 23rd the weather was hazy again, and the artillery aeroplanes which went out at 3.30 a.m. found conditions difficult for observation, but before the haze thickened a reconnaissance had been made of the First Army front which indicated unusual rail movements in Lens. To watch this and any further road movement during the dark, two night reconnaissances were made by No. 18 Squadron.

The first, between 1.30 a.m. and 2.30 a.m. on the 24th, could detect no lighted transport, but reported heavy shelling about Souchez and Givenchy. The second, between 2.40 a.m. and 4.40 a.m., reported minor train and troop movement at Lens, but that otherwise all was quiet in the area. This aeroplane was fired at, at 3.30 a.m., by anti-aircraft guns, which succeeded in damaging the tail-plane of the machine. The weather had, apparently, been too bad for the German pilots on the 23rd, but they were about again on the 24th, especially in front of the IV Corps, where, however, they were attacked as they appeared and could do little work.

A report on the 27th of May comparing the work of the kite balloon and of the aeroplane squadron says:

The balloon appears to have been the better for the purpose of reporting the general situation and the general artillery activity. Both by day and night the observer was able to keep the Artillery Group Commander informed as to the situation, whence hostile shelling was coming, what places were being most heavily shelled, the centres of greatest activity, the presence of gas, and the rough direction of its movement.

As regards ranging, the aeroplanes were the more successful, and conducted shoots under weather conditions which rendered observation for the balloon impossible. Aeroplanes located many more flashes than the balloon during daylight, but none at night. The balloon was able to report the direction of flashes at night, and in some cases to identify the battery owing to the observer's intimate knowledge of the ground. The advantage of the telephonic communication of the balloon over the wireless of the aeroplane was very apparent.

The Vimy fighting resulted in a small gain of ground to the enemy but, in view of the coming offensive, it was not judged worthwhile attacking to recover what had been lost. The attack at Hooge on the 2nd of June was a more serious affair. There the Germans captured trenches on a front of more than one and a half miles and penetrated to a maximum depth of 700 yards, over ground which commanded the British trenches north of the Ypres-Comines railway. Intermittent fighting followed the German success until the 13th of June, when a splendid Canadian advance restored the position. The air work in connexion with these operations was done by squadrons of the II Brigade, chiefly by No. 6 and, to a less extent, No. 5. A hint of what was about to happen came on the day before the action began, when a reconnaissance observer of No. 20 Squadron brought back news of abnormal railway movements in the Menin-Courtrai area.

The attack on the 2nd gave opportunity for the testing of a modified artillery scheme. Conferences between the artillery and flying commanders of the Second Army had led to an alteration in the arrangements for *General Artillery Action*: the revised orders were issued on the 21st of May. By these, each corps was to arrange for the aeroplane assistance it required and could call for help from neighbouring corps under prepared schemes. This arrangement, known as *Corps Artillery Action*, was put into practice on the 2nd of June at 10.15 a.m., involving Nos. 6 and 5 Squadrons, which at once abandoned their routine duties and gave their full attention to the immediate requirements, chiefly artillery work and tactical reconnaissance. Other reconnaissances were made by Nos. 1, 16, and 20 Squadrons, and bombing was done by Nos. 7 and 16 Squadrons with escorts from No. 29 Squadron. On the 13th of June, when the Canadians successfully counter-attacked, the weather did not allow of any flying to help the artillery, but the area had been so well registered with air observation that the artillery fire proved effective.

THE SOMME AREA: AIR WORK AND DISPOSITIONS FOR THE BATTLE.

We have considered, then, the broad development of the Flying Corps in the west and its various activities up to the eve of the Somme battle. We can now turn in more detail to the preparatory work done by the flying squadrons above the area of the coming struggle. The line north of the Somme River had been taken over from the French by the Third Army in July 1915. In the same month the Third Wing (Nos. 4, 8, and 11 Squadrons) of the Royal Flying Corps, under Lieutenant-Colonel J. F. A. Higgins, moved down from St. Omer. When, at the end of January 1916, the III Brigade, R.F.C., was formed for the Third Army, the Third Wing became the corps wing of the brigade.

Towards the end of February 1916, Sir Douglas Haig relieved the French Tenth Army in the Arras sector, by moving the Third Army north, and by putting the newly formed Fourth Army, under Sir Henry Rawlinson, along the front from Gommecourt to Curlu. The III Brigade of the Flying Corps moved north with the Third Army, but left behind the Third Wing and No. 1 Kite Balloon Squadron as the nucleus for the brigade to be formed for duty with the Fourth Army. (The army wing of the III Brigade—the Twelfth—was reconstituted as a corps wing to replace the Third Wing. The III Brigade was completed on the 10th of March 1916, by the formation of the Thirteenth Army Wing). This brigade—the IV—under Brigadier-General E. B. Ashmore, (he handed over the command of the I Brigade to Brigadier-General D. le G. Pitcher on the same day), was formed on the 1st of April 1916, to include the Third Wing (now Nos. 3, 4, 9, and 15 Squadrons), the Fourteenth (Army) Wing (Nos. 22 and 24 Squadrons), and No. I Kite Balloon Squadron (Nos. 1 and 3 Sections).

Thus, the corps air work over the area north of the Somme was the responsibility of the squadrons of the Third Wing not only through the many months of preparation but also during the battle. In October 1915 the first photographs of the enemy defences were taken. Gradually a complete air picture of the first and second line systems, as well as of many villages in rear, was built up. It was, however, at the beginning of March 1916, when the Fourth Army came into the line, that intensive air preparations for the battle began. It had been decided, in this month, that the strength of all squadrons should be raised from twelve to eighteen aeroplanes. The IV Brigade was the first to benefit from this increase. By the middle of June 1916 five of the six squadrons comprising its two wings were up to the new establishment, and the remaining squadron—No. 15—was completed by the 6th of July.

Meanwhile, on the 25th of April, an important reconnaissance brought back news that the enemy was constructing new and formidable defences behind the Somme front. The reconnaissance machine, a B.E.2c of No. 15 Squadron (Lieutenant A. B. Adams and Second Lieutenant C. R. Robbins), was escorted by four B.E.2c's of the same squadron, and by three D.H.2's of No. 24. The single-seater fighters followed the B.E.2c's in triangular formation. Soon after the lines were crossed Fokkers attacked the B.E.2c's, but were in turn dived on by the D. H.2's, which contrived to out-manoeuvre the enemy aeroplanes, and beat off the attacks.

One Fokker was driven down. The occupants of the reconnoitring machine were able to give their full attention to the ground below and discovered a third line system stretching from near Ablainzevelle by way of Achiet-le-Petit, Irles, Pys, and Le Sars to Flers. They reported also, in some detail, on the various defence works about the principal towns. When this information was brought back, photographs were ordered, and obtained, of the whole line. To keep pace with the extension of the enemy's defensive measures, photography continued at intervals. From the 15th to the 18th of May the whole trench system along twenty miles in front of the Fourth Army, that is the first, intermediate, second, and third lines, was photographed again. On the 20th of June and the two following days the defence system was covered once more, the Third Wing making twenty-four photographic flights, and the Fourteenth Wing eight.

The date fixed for the opening of the infantry offensive on the Somme was the 29th of June. General Foch, however, who was to conduct the attack on the British right, immediately north (the French had taken over the short sector Curlu-Maricourt on the 1st of June 1916), and south of the river, urged postponement until the 1st of July, and this was agreed to on the 28th of June. In a letter to General Joffre on that day. Sir Douglas Haig, after stating that arrangements had been made 'to continue the battle with such vigour as will force the enemy to abandon his attacks on Verdun', set out his immediate plans as follows:

1st. To aim at breaking the enemy's front first of all between the Somme and Serre.

2nd. To secure the positions about Bapaume and thence southwards to Ginchy, while the French forces aim at reaching Sailly and Rancourt (as agreed at our last meeting, Saturday, 17th June).

3rd. To enlarge the breach by gaining possession of the area lying between Bapaume and Arras. With this object an attack will be launched from the N.W. against Blaireville and Ficheux in co-operation with all available troops (including cavalry) working northwards from the line Miraumont-Bapaume.

4th. Having once broken the enemy's front between Arras and the Somme, opened the roads comprised in that sector eastwards and established our forces on the line Monchy-le-Preux-Bapaume-Rancourt, I shall then be prepared to move forward to the line Cambrai-Douai, with the object of continuing the operations against the enemy's forces, the direction of the further operations depending on whether he clings to his fortified positions to the north, or has succeeded in concentrating a force to oppose our advance eastwards.

In the operations outlined above the principal role was to be played by the Fourth Army. The army commander had at his disposal, for the air work required by his five army corps, the four squadrons of the Third Wing and No.1 Kite Balloon Squadron, comprising five balloon sections. He also had, in direct touch with his own headquarters, the two squadrons of the Fourteenth Army Wing. The aeroplanes of the Corps Squadrons were distributed as follows, reading from left to right of the line:

Corps	Squadron	Counter-Battery.	Contact Patrol.	Trench Flights.(a)	Special Missions.(b)
VIII	No. 15 (B.E.2c's)	8	3	3	2
X	No. 4 (B.E.2c's)	9	3	4	2
III	No. 3 (Moranes)	4	3	3	2
XV	No. 3 (Moranes)	4	Shared with III Corps	—	—
	No. 9 (B.E.2c's)	—		2	—
XIII	No. 9 (B.E.2c's)	5	4	4	3

(a) Close Reconnaissance and destructive bombardment.
(b) Destruction of kite balloons, close photography, &c. and reserve.

In addition, each corps had one kite balloon section for work with the corps heavy artillery. Further, the three balloon sections for which army observers had been specially trained in tactical duties at the school at St. Riquier, came into the area on the 18th of June and were allotted, No. 13 to the VIII Corps, No. 6 to the X Corps, and No. 4 to the XV Corps. The immediate protection of the corps aeroplanes was to be afforded by continuous line patrols by pairs of aeroplanes of the two army squadrons and by periodic offensive sweeps by formations of de Havillands. Army reconnaissance, photography, reconnaissance, and attacks on kite balloons were to be made with an escorting force of two or three de Havillands. An initial infantry attack, subsidiary to the main operations, was to be made by the VII Corps of the Third Army against the Gommecourt salient, the air co-operation in which was to be supplied by No. 8 Squadron (eighteen B.E.2c's) and by No. 5 Kite Balloon Section.

To complete the Flying Corps concentration for the battle, the headquarter Ninth Wing (Nos. 21, 27, and 60 Squadrons and one Flight of No. 70 Squadron) arrived at Fienvillers and Vert Galand on the 19th of June. A second Flight of No. 70 Squadron arrived on the 1st of July. The squadrons of this wing were to be responsible for strategical reconnaissance for General Headquarters, the organised offensive against the enemy air service, and distant bombing of communications.

The bombing offensive against the rear lines of rail communication aimed at the isolation of the area south of the Valenciennes-Arras railway and west of the Douai-Busigny-Tergnier lines. It was hoped to achieve this by the destruction of trains in cuttings, and of railway bridges, in the neighbourhood of Cambrai, Busigny, St. Quentin, and Tergnier, as well as by attacks on the junctions themselves. Furthermore, a blow was to be aimed at the ammunition supply by bombing the great depots at Mons, Namur, and at the St. Sauveur station at Lille. To help in the attacks on the railway communications, twelve B.E.2c's of the II Brigade were to deal with the lines Douai-Cambrai, and eight each from the I and III Brigades were to bomb respectively the lines Le Cateau-Busigny-Wassigny, and Mézières-St. Quentin.

The detachments from the I and II Brigades were to operate from Fienvillers and Vert Galand, but were to return to their own aerodromes each night. To ensure the maximum number of attacks on trains it was essential that the presence of bombing aircraft over the railway lines should be as continuous as possible. Furthermore, the destruction of a moving train did not call for massed bombing. Under these circumstances, the accepted scheme of bombing in formation was temporarily cancelled for these railway attacks, and brigade commanders were given discretion to send out their pilots in groups, pairs, or singly. Sufficient protection for the bombers, it was considered, would be provided by a special scheme of offensive patrols to be carried out by the Ninth Wing whilst bombing was in progress.

★★★★★★

The patrols were to be made by alternate formations of aeroplanes, supplied by Nos. 27 and 60 Squadrons, of the lines Arras-Denain-Valenciennes-Le Cateau-St. Quentin-Peronne and Arras-Aubigny-Cambrai-Marcoing-Bapaume.

★★★★★★

The main bombing was to begin on the opening day of the infantry assault. It was expected that reinforcements would be moved by rail only after the offensive began and that the earlier destruction of the lines might be made good in time. In addition to the bombing of communications, there were to be widespread attacks on troops, transports, dumps, billets, headquarters, &c., in the immediate battle area.

For the opening of the battle then, the Fourth Army had a total of one hundred and nine aeroplanes in direct support. The strength of the Ninth Wing was fifty-eight aeroplanes, bringing the concentration of the Royal Flying Corps in the battle area to one hundred and sixty-seven aeroplanes. To this number must be added the eighteen B.E.2c's of No. 8 Squadron which supported the subsidiary Gommecourt attack and the detachments (which varied in strength after the first day) of the bombing B.E.2c's from the other brigades.

To get a true measure of the Flying Corps achievement over the Somme, it will be necessary to know what air forces were opposed to them. (See also *Some Notes on the German Air Service at the Somme*, Appendix 7).

The German *Reichsarchiv* has stated that on the 30th of June the sector on both sides of the Somme river was held by the German Second Army, (this army had its right wing near Hannescamps, eighteen kilometres south-west of Arras, and its left wing near Ribecourt, ten kilometres southwest of Noyon), and that the air units with this army were six reconnaissance flights (*Feldflieger-Abteilungen*, forty-two aeroplanes) and four artillery flights (*Artillerieflieger-Abteilungen*, seventeen aeroplanes.) There were, in addition, a bomber-fighter squadron (*Kampfgeschwader*, No. 1), consisting of forty-three aeroplanes, a bomber-fighter flight (*Kampfstaffel*, No. 32), of eight aeroplanes, and one single-seater fighter detachment (*Kampfeinsitzer-Kommando*), of nineteen aeroplanes. Thus, the total air strength of the German Second Army (excluding the machines at the army aircraft park) was 129 aeroplanes.

✶✶✶✶✶✶

North of the Second Army to the sea, the German Sixth Army had, on the 30th of June, approximately 120 aeroplanes, and the German Fourth Army, 75. These figures are exclusive of the machines in the army aircraft parks. In addition, in the Fourth Army area, on the coast, were two naval reconnaissance flights of an approximate total strength of 25 machines. South of the Second Army (*i.e.* from near Ribecourt to Switzerland), there were approximately 490 aeroplanes, excluding those at aircraft parks. Of these, more than half were in the Verdun area. Compare the position on the 15th of October, 1916, in 'The Reorganisation of the German Air Service' chapter 4.

✶✶✶✶✶✶

It is not possible to say, definitely, what proportion of the Second Army air strength was opposed to the British, but what is clear is that, for the opening phase of the operations, the German air service in the Somme area was outnumbered by the Royal Flying Corps. The disparity, however, was substantially reduced in the middle of July. (See 'The Second Phase' chapter 4).

Before the battle opened the German air service suffered the loss of its leading fighting pilot. Second Lieutenant G. R. McCubbin of No. 25 Squadron, with Corporal J. H. Waller as gunner, was flying his F.E.2b over Annay at about nine in the evening of the 18th of June, when he saw three Fokker monoplanes. As he turned towards them, one dived away and the others made for another F.E. of the squadron which was working over Lens. McCubbin caught up with these as they dived on his comrade and, with an accurate burst of fire, sent one crashing down. Thereupon he turned to attack the second Fokker, but found that both the enemy and the F.E. had disappeared. It was learned a few days later that this F.E. had been forced to land and its two occupants taken prisoner, and, further, that McCubbin's victim was the famous Max Immelmann.

On the 27th of June the advanced headquarters of the Royal Flying Corps was set up in the village of Fienvillers, not far from the aerodrome on which were Nos. 21 and 27 Squadrons. Thirty minutes distant by motor car, in the village of Beauquesne, was General Headquarters. All was ready for the great struggle.

CHAPTER 4

The Battles of the Somme, 1916
(Order of Battle, Royal Flying Corps, Appendix 4)

The Somme valley, forming as it does a line of defence for Paris, has always been one of the great military barriers of northern France. The Romans in the days of their decline made full use of its defensive features. Edward III, hotly pursued by an overwhelming army, avoided surrender by a surprise fording of the river. Henry V marched along its bank vainly seeking a way over until he came to a point between Peronne and Ham, where his weary and half-starved force was led by a native through the marshes to a little-known and ill-guarded ford.

Edward crossed the Somme to the victory of Crécy and Henry to the triumph of Agincourt. Rain played its part in both those battles. At Crécy, King Philip ordered his Genoese crossbowmen to begin the attack, but a sudden storm wetted and made useless their bowstrings. At Agincourt, a downpour overnight softened the loam so that the tramping of thousands of infantry churned the plain to a bog, which made it impossible to bring artillery into action, robbed the heavily armoured French troops of mobility, and brought victory to Henry's more lightly equipped army. Rain was again to play a vital part in the great struggle of 1916.

The Somme, after flowing north from Ham to Peronne, takes a giant bend west to Amiens, whence it follows the general line of the rivers in this part of France in a north-westerly direction to the sea. Some seven miles before the river enters Amiens it receives the waters of its tributary, the Ancre, whose valley is immortalised in the records of the British Army. Between the two rivers is a deserted, arid country of wide monotonous uplands and shallow depressions. An observer flying over the district would be struck by the absence of human habitation outside the towns and clustered villages. The reason for this is one which was to affect profoundly the character of the battles.

Under the whole Somme region is a deep horizontal layer of chalk so heavily fissured that rain which falls upon it percolates to great depths before it is held. The sinking of deep wells, beyond the means of the small peasant, became a communal enterprise, and the peasants grouped themselves in close proximity to their water supply. From a defensive point of view, then, there is open unobstructed country where lines of trenches may be sited almost anywhere to give a wide clear field of fire, and there are the clustered villages which can be fortified as strong points. Chalk is easily quarried, and every village had extensive cellars and artificial excavations which enormously enhanced their defensive strength. It was this sort of underground labyrinth, for instance, that enabled the defenders of Beaumont Hamel to resist so fiercely and for so long. Into the slopes about the town deep and secret hiding-places had been tunnelled in the French wars of religion, and these catacombs were to serve their turn as a protection for German soldiers from British shells.

But whilst chalk is the dominant geological structure of the district, it is near the surface usually only in the valleys. The uplands have mostly a covering of fine grained reddish-brown loam with a clayey content liable in wet weather to turn to deep squelching mud. Between the loam and the chalk there is often a clay and flint formation which outcrops in irregular patches and is inimical to the growing of the sugar beet, the staple product of the region. Much of the Somme country was, of old, covered with thick forest, and the continuous clearing which has gone on down the centuries for the purpose of agriculture has left patches here and there where trees are embedded in this unfriendly clay and flint. Many of these patches of woodland were to earn world notice for the bloody fighting that was to mark their capture. To name some of them is to revive a crowd of memories: Mametz, Railway Copse, Fricourt, Bernafay, Trônes, Delville, Bazentin, High Wood.

If we follow an aeroplane flying to the lines sometime in June 1916, we may view the setting for the battle. It will be necessary to go out before the bombardment began which was to turn the woods into a few sorry stumps, raze the villages to the ground, and plough the whole land until it became a gigantic monotonous wound. From over Albert, flanking our right, we can see the green valley of the Somme River with its peat bogs and its string of small lakes, closely dogged on the south bank by a canal. Down beyond the bend of the Somme, with its opposing network of trenches, is water-patched Peronne set above the river in terraces of white.

Beneath the aeroplane the Ancre River, passing out of Albert, winds through woodlands and cuts straight across the German defences which show up as a maze of white lines. These are particularly complicated in front of Beaumont Hamel beyond the north bank of the river, and about Thiepval on the south side. The valley of the Ancre can be followed bending round towards the south of Bapaume, a great road and rail centre. The eleven miles of straight, poplar-lined road which connects Bapaume with Albert stands out with its crossing and recrossing of trenches. Where the road cuts into no-man's-land lie the giant mine-craters of La Boisselle, white beacons of guidance from afar.

The whole irregular front of Sir Henry Rawlinson's Fourth Army, which is to deliver the main attack, can be seen from near Serre in the north, down across the Ancre valley, turning off to the east south of Mametz, and partly rounding the wood of Maricourt where it joins up with the French who rest with their right in this sector at the top of a horseshoe bend in the Somme. Looking over the German area in front of him, the skilled observer will know at once that the enemy, from his high positions along the main ridge, must have many points which offer observation far back into the British lines.

The district, a wide mosaic of brown and green fields, is intersected by ravines which serve to accentuate the height of the uplands. The vast defence lines, like spider webs picked out by a hoar frost, show up with formidable vividness. The copses, curiously shaped, are dark green of aspect. A network of roads overspreads the whole tableland, centring in the villages soon to be known, even as they cease to be, to every cottage in England: Pozières, Martinpuich, Flers, Longueval, Montauban, Guillemont, Ginchy, and Combles, to name but a few of them.

To complete the picture on a day of June 1916, one would have to note a palisade of kite balloons stretching away behind the lines on both sides, a desultory shelling, British aeroplanes on a to and fro course over the German trenches quietly spotting for the artillery, patrols moving with set purpose to photograph or reconnoitre German back areas, more restless patrols at a greater height searching out enemy aircraft, perhaps an occasional rapid manoeuvring in the air which betokens an air fight, and, here and there in the sky, the constant forming and dispersing of smoke which tells of the bursting of anti-aircraft shells.

The First Phase.

From the middle of June there was an intermittent bombardment of the enemy defences along the whole front held by the British and along the French front north and south of the Somme. On Friday, the 23rd of June, the day before the shelling was to be intensified in the area of attack, a thunderstorm was suddenly loosed over the trenches at three in the afternoon. The kite balloons of Nos. 1 and 14 Sections along the Fourth Army front were struck by lightning and destroyed, and that of No. 12 Section was damaged and had to be ripped. The balloon of No. 5 Section in the Third Army area was wrenched from its winch and whirled away towards the trenches, rising rapidly. The two observers hurriedly tore up and scattered their notes, maps, and photographs.

At 13,000 feet the balloon was swirling in a snowstorm accompanied by vivid lightning and thunder. It crossed the German lines north-east of Monchy, but was almost at once blown back again and then began to fall. When the storm had first struck, the parachutes had been shaken from their cases and opened out below the basket. Second Lieutenant J. W. Jardine at once cut his away, but Second Lieutenant G. D. S. M. Pape had remained attached to his, resisting its insistent tugging until the balloon began to fall, when he was forcibly lifted from the basket and carried high above the envelope.

The ropes of the parachute carried also the guy ropes of the balloon with which they had become entangled. Pape as he looked down could see flames come from the valve and lick the snow-covered fabric of the gas-bag which was fast losing shape. Realising that his parachute was now holding the balloon up, he securely fastened the tail line. The procession parachuted into a British gun emplacement behind Arras. Both officers were badly shaken; Pape had had his left hand severely frost-bitten in the snowstorm; Jardine in his report of the adventure stated that he expected to be fit for duty in a week.

The storm left in its track banks of low cloud which, through the 24th, caused intermittent rain and hindered air observation of the bombardment. Pilots flew low and directed the artillery fire on forty targets, but this was a long way short of the pre-arranged programme.

At four in the afternoon of the 25th a concerted attempt was made to destroy the German kite balloons in front of all four British armies. Of the twenty-three balloons reported in the air, fifteen were attacked; four were brought down by aeroplanes firing Le Prieur rockets, and one was destroyed by phosphorus bombs.

★★★★★★

Le Prieur rocket was invented by Lieutenant Y. P. G. Le Prieur of the French Navy. They were attached to the interplane struts of the aeroplane and were fired electrically by the pilot. Their best range was under 400 feet; beyond this range the curved trajectory of the rocket made accurate aiming impossible.

The phosphorus bomb was designed by Lieutenant R. B. Bourdillon in co-operation with Captain P. H. Linthune and Major B. Hopkinson. The first deliveries (85 bombs complete with special carriers) arrived in France on the 16th of June 1916. The bomb contained converted phosphorus, the invention of Messrs. Allbright and Wilsons, of Birmingham.

★★★★★★

Three of the balloons which were shot down had been observing over the area of the Fourth Army. This success, achieved in spite of difficulties of weather and anti-aircraft fire, was enhanced on the following day when two of the Nieuport pilots of No. 1 Squadron, who had been so successful on the Fourth Army front, returned to the Second Army area and, with another pilot of the same squadron, shot down in flames three of the balloons on that front which had survived attacks on the previous day.

On this—the second day of the main bombardment—the German batteries strongly retaliated, and the positions of one hundred and two of them were quietly plotted by observers of the IV Brigade chiefly in front of the VIII and X Corps. Aeroplane and kite balloon observers who watched the bombardment through the day reported the uplands and valleys spurting as if alive. Blazing dumps and exploding ammunition over a wide area added to the inferno. Enemy airmen did little to interrupt the work of the British observers: a Fokker which was met by a de Havilland pilot of No. 24 Squadron near Courcelette was attacked and shot to pieces in the air.

Artillery observation was again the feature of the air work on the 26th. The air time-table had been drawn up so that disproportionate attention was not given to any one target. At half past three in the afternoon the bombardment was halted for an hour to allow the Flying Corps to photograph the area, so that the gunners might have an exact record of the damage their fire had so far accomplished.

A grey horizon and fog on the uplands during the next four days failed to rob the assembling British soldiers of their buoyancy but made air work difficult. Every hour of bad weather that kept aeroplanes away from the front brought respite to some German battery, and the full effect of the lost hours must be borne by the infantry when they advanced to the assault. No one realised this better than the airmen. Pilots flew in and under the low clouds and took advantage of every bright interval to continue their work of helping the artillery to destroy the enemy guns, but the grey days took their toll of flying time, and the effect on the day of attack, although it cannot be estimated, was none the less important. (It is significant that counter-battery orders issued from X Corps on June the 28th stated that so long as aeroplane observation continued to be impossible, the number of rounds on each target was to be doubled).

Reconnaissance and photography during the bombardment paid special attention to the extent to which the wire in front of the enemy defences had been cut. The wire formed a formidable obstacle. Each group of defences comprised several lines of deep, interconnected, well-sheltered trenches protected by barbed-wire entanglements often in two belts forty yards broad. The wire, interlaced about heavy iron stakes, was often almost as thick as a man's finger. One of the Corps Commanders said:

> The aeroplane photographs showed admirably the effect of the bombardment both on the wire and on the trenches and were of the greatest value.

On the eve of the battle the clouds suddenly dispersed and Saturday, July the 1st, dawned with the promise of a perfect summer day. There was an early buzz of activity on all the aerodromes. From the lines came the solid roar of the artillery. Aeroplanes went off at four o'clock to watch the bombardment, but the damp earth was obscured by patches of mist and accurate observation was impossible. As the rays of the sun pierced the shallow valleys, the mists began to dissolve and, at twenty-five minutes past six, when the bombardment rose to a fury, observers were able to signal its general effect. The contact observers, whose special mission it was to report the progress of the battle, could see, at the same hour, thin lines of infantry crawling from the British front trenches into no man's land to be ready for the assault at thirty minutes past seven.

As the value of the contact reports would depend on timely receipt by the commands concerned, each corps and divisional headquarters had a wireless receiving-station to take in urgent messages or calls from the observers for barrage fire. In addition, infantry officers, in telephonic communication with corps headquarters, were stationed at selected points to receive bags dropped from the aeroplanes containing messages or the special lithographed maps on which the observers had marked the positions of the British and enemy troops.

We may first consider the attacks north of the Ancre. In this area the Germans were particularly well prepared. Whole battalions could stay, careless of the bombardment, in catacombs below the fortified villages; underground passages went from the shelters to the front line trenches; machine-guns could be moved rapidly from deep dug-outs to their emplacements, many of them out beyond the parapets; and the German artillery commanders had direct observation from their higher ground over most of the front line area.

The subsidiary attack, against Gommecourt, was made by the VII Corps of the Third Army and was watched by No. 8 Squadron. When the weather had cleared on the previous evening this squadron had procured an excellent final set of photographs of the German front positions, and had distributed prints of them to the corps during the night. The attack was made by two divisions—the 46th and 56th—and from 6.45 a.m. to 3.25 p.m. one aeroplane was working over each division on contact patrol; after that hour one aeroplane patrolled for the two divisions. The attacking troops had red flares which they were to light for the information of the air observers, but no flares were seen from the aeroplanes over this corps, and observers found that the only way to get information was to have a close look at the men from a height from which it was possible to detect the colour of their uniform.

This meant flying through the storm of the barrage, and the aeroplanes were often tossed about in the disturbed air like surf-riding corks. It meant, too, unpleasant ground fire when the troops which were being inspected from a low height proved to be wearing grey instead of khaki. These risks, however, were lightly undertaken and, although by the end of the day three of the contact aeroplanes had been so shot about by rifle and machine-gun fire that they were no longer serviceable, no low-flying aeroplane was lost. One pilot on the way back from the lines in the afternoon to drop a message, hit and spun down the cable of the balloon of No. 5 Section, near St. Amand. The aeroplane was partly wrecked but the pilot and his observer were uninjured.

The information which contact observers brought back to the VII Corps commander did not make pleasant reading. It told of the misfortune of the left attack of the 46th (North Midland) Division with which, once it was launched, touch had been completely lost on the ground. The air observers had watched the leading waves of the Sherwood Foresters pass over the front line and make their way gradually towards the northern corner of what was left of Gommecourt Wood. Then they saw, as the waves passed on their way, the German infantry come scrambling from the shelter of their dug-outs and reoccupy their front line trenches. The rear waves, which had been given the task of clearing the dug-outs, never got across no man's land owing to the heavy artillery and machine-gun barrage.

The men who had been cut off behind the German lines fought desperately all day. It proved impossible to develop fresh attacks to help them, and, by the end of the day, those who had not been killed were captured. On the rest of the front attacked by the MI Corps the news was little better. The aeroplane observers watched the assaulting battalions of the 56th (1st London) Division move out across no man's land south of Gommecourt under cover of a smoke curtain. They saw them fight their way through the first line of trenches to the second, and then on to the third. They watched the German barrage develop to the point when there seemed to be no hope that reinforcements could get through to the help of the first waves which had done so well. They saw the enemy collect and begin to counterattack; they were witnesses of much of the desperate fighting which followed:—the loss of the third German line soon after midday; the gradual falling back in the afternoon; and then, late in the evening, the reoccupation by the enemy of all that had been so promisingly captured in the morning.

The left of the main attack by the Fourth Army, from Serre as far as Thiepval, that is to say in the area fought over by the VIII and X Corps, met with a somewhat similar fate. These corps were assisted from the air by Nos. 15 and 4 Squadrons respectively. Along this part of the front, forward ground observers were able to follow broadly the progress of the fighting, and ground communications, too, were fairly reliable. There were, however, isolated deep penetrations into the German defences which air observers alone could report, notably at Pendant Copse and, south of the Ancre, through the Schwaben Redoubt towards Grandcourt.

That the brilliant advance to the Schwaben Redoubt greatly shook the defence is revealed by a report of No. 4 Squadron received at two in the afternoon that a number of known batteries in the area beyond the ridge, that is between Grandcourt and Courcelette, had already moved or were hurriedly leaving. The position at 4.30 p.m.

as reported by the squadron was that nowhere was there a massing of German troops on this part of the front, but that our hold on Schwaben Redoubt appeared insecure. An hour later, an observer reported that we were still in possession of the Redoubt and the point known as the Crucifix to the south-east. The fortress village of Thiepval, however, was the key point of the position and this stubbornly held out.

Captain C. A. A. Hiatt of No. 4 Squadron was sent out specially to examine the position about the ruins of the village. This he did leisurely and with cool detail from no more than 600 feet. But Thiepval, indeed, proved unassailable, and, with Beaumont Hamel, sealed the fate of the northern part of the attack. The penetrations of the German defences, so hardly fought for, could not be maintained, and during that night and the next day such of our troops as were left were forced to withdraw to their own lines.

The northern attack had been made at great cost, but not in vain. It kept occupied the main part of the enemy defence, and its fruits were reaped farther south. The III Corps, with which the larger part of No. 3 Squadron cooperated, was held up at the strongly fortified villages of Ovillers and La Boisselle, but its right division—the 34th—penetrated as far as Peake Wood. This proved to be the point of the wedge driven into the line north of the village of Fricourt. The XV Corps hoped to capture this village by pinching out the blunt salient which it formed into their lines.

The attack was made by the 21st Division just west of the village, and by the 7th Division, south of it in the direction of Mametz. The air co-operation was provided by parts of Nos. 3 and 9 Squadrons. By the evening the 21st Division had succeeded, in conjunction with the 34th Division on its left, in biting deeply into the German line north of Fricourt, whilst the troops of the 7th Division had fought their way through and beyond Mametz. On their left they had formed a defensive flank, and, on their right, were linked up with the XIII Corps. On the fronts fought over both by the III and XV Corps, a number of red flares were lighted by forward troops and were promptly reported from the aeroplanes. Captain E. J. E. Hawkins, commanding No. 3 Kite Balloon Section, was responsible for some observation on this front which proved of direct help to the infantry.

On the right of the XV Corps the 22nd Manchesters, who had reached Danzig Alley soon after 8.0 a.m., had been pushed out again by Germans attacking from Fritz Trench. Captain Hawkins directed the 78th Siege battery on to this trench so effectively that the 2nd

Queens were able to take it in the afternoon with small loss.

The greatest advance of the day was reported by No. 9 Squadron flying over the XIII Corps on the British right. A contact observer watched the men of the 30th Division move forward, with little opposition, towards the line Dublin Trench-Glatz Redoubt, which they took at 8.30 a.m. He also saw the 18th Division take the Pommiers Trench and advance quickly to the capture of the Pommiers Redoubt. Another aeroplane, piloted by Captain J. T. P. Whittaker with Second Lieutenant T. E. G. Scaife as observer, got over the lines just after 10.0 a.m. The observer, as he looked forward, could see a line of flashes, reflected from the mirrors which men of the 30th Division carried on their backs, leaving Glatz Redoubt and moving along the trench known as Train Alley in the direction of Montauban.

Suddenly he saw a battery come into action in Bernafay Wood. His pilot at once flew across and attacked the crew with machinegun fire from 700 feet. The gunners were probably dispersed by the fire as the battery was out of action for some time. The airmen then came upon German troops in trenches east of the wood and turned their machine-gun on to them. They flew back to the front and were in time to see the 16th Manchesters enter Montauban in splendid formation. They could see, too, that the men of the 18th Division had fared equally well, and were now moving up the ridge to the west of the village. So exhilarated were they with what they saw that they flew low along the ridge, waving their hands to the victorious infantry, on whom their greeting had a heartening effect. The commander of the 55th Brigade wrote:

> My men were immensely cheered and delighted on reaching the Montauban ridge when one of your gallant fellows came down very low and exchanged a wave of the hand.

At a quarter past eleven the mirrors could be seen flashing along the northern edge of Montauban. Before the aeroplane returned from the front, soon after midday, Scaife plotted the general line which the XIII Corps had reached, and his sketch showed Montauban and the whole of the ridge to the west in our hands. After the aeroplane left, a company of the King's (Liverpool) Regiment captured the brickfields south-east of Montauban, and this completed the advance of the XIII Corps on the first day.

Whilst the contact observers were reporting the progress of the infantry, the artillery observers along the whole front of attack searched out targets for the guns and howitzers. They sent down a stream of messages giving the positions from which German batteries were firing and observed the counter-fire on to many of them. Owing to the enormous number of bursting shells they could, for the most part, give no more than general corrections to our own artillery.

The balloon observers, linked by telephone with the headquarters of the corps heavy artillery, did not confine their attention to the enemy batteries. They watched and reported the incidence and changes of the enemy barrage and put the artillery on to many fleeting targets. Their observation did not cease with the fall of night. They continued through the dark hours to pick up the direction of enemy gun flashes and to report what parts of our front were being shelled.

Air reconnaissances throughout the day revealed slight activity on the roads and railways behind the German lines. Special attention was paid to the great rail centre at Bapaume which was visited at frequent intervals from five in the morning. Aeroplanes of No. 70 Squadron which left to reconnoitre Cambrai at 6.0 a.m. were back on their aerodrome an hour and twenty minutes later. They had met with no opposition and reported no unusual movements. A later reconnaissance flight to Cambrai and beyond to Busigny and Etreux had to fight its way on the whole round. The escort of three Martinsydes kept the enemy away from the reconnaissance aeroplane—a Morane biplane—and forced two Rolands to land. The observer reported only normal movement.

The bombing programme had opened with an attack on St. Sauveur Station on the previous evening, the 30th of June, by six R.E.7 pilots of No. 21 Squadron, who reported hits on the sheds. The raid was repeated by the same number of aeroplanes shortly before six in the morning of the 1st of July when there were hits on the station and on the railway. On each raid the bombing aeroplanes were escorted by two Martinsydes and by two Morane biplanes. It had been arranged that, for the second raid, an additional escort of five F.E.2b's of No. 20 Squadron should join the bombers over Armentieres, but on their way these F.E.'s met a formation of Fokkers which they stopped to fight, sending two down to land in the German lines.

The railway bombing on the 1st of July was done by twelve B.E.2c's of the II Brigade and by sixteen supplied equally by the I and III Brigades. Each aeroplane carried two 112-lb. bombs and was flown without an observer. The detachments from the I and II Brigades flew to Fienvillers and Vert Galand respectively in the morning, and went out at intervals beginning soon after midday. Cambrai Station and the lines near it were hit with seven bombs, but one pilot failed to return. The best result in this area came soon after five in the evening when Second Lieutenant A. L. Gordon-Kidd of No. 7 Squadron saw a train on the line between Aubigny-au-Bac and Cambrai.

It so happened that the train was approaching a ten-foot cutting, on a curve south of Aubigny, which had been suggested to pilots as one of those spots where the clearing of train wreckage would offer the greatest difficulties. The pilot was therefore alive to his opportunity and went down to 900 feet before releasing his bombs. He was rewarded with a direct hit on the middle of the train which caught fire and began to explode. An hour later a pilot of No. 16 Squadron, who found the train still burning, dropped two more bombs on the rear coaches causing further explosions which left no doubt that the train had been loaded with ammunition. The last of the bombing pilots, as he left Cambrai at half past six, saw the train still blazing fiercely with frequent leaping flames to mark the blowing up of what yet remained of its freight.

Of the bombs dropped by the I Brigade on Busigny, only one hit the station. Nor did better luck seem to attend the bombing of St. Quentin by the III Brigade. The first of the pilots to go off, soon after midday, never came back. In the afternoon, of six aeroplanes which set out at various times only three got home.

******

Of the four officers of the III Brigade who did not return, one was killed and three were made prisoners. One of the latter, Second Lieutenant L. A. Wingfield who escaped from Germany in October 1917, reported that his bombs had on the 1st of July, blown up an ammunition train which sent smoke columns 2,000 feet into the air.

******

Two pilots had bombed the station without apparent damage, one surviving a continuous attack by three enemy aeroplanes, whilst the third had lost his way and had dropped his bombs on a camp near Vermand. The bombing of St. Quentin then had been costly and, so far as the pilots who returned could see, had not done much harm. But a consideration of what actually happened illustrates the difficulty of presenting the true effects of this role of aircraft. Prisoners who were captured by the French Army later in the month told how on the 1st of July their division—the 22nd Reserve—received urgent orders in the afternoon to entrain at St. Quentin for the Somme front.

At about 2.0 p.m. two battalions were in the station. Their arms were piled and their transport was being loaded on to a train, when British aeroplanes suddenly appeared and began to bomb. One bomb hit and exploded an ammunition shed. Lined up in the station sidings were two hundred ammunition wagons and, before these could be got away, the fire had spread to them and sixty wagons were destroyed. The fire, too, destroyed the troop train and the whole of the equipment which the two battalions had deposited on the platform. The panic-stricken men fled in every direction leaving a hundred and eighty dead and wounded. The 71st Reserve Regiment, which suffered most, was sent back to its billets at Etreillers and moved next day to Ham to be re-equipped.

Nearer the actual front, Bapaume, known to contain a German headquarters, was bombed by six Martinsydes in the morning and by six R.E.7's about midday. The first raid, made by No. 27 Squadron, started a fire which burnt for several hours. The second, by No. 21 Squadron, cut the railway line south of the town. An aeroplane of No. 27 Squadron, which accompanied the second bombing expedition, brought back photographs of Bapaume and of Achiet-le-Grand. In addition to the major bombing, all the corps squadron aeroplanes carried twenty-pound bombs which were dropped throughout the day on billets, transport, trenches, and batteries.

The special offensive patrols, in connexion with the railway bombing, were made by aeroplanes of Nos. 27 and 60 Squadrons from 11.30 a.m. until after 7.0 p.m. These patrols found little to do. The first of them in the morning, carried out by pilots of No. 60 Squadron, forced an L.V.G. biplane to land near Bapaume, but none of the others encountered enemy aeroplanes.

To protect the aeroplanes doing corps work along the fronts of the Fourth and Third Armies, there were two sets of patrols. One set, made by de Havillands of No. 24 Squadron, covered a line roughly stretching from Peronne through Pys to Gommecourt. The squadron had been reinforced by the addition to its strength of five scouts—three Bristols and two Moranes. The first patrol went out at 6.45 a.m. and the last left the lines at nightfall. The first met in all six enemy aeroplanes. Second Lieutenant S. E. Cowan had three fights. Over Peronne an aeroplane which he attacked escaped eastwards. Over Pys he saw two two-seater biplanes approaching the lines from Bapaume and attacked each in turn. The observer in one fell, apparently wounded, into his cockpit. The other aeroplane, hit at close range, fell into a cloud and did not seem to be under control. Five minutes later Cowan attacked and drove east a twin-fuselage biplane. The third patrol of this squadron when over Bapaume saw, far below, three German aeroplanes flying at about a thousand feet. Second Lieutenant T. P. H. Bayetto, on a Morane Scout, dived and forced one of them to land in a field: the other two flew away.

The second set of patrols, provided by No. 22 Squadron from 4.12 a.m. until dusk, was split up to cover a northern area from Douchy to Miraumont, and a southern area from Longueval to Cléry on the Somme. F.E.2b's were sent out in pairs for each area and each pair waited over the lines until they were relieved by the next pair, so that the patrolling was continuous. Whilst the officers of these two-seaters were out primarily to fight, they had other duties. The observers watched for enemy movements and concentrations, about which, indeed, they had much to report. For more immediate use each F.E.2b carried two 20-lb. bombs. The patrols met and fought a number of enemy aeroplanes. Two F.E.2b's were lost over the German lines and another was forced to land in the British lines with a damaged engine, but, by keeping the German aircraft engaged, the patrols afforded the best possible protection for the contact and artillery pilots and observers who, lower down in the air, went about their work unmolested.

On the right of the British front the French had made a brilliant advance on both sides of the Somme. Sir Douglas Haig now decided to concentrate his efforts between La Boisselle and his junction with the French. That Sir Henry Rawlinson might give his undivided attention to the pushing home of the offensive, the commander-in-chief relieved him of responsibility for the stretch from La Boisselle to Serre. The two army corps (X and VIII) along that sector he placed under General Sir Hubert Gough, commanding the Reserve Army, (the headquarters of the Reserve Army had been formed on the 22nd of May 1916), who was instructed to keep up a steady pressure and to act as a pivot on which the right could move forward.

The beginnings of a flying wing for the Reserve Army had been formed, under the command of Lieutenant-Colonel J. G. Hearson, on the 22nd of June. Now that General Gough was taking over two active corps, the reserve wing was designated the Fifteenth Wing, and the two squadrons—Nos. 4 and 15—which worked directly for those two corps, were transferred to the wing from the Third Wing. Nos. 1 and 11 Kite Balloon Sections became the corps balloon sections of the Fifteenth Wing, and No. 13 the army section. The air protection along the front of the Reserve Army remained the duty, for the time being, of the Fourteenth (Army) Wing.

By midday of Sunday, the 2nd of July, the XV Corps had captured Fricourt village, but Fricourt Farm, northeast of the village, stubbornly held out. In the afternoon the defenders of the farm yielded at last to the attacks of the 17th Division, newly brought up from corps reserve. The progress of the division was accurately followed by contact observers who reported the fall of the farm a few minutes after it took place. In the area of the III Corps a terrific struggle was waged all day in the village of La Boisselle. The positions of red flares, lighted in the ruins from time to time, were reported by observers of No. 3 Squadron. A little before ten in the evening the observer in the balloon of No. 3 Section was attracted by the urgent flashing of a lamp from a point on the outskirts of the village. He read the message:

> In contact with German bombing party. Am unable to push him farther back without a supply of rifle grenades. If possible please send a supply without delay. Needed, pickets, wire, and sandbags, for consolidation. Also, Very pistols and ammunition.

This call for help was passed on at once to the Royal Engineers and to the infantry command. The balloon of No. 12 Section was also of direct help to the infantry on July the 2nd. The observer caught sight of a German battery getting into position on the edge of Bernafay Wood. He telephoned the information to the artillery and was ordered to direct the fire of a French battery on the enemy guns. These, meanwhile, had opened rapid enfilade fire on the troops along the ridge west of Montauban. But not long did the German gunners work undisturbed. Responding to the balloon observer's corrections, the French commander was soon dropping shells among them. Their fire suddenly stopped. When Bernafay Wood was captured later, two guns, found battered and derelict, gave silent testimony to the use of the military kite balloon.

Aeroplane reconnaissances during the 2nd again revealed normal activity behind the German lines except that ten trains moving in the early morning from Douai towards Cambrai seemed to indicate the arrival of reinforcements from the Lens sector. Bapaume was attacked by six R.E.'s of No 21 Squadron in the afternoon. Their six bombs, weighing 336-lb. each, dropped on an infantry headquarters and on ammunition, dumps, started a fire which grew in intensity and still coloured the eastern sky when darkness had closed over the day's fighting.

******

These were heavy cased bombs, containing only 70-lb. of explosive, produced by the Royal Aircraft Factory. It had thick metal strips, fragments of which, on the explosion of the bomb, were thrown off radially with a velocity estimated at 2,000 feet a second.

******

The bombers were escorted by four Martinsydes of No. 27 Squadron, and an offensive formation of six Moranes of No. 60 Squadron patrolled the Bapaume area whilst the attack was in progress. German aircraft showed no disposition to interfere. Elsewhere along the front they were generally inactive through the day. On the Fourth Army front there were no more than four fights, all indecisive. There were seven fights opposite the Third Army which resulted in four German aeroplanes being brought down.

Reconnaissance observers who flew off early in the morning of the 3rd to look at the German movements about Cambrai, brought back news of many trains in the town, and reported that reinforcements were coming in from the east and south-east, and were moving on towards Bapaume and Peronne. Some of those who had gone on during the night were actually fighting on the front later in the morning, and were identified as having come from the Champagne.

The bombing of moving trains by the detachments of the I, II, and III Brigades which was resumed on this day met with failure. From 5.30 a.m. pilots went out, at intervals, in pairs. At the same hour the offensive patrols by Nos. 27 and 60 Squadrons began. (No. 27 Squadron—formation of five Martinsydes, Arras-Douai-Le Cateau-St. Quentin-Albert. No. 60 Squadron—formation of five Moranes, Marquion-Cambrai-Bapaume). The first two bombers from the I Brigade ran into a formation of six German aeroplanes and, after a fight in which one of the B.E.2c's was damaged, were compelled to return with their bombs. The next two from this brigade succeeded in slipping through to Busigny where they bombed the station.

The aeroplanes of the III Brigade were to fly as far as St. Quentin. The first pair were attacked on the way. One pilot dropped his bombs on Roisel and the other on Vermand, and both beat a hasty retreat with the enemy formation in hot pursuit. The next pair from this brigade had got no farther than Brie on the Somme when one of the pilots was wounded in the head by anti-aircraft fire. He dropped his bombs and made his way back. His companion was not seen again. The five pilots of the II Brigade met with little better success. Two failed to return from the Cambrai area, one brought his aeroplane back much damaged by machine-gun fire from a train which he was bombing near Cambrai, whilst the other two got back safely from bombing moving trains, on which, however, they reported no direct hits.

Whilst the bombing was in progress the offensive patrol of No. 60 Squadron, led by the Squadron Commander, Major F. F. Waldron, came in for heavy fighting over Cambrai. Major Waldron was killed in a fight with a Fokker: the other Moranes, badly shot about, eventually returned.

The railway attacks on this day and on the 1st of July had cost, in all, eight bombing aeroplanes missing, one pilot who got back wounded, and damage, more or less severe, to many of the aeroplanes which returned. The offensive patrols had proved inadequate to the protection of the bombing pilots who, flying without observers in their bomb-loaded B.E.2c's, were ill-equipped to protect themselves. Furthermore, the reported results of the bombing were incommensurable with the losses incurred. General Trenchard, after consultation with G.H.Q., cancelled further low bombing attacks on trains, by the B.E.2c's, and sent the detachments back to resume their routine corps work for the First and Second Armies.

Bombing in formation, under escort, once again became the general rule. In the afternoon the concentration of trains which had been reported in Cambrai by the morning reconnaissance was attacked by three R.E.7's of No. 21 Squadron with four Martinsyde escorts. Three 336-lb. bombs hit buildings south of the station.

Some of the most confused and bloody fighting on the ground, during the day, took place in the underground warrens of La Boisselle. In the evening a number of flares lighted in and about the village enabled the air observers to plot the line of the infantry's progress. On the front of the XIII Corps the interest centred about Caterpillar and Bernafay woods. The Corps received orders, in the afternoon, to take these places. An observer of No. 9 Squadron had reported in the morning that he examined Caterpillar Wood three times from a height of five hundred feet and that he could find no trace of the enemy there.

Another observer of the same squadron flew low over Bernafay Wood in the afternoon and confirmed infantry patrol reports that that place, too, was untenanted. Bernafay was taken, with little opposition, at nine in the evening, and its capture, reported by wireless from the air, was known to corps headquarters nine minutes after it happened. Caterpillar Wood was quietly occupied during the night.

Throughout the day aeroplane and balloon observers co-operated continuously in counter-battery work, and many photographs were brought in to show the effect of the artillery fire. Enemy balloons working for their own artillery were attacked by aeroplanes in the afternoon. One balloon, above Logeast Wood, north-west of Achiet-le-Grand, was registering an enemy battery on to guns in the Château de la Haie valley, west of Hébuterne, when Captain J. A. Crook on a Nieuport of No. 11 Squadron appeared over the wood. He dived at the balloon, fired his Le Prieur rockets into it at close range, and sent it down in flames. Against other German balloons the attacks were unsuccessful.

Tuesday the 4th of July was a comparatively quiet day on the ground, but by midnight the III Corps at last held the whole of the village of La Boisselle. Clouds were low all day, bringing occasional rain. No German aircraft were seen by the fifty-two pilots of the IV Brigade who flew low about the lines, chiefly on artillery work. A large enemy column marching on Bazentin-le-Grand in the evening was attacked by machine-gun fire from the air and partly scattered, and its position was notified at the same time to the artillery. The weather was no better on the following day and again there was little flying. On the ground bombing parties on the front of the XV Corps pushed forward to the southernmost point of Contalmaison, and the capture of the whole of the powerful first defence system from the Brickfields to La Boisselle was now complete.

Before the second system could be assaulted the enemy had to be ejected from the fortified tangled acres of the Mametz Wood, and from the pear-shaped Trônes Wood, the core of which was entrenched. In the afternoon of July, the 6th, No. 3 Squadron was instructed to reconnoitre Mametz Wood and the German trenches to the west, especially the Quadrangle Support trench which connected the wood with Acid Drop Copse. The report which the squadron sent in gave, in some detail, the condition of the trenches, stating exactly what portions appeared too damaged to be tenable. The small Acid Drop Copse had been pretty well levelled by shell fire, but the majority of the trees of Mametz Wood were still standing: not enough of them had been blown over, said the observer, to form much of a barrier. Attacks against the positions were made by the XV Corps through the next day, the 7th, but met with strong opposition which developed behind a heavy barrage. An observer of No. 3 Squadron dropped a message to say that at half past five in the evening the Quadrangle Support trench, fiercely assaulted all day, was still strongly manned by German infantry.

We could see their grey uniforms very plainly at 800 feet. They fired on us: others tried to take cover.

The attack on Mametz Wood itself fared no better, although a deserter came in during the day and stated that life in the wood was hell. The Quadrangle Support trench was again attacked at 5.50 p.m. on the 8th. A contact aeroplane of No. 3 Squadron was over the area for the beginning of this attack. As soon as our barrage opened the officers saw a rocket go up from behind Contalmaison, and almost at once a German barrage fell in a solid wall of fire from Bailiff Wood, west of Contalmaison, to Bottom Wood, south-west of Mametz Wood. The airmen flew behind the barrage along the whole line of enemy trenches. Until a quarter past six they saw no one at all in the Quadrangle Support trench, but at that moment men suddenly appeared in it. They counted their numbers; in one stretch of the trench there were six grey uniforms in each traverse, and in the rest double that number.

The British attack on the trench again failed. For the next two days fighting was ceaseless. The enemy stubbornly contested every step, and not until after midnight of the 10th/11th was Quadrangle Support trench and the bulk of Mametz Wood in our hands. The wood was finally cleared in the early morning of the 12th. On that day, too, we were still in possession of the southern part of Trônes Wood. At eight in the evening of the 12th the officers in an artillery aeroplane of No. 9 Squadron noticed that the enemy had begun a barrage between Bernafay and Trônes woods. Suspecting the beginnings of a German counter-attack, they called on our artillery for a counter-barrage which was at once put down. When the German attack came at 9.0 p.m. the sting had already been extracted from it and the attempt was easily repulsed. Now that the whole of Mametz Wood and a part of Trônes Wood were in our possession, the way was clear for the attack on the second line along the ridge from Longueval to Bazentin-le-Petit.

During the days of getting ready for the next step, air-observers kept a keen watch on the enemy rail and road movements. On the early morning of July, the 6th, a reconnaissance pilot of No. 3 Squadron had seen troops, (probably the 183rd Division), detraining at Vélu, east of Bapaume, into road transport presumably for conveyance to the front. He dropped down to 300 feet and bombed the troop train setting it on fire with a direct hit. Later in the morning much rail movement was reported in Cambrai and Marcoing. It was afterwards known that this was the 123rd Division arriving from Flanders. A further reconnaissance made as far over as Le Cateau and Landrecies revealed no unusual activity either towards Cambrai or to St. Quentin.

On the 7th many trains on the lines from Cambrai and Bapaume to Roisel showed that troops were being rushed down to reinforce the defences south of the Somme. On the 8th enemy movements slackened. At about five in the morning of the following day, many trains seen running both ways between Lille and Douai indicated the arrival of reinforcements from the north, and seemed to link up with other train activity on the lines from Bapaume to Cambrai.

On the 10th movements were normal again, but next day, although rail movements were still quiet, a long column of motor transport moving towards Tournai from the north was reported by a night reconnaissance of No. 20 Squadron. This, it was thought, was the supply and ammunition column of the division which had been seen arriving in the Cambrai-Marcoing area five days before. (The 123rd Division actually detrained at Gouzeaucourt and Epehy).

On the 12th—a showery day—aeroplane and balloon observers reported train movements which left no doubt that 'milking' of the line was going on between Thélus and Lens, and that either 'milked' or formed units were being moved to the Somme from the Lille area. (The German IV Corps—7th and 8th Divisions—left the Lens area for the Somme front at this time).

There was close co-operation with the artillery in preparation for the new advance. Our initial successes had compelled the German batteries to move back to new positions, a fact which led to increased demands on the air artillery observers. Perhaps the most important work of the Flying Corps during these days was the methodical location and registration of the new emplacements, an essential preliminary to counter-battery work. Special targets received immediate attention. On the morning of the 6th of July an observer of No. 9 Squadron saw an infantry and transport column making for Guillemont. He called up the 12th Heavy Battery and directed their fire on the column. The men were scattered in disorder, leaving many dead and wounded. Late the same evening a brigade of infantry was seen going into Ginchy by another observer of this squadron. His calls to the artillery went unanswered, so the pilot went down and dispersed part of the column with his machine-gun, and then returned to report the movement to XIII Corps headquarters. He went up again an hour later and, in failing light, his observer found a battalion near Ginchy. This time the artillery replied to his call at once and quickly got hits with shrapnel: German officers who were captured later stated that this battalion lost half its men.

The main bombing, whilst the enemy was bringing up reinforcements, was again aimed at his railway centres. At half past four in the morning of July the 9th six R.E.'s of No. 21 Squadron attacked Cambrai, each dropping a 336-lb. bomb, three of which fell into the station. At the same time six Martinsydes of No. 27 Squadron each dropped two 112-lb. bombs on Bapaume, hitting the line. The Cambrai bombers were escorted by six Morane Scout pilots who were joined by the Martinsydes after they had bombed Bapaume. There was a stiff fight over Cambrai, and two of the British aeroplanes were shot down.

At half past four in the afternoon dumps at Le Sars and a headquarters at Le Transloy were bombed by pilots of No. 21 Squadron who were strongly escorted, but met no German aeroplanes. In Havrincourt wood south-west of Cambrai bivouac fires had been seen for some days, and aeroplanes flying near the wood were subjected to increasing antiaircraft fire which seemed to indicate a desire to keep the Royal Flying Corps at a distance. It was therefore decided to make a big raid on the wood on the morning of the 11th. When the twenty bombers and their seventeen escorting pilots, flying in two groups, had gained height they ran into thick clouds and the groups became separated. One group got to the wood into which they dropped fifty-four 20-lb. bombs, starting a number of fires. Of the second group only three crossed the lines, and these were attacked and driven back by six enemy aeroplanes.

The railway movements from the Lens and Lille areas to the Somme, seen from the air on the 12th, called for action. On the 13th a special attempt was made to intercept trains between Douai-Cambrai and Valenciennes-Cambrai. Four Martinsydes of No. 27 Squadron crossed the lines in the clouds. Two of them attacked a train near Aubigny-au-Bac from 800 feet and derailed the front coaches, one of which overturned. The other two bombed a train on the Cambrai-Denain line without definite result. The bombing pilots made skilful use of the low clouds to screen their movements and encountered no opposition.

The general attack on the German second trench system, from Longueval as far as and including Bazentin-le-Petit Wood, was made on Friday the 14th of July. The whole of the new objective, as well as the third line behind it, had been previously photographed and reconnoitred in detail. Pilots had to fly low, and their aeroplanes were often seriously damaged by fire from the German infantry. The troops of the two attacking corps—the XV and XIII—assembled in their trenches before dawn on the morning of the 14th. The men of the XIII Corps, on the right, whose forward positions were, in places, distant as much as a mile from the enemy's lines, crept out into no man's land and lined up in the darkness below the German trenches on the crest. Whilst the two attacking corps were assembling, the III Corps on their left, whose task it was to form a defensive flank, greatly strengthened their position by occupying Contalmaison Villa and Lower Wood.

The assault made at 3.25 a.m. took the enemy by surprise; the first line of trenches was entered with little opposition and the men pushed on rapidly to the support line. Clouds were as low as 800 feet when the attack began and a ground haze made it impossible to see laterally for more than 600 yards. Nevertheless, a contact observer of No. 9 Squadron came back to the corps advanced landing ground and reported two hours after the attack began that the 3rd Division had taken two lines of trenches and were fighting for Bazentin-le-Grand, and that he had seen troops of the 9th (Scottish) Division forming for an attack on the fortified Waterlot Farm south of Delville Wood.

Other officers of this squadron reported that they had got glimpses of flares and infantry, through the mist, at various points in the German line. One of the aeroplanes was flying 500 feet above Longueval in an attempt to follow the fortunes of the attack, when a bursting shell wounded and temporarily blinded the pilot, Captain J. U. Kelly. The observer. Second Lieutenant H. A. V. Hill, less seriously hit, helped his pilot to bring the damaged aeroplane into the French lines near Maricourt, where it was wrecked.

Enough had been seen to indicate the success of the infantry, and cavalry were brought up to forward positions. The possibility of cavalry coming into action after the long stagnation of trench warfare was calculated to depress the enemy as much as it would electrify the British troops. To convey the news to the German defenders, already severely shaken, an aeroplane was ordered to fly over the lines and send out the following special message in the knowledge that it would be picked up by the German wireless along the front:

> Enemy second line of defence has been captured on a front of 6,000 yards. British cavalry is now passing through in pursuit of the demoralised enemy.

Although this message, which was flashed out at 10.30 a.m., deliberately exaggerated the situation at that time, the turn of events later in the day was to give it a measure of truth. Cavalry went through in the evening. Before they did so, air-observers from the fringe of the clouds glimpsed something of the further progress of the infantry. On the right, at 1.0 p.m., an observer saw men of the South African Brigade running at the double into Longueval. An hour later they had attacked and captured the northern part of the village which was wholly in our hands by 4.0 p.m.

An artillery observer, who had been in the air for two hours and had located a number of active German batteries, saw at three o'clock that men of the 7th Division were through and beyond the village of Bazentin-le-Petit. Here then was the opportunity for the cavalry. The 7th Division were ordered to move on High Wood with the Secunderabad Cavalry Brigade in support on their right flank. They began their advance about 6.50 p.m. with the knowledge that overwhelming opposition was unlikely, since an air reconnaissance of the country behind High Wood made between 3.30 p.m. and 4.0 p.m. had revealed no movements. The infantry went forward with little resistance until they approached High Wood.

On their right the 7th Dragoons and the Deccan Horse found that the going had been made slippery by the day's rain. A Morane monoplane of No. 3 Squadron (pilot, Captain A. M. Miller, observer. Second Lieutenant C. W. Short) watched the combined advance from the air. The officers saw, in front and to the east of High Wood, that German infantry were scattered in readiness in the standing crops. They quickly realised that the folds of the country hereabouts would help further to screen the enemy soldiers, especially from the cavalry. Captain Miller therefore dived and flew three hundred feet over the heads of the Germans to draw their fire, as this, he judged, would be the quickest way of revealing their positions and would, at the same time, serve to distract their attention from the advancing troops.

To make their intervention more effective, the two officers continued to fly up and down raking the German positions with fire from their Lewis gun, only giving up when the infantry—the 2nd

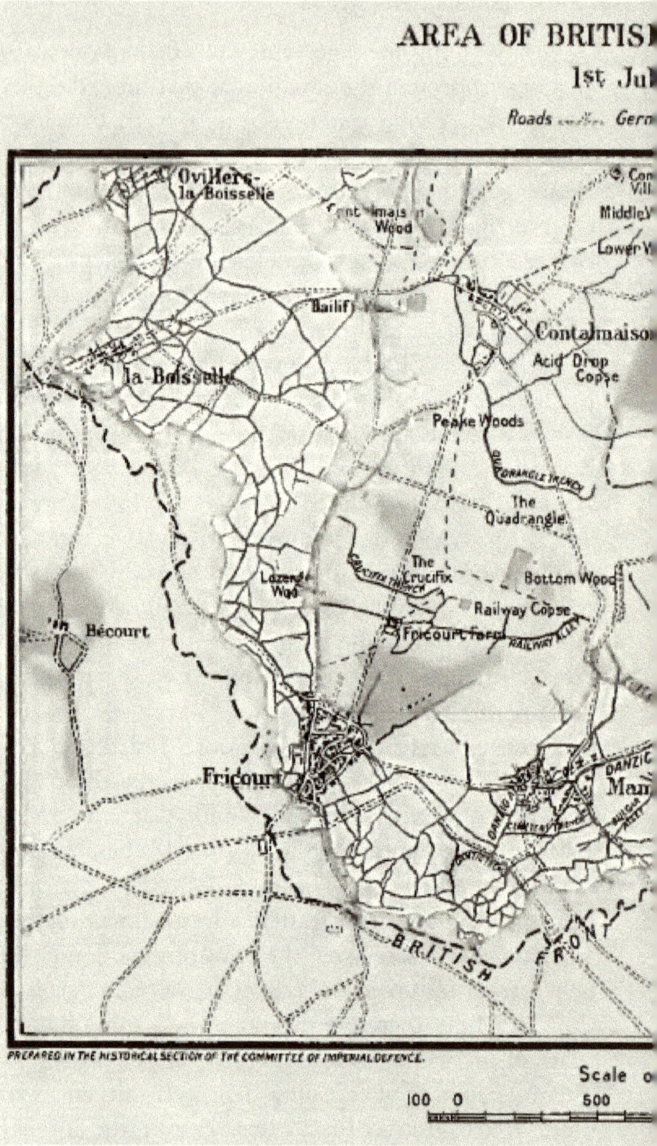

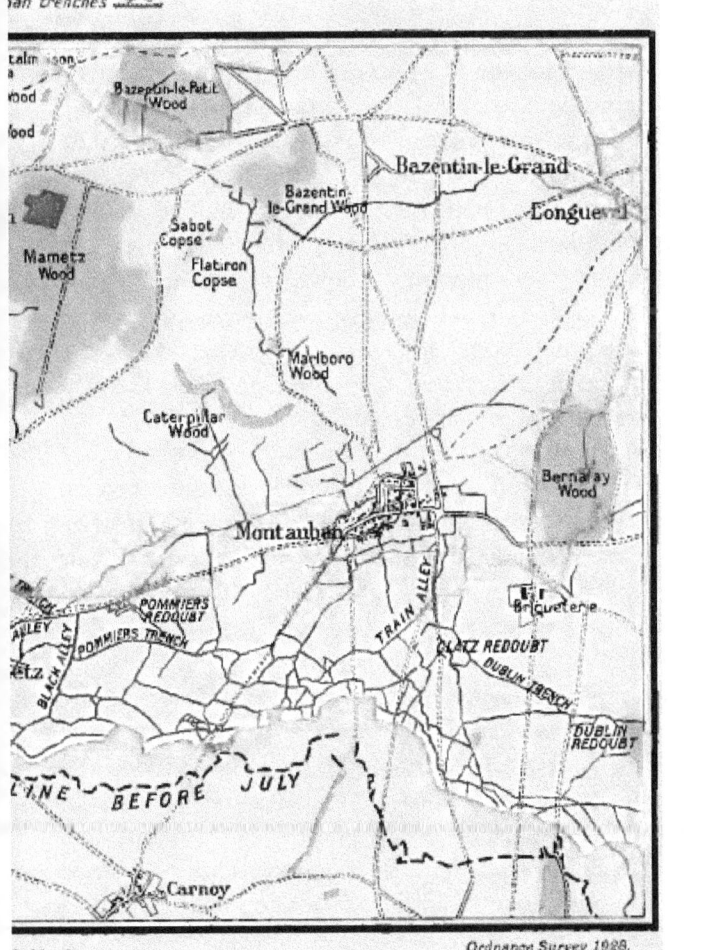

Queens—had made good their objective, and the cavalry had overcome the resistance which held them up. The Morane paid toll for this fine piece of co-operation. It was so badly holed by bullets that the pilot had, reluctantly, to turn for home. Before he did so his observer rapidly sketched the disposition of the German infantry and dropped the plan on the cavalry in a message bag. The cavalry commander said:

> This sketch of the enemy's position was of the greatest value to my gunners.

The further advance of the 7th Division was delayed by enemy counter-attacks from the direction of the Switch line which, striking off from the German second line east of Pozières, wound along the crest in an attenuated 'S' to High Wood, bit off the northern corner of the wood, and continued east along the ridge to Morval. The division, however, got into the wood at about 8.40 p.m., where their red flares, seen through the trees, were promptly reported by a contact patrol observer of No. 3 Squadron. The division worked through the night at the task of clearing the wood.

Meanwhile the cavalry had turned their attention to the German infantry in the crops east of the wood. Making the most of their rare opportunity they charged down on their enemy, speared sixteen of them and captured another thirty-two. When darkness came they fell back slightly and began the consolidation of a line linking up with the XIII Corps at Longueval. At dawn they were withdrawn. Their exhilarating co-operation, made with great precision and dash, had cost no more than two officers and one hundred men in casualties.

Throughout July the 15th the battle continued but on a reduced scale. Delville Wood was taken and held against heavy counter-attacks, and the strong points north of Longueval were the scene of fierce fighting, watched by officers of No. 9 Squadron who helped the artillery to keep down the enemy fire, took photographs, and reported the infantry's movements. A morning F.E.2b patrol of No. 22 Squadron, out to keep a friendly eye on the artillery and contact aeroplanes, found no enemy opposition in the air, and therefore went in search of targets on the ground.

One machine (pilot. Lieutenant E. G. A. Bowen, observer. Second Lieutenant W. S. Mansell) attacked fifty infantrymen near Flers: they scattered leaving some of their number lying on the road. Other troops coming from dug-outs in Flers ran off on the Le Sars road, chased by the machine-gun fire of the F.E. A party of cavalry hiding under trees then caught the pilot's attention, and three bursts of fire were enough to force them from their hiding place, some of the horses bolting riderless away. In the meantime, the second F.E. (pilot, Captain J. G. Swart, observer, Captain H. E. F. Wyncoll) was dispersing other parties of infantry in Flers.

The officers could clearly see many of the enemy fall where they were hit. The pilot then flew south on the look-out for further targets, and attacked, in turn, another small party of men, some wagons, and a gun limber, killing one horse attached to the limber and causing the others to bolt. Both aeroplanes survived strong anti-aircraft and machine-gun fire; their own attacks were helped by the new Buckingham tracer ammunition which was visible to the airmen all the way to the ground.

******

Buckingham tracer ammunition was an improved pattern of a bullet, designed by Mr. J. F. Buckingham of Coventry, which had been adopted by the Naval Air Service early in the war. It combined incendiary qualities with a marked smoke trace. It was designed, chiefly as a sighting aid, for use against other aircraft, and was only incidentally used against troops on the ground.

******

The situation in the Longueval area on the 15th made the position of the troops fighting for possession of the north-west corner of High Wood precarious, and they suffered heavily from shell-fire. In the afternoon a pigeon flew in with a message saying that the enemy were firmly established in the wood, and asking that heavy artillery be turned on a strong machine-gun emplacement in the northern part. From no point within our own lines was it possible to see what was going on in the High Wood area, and at 5.0 p.m. an aeroplane of No. 3 Squadron was sent to find out the exact situation. The observer reported that the British were holding a trench to the west of the wood and were also collected south of the Bazentin-le-Petit road.

From just in the wood on the west side flags were waved in reply to his signals, but on the east side the Germans were in strength and opened rapid fire on the aeroplane. The whole length of the troublesome Switch Trench, which dominated High Wood on the west, was seen to be full of German infantry. Until the Switch Trench was taken the cost of hanging on to High Wood must, it was realised, be exceedingly heavy. The wood, therefore, was wholly evacuated, without enemy interference, by 8.0 a.m. of the 16th.

Whilst the High Wood fighting was in progress in the afternoon of the 15th a fierce attack was made by the III Corps on Pozières. An observer flying over the front to report the struggle saw that the preliminary bombardment had wrecked many buildings, but had done little damage to the trenches commanding the village. As the bombardment lifted he watched the German infantry and machine-gunners come from their dug-outs and cellars. He saw them run down the trenches to their fire stations and open immediate fire. It appeared to him, he said in his report, that the British infantry had not got as close to the position during the bombardment as they might have done, and that this fact gave the German machine-gunners all the time they needed to man their positions. The attack failed and the troops were compelled to fall back, following which Pozières was rebombarded.

On July the 17th Ovillers was captured and the 48th Division moved thence along the spur towards Pozières where the bombardment had now increased to great violence. But the effects of the shelling of the village had been, for the most part, unobserved as rain and mist made flying useless. How disastrous this lack of observation was, was clear from a report made by an observer in a bright interval in the evening of the 17th. The bombardment, he said, had done little military damage. Indeed, the defences of the village had been greatly strengthened with new machine-gun emplacements and barricades. The truth of this statement was tested a little later in the evening when a preliminary infantry attack was completely mastered by the enemy's machine-gun fire. At once the main attack on Pozières, ordered for the morning of the 18th, was cancelled.

The first phase, which had given us a six thousand yard footing on the main ridge, was over. We may pause here to consider what was the effect of the part played by the Royal Flying Corps in the beginnings of the battle. Cooperation with the infantry, or contact patrol, had given results which made it clear that this new demand on the air would be a feature of all future ground operations. Of the devices arranged as signals from the ground, flares had easily proved most useful, the only complaint of air observers being that they had not been lighted in sufficient numbers. This was due partly to a shortage in the supply and partly to a disinclination of some of the troops to light them, since they feared that the possible exposure of their position to the enemy would draw artillery fire.

Another difficulty arose from the fact that when flares were lighted at specified places and times, it could not always be guaranteed that the aeroplane observers would be in a position to see them. Experience indeed showed that the alternative method, by which the infantry did not light the flares until called upon to do so by the aeroplanes, would prove more satisfactory whenever it could be arranged. At first this signal had been made by the observer by lamp or white Very light, but before the first phase had ended it was found that a continuous hoot from the aeroplane on a Klaxon Horn gave a distinctive note which could be readily heard on the ground. The reports of the contact observers left no doubt, however, that most information could be obtained by direct observation from a low height, and that any uncertainty as to the nationality of the troops could usually be set at rest by going low enough to draw fire.

A surprising fact that emerged from the fighting in the first phase was the comparative immunity of the low flying aeroplanes. The Royal Flying Corps was prepared to take extreme risks to give the infantry a helping hand, but the contact pilots and observers found that the German troops were often too distracted to pay serious attention to the air. Actually, no contact aeroplanes were shot down, although many of them were so knocked about that they had to be dismantled and rebuilt. The only machine destroyed in the air was blown up by one of our own barrage shells. That only one was lost in this way was remarkable since most low flying observers told of heavy shells visibly passing them as they went about their work.

The artillery co-operation, hampered by bad weather, was probably as good as it could well have been. The undulating nature of the country added enormously to the calls on the artillery aeroplanes: much of the counter battery work had to rely entirely on observation from above. When the weather stopped flying, as for instance for the Pozières attack on July the 17th, the lack of observation possibly made all the difference to the fate of the assault. The III Corps commander, commenting on the Pozières failure in his diary, comes to the conclusion that:

> Aeroplane observation now appears to be an essential preliminary to a successful attack.

Artillery officers who inspected the ground captured from the enemy were able to collect evidence of the effects of their fire directed from the air, especially against German batteries. On the 16th of July the commander of the X Corps forwarded some notes compiled by one of his officers. These showed that in Bailiff Wood fourteen emplacements had been totally destroyed and thirteen smashed guns abandoned; that several batteries west of Contalmaison Wood had been destroyed; that a number of guns and six railway trucks loaded with timber were lying smashed near Bottom Wood; and that many other broken guns were lying derelict in Mametz and Caterpillar Woods. The chief artillery officer of the 32nd Division testified that:

> The German artillery on our front has been in a great measure destroyed by our aeroplane observation for heavy artillery.

The brilliant advance on the right of the British line, made throughout the first phase by the XIII Corps, was rendered possible by the effectiveness of the support given to the infantry by the artillery behind the corps front. The artillery commander generously passed on the praise which came to him. He wrote to Major A. B. Burdett, the commander of No. 9 Squadron:

> The results obtained were entirely due to the gallant efforts of your observers and pilots.

General Trenchard, in his daily report to the commander-in-chief, had stated, on the 9th of July, that his policy was to try to keep German pilots from crossing our lines or from interfering with the work of the corps pilots and observers. How successful he was is brought out by the fact that on no single occasion were the co-operating aeroplanes prevented by enemy aircraft from doing the duty allotted to them. Furthermore, although it was impossible to seal the air so that no hostile aeroplane could break through, the offensive patrols over the enemy's back areas kept the German airmen so occupied that the assistance which they were able to give to their own artillery and infantry in the first phase of the battle was negligible.

To sum up, the contribution of the Royal Flying Corps was a double one. First, the direct help to the army. Pilots and observers photographed the whole area of attack; they reported on the condition of the wire and trenches and, at times, on the probable strength of the opposition which would be met with; they did much to keep the various headquarters in touch with the attacking troops, thus ensuring that the attack should not fail for mere lack of knowledge and, above all, that the men should not suffer from their own artillery fire if their progress was ahead of their time-table; and they took a hand in the fighting by making bombing and machine-gun attacks from a low height.

In co-operation with the artillery they helped, both before and during the struggle, to neutralize the fire of many German batteries, to destroy trenches and strong points, and to snap up any opportunities which were offered by open movements of the enemy. Of direct importance, also, was the spirit of defencelessness which they instilled into the German troops. A German officer says:

> The infantry had had no training whatsoever in the science of defence against low-flying aircraft, and, moreover, had no faith in their ability to shoot these machines down if they were determined to do so. In consequence of this they were seized with a fear almost amounting to panic, a fear which was fostered by the incessant activity and hostility of the enemy's aeroplanes. (Neumann, *The German Air Force in the Great War*).

Secondly, they helped the army, indirectly, by denying a similar latitude to the German air service. Where the enemy was without ground observation his artillery fire went, for the most part, unobserved. Our own battery commanders were not hampered by the fear, ever present to the enemy, that aeroplanes were above waiting to note their tell-tale flashes. The morale of the British infantry before they went into the line suffered nothing from aircraft bombing. Moreover, when the infantry moved up to attack they could do so in the knowledge that no spying aeroplanes would soon turn the German guns on to them; and they could go into battle reasonably assured that any rapid enemy movements to counter them would not go unnoticed by their own airmen. In a word the army enjoyed all the advantages that a local air superiority brings.

The Second Phase.

The second phase of the battle—a tense struggle for the main ridge—endured until the middle of September. The opening of the phase coincides with a marked change in the air situation. No longer is our superiority unchallenged. On the 19th of July the German First Army, which had been temporarily dispersed, was resuscitated under General Fritz von Below. This army became responsible for the right wing of the Second Army, along the front from Hannescamps to near Peronne. Meanwhile air reinforcements for the First Army had been coming into the area. The new units were three reconnaissance flights (*Feldflieger-Abteilungen*) of six aeroplanes each, one artillery flight (*Ar-*

tillerieflieger-Abteilung) of four aeroplanes, one bomber-fighter squadron (*Kampfgeschwader*) of approximately thirty-six aeroplanes, and one bomber-fighter flight (*Kampfstaffel*), consisting of probably eight aeroplanes.

In addition, the First Army, on its formation, took over from the Second Army, two reconnaissance flights (a total of fifteen aeroplanes), two artillery flights (eight aeroplanes), a bomber-fighter squadron (forty-three aeroplanes), and a bomber-fighter flight (eight aeroplanes). Further, by the 19th of July, two new fighter squadrons (*Kampfeinsitzer-Staffeln*) had been formed by concentrating single-seater fighters specially withdrawn from various artillery and reconnaissance units. The nominal strength of these squadrons was twelve aeroplanes each.

This gives the German First Army, on the opening of the second phase, a total air strength of one hundred and sixty-four aeroplanes, excluding those in reserve. From now onwards, the German air service on the Somme was consistently strengthened. To avoid discontinuity in the narrative of the intricate ground fighting, the air co-operation over the immediate battle front will first be dealt with to the end of the phase. How the enemy airmen, in spite of the reinforcements, continued to be fought and drawn away from the interlocking armies by our offensive and bombing formations must be told later in the chapter.

The fiercest fighting in the second phase was on the British right. At Delville Wood and at Longueval our lines formed a sharp salient overlooked by the enemy from Guillemont round to High Wood. The position offered the German artillery many opportunities for well-observed concentric fire, not only on the wood and the village, but also on the congested area behind the front. It was essential, before any further great progress could be hoped for, to bring our right flank into line with the centre. This meant taking Guillemont, Falfemont Farm, and Leuze Wood, and then Ginchy and Bouleaux Wood. Plans of attack were ready in the middle of July but bad weather intervened. The weather conditions were at their worst in the third week of the month, and the consequent failure of air co-operation led to various postponements of the attack, and so gave the enemy a breathing space during which he could strengthen his defences.

Another point making for delay was the unsatisfactory nature of the situation at Longueval. On the 18th of July a German counter-attack on Delville Wood was delivered in such force that it carried, too, the northern half of Longueval which had only been fully cleared again that morning. Through the 19th there was bitter fighting, watched from above, in the Scottish named streets of the village. Observers elicited, by frequent questioning, the fluctuating positions of the attacking battalions; many of the answers were spelt out on the ground panels and were easily read in the air. The struggle in Longueval continued next day, the 20th, but the air observers could report no headway against the stubborn enemy defence.

To help the Longueval attack a dawn assault had been made on the 20th, through mist, by the XV Corps at High Wood. Observers of No. 3 Squadron, who flew over the wood, caught glimpses of shadowy figures and flares and reported that, except in the northern part of the wood, the attacking troops had reached their objectives. Consolidation went on in the wood all day: in the evening the northern corner was taken but was lost again to a counter-attack.

The first general attack of the second phase took place in the early hours of Sunday, the 23rd, after two days bombardment along the whole front. As has been stated the enemy made full use of the delay caused by the bad weather. The mist, however, did not wholly obscure his preparations, and observers caught fleeting views of new positions. On the 21st of July No. 4 Squadron reported new entrenchments round Le Sars and Courcelette, and No. 3 Squadron discovered an extensive new line between Le Transloy and Warlencourt, and a doubling of the third line between Eaucourt l'Abbaye and Flers.

A morning patrol of No. 9 Squadron on July the 22nd reported in some detail on the strength and positions of the fortifications at Ginchy, where new digging was seen to be in progress behind the village. The officers also inspected the whole of the entrenchments from Combles to Gueudecourt and testified to their elaborate strength, but stated that nowhere were they occupied. Flers, they said, was strongly held, but they saw no traffic on any road. Of more immediate importance was a discovery made by Second Lieutenant T. S. Pearson, who was flying with Captain C. H. B. Blount of No. 34 Squadron.

★★★★★★

No. 34 Squadron equipped with B.E.2e's arrived at Allonville under the command of Major J. A. Chamier, on the 15th of July, from England. Of its seventeen observers, all except three were trained artillery or infantry officers who had transferred to the Royal Flying Corps, and its pilots had had more than the usual amount of training. The squadron was posted to the Third Wing of the IV Brigade and began work on July the 19th for the III Corps.

★★★★★★

There had been rumours of new digging in advance of that part of the Switch line which was to be the main objective of the III Corps in the coming general attack. But up to the morning of Saturday the 22nd there had been no confirmation as fog had shrouded the whole position from the air. On this morning, however, these officers dived clear of the mist north of Bazentin-le-Petit, and came upon a new trench which had been thrown up several hundred yards in advance of the Switch line, roughly parallel to our forward positions between Bazentin-le-Petit and High Wood (see map following). This intermediate line, which was connected with the Switch line by a communication trench along the Martinpuich-Bazentin road, was seen to be strongly manned by the enemy. This information, it was realised, completely altered the tactical situation in this sector, and on landing Pearson was sent at once to III Corps headquarters to explain all that he had seen. On his information the orders for the III Corps attack were amended to make the new trench, instead of the Switch line, the first objective of the 19th Division.

The bombardment along the whole front from Trônes Wood to Pozières began at seven o'clock that evening, and at half past one on the Sunday morning the infantry advanced. But they found the enemy in great strength everywhere, not only in his newly constructed trenches, but also in shell holes in front of his main positions, where he had spread a network of machine-gun posts. The brilliant tactical handling of his machine-guns, indeed, brought about the failure of the attack, except at Pozières, where a compensating advance was made by the Reserve Army over the tumble of battered trenches and buildings.

★★★★★★

For the Pozières attack, the I Anzac Corps, newly placed under General Gough, had taken over the sector in front of the village hitherto held by the III Corps. By the morning of the 25th the Australians had captured the village and the cemetery and had advanced along the trenches to the north-east. 'C' Flight of No. 7 Squadron had come south with the Australians and had been temporarily attached to No. 4 Squadron on July the 19th. No. 4 Squadron thereupon extended its area to cover the Anzac front.

★★★★★★

The failure of the advance on the Fourth Army front on the 23rd had clearly shown how necessary it was to drive in the German forward machine-gun posts and to capture the new trenches, before the

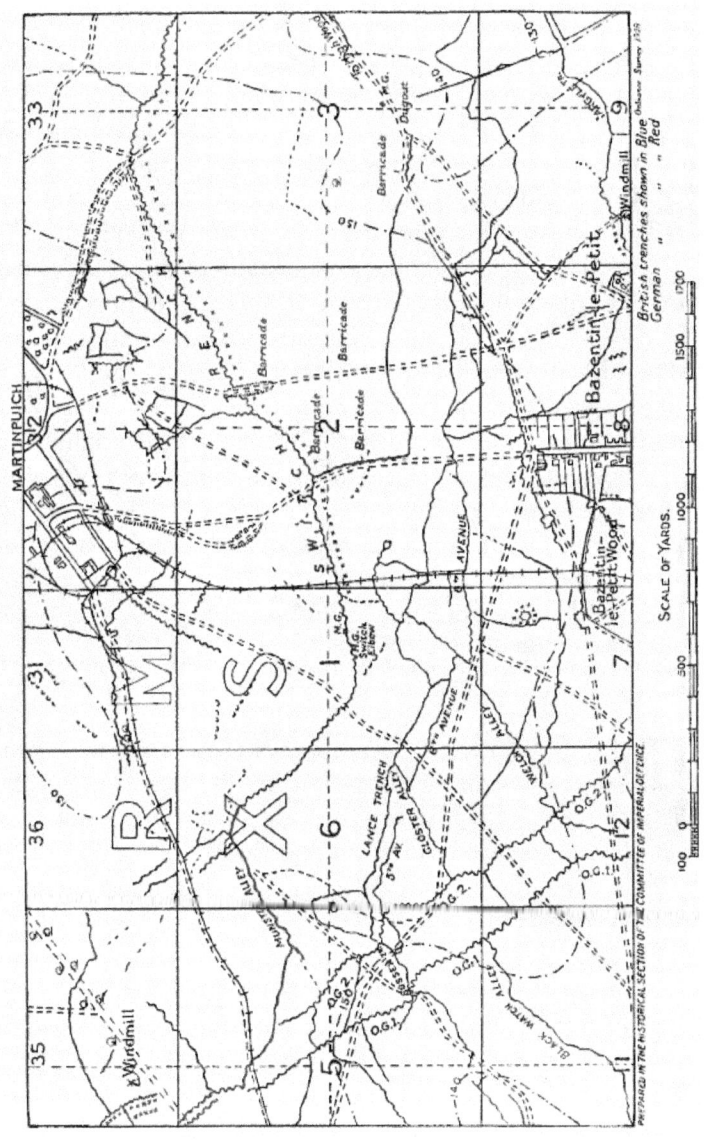

MAIN ENEMY POSITIONS
NORTH OF BAZENTIN-LE-PETIT.
30th July, 1916.

next general attack. An attempt to do this on the III Corps front on the 24th failed. On July the 25th operation orders were issued for this corps to attack again after dusk that evening. The orders, which had already gone out, allotted to the 1st Division the preliminary task of taking the old German communication trench known as Munster Alley. The division was then to proceed to the capture of part of the Switch line. Soon after midday the situation was suddenly altered, when an air report from No. 34 Squadron was received by the corps commander, showing that an important new German trench line had been constructed from Munster Alley, near its junction with the old German second line, westwards.

This new trench crossed the old second line and joined the German first line so as to form a prolongation of the Switch Trench. At once a telegram was sent out from III Corps headquarters modifying the plan of attack and instructing the 1st Division to concentrate its whole effort on the taking of Munster Alley. But the newly discovered German position proved strong enough to hold up all attacks, and the sinister Munster Alley was the scene of continuous hand to hand bombing and grenade fighting. Not until the 28th of July was the weather clear enough for air photography, and the prints that were delivered to the Corps headquarters on the following day revealed for the first time the complete intricacy of the new trench system and, in the words of the corps commander:

> Accounted for the obstinate resistance to any considerable advance up Munster Alley.

Had it been possible to produce these photographs earlier the character of the fighting must have been different. Such an instance showing the handicap under which the infantry fight when they are denied a clear picture of their task, emphasises the value of the routine work of photographing the defences. More serious, however, than the difficulty of getting photographs, was the effect of the weather on the air co-operation with the artillery.

Many of the new German battery positions taken up after the British advance on the 14th of July remained undiscovered. The III Corps artillery commander laments, for instance, on the 25th of July that he can do little to relieve the heavy shelling on the battery positions of the 19th Divisional artillery as 'we do not yet' know where the hostile batteries are. This must go on, 'as far as one can see, until the weather clears and the mist goes.' But observers of Nos. 3 and 34

Squadrons, watching through the mists, gradually plotted the positions of active guns on this front, and the artillery commander was able to say a day or two later that their information might 'save the situation which has become critical as regards counter-battery work.'

The position on the 28th of July may be thus summarized: the XIII Corps had wrested from the enemy what remained to him of Delville Wood; the XV Corps had taken Longueval village and had advanced their line in High Wood; the III Corps had a footing along Munster Alley; and, on the left, the Reserve Army were through and beyond Pozières. The main problem still was to swing forward the right flank. In conjunction, therefore, with a French advance north of the Somme the XIII Corps attacked Guillemont and Falfemont Farm to the south-east of the village on the morning of the 30th of July. The infantry started off at a quarter to five in a white fog which did not disperse until about ten o'clock so that No. 9 Squadron were helpless up to that hour. The Royal Scots got through the village, but receiving no support from either of their flanks were compelled to withdraw, and the net result of the day was a slight advance north of Maltz Horn Farm as far as Arrow Head Copse.

After the weather cleared No. 9 Squadron had every available aeroplane out for artillery, contact, and photographic work; plates were exposed from Guillemont to Falfemont Farm and reports of the positions of our own and of the enemy troops were brought back. The German artillery had increased to such an extent that ground arrangements to keep touch with the attack were becoming more and more unreliable, a fact which threw an increasing responsibility on the air, a responsibility which the contact observers shared with the carrier pigeons.

It increased, too, the urgency and importance of counter-battery work. In the improved weather which August brought, leeway was made up and the German shelling along the whole Fourth Army front showed a daily decrease. On the 8th of August the attack on Guillemont was renewed: it began well, but as our troops passed through the village the Germans came from their colony of subterranean passages and cut them off. As in the previous attack the men who penetrated through the village received no help from their flanking battalions, which failed to make progress.

Second Lieutenant M. G. Begg of No. 9 Squadron, flying in the morning for two and a half hours, sketched on a map the points in and about Guillemont where he had seen mirrors flashing from the backs of the British troops and dropped his map on the corps headquarters.

He was sent up again in the afternoon and located the headquarters of three of the attacking battalions. The experiences of the day, however, made it clear that Guillemont was too strong to be taken by a local attack and a more elaborate combined effort was therefore planned.

Meanwhile, on the 12th of August, there was an offensive movement along the British front in concert with an attack by the French. Minor gains were made particularly on the Reserve Army front, where the lines beyond Pozières were pushed forward within a short distance of Mouquet Farm. At a quarter past eight next morning, a massing of troops along 1,500 yards of the German front line trenches near the Farm, in preparation for a counterattack, was seen by Second Lieutenant E. O'Hanlon flying with Sergeant H. L. Pateman of No. 4 Squadron. The observer at once dropped a message for the II Corps headquarters who ordered an immediate barrage. (The II Corps headquarters had relieved the X Corps headquarters in the line on July the 24th). Within a few minutes of their return to Mouquet Farm the airmen had the satisfaction of seeing the enemy line quiver and leap, a solid mass of flame and smoke. After a hurricane ten minutes the fire was reduced and when the smoke had cleared a little the observer was able to report that the German concentration had vanished, and the barrage was then called off.

The combined attack planned after the Guillemont failure on the 8th of August was made on the 18th, along the whole line from Thiepval to the Somme. The Reserve Army with heavy fighting made slight progress. Before the attack on the II Corps front, launched at 5.0 p.m., No. 4 Squadron was called on to get photographs of the line for the artillery commander, whose five-day bombardment had aimed at complete isolation of the corps objectives. Final pictures were required with a view to readjusting the fire, if necessary, immediately before the attack. The clouds were low, but some successful photographs were taken from under them.

Once the attack was started, contact observers of the squadron followed and reported its progress. On the right of the II Corps the Anzac corps made their attack at Mouquet Farm and at Munster Alley at 9.0 p.m. The advanced positions of the front of this corps had not been definitely known at the corps headquarters in the morning, but an aeroplane of No. 7 Squadron, sent up on early trench reconnaissance, had cleared up the uncertainties before the attack began.

******

The remainder of No. 7 Squadron arrived at Warloy from Bailleul on the 30th of July and reabsorbed 'C' Flight which had been attached, temporarily, to No. 4 Squadron. No. 7 Squadron took over the air work for the I Anzac Corps with which it had previously co-operated in the Ypres Salient.

******

On the Fourth Army front the III Corps, who attempted to complete the capture of the intermediate line north of Bazentin-le-Petit and to extend their positions about High Wood, could not maintain their gains. On their right, however, the XV Corps at Delville Wood had better success. The infantry of this corps left their trenches at 2.45 p.m., and the first message and map were dropped by an observer of No. 3 Squadron on corps headquarters at 3.55 p.m.: they gave the infantry positions as signalled to the aeroplane by the battalion headquarters, and some information on the strength of the enemy in trenches and shell holes. The corps operation orders had instructed the infantry to light their flares, which were of a vivid green, at 7.30 p.m., and an observer over them at this time was able to plot very clearly on a map the whole front line reached at that hour by the 14th Division, and part of the front of the 33rd Division.

The map was received at corps headquarters at 7.55 p.m., and showed that most of the objectives of the 14th Division had been gained but that the 33rd Division had been less successful. Twenty minutes later another observer of No. 3 Squadron confirmed this information which was passed on to the divisional headquarters. The accuracy of these reports was commented on by the corps commander; the detail with which the observers were able to follow the line resulted from the fact that flares were lighted with more continuity and completeness than in any previous attack on this corps front.

The attack against Guillemont by the XIV Corps, which had relieved the XIII Corps in that sector, had begun at the same hour in the afternoon. On the left the 24th Division reached the fringe of the village and secured and held the station against numerous counter-attacks. The fighting on the front of this division was reported during a two and a half hour flight by Second Lieutenant Scaife (pilot. Lieutenant B. T. Coller) of No. 9 Squadron. During the flight Scaife called for fire on a closely manned trench north of Ginchy, and he sent down corrections until the shells were getting direct hits on the trench. Other observers of the squadron were over the area without break until dark, and were successful in locating signalling panels and ground sheets which gave the positions of the headquarters of the attacking battalions; their reports showed that the right division of the XIV Corps had failed to secure their objectives. The flying officers enlivened their work throughout the day by diving to attack parties of German infantry not only behind the front, but also in the trenches.

On August the 19th there were indications from the air that, as a result of the previous day's fighting, the enemy was readjusting his line farther back and that our infantry patrols could profitably be pushed forward in various places. Further enemy readjustments during the next two days were cleared up by reports sent in by the contact observers of Nos. 34, 3, and 9 Squadrons, many of whom made their observations from 500 feet.

On the 22nd of August the Reserve Army pushed forward its lines at the Leipzig Salient, and the Australians bombed their way to the edge of what was once Mouquet Farm. The 1st Australian divisional war diary says:

> The 7th Squadron R.F.C. have been called upon daily during the operations for photographs, and have supplied them about 4 to 5 hours after the demand. These photographs have been of the greatest assistance in locating our own and the enemy's position, and have formed the basis on which orders have been issued.

Next evening and again on the morning of the 24th the centre of the fiercest fighting shifted to Guillemont, where there were determined attempts to retake the ground we had won on the 18th. The attacks were everywhere repulsed, but they had the effect of making an assault on the village, which the XIV Corps was preparing for the afternoon of the 24th, impossible. The advance on this day was confined, therefore, to the front of the XV Corps, where a further stretch of Delville Wood, as well as much ground to the north and west of it, was captured, and to the front of the Reserve Army which was pushed closer to Thiepval.

A feature of the XV Corps advance was the completeness once again of the story brought back by the contact observers of No. 3 Squadron, made possible by the lighting, everywhere along the front gained, of enough red flares to define the line to the overlooking air observers, with almost perfect clearness. At one point, north of Delville Wood, an observer (Second Lieutenant F. E. S. Phillips) saw that at 6-40 p.m. the line of our infantry, marked by the blazing of fourteen flares, was still under shrapnel fire from our own artillery. He flew back at once and dropped an urgent message giving the information to corps headquarters. The barrage was ultimately lifted a hundred yards. (The 2nd Worcesters and the 16th K.R.R.'s had, indeed, overshot their objectives as the obliterated enemy trenches could not be recognised amongst the mass of shell holes).

The pilot returned to the fighting, and the observer completed his map and dropped this and a further message which were received at Corps headquarters at 8.0 p.m. The map showed that a part of the 14th Division was held up on the right of Delville wood. The wood was finally cleared of the enemy by the division next morning, August the 25th, and the forward progress of the troops to their various objectives was once more followed and reported from the air, step by step.

Throughout the next week there was comparative quiet on the ground, where small but steady progress was made and counter-attacks defeated. In the air, too, thunderstorms brought a lull. During this period there was a reorganisation of the flying squadrons on the Reserve Army front. On the 2nd of August No. 32 (fighting) Squadron had been attached to the Fifteenth Wing and, as the Wing Commander was fully occupied in directing the work of the corps squadrons (Nos. 4, 7, and 15) and kite balloon sections (Nos. 1, 11, and 13), it was deemed necessary to form the additional Flying Corps brigade which had already been sanctioned. Consequently, on the 27th of August these units were grouped under the command of Brigadier-General C. A. H. Longcroft to form the V Brigade.

★★★★★★

A further fighting squadron, No. 23, joined the brigade on the 5th of September, and, together with No. 32 Squadron, formed the Twenty-Second Wing on the 14th of September. In addition. No. 18 Kite Balloon Section came under the orders of the brigade on the 8th of September.

★★★★★★

Just at this time there was an interesting attempt at night reconnaissance by a specially constructed naval airship of the 'S.S.' type. This was the S.S. 40 which had first been flown to France on the 6th of July 1916. The ship, however, had been sent home again for the fitting of a larger envelope (the original one giving insufficient height), and eventually returned on the 10th of August with an all-black envelope of 83,000 cubic feet capacity which, on test, took the ship to a height of 8,000 feet. On the night of the 28th/ 29th of August the airship, carrying a Royal Flying Corps observer, made a four hour reconnaissance flight over the enemy lines. The observations were made from about 8,000 feet, but little of value was reported.

******

The airship was too vulnerable to go much lower and 8,000 feet was too high for night reconnaissance of any value. After two further reconnaissance attempts, the airship was sent back to England on the 22nd of October 1916.

******

The execrable weather culminated in a violent storm on the 29th of August. On the aerodrome of No. 21 Squadron a hangar was blown away and five B.E.12's were totally destroyed and nine others damaged. This squadron had only returned to the Somme front four days earlier after being re-equipped at Boisdinghem with its new machines. An aeroplane of No. 34 Squadron, caught in the storm over enemy territory, did not return.

At noon on the 3rd of September, after two days of preparation in which trench reconnaissances, counterbattery co-operation, and photography were the features of the air work, there was an attack along the whole front between the two rivers and across the Ancre as far as Beaumont Hamel. On the Reserve Army and III Corps fronts gains were made, but were lost to German counterattacks except near Mouquet Farm where the Australians maintained a slight advance.

The XV Corps had early success at Ginchy. Before their advance began an observer of No. 3 Squadron had examined the enemy trenches about the village and had reported no concentrations. Nowhere was the aeroplane fired on, and at one point where the pilot flew low over huddled Germans he concluded from their complete inactivity that they were corpses. Another observer of this squadron. Second Lieutenant F. E. S. Phillips piloted by Second Lieutenant L. C. Kidd, watched the beginning of the attack and saw men of the 7th Division enter the village.

At one o'clock he watched them fighting in the centre of the ruins, and soon afterwards saw them advancing in open and irregular order towards the eastern outskirts. North of the village he saw Germans massed in Switch Trench, and others striving to get to the village down the communication trench known as Lager Lane. He worried them with machine-gun fire until his drums were exhausted and sent an urgent wireless message calling up the artillery. He flew back to the corps report centre and dropped a bag with a map and, although the aeroplane had been damaged by bullets, the pilot returned to Ginchy where our shrapnel and heavy shells were now dropping amongst the Germans in the trenches.

Before the aeroplane left the line at 2.40 p.m. the observer saw our troops on the eastern edge of Ginchy, so that we now occupied most of the village. But not for long. The German troops who had been reported by the observer massing in the trenches to the north succeeded, despite our artillery fire, in making a strong counter-attack at three o'clock and, although detachments held stubbornly to various parts of the village, the division was pushed out bit by bit, and by the evening held only the western outskirts.

The greatest advance of the day was made on the right. The progress in this area may be followed in a typical contact patrol report of No. 9 Squadron (pilot. Second Lieutenant E. R. H. Pollak, observer. Second Lieutenant T. E. G. Scaife), made between noon and 3.0 p.m. The flying officers watched our men leave their trenches and move on Guillemont. They saw the heavily pressed Germans sending up a stream of lights—signals of distress. They watched our troops attack and drive them from their positions, and south of the village they saw khaki figures occupy, in force, the trench connecting up with Wedge Wood. Soon after two, British discs were flashing along the whole eastern edge of Guillemont. Half an hour later the officers saw that Wedge Wood was strongly occupied and that we were established along the Ginchy road as far as the Leuze Wood-Guillemont cross road.

South of Wedge Wood, however, at Falfemont Farm, where the 5th Division had attacked three hours before the main assault, the enemy was still in possession. At one point near the farm the flying officers could see, showing up plainly against the white chalk background of a shell hole, about fifty men of the Royal Warwicks pinned to their ground by a German machine-gun detachment in a trench just in front of them. They dived and attacked the Germans with their Lewis guns to such effect that our men were at once able to advance. Later reports by observers of No. 9 Squadron showed that Falfemont Farm had resisted all efforts to take it, but that farther north we had extended our gains along the Ginchy road north of the Guillemont-Leuze Wood cross road and that the whole position had been consolidated.

Next afternoon, Monday September the 4th, the 5th Division attacked Falfemont Farm again. No. 9 Squadron saw the frontal attack held up by machine-gun fire, but saw some of the troops bombing their way slowly round the northern end of the farm. One of the air-observers watched a crowd of Germans come out of the quarry north-east of the farm and run out to man shell holes to oppose these troops. He sent out a wireless call to the artillery, and within a few minutes a curtain of fire dropped on the quarry and its outlying shell holes. Further reports from No. 9 Squadron in the evening showed that the left brigade of the 5th Division had pushed as far as the western edge of Leuze Wood. Through the rain of the night, Falfemont Farm was being taken piece by piece; it was completely in our hands by the morning of the 7th. By the evening of that day, too, we occupied most of Leuze Wood, and the air reports showed that the enemy, thrown into some confusion by our success, had scraped a hurried irregular line of trenches connecting shell holes between Leuze Wood and the railway south-east of Ginchy.

The four days fighting from the 3rd of September had given better results than any of the operations since the 14th of July. The possibilities, especially on the right, were now distinctly promising, and preparations for a further attack on Ginchy went ahead. On the 9th of September the whole Fourth Army sprang into action once again from Leuze Wood to High Wood. Between Ginchy and High Wood the attack failed except for a small advance south-east of the wood, but the whole of Ginchy was captured and gratifying progress was made north of Leuze Wood. When the infantry went over the top late in the afternoon a haze lay over the battlefield, but three contact observers of No. 9 Squadron followed the taking of Ginchy in detail and reported each stage of the progress north of Leuze Wood.

The captures of the day marked the end of the second phase of the campaign. We had now overrun the elaborate fortifications of the main positions. From the road above Mouquet Farm round to Delville Wood we were looking down from the forward crest of the ridge on the slopes beyond, and along the remainder of the ridge as far as Leuze Wood we had a firm footing. In front of us now were improvised positions manned by an enemy whose morale had been lowered by the relentless fighting, and the knowledge that his best endeavours in positions that had been perfected over a period of two years had failed to stem the advancing tide of the British armies.

We have followed the fighting through the eyes of the observers of the corps squadrons doing their vital jobs of contact patrol, artillery spotting, trench reconnaissance, and photography. The balloon observers were in the air day and night for long stretches and reinforced the work of the aeroplanes. General von Below, the German First Army commander, in a memorandum written after the battle deals with the moral effect of the aeroplane observation for the British artillery and goes on to say:

> The innumerable balloons, hanging like grapes in clusters over the enemy's lines, produced a similar effect, for the troops thought that individual men and machine-guns could be picked up and watched by them and subjected to fire with observation.

The balloons, in common with the corps aeroplanes, worked with little fear of attack from enemy airmen; they were a target for the German artillery, but their worst enemy at this time was the weather which often made their observation uncomfortably difficult. At times the weather brought disaster. On the 20th of August the balloon of No. 1 Section broke away in a high wind and was carried towards the trenches. The two observers, Captain B. H. Radford, and Second Lieutenant P. B. Moxon, who had been registering artillery of the V Corps, hurriedly threw overboard their instruments and maps before jumping themselves. Moxon landed safely, but Radford, whose parachute failed to open, was killed. As Basil Hallam he had been a figure of the London stage on the outbreak of war, where his most popular song had emphasised the lighter qualities of the country's youth. It was not unfitting that many who had applauded his lesser part should be silent witnesses of his last act.

The Bombing Offensive.

It must now be told how it was possible for the Royal Flying Corps to do its work for the army little hindered by the German air service. This was brought about in two ways—by seeking out and fighting the enemy's aeroplanes far over his own lines and by creating such a threat to the vitals of his communications, through incessant bombing, that he was compelled to use up much of his fighting strength in defence. The activity of the German air force in the battles of the Somme may be represented by a steep ascending curve, governed by the arrival in the area of new squadrons. This curve would show sharp accentuations about the third week in July and again at the beginning of September.

The July increase was coincident with the arrival of the first big air reinforcements on the front, whilst the September increase followed the drastic change in the German direction of the war. On the 29th of August General von Falkenhayn was succeeded as Chief of the General Staff by Field-Marshal von Hindenburg who had General von

Ludendorff as his Quartermaster-General. Hindenburg, recognising the extreme gravity of the position in the west, ordered the immediate suspension of the Verdun offensive and began a defensive concentration on the Somme front. A thinning of the German air forces at Verdun and on all other fronts began at once, and, by the middle of October 1916, when the air concentration reached its peak, more than a third of the whole German air force was opposed to the British and French at the Somme.

We may consider first the measure and effects of the bombing. This had not only the result, as has been said, of pinning much of the attention of the enemy airmen to their own vulnerable centres, but it inflicted material damage which influenced, in greater or less degree, the day to day operations. Equally important was the wearing effect of the air attacks on the enemy's spirit of resistance. The statements of prisoners captured through the battle are monotonous in their insistence on the feeling of helpless irritation which the bombing caused. The billets and dumps behind the immediate battle front were visited most often. The IV Brigade, concerned as it was in giving its full support to the army, could do no systematic bombing, but the two-seater squadron, No. 22, of its army wing used any time left over from its reconnaissance, photographic, and patrol work to attack the German billets with phosphorus and twenty-pound bombs.

The squadrons of the Fifteenth Wing, working for the Reserve Army which was acting as the pivot for the main advance, found time to make occasional raids on Grandcourt, Miraumont, Courcelette, Le Sars, and Le Barque. But the main bombing, in the area south of the Ancre, fell to the Martinsydes (No. 27 Squadron), the R.E.7's (No. 21 Squadron), and the B.E.12's (No. 19 Squadron) of the headquarter wing.

******

No. 19 Squadron arrived from England on July 30th and took the place of No. 21 Squadron, which had gone temporarily to Boisdinghem on July 28th to be re-equipped. The B.E.12's of No. 19 Squadron were fitted with the Vickers interrupter gear to give machine-gun fire through the propeller. No. 21 Squadron was re-equipped with B.E.12's similarly fitted.

******

The normal load for each bombing aeroplane was two 112-lb. bombs or eight twenty-pounders. The villages along the Bapaume-Peronne road, such as Beaulencourt, Le Transloy, and Sailly-Saillisel, were usually filled with troops and stores and were repeatedly attacked. Le Transloy, perhaps, suffered most. Explosions and fires amongst the houses were, time and again, reported by the bombers. The nearer congested villages of Le Barque, Ligny-Thilloy, and Thilloy were also severely bombed, especially after the arrival of No. 19 Squadron.

Beyond the Bapaume-Peronne road were the two great feeding railways of the front coming south from Cambrai. At Marcoing, about six miles south-west of Cambrai, a branch line leaves the main Peronne line for Bapaume. At Epehy, some eight miles farther south, a second winding branch line goes off to the north-west, to connect with the Bapaume line at Vélu. The three junctions of the triangle, Marcoing, Epehy, and Vélu, and the stations at Bapaume and Cambrai were the main bombing objectives on the railway system. The raids on these places stung the enemy to such an extent that the bombing formations were attacked over their area with greater determination than over any other points behind the front. This resistance was made easier by the proximity of important German aerodromes.

In the afternoon of the 30th of July eight Martinsydes of No. 27 Squadron which bombed Epehy junction were attacked, out and home, and lost two of their number. Seven pilots of the same squadron, flying this time with an escort of four of No. 70 Squadron's Sopwiths, went off in the evening to bomb Marcoing. A thick mist closed over the lines as the aeroplanes crossed, and the pilots soon became detached from one another. Only two got as far as Marcoing. Let one of them, Second Lieutenant R. H. C. Usher, tell what happened, he says in his report:

> The patrol seemed to break up just as we were crossing the lines. As I didn't see any signals to return and as I still had a Sopwith with me I went on to Marcoing and dropped my bombs both of which fell in the village—I turned quickly round and almost ran into an L.V.G., I gave him a drum and he went down underneath me, I saw the Sopwith take him on and whilst I was changing drums I was attacked again in front by a Roland, I gave him a drum and at the same time I heard a machine-gun behind me, looked round and I saw three Rolands on my tail. I was hit in the leg almost immediately, but managed to give them a drum of my side gun and they went away, my engine started spluttering and I saw a hole in my petrol tank—my engine stopped so I started gliding down thinking I should have

to land—petrol was flowing all over my left leg so I put my left knee over the hole in petrol tank. It struck me that by pumping I might be able to get a little pressure, by this time I was about 200 feet up—the engine started and I was then about 15 miles from our lines, I kept pumping hard all the time and managed to just keep enough engine to keep going—I thought I should have to land three or four times, once I had actually flattened out to land but my engine just picked up in time—I came back to the lines for about 15 miles at an average height of 50 feet.

I had lost myself and was so low, that I could see very little of the country, I then picked up a "Horace" French biplane that was flying low and followed him and eventually landed at Moreuil aerodrome—crashing the machine on landing—I was feeling very weak as I had lost a lot of blood and was exhausted by having to pump so long. After having engaged the first machine I did not see anything of the Sopwith. During the time that I was flying so low I was subject to a lot of rifle and machine-gun fire.

******

The Sopwith pilot, who returned safely, had fought the enemy two-seater within 1,000 feet of the ground, where it was lost in the mist. Flight Lieutenant Usher, the Rugby footballer, was killed in an aeroplane accident, June 5th, 1924.

******

Inside the railway triangle, Havrincourt Wood, reported to conceal troops within its shades, was an important bombing objective, but it took heavy toll of the raiding machines. On August the 26th five of No. 19 Squadron's B.E.12's encountered a storm after raiding the wood, and not one of them got home. Five days later four bombers of No. 27 Squadron were shot down in a fierce fight after dropping their bombs in the wood. On September the 2nd No. 19 Squadron, after releasing fifty-six twenty-pounders over bivouacs in the wood, were heavily attacked, but were extricated from a difficult position by the daring of their leader, Captain Ian H. D. Henderson. (Only son of Lieutenant-General Sir David Henderson, G.O.C. Royal Flying Corps. Killed flying at Turnberry 21st June 1918).

The most ambitious raids of this period, however, were made by No. 27 Squadron to objectives far beyond Cambrai. On the 28th of July four Martinsydes of the squadron dropped two 112-lb. and eight

20-lb. bombs on ammunition sheds and rolling stock at Mons, leaving four fires burning as they turned for home. They got without incident. On August the 3rd they went farther over, to the Ronet sidings at Namur and to the airship sheds at Cognelée. At the Ronet sidings, six 112-pounders, dropped from eight hundred feet, were reported to have hit the engine-shed, power-house, and rolling stock.

Of the two Martinsydes which went on to Cognelée, one failed to return. The pilot of the other went low enough to see, through the open door of the shed he was to bomb, that the Zeppelin was out, so he dropped his bombs on the corner of another shed, and then enfiladed, with machine-gun fire, a company of men lined up in front of the shed, causing several to fall. Five days later the same squadron attacked factories and the railway at Quievrechain east of Valenciennes, where a reconnaissance of No. 70 Squadron had told of great activity. Their four 112-lb. and forty 20-pounders, some of them dropped from 300 feet, hit three of the factory buildings and two trains.

On August the 23rd the squadron blew up an engine and damaged rolling stock in the station of Aulnoye, south-west of Maubeuge, and on September the 6th visited the station again, being rewarded with hits on the buildings and trains in the yard. In the two raids fourteen 112-lb. and forty 20-lb. bombs were dropped from between 400 and 800 feet. Meanwhile Mons had been visited again on the 24th of August when two 112-pounders got a direct hit on a train in the station. On the 25th a new objective was bombed by No. 27 Squadron, Busigny station, south-west of Le Cateau, and one of their 112-lb. bombs blew up what appeared to be a gas-works. All this long-distance bombing was done with no loss to the raiders other than the one aeroplane which failed to return from the airship sheds at Cognelée.

The bombing to the north of the Ancre, which served to divert much of the German air activity from the immediate battle area, was done by the squadrons of the III Brigade. This brigade, too, found time for many attacks on Bapaume and on the villages west and south of it. The raids were made chiefly by B.E.2c's of Nos. 8 and 12 Squadrons and, to a less extent, of No. 13 Squadron. Escorts were provided, up to the end of August, by Nos. 11 and 23 Squadrons, after which date No. 60 Squadron, on their return to the front from a temporary rest, took on the duties of No. 23.

✶✶✶✶✶✶

On August the 3rd General Trenchard, referring to No. 60

Squadron, had written to Sir Douglas Haig:

> I have had to withdraw one of the G.H.Q. fighting squadrons from work temporarily and have sent it to St. André-aux-Bois. This squadron, since the battle began, has lost a squadron commander, two flight commanders and one pilot—all killed or missing, and yesterday it lost two more machines with two pilots and two observers by anti-aircraft gun fire. Besides this, they have had several officers wounded. They have a very difficult machine to fly, and I think a rest away from work is absolutely necessary.

No. 60 Squadron (two flights having exchanged their Moranes for Nieuport Scouts) returned on August the 23rd to an aerodrome at Le Hameau where they came under the III Brigade, relieving No. 23 Squadron which, on the 1st of September, moved to Fienvillers to work under the headquarter wing, passing to the V Brigade four days later at Vert Galand.

★★★★★★

Each bombing pilot carried usually two 112-lb. bombs and the escorting pilots often dropped, in addition, a small number of twenty-pounders.

The main raids of the III Brigade, in July, were made on Bapaume; on the important junction at St. Léger, where a light railway, used for carrying stores and ammunition to the front, joined the main line; the great dumps at Corons on the Arras-Douai railway; the sidings at Boyelles; and on the junction and railway bridge at Aubigny-au-Bac. At Bapaume station, on the 15th of July, twenty-seven 112-lb. bombs dropped by Nos. 8 and 12 Squadrons started fires. The raiders were attacked over the station by seven enemy aeroplanes, one of which, a twin-engined machine, was shot down in flames. St. Léger was attacked by the same squadrons in the evening of the same day with twenty-six and again in the afternoon of the 30th with thirty 112-lb. bombs, which blew up and set fire to a moving train and exploded a dump near the station. A formation of Fokkers which watched the second raid from above the escort made no attempt to interrupt its progress.

Night raids on Corons dump were made by No. 13 Squadron on the 18th, 20th, and 28th of July. They lost an aeroplane on the first raid, but twice caused explosions in the dump. A day raid on the dump was made at the end of July by Nos. 8 and 12 Squadrons with thirty-two 112-lb. bombs. The sidings at Boyelles, and stores near, had been damaged by a similar number of bombs from these two squadrons on the 19th. North of the village of Aubigny-au-Bac the Douai-Cambrai line is joined by a branch line from Aniche just before it crosses the wide marshes of the Sensée River.

The junction and the bridge were attacked on the morning of the 21st, and the evening of the 28th, with a total of fifty-seven 112-lb. bombs dropped by Nos. 8 and 12 Squadrons. Some of the bombs were released from two hundred feet, but the narrow bridge escaped destruction, although the railway and station buildings were damaged. Both raids were protected by F.E.'s of No 23 Squadron which had to fight continuously. They fought so well on the first raid that two enemy aeroplanes were shot down to crash, and a number of others to land, under control, away from their aerodromes. One of the B.E.'s of No. 12 Squadron was lost, but the other aeroplanes, much shot about, returned safely. An escorting pilot said:

> Had the hostile machines been more enterprising, our losses in B.E.'s would have been heavy.

On the second raid a formation of attacking Fokkers was driven off, one of them out of control. Two officers in the escorting F.E.'s arrived home wounded, and one of the bombing aeroplanes of No. 8 Squadron, which was hit on the way back by an anti-aircraft shell, landed in flames behind the British trenches, where its destruction was completed by the enemy artillery, the pilot escaping with minor burns.

Two days after their second raid on Aubigny, the same squadrons attacked the billeting villages of Rocquigny and Villers-au-Flos, south-east of Bapaume, and left parts of them burning. But best visible results of the day's bombing by the III Brigade came from a few twenty-pounders released by No. 23 Squadron on Martinpuich. These caused an explosion which sent clouds of sulphurous smoke thousands of feet into the air, and was followed by a fire which was still burning fiercely when aeroplanes of the same squadron bombed the village again at half past ten next morning.

In August the targets attacked by the III Brigade increased in number. A new objective was the village of Grévillers west of Bapaume which, on three visits, received seventy-six 112-pounders. Other new targets were Oppy, an important centre north-east of Arras, Loupart

Wood, south-west of Grévillers, which gave cover to batteries, ammunition, and troops, an ammunition depot at Croisilles, the billeting village of Beugny east of Bapaume, and batteries and hutments in the valley between Irles and Warlencourt. In addition, the station and sidings at Boyelles were again attacked on the 7th and 8th of August with fifty-eight ii2-lb. bombs which set a train and dumps on fire. There were, too, many minor attacks by the brigade on such places as Le Sars, Courcelette, Thilloy, and on the numerous small villages behind the Third Army front. Ball, on his Nieuport, had notable fights on two of the bombing raids.

On August the 22nd he accompanied the escorting F.E.2b's of his squadron. No. 11, to the Warlencourt valley. The formation met about twenty German aeroplanes flying in three groups. Ball picked out and attacked, from under fifty feet, the rear machine of seven Rolands and sent it down to crash. One of five which he next fought went down in flames, whilst another, shot down with the last of his ammunition, crashed on a house. He returned at a low height, attacked all the way, took in a supply of ammunition on the nearest aerodrome which happened to be that of No. 8 Squadron, and flew back into the fight to find that the F.E.'s had now dispersed the enemy.

On his way home again Ball, with no petrol and little ammunition, was attacked by two formations, and his Nieuport was damaged by many bullets. He was compelled to land near Senlis where he slept by his aeroplane, flying it next morning, after repair, to the aerodrome of his new squadron—No. 60—which had just returned to the area. A week later he was fighting in protection of the bombers again. On the 28th he went over with the raiders to Loupart Wood and shot down three attacking aeroplanes. Two of them landed, apparently undamaged, in a field, but the third, which Ball fought down to within five hundred feet of the ground, crashed on to its nose.

The biggest raid made by the III Brigade in the first half of September was against Achiet-le-Grand on the 6th, with sixty-two 112-lb. bombs, many of which fell directly on the station and started an extensive fire. Considerable damage was done also to a large dump on the railway near Irles which was bombed on the 8th, 9th, and 14th, with a total of eighty-three 112-pounders, many of them falling on the dump or on the railway which fed it. The Irles raiders were hotly opposed by enemy pilots, but each time the escort of No. 11 Squadron kept them away from the bombers. On the second raid two of twenty Rolands which attacked were shot down, one crashing in no man's land, the other just behind the German trenches. Two of the escorting F.E.'s, damaged by bullets, made forced landings in their own lines, but there were no British losses on any of the raids.

THE DIRECT OFFENSIVE AGAINST THE GERMAN AIR SERVICE.

Although the bombing formations drew to themselves much enemy air activity, it is remarkable that not a single raid was prevented by enemy action and that some of the raids, especially to such distant objectives as Mons, Aulnoye, and Namur, went almost unchallenged. The reason, in part, was the determination with which the escorting pilots did their job, but, chiefly, the effectiveness with which the direct offensive against the German air force was waged. In addition to the organised fighting patrols, this direct offensive was extended by the bombing of the enemy aerodromes. Those which were singled out for attack were situated at Douai, Quéant, Bertincourt and Vélu, Beaucamp, Trescault, Hervilly, and south of Valenciennes. The most crowded aerodrome on the III Brigade front was at Douai, and this received chief attention.

On the 19th of July Nos. 8 and 12 Squadrons dropped twenty-eight 112-lb. bombs on it, and set fire to a petrol store and a hangar and damaged other hangars. Ten days later the same squadrons, with thirty-two 112pounders, destroyed an aeroplane standing on the aerodrome and two further hangars. During this raid German pilots took the air but made no attempt to interfere. On the 2nd of August Nos. 8 and 12 Squadrons were over the aerodrome again and dropped thirty 112-pounders which set fire to a hangar and caused an explosion.

On the 13th it suffered three further attacks, in the course of which three hangars were destroyed, two of them in flames. On the 7th of September No. 13 Squadron distributed fifty-six 20-pounders on the sheds in the southwest corner of the landing-ground. Quéant aerodrome was bombed by Nos. 8 and 12 Squadrons on the 1st of August when one hangar was destroyed and another damaged. The aerodromes between Bertincourt and Vélu were attacked with eight 112-pounders by No. 27 Squadron on the 29th of July.

The escort, provided by the squadron itself, had to fight to protect its bombers, and sent down one of the attacking aeroplanes to crash near Bapaume. One of the Martinsydes received many hits but the pilot, wounded in the shoulder, brought his aeroplane safely back. These aerodromes were attacked again on the 6th of September by pilots of Nos. 4, 7, and 15 Squadrons of the V Brigade who dropped one and a half tons of bombs. As the bombers neared their objectives the Germans wheeled their aeroplanes from their sheds and three of them got into the air. One of the others was destroyed on the ground by a bomb. A number of fleeting attacks were made on our formation, but the fighting was indecisive.

On the 8th of September No. 21 Squadron bombed and destroyed a hangar on Vélu aerodrome. The flying-grounds at Beaucamp and Trescault were attacked by No. 27 Squadron on the 7th of September with forty-five 20-pounders without apparent damage, but next day the same squadron went to Beaucamp again and blew up two hangars and a shed. Hervilly was bombed by No. 27 Squadron on the 29th of July with seven 112-pounders. Four Sopwith pilots of No. 70 Squadron, who escorted the bombers, fought a number of enemy aeroplanes over the aerodrome and sent one of them down out of control. The two distant aerodromes south of Valenciennes were bombed on the 7th of September by No. 12 Squadron led by Captain E. J. Tyson, who steered by compass for seventy minutes through and over thick clouds and took his formation down through the clouds directly over their objectives.

The offensive patrols of the army wings were made from five to ten miles behind the German lines. The nodal point was Bapaume, and over this town, and along the great highway connecting it with Peronne, an observer looking up at any time on a fine day during this period would hardly fail to witness the drama of battle in the air.

The headquarter squadrons flew beyond the area watched over by the army squadrons. Their patrols extended eastwards to Marcoing and Epehy, and at times to Cambrai and Le Catelet, whilst two of them, Nos. 70 and 27 Squadrons, carried the air war to Valenciennes, Solesmes, Le Cateau, and Bohain. The Sopwith two-seaters of No. 70 Squadron were responsible for all the most distant reconnaissances and much of their fighting came to them on this duty. The Sopwiths of the third flight of this squadron, which arrived from England on the 30th of July, had been handed over to the Royal Flying Corps by the Admiralty, (see chapter 7, 'The Luxeuil Bombing Wing'), and were equipped with a new Lewis gun mounting for the observer that completely outclassed all the heterogeneous mountings then in use.

This was the Scarff No. 2 Ring Mounting, and was the invention of the same naval warrant officer who had designed the Scarff-Dibovsky synchronizing gear for the Vickers gun. Round the observer's cockpit (behind the pilot) was a fixed ring, on which a movable ring rolled. Pivoted to the latter was an elevating bridge on which the gun was mounted. The weight of the gun was balanced by elastic cords. By means of a single lever, the observer could move his gun easily and quickly to fire in any direction and the gun was locked automatically when the lever was released. At once General Trenchard pressed for the Scarff mounting for all his Sopwiths. As further supplies became available it gradually came into universal use, not only in the British air services but also in those of our Allies. It remained, to the end, the standard observers' gun mounting.

For the first three weeks in July it was not unusual for pilots to come in from offensive patrols and report that they had found no enemy to fight. But this complaint was not repeated after the arrival of the German reinforcements between the 14th and 18th of July. (See earlier 'The Second Phase'). The duties assigned to the two bomber-fighter squadrons (*Kampfgeschwader*) of the newly formed German First Army were so-called barrage patrols (*Sperrefliegen*) behind and parallel to the German front. Their aeroplanes had, however, been designed primarily for bombing, and although the enemy acknowledged the importance of bombing at the Somme, he recognised his inability to undertake it in face of the British air offensive, and relegated these bombing aeroplanes to defensive flying, the ineffectiveness of which was soon to be proved.

But what was more important from the fighting point of view was the concentration of the single-seater fighters into two squadrons (*Kampfeinsitzer-Staffeln*). General Trenchard, although as yet unaware of the increases to the German strength, had foreseen that greater activity must be looked for, and had ordered No. 32 Squadron to move down from the north with some urgency. This squadron, equipped with de Havilland Scouts, arrived at Vert Galand to reinforce the headquarter squadrons on the 21st of July. On this day the weather was fine, and the effect of the arrival of the new German aeroplanes was at once shown in the strenuous fighting that went on throughout the day.

In this fighting No. 24 Squadron added to its reputation. On the previous evening four of this squadron's de Havillands, led by Captain R. E. A. W. Hughes-Chamberlain, had fought a formation of eleven German aeroplanes over Flers, destroying three of them, driving down two more, and dispersing the remainder. The squadron was therefore in high spirits on the 21st of July and eager for all comers. Its first patrol of five led by Captain J. O. Andrews, in company with two F.E.'s of No. 22 Squadron, went off at half past six, and was in its first fight, with five Rolands and five Fokkers, an hour later over Roisel.

One of the Fokkers was shot out of the fight and went down to crash its undercarriage as it Landed in a field. Lieutenant S. E. Pither followed it to the ground and scattered with his fire a group of men who had run to the wreckage. In the meantime, a general fight was in progress above, and eventually all the enemy were dispersed, three Fokkers having gone down, but under control. One of the de Havillands and the two F.E.'s, hit many times, were compelled to return. The other four closed up and continued their patrol towards Peronne, where they were joined by their squadron commander. Major L. G. Hawker. They soon discovered below them four L.V.G.'s flying towards the British lines. Hawker led his formation down and fought the Germans back to their aerodrome.

The squadron's next fight came in the evening when three of its pilots, flying with two from No. 22 Squadron, joined a Morane Parasol pilot of No. 3 Squadron in an attack, lasting half an hour, on fifteen German aeroplanes over Bapaume. One enemy machine crashed near Warlencourt, another fell into the village of Combles, and a third dropped to earth at Beaulencourt. Two others were forced to land in a field, after which the remaining aeroplanes in two's and three's flew away east leaving the air to the British formation which had inflicted its defeat without loss to itself. Whilst this dog-fight was being fought out west of Bapaume, an offensive patrol of six Martinsydes of No. 27 Squadron, led by Captain O.T. Boyd, was attacking isolated aeroplanes above their aerodrome at Bertincourt. They drove three down, fighting them to within a thousand feet of the ground. Captain Boyd's two guns had been put out of action by bullets early in the fighting, but he continued to lead his patrol for the full specified time and brought his formation safely back.

A few German pilots got through during the day and tried to interfere with our artillery and photographic aeroplanes, but found they had to contend with the same fighting spirit. There were three attacks on artillery machines, but in each instance, they were easily driven off. An F.E. of No. 22 Squadron, quietly taking photographs between Flers and Combles, was attacked by a Roland from below. The F.E. pilot side-slipped to give his observer a level target at forty yards; the Roland, vitally hit, crashed into Leuze Wood, and the F.E. continued its photography. General Trenchard, in his report on the day's work to General Headquarters, referring to the very large increase in the number of German aeroplanes on the front, expressed a hope that he would be able to keep the situation in hand.

For the next week, although offensive patrols went out in the rain and clouds, they found few German aeroplanes, but on the 30th of July, a slightly clearer day, more enemy aeroplanes were met with than on any day since the battle began, and about twenty-five of them succeeded in crossing the lines of the Fourth Army. From midday fighting was ceaseless, but so rapid and continuous were the exchanges that pilots had no time to watch the fate of the many enemy aeroplanes that went down, although at least two were believed to have been destroyed. In every attack the German formations were dispersed and driven off without loss to ourselves.

There was a marked decrease in enemy flying next day on the Somme front, and no activity on the three British Army fronts to the north. To bring home to the enemy the danger which lay in a weakening of his air units on other fronts, General Trenchard ordered the bombing of the airship sheds at Brussels, and arranged for the Naval Air Service to help by bombing the big aerodrome at St. Denis Westrem and the ammunition dump at Meirelbeke near Ghent. The raids were made on the 2nd of August. The H Brigade sent five B.E.'s and three Moranes to Brussels. One B.E. was shot down on the way by anti-aircraft fire from Ledeghem. The remainder dropped their bombs from a thousand feet without direct hits.

To divert attention from this raid, the same brigade sent thirteen aeroplanes to bomb Courtrai, where the station and main line were hit and an oil store set on fire. This formation had some fighting but, except the one B.E., all the bombing aeroplanes returned without mishap. The Naval Air Service attack, from the aerodromes near Dunkirk, was made in the morning by ten twin-engined Caudrons and one Henri Farman escorted by five Sopwith two-seaters. Their forty-four 65-lb. bombs fell among eight aeroplanes on the aerodrome at St. Denis Westrem, and on sheds and buildings at the side of the landing-ground. At Meirelbeke, where three Sopwiths each dropped twelve le Pecq bombs, the ammunition dump and railway trucks in its sidings received direct hits, but there were no explosions. One of the Sopwiths was shot down by anti-aircraft fire.

On the 3rd of August, as has been told. No. 60 Squadron was withdrawn from the front, but its loss had been partly compensated for by the arrival of No. 19 Squadron two days previously. On the day it was withdrawn No. 60 Squadron lost a pilot who had some amazing adventures before he was to see a Flying Corps mess again. Second-

Lieutenant C. A. Ridley, who set out to land a French agent, was forced down with engine trouble near Cambrai. For weeks the two moved discreetly about enemy country picking up what military information they could. Towards the end of August, they crossed the frontier into Belgium.

Here, for part of the time, Ridley, who spoke neither French nor German, painted his cheeks with iodine, bandaged his head, and went about as one deaf and dumb. So disguised, he was arrested on a tramcar near Mons, but escaped by punching the military policeman who was taking him, and jumping from the car which was moving at the time at fifteen miles an hour. He lost touch with his agent comrade after this adventure but, ultimately, in company with a Belgian from Hal, carried a ladder to the frontier and climbed over the electrified wire into Holland, setting foot on Dutch soil in the early hours of the 8th of October. A week later he was back on the Somme front with a mine of information on the enemy ammunition depots, aerodromes, and billets, which he had patiently compiled, under conditions of difficulty and extreme personal danger, during his two months of wandering behind the German lines.

Ridley's adventures have taken us ahead of the story and we must go back to August. Throughout the month there was much thick cloud over the Somme uplands, and enemy pilots made skilful use of the clouds as cover when they were attacked, but whenever the weather was clear our patrols hunted the enemy in every direction. The following episodes chosen here and there from the records of the fighting squadrons up to the eve of the reopening of the battle on the 15th of September will illustrate the variety and success of the fighting, and will show how the hope expressed by General Trenchard, that he could keep the situation in hand, was fulfilled.

On the 6th of August, at a quarter to seven in the evening, a patrol of No. 70 Squadron, led by Captain W. D. S. Sanday, met ten German aeroplanes near Bapaume flying west with a load of bombs. The Sopwiths fought the enemy formation back again to its aerodrome, where all the aeroplanes landed, as they had left, with their bombs. On the morning of this same day Lieutenant H. C. Evans of No. 24 Squadron had attacked a two-seater biplane, one of a patrol along the Bapaume-Peronne road. His first burst hit the German observer who ceased firing and waved his arms. Evans, interpreting this as a sign of surrender, indicated to the observer that he must fly back with the de Havilland. This invitation was misunderstood or refused and the de

Havilland pilot reopened fire, sending his enemy down, turning over and over, to crash east of Bois des Vaux.

On the 16th of August Ball attacked and dispersed a formation of five, forcing three down. On the following day, two F.E.2b's of No. 22 Squadron, suddenly attacked from behind by one aeroplane, turned at close range and sent it down in flames. On August the 21st a patrol of No. 24 Squadron attacked ten bomb-carrying German aeroplanes near Grandcourt: the enemy pilots dropped their bombs on ground occupied by their own troops, and flew home, escaping without apparent loss. On August the 22nd, after the clouds cleared at five o'clock in the evening, our pilots were fighting without respite.

A patrol of No. 11 Squadron attacked a formation of fifteen Rolands and L.V.G.'s; a long complicated fight ensued and, without loss to themselves, the British patrol crashed two and sent three more down out of control. The long reconnaissance made by No. 70 Squadron on the same day to Cambrai and Valenciennes had to fight the whole way. It first met and drove back a group of four before it crossed the trenches, forcing one to land in a corn field. It then scattered a formation of ten and fought continuously with other groups afterwards. Each reconnaissance aeroplane carried about 550 rounds of ammunition, but they came back with no more than thirty rounds amongst them all.

On the 24th Second-Lieutenant A. M. Vaucour, with Second-Lieutenant A. J. Bott of No. 70 Squadron, was flying south-west of Cambrai when the burning wad from an anti-aircraft shell set fire to the Sopwith's fuselage. Bott tore away the canvas surrounding the burning patch and beat out the flames with his hands. On the way home the Sopwith, in a fight with two enemy aeroplanes, had the petrol pressure pipe of its engine broken by bullets with the result that the engine was put out of action. The pilot glided over the trenches and landed south of Carnoy.

First air mechanic Herbert P. Warminger was sent out to help to repair the machine, and next morning, his task finished, he flew back as passenger with Lieutenant Vaucour. When the aeroplane was on its way, about three miles north-west of Albert, it was suddenly attacked by three enemy pilots. During the fight the Sopwith was hit by a shell, probably fired from an anti-aircraft gun, which wounded the mechanic and stopped the engine. The pilot safely landed his damaged aeroplane, but his passenger, who had behaved with great pluck in an unfamiliar predicament, died of his wounds the same evening.

On August the 31st, a fine day after a week of wet weather, there were signs of a further increase in the German aircraft on the front. New aerodromes were discovered, especially around Cambrai, and a bustling activity was seen on the old ones. Fighting went on all day behind the German lines to a depth of thirty miles. The de Havillands had a number of fights with fast scouts of a new type which gave small chance of getting to close grips, but all other fighting was successful. Ball, on his Nieuport, broke up a formation of twelve Rolands over their own aerodrome, near Cambrai. One of them, which he attacked from fifty feet below, crashed south-east of Cambrai; another, hit with the last of his ammunition, went down to land in a gap between two copses. The engine of the Nieuport, damaged by bullets, stopped, but Ball was able to clear the trenches west of Serre and land near Colincamps, returning to his aerodrome next morning.

On the 6th of September a reconnaissance by three Sopwiths of No. 70 Squadron to Cambrai and Busigny was attacked west of the latter town. The Sopwiths beat off the attacks. Captain Sanday sending one biplane down in flames. An offensive patrol of the same squadron attacked four German aeroplanes near Bapaume and sent one of them down in a spinning nose dive. Captain G. L. Cruikshank of the same squadron sent down another which ran into the parapet of a trench near Flers. Later he attacked, single-handed, three Rolands and drove down one.

To keep the enemy airmen busy all along the front, General Trenchard again ordered an intensive bombing of their aerodromes on September the 7th. Once more the naval aeroplanes co-operated by bombing the aerodrome at St. Denis Westrem. (See chapter 7 'Air Operations from Dunkirk'). Two aerodromes in front of the First Army were attacked by the I Brigade with no bombs, and six in front of the Second Army by the II Brigade with 265 bombs. These raids were additional to the bombing of the aerodromes at Douai, Valenciennes, and Beaucamp which have already been noticed.

In spite of the German air reinforcements, now making their presence felt, the corps pilots and observers continued to do their work with no effective interference whilst the fighting pilots continued to dominate the situation higher up. Two final examples of the fighting may be quoted, one to illustrate the eagerness of the fighting pilots, the other, the readiness of the corps aeroplanes to look after themselves. On the 9th of September three de Havillands of No. 32 Squadron fought five enemy pilots over Thiepval. Captain L. P. Aizlewood, choosing one of the hostile biplanes, held his fire until his dive had carried him to within twenty yards of his opponent. He emptied a complete drum before his eager dive caused his machine to strike the tail of his enemy. The propeller and undercarriage of the de Havilland were smashed, and the tail booms damaged, but, by skilful piloting, Aizlewood took his aeroplane to the ground and landed near the trenches without injury to himself. The German aeroplane which he fought crashed near Miraumont.

The other instance concerns an artillery aeroplane of No. 7 Squadron which, on the 12th of September, was directing fire near Pozières, when the observer was interrupted by a burst of machine-gun bullets. He looked round, in some surprise, and saw a squat German aeroplane, of a type unknown to him, diving from the clouds. He took up a kneeling position on his seat and fired. His shots were followed by a leap of flame from the enemy fuselage. He saw the German pilot stand in his cockpit and throw up his arms as his aeroplane paused before its final dive. Its charred wreckage fell in the British lines near Pozières.

Reference has been made to the laments of German soldiers on the measure of our dominance. Some of them are worthy of quotation, not to confirm what is beyond dispute, nor to discredit the German air service which admittedly found itself in a difficult position, but to illuminate the depressing effect of air superiority on the spirits of the infantry. An extract from the diary of a prisoner taken at Delville Wood reads:

> During the day one hardly dares to be seen in the trench owing to the English aeroplanes. They fly so low, that it is a wonder they do not pull one out of the trench. Nothing is to be seen of our German hero airmen.... One can hardly calculate how much additional loss of life and strain on the nerves this costs us....

An unfinished letter in the pocket of a dead soldier stated:

> We are in reserve for the time being but we can't remain here too long on account of hostile aircraft.... Now just a word about our own aeroplanes, really one must be almost too ashamed to write about them, it is simply scandalous. They fly up to this village but no farther, whereas the English are always flying over our lines, directing artillery shoots, thereby getting all their shells, even those of heavy calibre, right into our trenches. Our artillery can only shoot by the map as they

have no observation. I wonder if they have any idea where the enemy's line is, or even ever hit it...

Another prisoner writes:

> Our airmen are so inferior that they do not hold the field even as far behind the front as this.... No one shakes off the pests which stick to us continually all day and into the night. This moral defeat has a bad effect on us all.

Prisoners stated, too, that often they could see our troops in the open but made no attempt to fire at them, as any movement seemed to be reported from the air and to bring immediate artillery fire.

What the prisoner says is not always evidence, but any doubt of the insidious and pervasive effect of the work of the Royal Flying Corps in the first two and a half months of the battle is dispelled by a further extract from General von Below's famous memorandum on the experiences of the German First Army in the battle:

> The beginning and the first weeks of the Somme battle were marked by a complete inferiority of our own air forces. The enemy's aeroplanes enjoyed complete freedom in carrying out distant reconnaissances. With the aid of aeroplane observation, the hostile artillery neutralised our guns and was able to range with the most extreme accuracy on the trenches occupied by our infantry; the required data for this were provided by undisturbed trench reconnaissance and photography.
>
> By means of bombing and machine-gun attacks from a low height against infantry, battery positions and marching columns, the enemy's aircraft inspired our troops with a feeling of defencelessness against the enemy's mastery of the air. On the other hand, our own aeroplanes only succeeded in quite exceptional cases in breaking through the hostile patrol barrage and carrying out distant reconnaissances; our artillery machines were driven off whenever they attempted to carry out registration for their own batteries. Photographic reconnaissance could not fulfil the demands made upon it.
>
> Thus, at decisive moments, the infantry frequently lacked the support of the German artillery either in counter-battery work or in barrage on the enemy's infantry massing for attack. Heavy losses in personnel and material were inflicted on our artillery by the enemy's guns, assisted by excellent air observation,

without our being able to have recourse to the same methods. Besides this, both arms were exposed to attacks from the air by the enemy's battle-planes, the moral effect of which could not be ignored.

CHAPTER 5

The Battles of the Somme, 1916 (continued)

The 15th of September, which marked the opening of the third phase of the battle, was an outstanding day, not only on the ground where the army went into action for the first time behind a new and fantastic engine of warfare, but also in the air where the officers of the Royal Flying Corps flew more hours and had more fighting than on any day since the war began. The military operations were ambitiously planned. The Fourth Army was to seize the enemy's third line system between Morval and Le Sars, following which cavalry were to break through to the high ground between Rocquigny and Bapaume. The Reserve Army was to secure the left flank of the Fourth Army by taking Courcelette and the high ground north-east of Thiepval.

Of the new and secret weapon, the tank, forty-nine were to go into action, seven with the Reserve Army, and the remainder with the Fourth Army, and their doings in the battle were to be reported by the contact observers of the corps squadrons. For co-operation with the cavalry advance. No. 18 Squadron had been specially brought down from the First Army front. This squadron, equipped with F.E.2b's, had come under the orders of the Fourteenth Wing of the IV Brigade on the 7th of September. Although it was a fighting reconnaissance squadron, its pilots and observers had had experience of artillery and other corps work on the First Army front.

The tanks moved up to their jumping-off places during the night before the attack. To drown the roar of their engines in the ears of German troops in the front trenches a few aeroplanes flew all night about the lines. But the new weapon did not come as a complete surprise to the enemy infantry. They had been warned, five or six

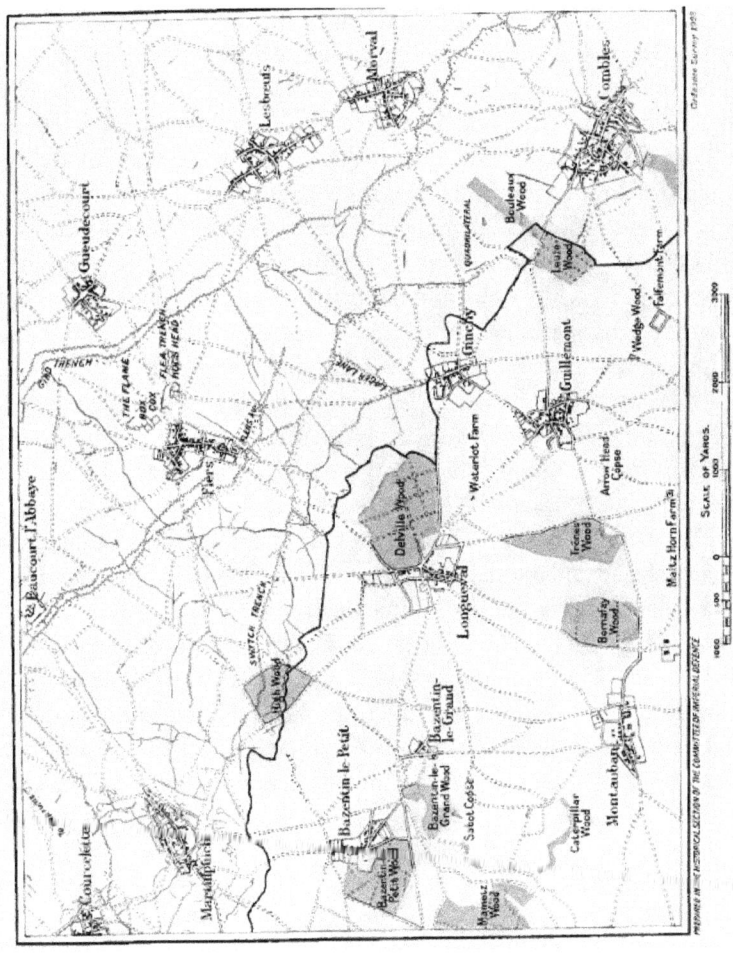

AREA OF FOURTH ARMY OPERATIONS.
15TH SEPTEMBER, 1916.

weeks before, that some sort of armoured car might be used during the battle, and on the afternoon of the 14th of September a German kite-balloon observer had seen and reported some of the tanks moving up, whereupon a special warning had been sent out to German commanders in the front line.

The artillery bombardment which had begun at six in the morning of the 12th went on steadily until 6.20 a.m. on the 15th, when it was increased as the infantry moved forward through a light mist. The advance on Courcelette was made by the Canadian Corps which had taken over from the 1st Anzac Corps on the 3rd of September. Observers of No. 7 Squadron watched the Canadians move down the slope to the western face of the village whence, at half-past seven, flares were reported burning in a line to a point near Martinpuich. The Canadians advanced to the capture of Courcelette at six in the evening, and within an hour, observers of No. 7 Squadron sent down the news that flares had been lighted in a semicircle round the village showing that it was wholly in our hands.

The progress of the III Corps on the right of the Canadians was watched by observers of No. 34 Squadron. At half-past nine in the morning their reports showed that the 15th (Scottish) Division had reached the outskirts of Martinpuich and that the 50th (Northumbrian) Division were well forward east of the village, but that farther south the advance was held in High Wood. The taking of High Wood was to provide a good example of the life-saving value of contact patrol. Captain C. H. B. Blount and Lieutenant T. S. Pearson of No. 34 Squadron dropped a message soon after 10 a.m. which told of the misfortune that had befallen the three tanks allotted to the wood. One was ditched in our own trenches, one was on its end against a tree, and the third was in flames in the German trenches. Deprived of the assistance of the tanks, the infantry were held by uncut wire and fierce machine-gun fire, and were scraping a hurried position in shell holes in front of the enemy trenches.

After dropping this information, the airmen flew back to the front and found that on either side of the wood the attacking troops had now pushed well forward, and had extended to meet one another north of the wood where they were digging along a roughly continuous line. They flew home to make a verbal report. When they reached the corps headquarters they found that an immediate frontal attack on the important German line across High Wood was being organised. Lieutenant Pearson says:

This would have resulted in the complete wiping out of the attacking force, for the enemy trench was manned literally shoulder to shoulder with a machine-gun every few yards, and most of the wire uncut.'

After a full discussion of the situation with the two flying officers, it was realised that, with the wood surrounded, the surrender of the garrison was a matter of time. The orders for a frontal attack on the formidable northern corner were therefore cancelled. The two officers then flew on a second patrol over the wood. At 12.30 p.m. they reported that the troops which had been digging north of the wood had consolidated their position. Half an hour later the isolated northern corner was quietly taken with its full garrison.

Although the capture of Martinpuich was not part of the day's objective for the III Corps, troops of the 15th Division, with the help of a tank, which ambled through the streets blowing in dugouts as it went, took the village soon after 5 p.m.

But most exhilarating reports of all came in from observers of No. 3 Squadron who followed the attack of the XV Corps on Flers. The first message was dropped on the Corps headquarters at twenty minutes past seven. The observer had watched the infantry move over the open behind the barrage which crept ahead with uncanny precision. He saw a continuous stream of emergency signals bursting above the German trenches. Within ten minutes of the British infantry starting forward their flares were being lighted along the Switch Line, and a quarter of an hour later were burning as far over as the sunken road known as Flers Avenue, south of the village. So rapidly indeed had the troops moved that they had outdistanced their supporting tanks.

At half-past eight, however, three tanks were seen moving towards Flers, and fifteen minutes later one of them was advancing down the main street surrounded by a crowd of khaki figures, who were soon afterwards seen to occupy the north and west side of the village. Just after midday an aeroplane flew over an adventurous tank which was pushing forward to the outskirts of Gueudecourt whence many Germans had retreated from Flers, but even as the observer picked up its position he saw it hit and set on fire.

The air reports in the early afternoon showed that, north of Flers, we were holding the system of trenches known as Box and Cox and The Flame, and to the northeast were strongly established in the group of defences known as Flea Trench and the Hogs Head, and that elsewhere the XV Corps was holding its third objective. At half-past three the divisions in the line were ordered to consolidate and not advance beyond these positions. The reason for this order was the partial failure of the attack of the right corps, the XIV, which was held by the strong work east of Ginchy known as the Quadrilateral. To this corps had been allotted sixteen tanks, but six broke down before reaching their jumping-off points and of the remainder there was only one to co-operate in the attack on the Quadrilateral.

An observer of No. 9 Squadron reported at eight o'clock that this formidable work was holding up the 6th Division and that the one tank seen in front of the position was apparently of no help. This tank, in fact, had been blinded by having its periscope shot away within fifty yards of the enemy's forward trench. Whilst the 6th Division was being held, an observer had watched the Guards Division on their left make early and rapid progress to their first and second objectives and then advance to near their third before they were stopped. The division reported that they had in fact taken their third objective, but the air reports showed their forward troops in isolated posts along a series of shell holes about two hundred yards short of it, and, as was proved later, this statement of their position was correct.

Despite the setback on the right and the fact that the larger objectives had not been realised, the day's advance had been highly satisfactory. On a front of over six miles we had broken through two of the enemy's main defensive systems and had taken, with only light losses, Courcelette, Martinpuich, and Flers, each elaborately fortified for prolonged resistance.

Only enough has been picked from the reports of the contact observers to outline the advance, but they kept the corps commanders almost continuously informed of the progress of their divisions. With no break all day the contact aeroplanes were over the troops, many of the observers totalling eight hours of flying. Nor did they confine their help to a report of the infantry's movements, but they passed on also demands for ammunition, and sent down many calls to the guns for fire on to fleeting targets offered by enemy formations.

Air artillery observers made many notes on the positions of the infantry to supplement and confirm the contact reports. But the best work of the artillery aeroplanes was the rapid engaging of enemy batteries, some of which were seen to be withdrawing as our line advanced, and of moving troops. The call used for these fleeting targets was the area or zone call, and on every occasion fire was opened almost as the signal was tapped out. On the Reserve Army front the positions of four separate formations of troops were so reported; on to three of them fire fell at once and inflicted heavy casualties. On the Fourth Army front no less than one hundred and fifty-nine active batteries were located, and most of these were reported by area call. Seventy of them were engaged with air observation, and of these twenty-nine were silenced, thirteen by direct hits.

Two examples typical of the work of the artillery aeroplanes may be given. An observer of No. 7 Squadron, on artillery patrol, saw in the evening eight field guns firing from a sunken road east of Courcelette. Shrapnel fire was opened on them on receipt of his message, but the enemy continued doggedly to work his guns. The pilot. Lieutenant A. L. Gordon-Kidd, thereupon dived and fired at the gun crews whom he could see outlined against the dusty road. His fire was returned and his aeroplane many times hit, but he killed and wounded some of the gunners.

Another artillery aeroplane of No. 3 Squadron, during a morning patrol, sent down by area call the positions of eight active batteries between Lesboeufs and Gueudecourt, and then gave corrections of lire on to them. The officers themselves engaged another battery with machine-gun fire with such effect that its two guns did no more firing whilst the aeroplane was about. In the course of their patrol they watched a Nieuport shoot down a balloon near Thilloy.

This balloon was one of two shot down during the day, both by pilots of No. 60 Squadron, one of whom failed to return from his adventure. This squadron had destroyed a balloon in the air west of Bapaume on the previous evening. Good as these successes were, they fell short of what had been hoped for. They were won each time against attacks by German aeroplanes, but that more were not destroyed was due to the sharp lookout kept by specially posted ground observers, on whose warning of the approach of aeroplanes, balloons were rapidly hauled down. Anti-aircraft guns, too, were arriving in increasing numbers and added to the difficulty of driving home the attack.

The British balloons, aided by the clear visibility all day, gave uninterrupted support to the artillery, and with their help many batteries, trenches, and strong points suffered severe damage. As a result of the jump forward made by the infantry in the morning, some of our balloons were moved to positions from which they could overlook a new stretch of the enemy back area. The balloon of No. 3 Section was shifted in the afternoon to the outskirts of Montauban. The observer had begun work from his new position when he was asked by a siege battery commander to move again as the cable of the balloon was in his line of fire. Overhead telephone wires and other military impedimenta in the neighbourhood made a quick move impossible, and the observer judged that the very slight risk of the cable being hit was outweighed by the interruption to his work that a move would entail. He therefore remained. But not for long. A shell from the battery cut through the cable, the balloon soared away, and the observer had to rip it open before he parachuted to the ground.

Sometime before the infantry attack was launched in the morning, bombing aeroplanes had gone out, and they continued to fly backwards and forwards to German centres through the day, dropping a total of eight and a half tons of bombs. The first bombs, dropped by No. 27 Squadron, hit outhouses at General von Below's headquarters at Bourlon, and at the same time pilots of No. 19 Squadron blew out a wall of a *château* at Havrincourt which was believed to house a corps headquarters. No. 27 Squadron flew over Bourlon again about 9.0 a.m. and dropped eight 112-lb. and sixteen 20-lb. bombs. The bombers were attacked as they were getting into position over the *château* and had little opportunity to watch the impact of their bombs, but four were seen to fall on the main building.

In the fighting four enemy aeroplanes went down, one of them being seen to crash, and one of our machines was lost. At 9.45 a.m. five aeroplanes of No. 27 Squadron left to bomb Achiet-le-Grand and Vélu stations where they hit rolling-stock and buildings. But the best bombing by this squadron was done in the afternoon. No. 70 Squadron had reported forty trains on the lines about Cambrai in the morning. Most of the movement was in a westerly direction and probably represented the arrival of the infantry of a whole division. Eight Martinsyde pilots flew off soon after 2.0 p.m. to find and bomb the arriving troops. Three of them were near Gouzeaucourt when they saw a train going into the station. All pilots dived. The first bomb hit the engine and stopped the train. Men jumped out.

The bombs from the second Martinsyde blew up the rear truck and the pilot then turned and dropped a 112-pounder in the midst of troops who had collected on the side of the railway line. The bombs from the third aeroplane hit an ammunition truck in the middle of the train, which exploded and blew up several other trucks one after the other. Whilst these three pilots were bombing at Gouzeaucourt, the remaining five, which had become detached from the formation in the clouds, hit trains at Ribecourt and Epehy and a stores dump at Bantouzelle.

Bapaume was bombed in the morning by the III Brigade. No. 12 Squadron supplied five bombing aeroplanes which dropped six 112-lb. and thirty-two 20-lb. bombs from between two hundred and eight hundred feet. Hits were seen on a train, standing trucks, the railway, and on the station buildings. The bombers and their escort of five F.E.'s from No. 11 Squadron had many fights over the town. The escort shot down four enemy biplanes which were seen to crash, and forced two others to land, and one of the bombing B.E.'s sent down another with a wounded observer. The bombing leader was wounded in the arm over Bapaume as he flew low to drop his bombs, but returned safely, crossing the trenches at five hundred feet. A sergeant observer in one of the escorting aeroplanes was also wounded and died later.

A reconnaissance of Vélu in the early morning had reported trains in the station, and eight aeroplanes from No. 13 Squadron were sent over to bomb them. The pilots reported that their ten heavy and twenty-four 20-lb. bombs hit three trains, derailed coaches and trucks, and set fire to a store on the side of the line. Other bombs were dropped, without observation of effects, on Vélu aerodrome by No. 11 Squadron, and, without direct hits, by No. 13 Squadron on the *château* at St. Léger where a divisional headquarters was established.

Most of the day's air fighting was above Bapaume and in front of the Third Army. No. 60 Squadron destroyed three enemy aeroplanes in the day, two in somewhat unusual circumstances. Lieutenant Ball and Second-Lieutenant A. M. Walters on Nieuports had set out to shoot down balloons with Le Prieur rockets, but found that the balloons allotted to them were not in the air. Instead they picked out enemy aeroplanes. Ball, who fired his rockets at a Roland biplane, missed, but shot it down with a drum from his machine-gun. Walters had better luck with his rockets, one of which pierced the fuselage of an L.V.G. biplane and sent it burning to earth.

Three de Havilland's of No. 24 Squadron, which dived into a formation of seventeen German aeroplanes near Morval at 8.30 in the morning, sent one down in flames and another to crash in a field, and scattered the remainder. Another patrol of this squadron in the afternoon met four aeroplanes over Bapaume and destroyed one of them. Pilots of No. 23 Squadron also destroyed two machines over Bapaume, and a pilot of No. 32 Squadron, who was attacked from behind as he dived on a formation of five south of Bapaume, turned and shot down the attacking aeroplane, a Roland, in flames.

An offensive patrol of seven Sopwths of No. 70 Squadron which went out at a quarter to six in the morning had some of the bloodiest fighting of the day. They were led by Captain G. L. Cruikshank, a pilot who had gone to France with No. 3 Squadron in August 1914. His ambition was to meet Böelcke.

Over Havrincourt Wood he saw a fighter below him and dived to attack. Although he could not know it his enemy was indeed the German star pilot who, after a brilliant duel, shot down the British aeroplane, to fall to pieces in Havrincourt Wood. Another of the Sopwiths, with a pierced petrol tank and an observer mortally wounded, was compelled to land in enemy territory, and two others, badly damaged, reached the Allied lines with dying observers. The formation had been split up when the fighting began and the Sopwiths had, individually, to fight enemy groups. Three German aeroplanes were reported as driven down, one of them being seen to crash, whilst, in a further fight on the way home, two enemy aeroplanes collided as they attacked and one of them dropped like a stone.

All the day's fighting, once again, had taken place over and behind the German lines. Our casualties had been somewhat heavy. In all six aeroplanes with their nine officers were missing, four officers and a sergeant gunner had come in from the fighting wounded, and three of these, including the non-commissioned officer, had died of their wounds. Against these losses, fourteen German aeroplanes had been seen to crash and many others had been driven down damaged. The best testimony to the effect of the fighting on the German air service came in the late afternoon and evening when our offensive patrols, as numerous as they had been in the morning, met few German pilots in the air, whilst a reconnaissance of No. 70 Squadron, which reported on train movements as far over as Valenciennes and Cambrai in the afternoon, was wholly unmolested by enemy airmen.

At 9.25 on the morning of the 16th the infantry attack was renewed, slight gains were made, and many counter attacks, especially between Flers and Courcelette, broken up. The ground fighting was confusing all day, and aeroplanes were sent out time after time to clear up the situation. Aeroplanes of the Fifteenth Wing sent down to the II Corps 179 zone calls on to active enemy batteries and nine on to parties of infantry. In the early morning eight I 12-Ib. bombs were dropped on Bapaume station by No. 12 Squadron. An aeroplane of No. 18 Squadron going off to reconnoitre fouled the cable of No.

6 Section Kite Balloon, which broke away and landed a few yards behind the French front line. The balloon observer, whose parachute failed to open, was picked up dead two thousand yards from his balloon. The aeroplane crashed, the pilot being injured and the observer killed.

THE NEW GERMAN FIGHTING SQUADRONS.

Sunday the 17th of September was a day of somewhat heavy air casualties for the Flying Corps, most of the victims falling to a new fighting squadron which, under Böelcke's brilliant leadership, came out in force for the first time on this day. The single-seater fighter (*Kampfeinsitzer*) squadrons which had been formed in the middle of July could do little to affect the predominance which the Allied air forces had established. When the enemy air commander, Lieutenant-Colonel Thomsen, realised how inadequate these squadrons were, he suggested a reorganisation of the fighting units into special pursuit squadrons (*Jagdstaffeln*), equipped with the fastest types of fighters manned by carefully selected officers who had already proved their fighting worth on active service.

It was proposed to use these squadrons defensively. It was recognised that the Fokker monoplane was no longer a match for the British fighters and, in August, the Fokker was replaced by the fast Halberstadt and the D type Albatros, which had as armament two fixed machine-guns firing through the propeller, a new and surprising innovation. As fighters they outclassed every contemporary British aeroplane opposed to them. The enemy left no stone unturned to get the very best from his new fighting units. Not only were the officers carefully selected, but they were given a special course at single-seater fighting schools in Germany, and then passed on to an advanced fighting school at Valenciennes, finishing their training when they joined their fighting squadron at the front. The formation of these pursuit squadrons was to have a profound influence on the whole future air war on the western front.

Böelcke, after making a reputation at Verdun, had gone off on a visit to the Turkish, Macedonian, and Russian fronts. He was at Kovel in the middle of August visiting his brother who was flying with a squadron near the town. Another officer at Kovel was Manfred Freiherr von Richthofen. (*Richthofen & Böelcke in Their Own Words* containing both *The Red Battle Flyer* by Manfred Freiherr von Richthofen & *An Aviator's Field Book* by Oswald Böelcke is also published by

Leonaur). Böelcke, who had been empowered to organise one of the new pursuit squadrons for the Somme, had a free hand in the choice of his officers, and invited Richthofen to join his new unit, an invitation which was readily accepted. The new unit, known as *Jagdstaffel 2*, was formed on the 30th of August 1916 at Lagnicourt, where the pilots impatiently awaited the arrival of their new aeroplanes. Meanwhile Böelcke made occasional patrols alone.

On the 16th of September the first batch of new aeroplanes arrived and, on the following morning, Böelcke led five of his pilots in close formation towards the British lines. At the same time as the German fighters were getting into the air, eight B.E.'s of No. 12 Squadron, carrying eight 112-lb. and thirty-two 20-lb. bombs, escorted by six F.E.2b's of No. 11 Squadron, were leaving for a visit to Marcoing station. Böelcke saw them soon after they had crossed the lines and followed to cut them off. But the British pilots reached Marcoing and, taking deliberate aim, dropped their forty bombs about the station, which was set on fire. Just outside the station an explosion which followed the burst of a bomb sent clouds of smoke high in the air. Almost as they released their bombs the aeroplanes were mixed up in a fierce fight. In addition to Böelcke's five, some seven other German fighters appear to have joined in.

The F.E.'s did all they could to protect the bombing aeroplanes and in doing so four of them were shot down. In spite of the self-sacrifice of the escorts two of the bombers also fell victims to their more speedy opponents. The remainder, extricated from further fighting by an offensive patrol of No. 60 Squadron, got safely home. Richthofen, in his book, states that each of the five pilots of his squadron shot down one opponent, and that for all of them, except Böelcke, it was their first victory against the Royal Flying Corps.

★★★★★★

Their success, against seasoned opponents, achieved on aeroplanes which had only arrived the previous evening, constituted a remarkable performance. It gave Böelcke's new fighting squadron immediate prestige.

★★★★★★

Richthofen gives particulars of his own victim, one of the F.E.'s, which was landed by its pilot in a field. The engine, he says, had been shot to pieces, and the pilot and observer severely wounded. The observer died in his cockpit and the pilot did not survive the journey to the nearest dressing-station. These were not the only losses of the day. No. 27 Squadron, which had successfully attacked Cambrai station without loss at dawn with eight 112-lb. bombs, lost an aeroplane a little later in the morning during a raid on Valenciennes in which four 112-lb. bombs exploded on trains in the station sidings. A reconnoitring Sopwith was lost, too, over Cambrai by No. 70 Squadron, and another aeroplane by No. 23 Squadron during a reconnaissance of the Vélu-Epehy-Marcoing triangle. To offset these losses, four German aeroplanes were destroyed in fighting near the lines.

In addition to the bombing already mentioned, successful raids were made, without loss, on Miraumont station and on the station and *château* at Havrincourt Wood. Major-General Trenchard in his report to Headquarters says:

> I have come to the conclusion, that the Germans have brought another squadron or squadrons of fighting machines to this neighbourhood and also more artillery machines. One or two German aeroplanes have crossed the line during the last few days . . . and new wireless calls have been intercepted. With all this, however, the anti-aircraft guns have only reported 14 hostile machines as having crossed the line in the 4th Army area in the last week ending yesterday, whereas something like 2,000 to 3,000 of our machines crossed the lines during the week. Also, the artillery and contact patrol machines have practically not been interfered with at all for the last three days. Most of the fighting has been done well behind the lines, and the places we have bombed well back have more aeroplanes near them than ever before which I think shows the enemy keeps the majority of his machines away from the lines.

On Monday the 18th the weather broke and little flying was possible, but on the ground the stubbornly-defended Quadrilateral, east of Ginchy, was surrounded and captured by the 6th Division in the morning. An attempted reconnaissance on the 19th by F.E.'s of No. 11 Squadron escorted by fighters of No. 60 Squadron, was attacked by Böelcke's formation near Quéant. A Morane flown by Captain H. C. Tower was shot to pieces in the air by Böelcke, the pilot of one of the F.E.'s was wounded, and another F.E. with a damaged engine and wounded observer had to be landed in Delville Wood where it was destroyed by shell fire. So effective was the enemy opposition that the reconnaissance could not be completed. For the rest of the week the weather continued dull, but it cleared in time for air work for the new general attack to take place on Monday the 25th.

On the 22nd photographs and reconnaissances and artillery registration on trench points and destruction of German batteries kept pilots of the IV Brigade in the air for 303 hours. A valuable reconnaissance of this brigade revealed the construction of new lines consequent on our recent successes. The fourth line had been doubled between Sailly-Saillisel and Le Transloy, a fifth was being feverishly thrown up in front of Bapaume southwards to Manancourt, and a sixth line had been begun some three miles farther east. As was usual on a fine day after a spell of bad weather the enemy air service was intensely active, and our pilots had many encounters with the new German fighters. Fifteen enemy kite balloons were reported along the corps fronts of the Fourth Army directing fire with damaging accuracy on our trenches and communications, and thirteen enemy aeroplanes crossed the lines of this army during the day.

An attack, with phosphorus bombs, was made on the German balloons, but they were rapidly hauled down as the aeroplanes approached and none of them, so far as could be seen, was destroyed, although the bombs appeared to burst directly over them. The aerodrome at Vélu was bombed by six pilots of No. 21 Squadron who found many aeroplanes lined up on the landing-ground when they arrived. The bombs fell amongst the machines, but so vigorously were the Martinsydes attacked that pilots had no time to watch the effects of their bombs. One Martinsyde pilot, mortally wounded, eventually fell with his aeroplane in the French lines. The pilots of two independent offensive patrols of No. 19 Squadron also bombed the Vélu aerodrome. They all reported hot fighting: the first patrol lost two aeroplanes and the second, one, whilst one enemy aeroplane was sent down in flames.

A morning bombing attack on the station of Quievrechain, east of Valenciennes, by No. 27 Squadron, met with little opposition. A bomb which struck the middle carriage of a train in the station failed to explode, and the pilot then went down to within a hundred feet of the train and fired a drum from his machine-gun at the engine-driver. Only two enemy pilots were encountered on the long journey and these made but half-hearted attacks. The same squadron attacked Havrincourt Wood with fifty-six 20-lb. bombs in the afternoon, having only one indecisive fight on the way home. The offensive patrols on the Ancre and Somme fronts had many fights throughout the day, four enemy aeroplanes being destroyed and six others driven down damaged. There were isolated enemy attacks on our photographic aeroplanes.

One photographic machine was brought down by an anti-aircraft shell, and another, with its engine put out of action by bullets from an enemy aeroplane, was compelled to return before it had completed its task. All other attacks were beaten off, and the photographs, urgently asked for by the army, were all procured. The pilot, Second Lieutenant F. Hall, of the aeroplane of No. 18 Squadron which was hit by a shell, became unconscious in the air. The F.E.2b was then attacked by a Roland but fell into a spin. It came out of the spin and the observer. Lieutenant B. Fitz H. Randall, took control and brought the aeroplane into our lines where, on landing, it ran into a shell hole and overturned. The observer dragged his pilot from the aeroplane and, assisted by infantry who rushed to help, carried him towards a dressing-station, but he died on the way.

An F.E.2b pilot of No. 22 Squadron, who was escorting a photographic aeroplane, attacked and shot down a German aeroplane over Sailly-Saillisel, and then went to the assistance of two French aeroplanes which were being attacked by two Rolands over Morval. He dived to attack one of the enemy pilots, but the other by a rapid manoeuvre got on the tail of the F.E. in which the gunner sits in front of the pilot. The F.E. pilot, Second Lieutenant H. J. Finer, therefore pulled back the nose of his machine, to allow the gunner. Corporal A. Winterbottom, to turn and fire the rear gun over the top plane. As the corporal undipped the gun to get it into position, he was killed, and the gun then fell back to strike the pilot on the head. Finer remembered nothing afterwards until he recovered consciousness on the way to a French Army headquarters. What happened was that he got his aeroplane down behind the French lines where it turned over on landing and was completely wrecked.

Saturday the 23rd was another day of bright weather and great air activity. The corps squadrons continued their reconnaissance and artillery work and reported explosions in batteries and dumps, especially at Le Transloy and Thilloy, where fires started in the morning were followed by explosions throughout the day. Before daybreak six aeroplanes of the V Brigade bombed and set fire to buildings in Bapaume station, and four pilots of No. 9 Squadron got similar results from bombing the station at Roisel, whilst, to the north, Douai was attacked at the same hour by No. 13 Squadron.

At noon this squadron, in company with No. 12 Squadron, dropped one hundred and eight 20-lb. bombs on the railway station at Quéant.

A distant raid to the Zeppelin shed at Maubeuge, now reported to be used as an ammunition store, was made by five Martinsydes of No. 27 Squadron, three of which were acting as escort. The bombs just failed to hit their target: all the aeroplanes returned safely. The squadron, however, had suffered severely in the morning. Six Martinsydes had gone off at half-past eight to patrol as far as Cambrai where they flew into a formation of the new German single-seaters. In the sharp fighting which ensued three Martinsydes were shot down.

Another (pilot, Second Lieutenant L. F. Forbes) collided with a German aeroplane, which at once dropped abruptly to earth. The Martinsyde came from the collision with a smashed wing. Although thus severely handicapped, Forbes shook off all further attacks and, by a fine feat of piloting, flew his aeroplane back from Cambrai to the aerodrome of No. 24 Squadron. There he found that the Martinsyde became entirely uncontrollable when he tried to throttle down his engine to land. He ran his aeroplane into a tree and was severely injured.

The morning of the 24th brought a dense haze which, until ten o'clock, delayed observation of the bombardment. Thereafter the weather was clearer, but although the broad effects of the shelling were reported and photographed, mist continued to interfere with the air work.

In the afternoon a special offensive sweep was made to catch the new enemy fighters working from the aerodromes around Cambrai. Sixty pilots set out, in groups, at various heights. One of the formations—five B.E.12's of No. 19 Squadron—was attacked over Havrincourt Wood by two single-seaters which completely outmanoeuvred them and shot one of them down in flames and another to pieces in the air, and then dived clear away to their aerodrome.

Six Martinsydes of No. 27 Squadron were more successful. They lost one of their number but destroyed a Fokker. The formation of six pilots of No. 23 Squadron had many fights and got split up. Over Bertincourt a Roland, which attacked one of the F.E.'s from a range of fifteen yards, killed the observer and put bullets through the propeller, planes, and engine, but left the pilot untouched. Another F.E. pilot, seeing the fight, dived to attack the Roland and shot it down: it was last seen diving vertically near the ground. Five F.E.'s of No. 22 Squadron were fighting an equal enemy formation at the same time over Bus, south of Bertincourt, with greater success. Without loss to themselves they shot down one which crashed on to a telegraph line, another which fell and overturned near the wood of St. Pierre Vaast, and two others which were last seen in steep dives close to the ground. The other formations which made up the sixty had no decisive fights.

The chief bombing raid of the day was made on the ammunition dumps at Irles where twenty-three 112-lb. bombs were dropped in the morning by Nos. 12 and 13 Squadrons. Bursts were seen near the dump, but mist made observation of results impossible. Elsewhere along the battle front all brigades distributed 20-lb. bombs on the enemy billeting villages in their areas.

Monday the 25th was a bright, cloudless day, but again there was a ground haze. The reports which came in on this day from the contact observers were the most exhilarating and accurate that had yet been received. The main objectives of the infantry were Gueudecourt and a belt of country about a thousand yards deep curving round the north of Flers, the task of the XV Corps, and the villages of Lesboeufs and Morval, assigned to the XIV Corps. The air observers watched the troops move forward, close up to their barrage, with methodical precision and small loss.

Only at Gueudecourt did they have to report a check. Here the 21st Division were held by insufficiently cut wire in front of part of the Gird Trench, south-west of the village. Elsewhere their reports referred to the advance as 'wonderfully carried out in perfect order', and showed the whole objectives of both corps carried with the exception of a corner of Morval village. The final advance of the XIV Corps from a line on the western outskirts of Lesboeufs and Morval was begun at 2.35 p.m., and twenty-one minutes later an observer in No. 12 Section's balloon reported that the whole of the final objective, except the south-east corner of Morval, was taken. This information, the first to come in of the complete success of the day's attack, was thus known at corps headquarters almost as it happened.

At the end of the day a map was issued showing the positions of the infantry as seen from the air, and when it was possible later to correlate all the reports of the day's advance, this air map proved to be of greater accuracy than the reports of their positions received from the troops themselves after they had made good their gains. The southeast corner of Morval fell during the evening, and with the completion of our captures here the last of the high ground on the main ridge was in our possession. The German position in Combles was now highly dangerous. The village indeed would have fallen on this day but that the French enveloping attack towards Frégicourt was held up, a fact which was reported by the British kite balloons.

German pilots were extremely active in the morning, but most of them were reported cruising about at 14,000 feet where not many of our pilots could get up to them. Some of them crossed our lines, and some flew low but did little to worry our corps aeroplanes. There were one or two instances of shoots being interrupted by the presence of enemy aircraft over the batteries, but these interruptions were temporary. Four German aeroplanes were destroyed and others were driven down damaged, but on the whole the day's fighting was less definite, chiefly because the superior speed and climbing power of some of the enemy fighters enabled them to break off the combat at will.

No casualties were suffered by the British fighting machines. Nos. 12 and 13 Squadrons, with a strong Nieuport and F.E.2b escort, made a morning attack on the aerodrome at Lagnicourt, south of Quéant, with fifty-six 20-lb., two 112-lb., and nine 40-lb. (phosphorus) bombs. Hangars and machines standing outside were damaged and a building on the aerodrome was set on fire. Thirty-two 20-lb. bombs were dropped on a divisional headquarters at Manancourt, east of Sailly-Saillisel, one of which caused an explosion in the village.

A German officer, captured at Morval in the evening of the 25th, stated that Combles was to be evacuated during the coming night. As soon as darkness fell the XIV Corps began a heavy barrage of the valley east of the village. In the early morning infantry patrols occupied the northern half of this strongly fortified centre and linked up with the French who came in from the south.

The positions of the British and French at this point were cleared up by a report brought back at noon by Second Lieutenant Scaife who had flown over the area with Lieutenant B. T. Coller. These two officers went off again at 2.20 p.m. to report on further adjustments of the line, but at three o'clock, in view of the troops whose movements they had so often reported, their aeroplane was blown up by a direct hit from an anti-aircraft shell and fell near Lesboeufs.

The quiet work of the pilots and observers who flew in direct co-operation with the infantry is apt to be obscured by the more spectacular attraction which attaches to air fighting. Something of the value of that work and the spirit with which it was performed has, it is hoped, been brought out in this story. They, alone, were the witnesses of the whole titanic struggle, and through their eyes the army commanders could follow the fortunes of their troops. Amongst all their hundreds of reports, those of Second Lieutenant T. E. G. Scaife stand out for their completeness, accuracy, and appreciation of the tactical position. He grew to a detailed knowledge of the battle area and he was, when he made his last flight, at the height of his usefulness to the army corps for which he worked.

Of the places which formed the objectives on the 25th, there still remained to the enemy on the morning of the 26th the village of Gueudecourt. Before this could be stormed it would be necessary to eject the German infantry from what they still held of the Gird Trench which protected the village from the south-west. The capture of this trench was to provide an example of perfect cooperation between the air, tanks, artillery, and infantry. The 21st Division had, on the 25th, occupied that part of Gird Trench which was on the west of the village, whilst the Guards Division had taken another part of it farther south. Between the two divisions fifteen hundred yards remained in the enemy's possession.

At 6.0 a.m. on the 26th a party of the 7th Leicesters began to bomb down the trench in the direction of the Guards Division. Twenty-five minutes later an aeroplane of No. 3 Squadron (pilot, Second Lieutenant L. G. Wood, observer. Lieutenant H. J. L. Cappel) was sent out to see how the Leicesters were getting on. When the aeroplane got over the trench, the officers found that the bombers had already made some progress and that a tank was getting into position to help them. They saw this tank begin its crawl along the line in company with the bombers at a quarter-past seven.

Half an hour later the German infantry were compressed in great strength along about 500 yards of the trench between the oncoming bombers and the Guards, and the observer, giving the pin-points of their flanks, sent down an area call to the artillery for fire on them. Shells fell thickly at once. Within a few minutes the tank and its bombing party had got as far as the sector which was being bombarded, and a second call to the artillery to cease fire was tapped out. As the shelling ceased, the pilot dropped to three hundred feet and flew along the trench raking the unhappy occupants with machine-gun fire. Their endurance snapped, and they waved arms and white handkerchiefs in surrender to the airmen.

This fact was transmitted to the infantry by message bag, and they advanced and accepted the surrender of eight officers and three hundred and sixty-two men. The total of British casualties in this brilliant little action numbered five. Now that the Gird Trench was in their hands, the 21st Division pushed patrols into Gueudecourt. The village was reported clear of the enemy, and the division then occupied it and, by the evening, had made good its full objective north and east of the village.

Whilst the Fourth Army was thus easily completing its task of the previous day, the Reserve Army, which had not attacked on the 25th, was making a jump forward at Thiepval. Sir Douglas Haig judged that the time had now come to take the village and to advance his left flank along the main ridge stretching away above it. The objectives included the strong works known as the Schwaben, Stuff, and Zollern Redoubts. (See map following). The attack was launched at 12.35 p.m. by the II and Canadian Corps, with the assistance of eight tanks, and watched by Nos. 4 and 7 Squadrons which had previously, by low reconnaissance, reported in some detail on the condition of the German wire and trenches. Almost everywhere the enemy was taken by surprise.

Observers saw the infantry move in good order close up to the artillery barrage, and watched them into Thiepval where they saw enemy infantry running from two tanks which had got into the village. They then watched the taking of nearly a thousand yards of trench east of Thiepval. They saw that at Mouquet Farm the German garrison put up a fierce resistance, but that the waves of khaki passed through the outer defences of the farm and went on to storm the Zollern Redoubt. Farther east they saw the Canadians, within fifteen minutes of starting, enter the Zollern Trench.

At 1.10 p.m. observers watched the advance reach the line of defences known as Hessian trench, north of the Zollern Redoubt, and they secured photographs of the position. Later in the day the air reports showed that most of Thiepval was captured, but that the enemy was still holding out in a bit of his old trench in the north of the village. Fighting went on in the outskirts of Thiepval all night, and by 8.30 a.m. on the 27th the whole of it was at last in our hands.

In addition to the contact patrols by the corps squadrons, low reconnaissances made by machines from G.H.Q. squadrons kept Headquarters informed of the general progress of the attack. Captain Ian Henderson of No. 19 Squadron tells, in a letter home, of what he saw whilst flying over the Canadians:

> I saw all the Germans huddled in their trench, and I saw our men advancing towards them. Then one of our men suddenly ran out and into the German trench. I expected to see him shot. No! All the Germans got out of the trench and followed

him back to our lines, running as hard as they could. . . .

The artillery work of the aeroplanes and of the balloons drew commendation from the Reserve Army Commander. The balloons on the front of the II Corps reported sixty-four active German batteries in the twenty-four hours following the opening of the attack, and, during the same important period, the aeroplanes gave the corps artillery commander the positions of one hundred and three more. Twenty-two German batteries, on the corps front, were engaged with aeroplane observation as compared with only six for which ground observation was possible. A formation of a thousand men, reported on the road south of Miraumont by an aeroplane of No. 4 Squadron, was scattered, with heavy casualties, by artillery, for the fire of which the observer sent down corrections.

The squadrons of the IV and V Brigades in the course of their normal work dropped one hundred and thirty-five 20-lb. bombs on trenches, batteries, and billeting villages. Lagnicourt aerodrome, whence the Germans continued to be very active, was again bombed by the III Brigade, but a thick haze made observation difficult, although hutments near the aerodrome were seen to catch fire. This brigade, too, made an attack on the kite balloons. Two which were caught in the air were shot down in flames by Le Prieur rockets fired by Nieuports of No. 60 Squadron, and others on the ground were attacked with phosphorus bombs, with what results could not be seen. An enemy divisional headquarters at Barastre was attacked by No. 19 Squadron with sixty-four 20-lb. bombs which burst among the billets.

In the day's fighting two German aeroplanes were shot down and four others driven down damaged, but our offensive patrols found once again that often they could not get to close grips with their faster opponents. A Sopwith of No. 70 Squadron, one of a patrol of six which fought six German aeroplanes over Bapaume, was lost.

On September the 27th the offensive patrols found numerous enemy formations in the morning before the weather broke with drenching rain. One patrol of six Martinsydes of No. 27 Squadron was attacked near Bapaume by five biplanes led by Böelcke, who gives an account of the fight in a letter home. (*Hauptmann Böelckes Feldberichte*). He tells how his first victim, (Second Lieutenant H. A. Taylor), after a brief fight, fell like a sack. He goes on to recount how he then got behind another Martinsyde which tried in vain to shake him off, and how he was surprised, after hitting the aeroplane with many bullets at close range, to see it fly round in continuous circles. Böelcke writes:

> I said to myself the fellow is long since dead, and the machine is flying so because its steering apparatus is fixed in the right position. I flew therefore quite close and saw the occupant, leaning over to the right, dead in his cockpit. So that I should know which of the machines I had shot down (surely it must go down), I noted the number: 7495, (flown by Second Lieutenant S. Dendrino), left him, and took on the next. This one escaped fighting in circles towards the front, but as I once got close under him, I saw that my hits had ripped his fuselage. He also would have cause to remember the day. All the same I had to work like a nigger.

The pilot who would have cause to remember, returned with bullets in the petrol tank, in the seat and seat bearers, radiator, engine, planes, centre section strut, and controls of his aeroplane. Of the remaining three aeroplanes of the patrol one, riddled with bullets, was landed by its wounded pilot in our lines, and two got back undamaged. In addition to this fighting, the early railway reconnaissance, made by No. 70 Squadron, lost one of its Sopwiths to an attack by a fast single-seater. No casualties to enemy aeroplanes were reported by any of our pilots as a result of the day's fighting. A German balloon which broke away from near Bapaume during the day drifted over our lines where it was blown northwards towards Ypres.

A pilot of No. 40 Squadron was about to shoot it down when he saw the observer hanging from the rigging, waving a large handkerchief. He thereupon held his fire and signalled to the observer to go down. The balloon was about 1,200 feet from the ground when a de Havilland pilot of No. 29 Squadron came up from the opposite side and, before he had realised what the position was, shot the balloon down in flames. The passenger in the balloon was taken prisoner; he had tried to jump but his parachute had got entangled in the rigging.

On the Fourth Army front on the 27th observers reported the progress of infantry patrols towards the line between Eaucourt l'Abbaye and Le Sars, on which the enemy had fallen back after a successful attack on part of his line north-west of Gueudecourt in the afternoon. In addition to the usual contact, artillery, and photographic work, the day was notable for many air attacks with machine-gun fire on infantry, and horse and motor transport behind the battle front.

On Thursday the 28th the Reserve Army, which had got a footing in the Stuff Redoubt on the previous day, followed up its success with the capture of the southern face of the Schwaben Redoubt. Aeroplanes of the V Brigade reported the success of this attack, and also enabled the artillery on their front to destroy sixteen gun-pits, damage fifteen others, and blow up nine ammunition pits. There were not many German aeroplanes flying throughout the day, but in the evening Captain Ball found and attacked an enemy formation and destroyed one and sent two others down damaged. Captain E. L. Foot, of No. 60 Squadron, flying a new fighter, the French Spad, destroyed another of a formation of four.

★★★★★★

Designed by Monsieur Béchereau for the old Deperdussin firm which Monsieur Bleriot had taken over soon after the outbreak of war as the *Societé pour les Appareils Deperdussin* (afterwards the *Societé pour Aviation et ses Dérives*). The initials were borrowed for the new machine which, fitted with the 150 horsepower Hispano-Suiza engine and a Vickers gun firing through the propeller, had a ceiling of about 19,000 feet, could climb to 10,000 feet in ten minutes, and had a speed at this height of 115 miles per hour.

★★★★★★

There was little useful flying in the rain on the 29th, but the 30th, a brilliant autumn day, brought a fresh burst of air activity. Five hundred air photographs were brought in from the battle area showing the details of the new country to be attacked: information on the wire and on the condition of the enemy's trenches was compiled by low reconnaissance. The Reserve Army, by the 30th, had captured the whole of the Stuff Redoubt and all except a corner of the Schwaben Redoubt, and thus the whole of the Pozières ridge and the ground dominating the Ancre valley from the south was at last in our grip.

So, went the final stretch of the main ridge and with it the last of the enemy's direct ground observation. It was now more important than ever that the Flying Corps should try to deny air observation to the enemy. The Nieuports showed that they could put up a good fight against the best of the enemy aeroplanes. Eleven aeroplanes of Nos. 12 and 13 Squadrons which dropped eighty-eight 20-lb. bombs on Lagnicourt aerodrome were escorted by six Nieuports and two Moranes of No. 60 Squadron, and by F.E.2b's of No. 11 Squadron. As the formation approached the aerodrome, many enemy pilots got off the ground. On the homeward journey there was fighting all the way.

Three German aeroplanes were destroyed—one in flames—and one was driven down out of control, whilst an F.E. was lost.

The German air resistance, following the appearance on the front of the new enemy fighting units, was growing apace. General Trenchard was quick to realise that the new fighters were the first sign of a reawakening of the German air service, and that every effort would be made by the enemy to profit by his experiences on the Somme and become more and more aggressive. On the 29th of September he had intimated to the War Office his intention of sending, through Sir Douglas Haig, a demand that the number of fighting squadrons with each army should be increased from four to six and eventually to eight, and on the next day Sir Douglas Haig sent the following letter home:

> I have the honour to request that the immediate attention of the Army Council may be given to the urgent necessity for a very early increase in the numbers and efficiency of the fighting aeroplanes at my disposal. Throughout the last three months the Royal Flying Corps in France has maintained such a measure of superiority over the enemy in the air that it has been enabled to render services of incalculable value. The result is that the enemy has made extraordinary efforts to increase the number, and develop the speed and power, of his fighting machines. He has unfortunately succeeded in doing so and it is necessary to realise clearly, and at once, that we shall undoubtedly lose our superiority in the air if I am not provided at an early date with improved means of retaining it.
>
> Within the last few days the enemy has brought into action on the Somme front a considerable number of fighting aeroplanes which are faster, handier, and capable of attaining a greater height than any at my disposal with the exception of one squadron of single-seater "Nieuports", one of "F.E. Rolls Royce", and one of "Sopwiths",—the last mentioned being inferior to the enemy's new machines in some respects though superior in others. All other fighting machines at my disposal are decidedly inferior.
>
> The result of the advent of the enemy's improved machines has been a marked increase in the casualties suffered by the Royal Flying Corps, and though I do not anticipate losing our present predominance in the air for the next three or four months,

AREA OF
RESERVE ARMY OPERATIONS AT THIEPVAL.
26th September, 1916.

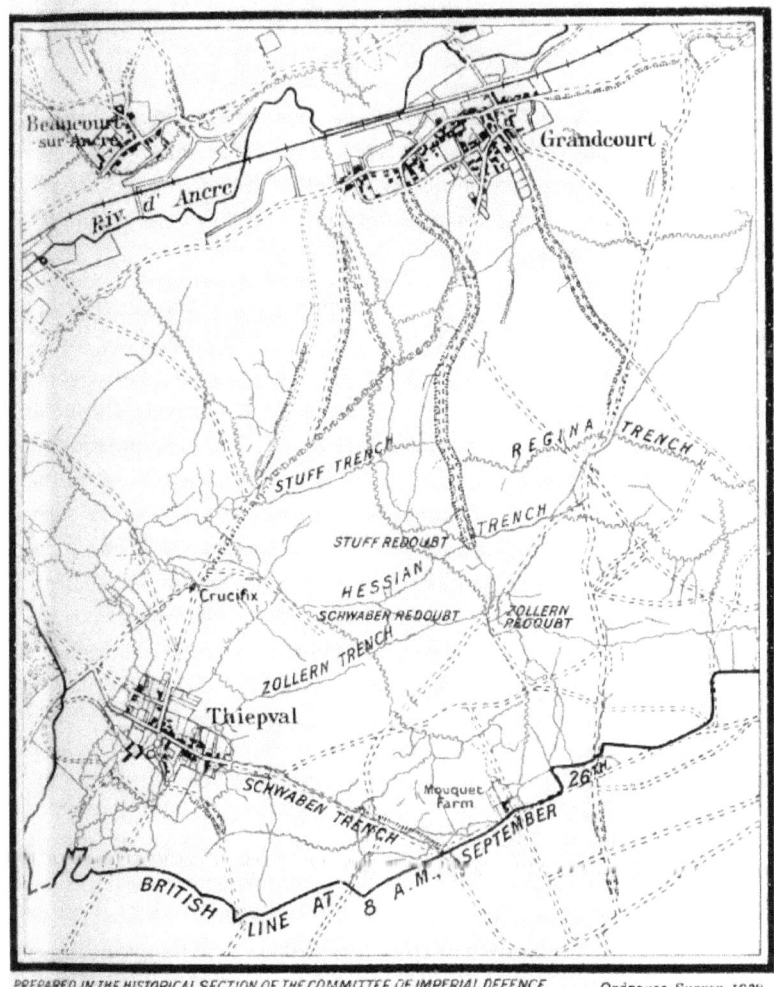

the situation after that threatens to be very serious unless adequate steps to deal with it are taken at once. I have directed the G.O.C. Royal Flying Corps in France to put forward a statement of our estimated requirements.

In a personal letter to Sir William Robertson, the Chief of the Imperial General Staff, written on the same day, Sir Douglas Haig pointed out that the jump in the Flying Corps losses in the last fortnight of September meant that we were now doing less distant fighting:

> With the result that an increasing number of German machines now come up to the lines, and a few cross them, whereas practically no German machines crossed the line in the first two months of the battle. It is the fighting far behind the enemy's lines that tells most.

On the 1st of October, at a quarter-past three in the afternoon, an attack was made by the III Corps and by the left division of the XV Corps against Eaucourt l'Abbaye and the enemy entrenchments east and west of it, along a total front of about 3,000 yards. In the village itself the enemy held out, (the whole Eaucourt l'Abbaye position was finally taken by the evening of October 3rd), but elsewhere the infantry, advancing under a well-timed barrage, gained all their objectives and even pushed patrols into Le Sars. The attack was reported by contact observers of Nos. 34 and 3 Squadrons. One of the aeroplanes of the latter squadron had its wing cut clean through by one of our own passing shells, and had to return. The commander of No. 34 Squadron, Major J. A. Chamier, who piloted one of the contact observers over the battle front, wrote his impression of the attack as follows:

> At 3.15 p.m. the steady bombardment changed into a most magnificent barrage. The timing of this was extremely good. Guns opened simultaneously and the effect was that of many machine-guns opening fire on the same order. As seen from the air the barrage appeared to be a most perfect wall of fire in which it was inconceivable that anything could live. The first troops to extend from the forming up places appeared to be the 50th Division who were seen to spread out from the sap heads and forming up trenches and advance close up under the barrage, apparently some 50 yards away from it. They appeared to capture their objective very rapidly and with practically no losses while crossing the open.

The 23rd Division I did not see so much of owing to their being at the moment of Zero at the tail end of the machine. The 47th Division took more looking for than the 50th, and it was my impression at the time that they were having some difficulty in getting into formation for attack from their forming up places, with the result that they appeared to be very late and to be some distance behind the barrage when it lifted off the German front line at Eaucourt l'Abbaye, and immediately to the west of it.

It was plain that here there was a good chance of failure and this actually came about, for the men had hardly advanced a couple of hundred yards apparently, when they were seen to fall and take cover among shell holes, being presumably held up by machine-gun and rifle fire. It was not possible to verify this owing to the extraordinary noise of the bursting shells of our barrage. The tanks were obviously too far behind, owing to lack of covered approaches, to be able to take part in the original attack, but they were soon seen advancing on either side of the Eaucourt l'Abbaye-Flers line, continuously in action and doing splendid work. They did not seem to be a target of much enemy shell fire.

The enemy barrage appeared to open late, quite five minutes after the commencement of our own barrage, and when it came it bore no resemblance to the wall of fire which we were putting up. I should have described it as a heavy shelling of an area some 300 to 400 yards in depth from our original jumping off places. Some large shells were falling in Destrémont Farm but these again were too late to catch the first line of the attack, although they must have caused some losses to the supports.

Thirty minutes after Zero the first English patrols were seen entering Le Sars. They appeared to be meeting with little or no opposition, and at this time no German shells were falling in the village. Our own shells were falling in the northern half. To sum up: the most startling feature of the operations as viewed from the air was (1) the extraordinary volume of fire of our barrage and the straight line kept by it. (2) The apparent ease with which the attack succeeded where troops were enabled to go forward close under it. (3) The promiscuous character and comparative lack of volume of enemy's counter-barrage.

Whilst the Fourth Army were attacking on the 1st of October at Eaucourt l'Abbaye, the Canadians on their left were attempting to push forward their line north and west of Courcelette, but they could make little progress against a terrific artillery fire and in face of numerous counter attacks. The attack began at 3.0 p.m., and during the following three hours sixty-seven area calls on to active batteries were sent down from the air to the II Corps counter-battery group, whilst the positions of thirty-nine batteries which were firing were reported by the kite balloon observers.

Before the Canadian attack began the station at Miraumont had been bombed by Nos. 12 and 13 Squadrons of the III Brigade. Twenty-five 112-lb. bombs were dropped at 11.45 a.m. and started fires in the station which were still burning five hours later. In the afternoon No. 19 Squadron dropped forty-eight 20-lb. bombs on the rest billets in Havrincourt without enemy opposition from the air.

On the 2nd of October rain poured continuously, and what was unusual was a patrol of eight German pilots low over our trenches between Morval and Lesboeufs at a time when no British aeroplanes were working in the air. One of the German biplanes was shot down by an antiaircraft battery.

On the 7th of October the Fourth Army, in dull and tempestuous weather, attacked from Destrémont Farm to Lesboeufs to help a French advance against Sailly-Saillisel. (To facilitate this advance Sir Douglas Haig had handed over Morval to the French at the end of September). On the previous day German airmen had flown over our forward positions, possibly taking photographs, and some of them, from a few hundred feet, had attacked troops of the XV Corps with machine-gun fire. Whilst the bombardment, in preparation for the attack, was in progress on the morning of the 7th, they appeared again, particularly over our battery positions behind Flers and Gueudecourt, and on to some of these they directed the fire of their own artillery.

Fighting pilots of the IV Brigade who went out when news of the enemy's activity was received found that the German pilots had ceased work and had gone home. The contact observers who went out to report the attack were seriously impeded by the strong westerly wind. So that the observers might have an opportunity to study the ground, pilots had to turn into the wind, when they at once became almost stationary and therefore perfect targets for the German infantry. Officers in two aeroplanes flying over the attack were wounded, and many other aeroplanes suffered so much damage from bullets that their pilots had to return forthwith to their aerodromes where many of them landed with difficulty. It is not surprising, therefore, to read in the army commanders' account of the attack, that the number and accuracy of the air reports was not up to the usual standard. Furthermore, the lack of air observation during the rainy days before the attack was launched seriously affected the accuracy of the supporting bombardment, and this fact was a part cause of the failure of the infantry to achieve their objectives, except at Le Sars and east of Gueudecourt. The other cause was the timeliness and accuracy of the enemy barrage, the latter aided, no doubt, by the earlier work of the German air observers.

We may pause to consider the wider effects of the break in the weather. Already many trenches were crumbling to lines of mud and the shell-pocked roads were fast becoming impassable. We had advanced to a position from which great happenings might have been looked for. All the enemy's laboriously prepared positions south of the Ancre had fallen and his armies had been consistently beaten. However feverishly he might work on new entrenchments farther back, he could not hope, unless time were allowed him, to make those defences formidable. And it was no intention of Sir Douglas Haig to give the enemy time.

The Allied scheme aimed at an immediate exploitation of the successes so long and so hardly fought for. That scheme included an advance to the general line Le Transloy-south of Bapaume-Bois de Loupart, after which the British forces were to swing to the north and northeast to turn the whole of the enemy defence system south of the Scarpe, and so threaten his armies in that area with capture or destruction. From a dispassionate consideration of all the circumstances it is difficult to see what, given fair weather, could have stopped the steady progress of these plans. Along the whole western front, the Allied forces outnumbered the Germans.

The British infantry and artillery had already shown their ability to drive the enemy from the strongest defences which time and science could provide; the Royal Flying Corps could look forward for a time to a continued superiority which, although modified, would still enable the corps pilots and observers to meet the requirements of the infantry and artillery. But the appalling weather continued far into November, the offensive plans were constantly reduced in scope, and the full fruits of the victory slipped irrevocably from our grasp.

On the 9th of October, at 11.20 p.m., German aeroplanes bombed the back areas of the III Corps. Within ten minutes three pilots of No. 18 Squadron and one from No. 21 Squadron were sent out to attack lighted aerodromes from which these enemy bombers might have come. No lighted aerodromes were found and the bombs were dropped on the station at Cambrai and on villages near Bapaume. At Cambrai the bombs were seen to burst on a train which had already been hit a little earlier by a pilot of No. 13 Squadron. At the same time another pilot of No. 13 Squadron had hit a train in Bapaume station, whilst a third, without observation of his results, had dropped two 112-lb. bombs on two trains in Quéant station.

The 10th of October saw a brief respite in the severity of the weather. Although there were no major ground operations both air services were on the wing all day, the enemy showing his usual burst of activity after a spell of wet. Every one of our offensive patrols had fights, and those which went in favour of the enemy were all with pilots of Böelcke's squadron. A patrol of No. 70 Squadron attacked seven fighters over the German aerodrome at Vélu. Some F.E.'s and de Havillands flew to the help of the Sopwiths and, although our pilots and observers found it impossible to hold their sights on the enemy aeroplanes owing to the rapidity of their movements, they succeeded in driving the enemy off. One German aeroplane was shot down and apparently destroyed, and one of the Sopwiths was lost.

In other fighting over the Somme area during the day, three German aeroplanes were destroyed. Two British machines were missing, and another, shot down near Morval, was completely wrecked, but both its occupants escaped unhurt. A pilot of No. 32 Squadron had the main controls of his aeroplane shot away. His machine turned a somersault and was wrecked near Pozières, but the pilot escaped unhurt. Another aeroplane of No. 23 Squadron, on photographic work near Bapaume, was attacked by a formation of five.

The pilot. Captain R. N. Adams, mortally wounded, fell on the control lever and the F.E.2b dived steeply. The observer. Second Lieutenant G. J. Ogg, leaned over the pilot's cockpit, pushed the pilot off the lever and, holding him back with one hand, worked the controls with the other, and landed the aeroplane within our lines near Morval. There it ran into a deep shell hole and was wrecked. The observer was unhurt but the pilot died without regaining consciousness.

During the following night bomb raids were made on Cambrai by No. 18 Squadron, on Marcoing by No. 19 Squadron, and on Vitry station and Douai aerodrome by No. 13 Squadron.

An infantry attack on the 12th of October along the whole Fourth Army front won only a small stretch of ground north and northeast of Gueudecourt; elsewhere the attack was repulsed. The reason of the failure was again the inadequate artillery preparation due to bad weather and the consequent restriction of air observation. The 16th was unexpectedly fine and the change in the flying conditions was welcomed on every aerodrome. The air activity opened long before dawn when three aeroplanes of No. 18 Squadron, one of which failed to return, bombed Cambrai. The enemy, in the dark, also made a raid, bombing the aerodrome of No. 9 Squadron where they destroyed one aeroplane, damaged another, and wounded two mechanics.

Seven B.E.12's from No. 19 Squadron bombed Hermies station and aerodrome, and Ruyaulcourt in the afternoon. The formation was attacked and two of the B.E.'s were shot down, one in flames. An earlier raid on Havrincourt by the same squadron had met with no opposition. Pilots and observers of the IV and V Brigades, who took full advantage of the fine spell to get photographs and to do artillery work, had to meet many attacks. One artillery aeroplane of No. 15 Squadron, attacked over the front line trenches at Hebuterne by five enemy pilots, crashed into the wire in front of the trenches and the pilot and observer were killed. Another, of No. 34 Squadron, got back damaged from an attack over Warlencourt, with a wounded observer. The numerous offensive patrols from both these brigades were fighting all day. One aeroplane was lost and one pilot returned wounded from IV Brigade patrols which destroyed three enemy machines during the day. Another was destroyed by the patrols of the V Brigade.

The next morning was again fine. Nineteen 112-lb. bombs were dropped on a dump and sidings north of Bapaume, causing an explosion. The Third Army reconnaissance, made by a formation from No. 11 Squadron, was attacked by about twenty fighters, two of which were shot down, whilst two of the reconnaissance aeroplanes were also lost. Another aeroplane was lost over Vélu by No. 23 Squadron a little later in the morning. A patrol of No. 24 Squadron, without loss to themselves, drove down two enemy machines. For the next two days there was rain and sleet, but on the 20th, 21st, and 22nd an interlude of fine weather brought some of the fiercest air fighting in the whole battle.

The Reorganisation of the German Air Service

The German air concentration at the Somme, it will be recalled, reached its peak in the middle of October. Furthermore, a complete reorganisation of the enemy air service had now begun. By an order of the new German High Command a strictly centralised control of all air units, including anti-aircraft defences, had been established on the 8th of October under General von Hoeppner with Colonel Thomsen, the former chief of the air forces in the field, as his Chief-of-Staff. General von Hoeppner was, by his enthusiasm and administrative ability, well fitted for his new command. He was born on the Baltic island of Wollin, in 1860, and had become a cavalry officer at the age of nineteen. He received rapid promotion and began the war, as a major-general, on the general staff of the Third Army.

He was commanding a reserve division when the new air command was offered to him. He took up his appointment at the moment when the German air service was recovering its morale, and his foresight was to ensure that the German airmen were never again to suffer such a spirit of helplessness as was their fate in the first weeks of the struggle on the Somme.

By the 15th of October the number of air units with the German First Army had increased to thirty-eight. These were seventeen reconnaissance lights (*Feldflieger-Abteilungen*), totalling one hundred aeroplanes, thirteen artillery flights (*Artillerieflieger-Abtelungen*), totalling fifty-three aeroplanes, three pursuit squadrons (*Jagdstaffeln*), totalling forty-five aeroplanes, three bomber-fighter squadrons (*Kampfgeschwader*) of a total of one hundred and seventeen aeroplanes, and two independent flights of a total of eighteen bomber-fighters. This represented an actual strength of 333 aeroplanes with the German First Army along the front from Hannescamps to Peronne.

On the morning of October, the 15th, the actual strength of the squadrons of the IV and V Brigades and of the headquarter Ninth Wing was 293 aeroplanes. (These included, in addition to the corps two-seaters, fifty-two F.E.2b's; thirty-six de Havilland Scouts; eighteen Martinsyde Scouts; thirty-five B.E.12's; twenty-six Sopwith two-seaters; and one Spad).

In addition, the five squadrons of the III Brigade had an actual strength of ninety aeroplanes of which eighteen (No. 11 Squadron) were F.E.2b's and eighteen (No. 60 Squadron) were made up of fifteen Nieuport Scouts, two Morane Scouts and one Spad. This brigade had, however, to meet some of the air units working with the German Sixth Army, especially in the neighbourhood of Douai. On the other hand, the air units with the German First Army were also concerned with a part of the French front from the British right to Peronne. It may be stated, very generally, that the superiority, in numbers, of the Royal Flying Corps over the German air service in the battle area, in the middle of October, is represented by half the strength of the III Brigade.

But it should be remembered that the forty-five aeroplanes of the three Pursuit Squadrons, or *Jagdstaffeln*, with the German First Army, were more effective as fighters than anything we could oppose to them. North of the III Brigade area, the two brigades of the Royal Flying Corps, together with the Naval Air Service units at Dunkirk, were more than double the strength of the enemy air units opposite their fronts.

★★★★★★

North of the German First Army, to the sea, were the Sixth and Fourth Armies. The Sixth Army had seven *Flieger-Abteilungen* (forty-one aeroplanes), and one *Jagdstaffel* (eleven aeroplanes). The Fourth Army had one *Flieger-Abteilung* (six aeroplanes), two naval reconnaissance flights (thirty-one machines), and one *Jagdstaffel* (12 aeroplanes) which gives one hundred and one machines in all. The two Royal Flying Corps brigades, north of the area covered by the III Brigade, had an actual strength of 180 aeroplanes as follows: I Brigade (five squadrons), fifty-four corps aeroplanes, and thirty-five fighters (No. 25 Squadron, seventeen F.E.2b's, and No. 40 Squadron, eighteen F.E.8's—single-seater fighters); II Brigade (five squadrons), fifty-five corps aeroplanes, and thirty-six fighters (No. 20 Squadron, eighteen F.E.2d's—the improved F.E. 2b with 250 horse-power Rolls Royce engine—and No. 29 Squadron, eighteen de Havilland Scouts).

Thus, the total strength of the Royal Flying Corps squadrons on the 15th of October was 563 aeroplanes, and of the German air service, north of Peronne to the sea, 434 machines (approximately) With the German armies, south of Peronne to Switzerland, were, approximately, 451 aeroplanes of which 120 were fighters. Of these, 207 aeroplanes (forty-four of which fighters) were attached to the German Second Army. Only 114 aeroplanes (twenty-five fighters) were now in the Verdun area. To get the true measure of the comparative strengths of the two air services at this time there must be added the Dunkirk units of the Royal Naval Air Service, namely, eighty aeroplanes (forty of which fighters) and fifteen seaplanes.

★★★★★★

It was natural, then, that the first fine day, following the zenith of the German air concentration at the Somme, should bring great activity on the part of the enemy air service and more determined attempts to interfere with our reconnaissance and artillery aeroplanes. The Third Army reconnaissance, for instance, on October the 20th, sent out by No. 11 Squadron, had completed its photography at Douai and was moving off to the south when Böelcke's squadron attacked.

The German leader severely wounded the pilot of one of the F.E.'s and shot many of his controls away. As the aeroplane went down the observer was thrown out and fell behind the German lines. The F.E. crashed in the British lines south of Arras, and was completely wrecked. Another of the F.E.'s was shot down, but was seen to land under control west of Douai, whilst a third, with its petrol tank smashed by bullets, got back to its aerodrome.

The German fighters, after their success, withdrew, and Captain H. B. Davey, the leader of the reconnaissance, undaunted, headed towards Bapaume to complete his work. On the way the three remaining F.E.'s were again attacked, and one was forced to retire with a damaged engine and propeller. Captain Davey with his sole surviving companion kept on in the hope that he would pick up a Nieuport patrol which had been warned to look out for his formation over Havrincourt Wood, but he failed to find them, and, surrounded by German aeroplanes, made his way back to the lines.

Despite the widespread activity of the enemy, No. 27 Squadron succeeded in making a raid on Aulnoye junction, south-west of Maubeuge. Nine of their Martinsydes dropped twelve 112-lb. bombs on the station buildings, and the pilots got back without encountering opposition although they had been out for four hours. No. 70 Squadron similarly met with no opposition on their long reconnaissance to Valenciennes and Le Quesnoy. Perhaps a reason for their immunity was that the enemy was paying more attention to the immediate battle area, where the patrols of the army squadrons were engaged in incessant fighting to protect our own corps aeroplanes and to keep off enemy machines, of which thirty-three crossed the lines of the Fourth Army during the day. One of these, a new single-seater fighter, was shot down into High Wood by F.E.'s and de Havillands. The total loss to the enemy in the day's air fighting was three aeroplanes destroyed, and seventeen forced down damaged.

During the crisp frosty night of the 20th/2ist of October German aeroplanes bombed Querrieu, Corbie, and Longueau, blowing up an ammunition wagon at the latter place. In retaliation four pilots of No. 18 Squadron went off just after three in the morning and bombed the neighbourhood of Vélu and Peronne.

The enemy took advantage of the clear weather to make a determined infantry attack, in the early morning of Saturday the 21st, on the Schwaben Redoubt. The German attack which was repulsed came at an opportune moment. The Reserve Army had made full dispositions for an assault on the Regina and Stuff trenches as far as the Schwaben Redoubt for later in the day, and when the troops went forward, just after midday, they caught the enemy on the rebound and took their objectives with great rapidity and small loss. Contact patrols by Nos. 4 and 7 Squadrons kept touch with the attack, and artillery observers of the same squadrons, favoured with perfect visibility, directed fire so effectively that ten gun pits were destroyed, fourteen others damaged, and seven ammunition pits blown up.

As the infantry attacked, many other German batteries were compelled to cease fire by observers who got our guns quickly on them by means of the zone call, the artillery being content to silence as many batteries as possible rather than to destroy a few. Two officers of No. 4 Squadron, by their observation for the artillery, aided in the capture of the Regina Trench. Between them they engaged and silenced, with heavy howitzer fire, nine German batteries which they saw plastering the area as our men went forward.

There were two brilliant bombing raids during the day, one by No. 27 Squadron as far over as Ath, north of Mons, and the other by Nos. 12 and 13 Squadrons on Quéant. At Ath the Martinsydes dropped ten 112-lb. bombs on a reported ammunition dump, photographs of which had been supplied by a French agent. Pilots went down low, one of them to 300 feet, to ensure accuracy of aim, and they were rewarded with four direct hits which set fire to the dump. The formation met with no opposition and returned safely. At Quéant, thirty 112-lb. bombs hit the station and railway line. Our formation of thirty aeroplanes, including escorts from Nos. 11 and 60 Squadrons, was attacked over the objective. One of No. 12 Squadron's B.E.'s was shot down, but all other aeroplanes got back safely.

After the formation had recrossed the lines a Nieuport pilot turned back to attack a fast biplane which, however, outmanoeuvred him, shot most of his controls away, and forced him to land between our front and support trenches. The pilot jumped clear as the Nieuport ran into a trench and turned over. Enemy airmen on the whole were less active than on the previous day, and made fewer attempts to interrupt the work of the corps squadrons. All the offensive patrols were successful in the fighting that came their way; one pilot of a patrol of No. II Squadron destroyed two enemy aeroplanes, one in flames, and other patrols drove down thirteen more, three of them damaged.

On the 22nd of October, the last fine day of the month, the enemy airmen made full use of their opportunity. Three Sopwiths of No. 45 Squadron, failed to return from an offensive patrol. (This squadron had arrived at Fienvillers from England on October 15th. The Sopwiths of the squadron were fitted with the Scarff-Dibovsky interrupter gear and with the Scarff Ring Mounting for the observer's Lewis gun). Earlier in the morning a patrol of this squadron had got split up and one of the Sopwiths was attacked by six single-seater fighters.

The observer was severely wounded in the stomach with the first burst of fire, but he continued to work his gun, sent one enemy aeroplane down out of control, and was successful in keeping off further attacks, and so enabled his pilot to make a landing behind our lines. An F.E.2b of No. 18 Squadron, which was escorting an aeroplane taking photographs near Bapaume, came into action with many enemy fighters, but drove them off and turned for home.

On the way the observer, Lieutenant F. S. Rankin, shot down one of three aeroplanes which attacked, whereupon the remaining two redoubled their efforts to bring the F.E. down. They were firing from behind, and the observer stood up to engage them over the top plane. He sent one of them down with a damaged engine, and was swinging his gun on to the third German machine when he was mortally wounded in the head and fell out over the side of the aeroplane.

The pilot. Second Lieutenant F. L. Barnard, caught his observer by the coat as he fell, and held on grimly as he climbed into the front seat whence he was able to pull his companion back into the F.E. Barnard returned to the pilot's seat under constant fire from the enemy fighter and found that most of the controls in his aeroplane had now been shot away. He succeeded, however, in getting back to the British front line where he landed behind the forward trenches. (Captain F. L. Barnard, the well-known civilian airman, was killed at Winterbourne, near Bristol, July 28th 1927, in a flying accident whilst testing an aeroplane entered for the King's Cup Race).

Elsewhere in the air the fighting was equally determined. Second Lieutenant A. Cropper, whilst patrolling with a companion aeroplane of No. 22 Squadron, was wounded in the leg in an attack by three fighters. He got his machine to the nearest aerodrome and safely landed his observer, but himself died as soon as he reached the casualty clearing station. Four British aeroplanes failed to return from fighting over the German lines.

On Monday the 23rd of October an attack was made by the XIV Corps of the Fourth Army in conjunction with the French Sixth Army to secure a good jumping-off position for an advance against the Le Transloy line. A dense fog had caused a postponement of the attack from 11.30 a.m. to 2.30 p.m. Although the fog lifted at noon the clouds remained low, and contact observers had the greatest difficulty in following the advance. By 4.0 p.m. they were helped by a plentiful lighting of flares which showed that our footing on the Le Transloy spur had been extended. Further progress, however, was held by a devastating long-range machine-gun fire, whilst some of our gains were wrested from us by counter attacks later in the day. During the progress of the attack, German aeroplanes flew over the gun positions of the XIV Corps; special patrols which were sent up after them were too late to engage them.

Enemy air observers were again registering on to batteries of the XIV Corps in the morning of the 25th. The railhead of Dernancourt, south of Albert, also came in for long-range artillery fire, for which an aeroplane gave corrections. At the time when these registrations were being made the Flying Corps fighting patrols were well over the German lines, where they had a few isolated combats in one of which a B.E.12 of No. 21 Squadron was shot down. Two artillery aeroplanes were also lost on the Reserve Army front, one, of No. 7 Squadron, being shot down in flames and another, of No. 4 Squadron, failing to return from its patrol. It was known later that both its occupants were killed. All three British aeroplanes which were shot down on this day fell to Böelcke's *Jagdstaffel 2*.

The 26th, although again squally, brought two big air fights. The first one began at 7.15 a.m., and was waged near Bapaume by five de Havillands of No. 24 Squadron against about twenty single-seater fighters, most of them Halberstadts. The de Havilland pilots found that although the Halberstadts were faster and could outclimb them, they had the disadvantage, as compared with the British fighter, that they lost height in turning, a fact of which the de Havillands made full use. The struggle was kept up at a fierce pace until the British pilots were left with only enough petrol to get them home, and by this time half the German formation had disappeared.

As the de Havillands turned for home, impeded by a strong head wind, the enemy pilots increased their attacks, but they had no success and gave up the fight before the lines were reached. The only British casualty was one officer slightly wounded. The second fight, in the afternoon, was more favourable to the enemy, and was notable for the last of Böelcke's successes. He led eight fighters of his squadron against artillery aeroplanes in the Ancre area. Of these, one was shot down in the enemy lines, and two into our own trenches where they were wrecked. The pilot of one of the aeroplanes which fell in our own lines was wounded and the observer killed, and the pilot of the other, who was flying alone, was picked up dead with a bullet through the head.

Captain Foot of No. 60 Squadron was returning alone in his Nieuport from chasing a German formation when he saw, from a distance, the attack on the artillery aeroplanes. He dived straight down towards a single-seater which was on the tail of one of the B.E.'s; he was too late to save the B.E., but he got a burst of fire into the enemy aeroplane from close range. The German pilot turned head on to the Nieuport, got slightly above it and, with his first few rounds, put the Nieuport's gun out of action; he then got on to the tail of the Nieuport and easily held it in the quick manoeuvring which followed. Foot dived steeply but could not shake off his enemy, who followed him down and set fire to his petrol tank when he was no more than a few feet from the ground. The Nieuport crashed at once and burnt itself out but the pilot escaped without injury. In the meantime, a de Havilland patrol of No. 32 Squadron, which had also seen the attack on the artillery aeroplanes, joined in the fighting and shot down one German machine which fell near the wreckage of the B.E. in the enemy lines.

On the 28th of October two de Havilland pilots of No. 24 Squadron, Lieutenant A. G. Knight and Second Lieutenant A. E. McKay, were on patrol in the afternoon near Pozières when Böelcke at the head of six fighters attacked them. Soon after the fight began six other German pilots joined in. In diving on Knight's aeroplane two of the enemy fighters collided, and bits were seen to fall off the planes of one of them as it glided away east, apparently under control. For another fifteen minutes the two de Havillands, by brilliant manoeuvring, beat off all attacks; by this time the fight had drifted east of Bapaume, but the enemy pilots lost heart and broke off the engagement allowing the de Havillands to make an unmolested return.

It was afterwards learned that the aeroplane which had gone down, in trouble as a result of the collision was piloted by Böelcke, that it broke up in the clouds, and that in the crash which followed the German leader was killed. In less than two months' air fighting in the Somme battle Oswald Böelcke had shot down twenty British aeroplanes. The aeroplane on which he did so well was handier, faster, and more effectively armed than anything flying against him, and all his combats were offered to him in the air above his own troops. Nevertheless, he proved a determined, resourceful, and gallant foe, and his successes inspired the members of his own squadron and put heart once again into the whole German air service. One may regret the manner of his passing, but the spirit which he bequeathed to his service lived on. (A laurel wreath, dropped by parachute over the German lines, bore the inscription: 'To the memory of Captain Böelcke, our brave and chivalrous foe. From the British Royal Flying Corps.')

The Royal Flying Corps on the Somme front had been reinforced, as we have seen, since the beginning of the battle, by three squadrons from England (Nos. 34, 19, and 45). Further, General Trenchard had drawn from the two brigades to the north, by the 23rd of October, three corps squadrons (Nos. 7, 18, and 5), and two fighting squadrons (Nos. 32 and 29). No. 5 (B.E.'s) had been transferred to work with the Reserve Army on the 2nd of October, and No. 29 (de Havilland Scouts) to the Third Army front on the 23rd of October, four other new squadrons which had arrived from England were used to take the place of the more experienced squadrons which had been withdrawn to the Somme. (These were No. 40, F.E. 8's, one Flight August 2nd., remaining two Flights August 25th; No. 42, B.E.'s, August 15th; No. 41, F.E. 8's, October 21st; and No. 46, Nieuport two-seaters, fitted with the Scarff-Dibovsky interrupter gear, October 26th. The dates given are those on which the squadrons arrived on their aerodromes after allocation to the brigades).

But against the added strength which these reinforcements brought, must be set down the fact that most of the squadrons in the line had been flying without break or rest since long before the battle opened and had suffered many casualties, and that after the middle of September the B.E.12's (Nos. 19 and 21 Squadrons) ceased to be used as fighters. The machine had proved too clumsy and incapable of useful work against the hostile fighters. General Trenchard said:

> I realise fully that I shall lose two squadrons if I stop using the B.E.12 and delay, I suppose, for some considerable period two

other squadrons. Although I am short of machines to do the work that is now necessary with the large number of Germans against us, I cannot do anything else but to recommend that no more be sent out to this country.

He went on to say that he would use the B.E.12's for the time being for night work, defensive patrols, and bombing with an escort.

Meanwhile, at a meeting of the War Committee in London, held on the 17th of October, at which Sir Douglas Haig's letter of the 30th of September on the subject of air reinforcements was discussed, it was decided that a Naval Air Service squadron, made up from the units at Dunkirk, should be sent down to the Somme to help the Royal Flying Corps. This squadron, under Squadron Commander G. R. Bromet, went to Vert Galand aerodrome, where the first of its aeroplanes arrived on the 26th of October and the rest within a few days. The unit, known as Naval Squadron No. 8, had one flight of Nieuports, one of Sopwith two-seaters, and one of Sopwith single-seaters ('Pups'), and made its first patrol on the 3rd of November.

The work of the Royal Flying Corps during the remainder of the battle had little in it that was spectacular, but it deserves to rank high for the pertinacity with which pilots and observers struggled through the rain, mist, and sleet to give their help to the army. In the teeth of the westerly gales, they flew perilously low, registering the guns, reconnoitring the trenches and villages, and attacking infantry and transport with bombs and machine-gun fire, or calling up the guns to get on to them. If the conditions were uncomfortable in the air, they were far worse on the ground. In the minor fighting troops often stuck waist deep in mud from which they had to be dug out. The German forward trenches when captured were often found to be a series of shell-craters joined by ditches knee deep in water.

Bright intervals on the 3rd of November brought out many German fighters. Five of our aeroplanes were shot down during the day, three of them from a photographic reconnaissance formation of No. 22 Squadron led by Captain Lord Lucas who, it was afterwards known, had been attacked by three enemy pilots and shot in the head and leg. His aeroplane was landed by the wounded observer, Lieutenant A. Anderson. Lord Lucas never regained consciousness after he was hit, and died the same day. He had lost a leg from wounds received in the South African War.

In 1914 he was Under Parliamentary Secretary for Agriculture, but in spite of his disability and his work in Parliament, he remained restless for more active service. In May 1915 he left politics for the Royal Flying Corps, and qualified first as observer and then as pilot. He flew on active service in Egypt and instructed at Dover before he went to France in October 1916. He was the oldest in years, but youngest in heart, of all the pilots of his squadron. (The death of Lord Lucas is commemorated in a poem, *In Memoriam A.H.* by the Hon. Maurice Baring). Of the four officers in the two aeroplanes shot down with him, one was killed, and two were wounded. Two of them had fallen, with their machine, on to an enemy kite balloon on the ground, and set it on fire.

On the 5th of November the Fourth Army attacked in conjunction with the French. Ground was won and maintained north-east of Lesboeufs but, elsewhere, gains could not be held in face of severe counter-attacks. Although a heavy gale blew all day a contact patrol observer, in a three and three-quarter hours' flight, was able to report the progress of the attack on the Butte de Warlencourt, which was taken but lost to counter-attacks.

On the night of the 6th German airmen made a raid down the valley of the Somme, attacking various villages. At Cerisy, an ammunition train, near which stood a cage filled with German prisoners, was blown up by a direct hit and the immediate area was devastated.

When the weather showed signs of improvement on the 8th German aeroplanes were reported in large numbers, especially along the front of the Australians north of Gueudecourt, where many of them flew low and attacked troops in the trenches with their machine-guns. This form of attack, indeed, was now being newly developed by the enemy. To force some of this activity away from the front, General Trenchard ordered the bombing of the enemy's back areas on the 9th, a bright, cold day. The station at Arleux, north-west of Aubigny-au-Bac, was attacked in the morning by No. 27 Squadron and after dark by No. 19 Squadron. The sheds at the station, reported to contain ammunition, were hit but no explosions resulted; a train in the station was attacked with machine-gun fire.

A raid on the ammunition dump at Vraucourt northeast of Bapaume, made by twelve bombers with fourteen escorting machines, was attacked by thirty or more aeroplanes, and led to the biggest air fight which the war had yet seen. Some of the enemy pilots attacked soon after the lines were crossed, but most of the eighty 20-lb. bombs carried by the aeroplanes of Nos. 12 and 13 Squadrons were dropped on their objective. As Vraucourt was neared the German attacks were intensified, some fighters getting inside our formation, and over the village itself the fighting became general. The escorting aeroplanes were supplied by Nos. 11, 60, and 29 Squadrons.

The first casualty was suffered by No. 60 Squadron soon after the trenches were crossed. Lieutenant A. D. Bell-Irving, in the last of three fights, was wounded in the leg, and had his Very lights set on fire and his engine and petrol tank hit, but he was able to land near the trenches, where his aeroplane was wrecked. Meanwhile, the remainder of the escorting machines were fighting hard to protect the bombers, but two of these, both from No. 12 Squadron, were shot down, and the pilot of another was wounded but got home. Two of the escort, both de Havillands of No. 29 Squadron, were fought down by several enemy fighters, and were last seen still keeping up the fight close to the ground. Lastly, one of the F.E.'s of No. 11 Squadron, with a dead observer and a wounded pilot, crashed into no man's land whence the pilot escaped into the front line trenches.

The enemy airmen delivered their attacks from all sides in groups of two or three and succeeded in splitting up our formation, which resulted in many isolated combats at various heights. The fighting was so rapid and detailed that it is impossible to say what losses the enemy suffered, but three of his aeroplanes appear to have been destroyed. One of the bombing pilots who was shot down. Lieutenant G. F. Knight, eventually escaped from his prison camp in Germany. He died soon after his return to England, but he lived long enough to set down the story of his adventures in a small book, *Brother Bosch*, one of the best of its kind which the war produced, and one which epitomises the spirit of his Service. (This is published by Leonaur in *Wings of War* which contains both *The Airman* by C. Mellor and *"Brother Bosch"* by Gerald Featherstone Knight).

The offensive patrols which the III Brigade sent out during the day had twenty-six fights. On one of the patrols Flight Sergeant J. T. B. McCudden had his first fight in the Somme battle. This pilot, who was to do great work on the Western front, must here be introduced to the reader. He was born at Gillingham in Kent in 1895, son of Sergeant-Major W. H. McCudden of the Royal Engineers, which he himself joined as a bugler at the age of fifteen. He transferred to the Royal Flying Corps in April 1913, and went overseas on the outbreak of war as a mechanic in No. 3 Squadron. Before he returned to England to learn to fly in January 1916 he had had some experience as an observer. He was back in France as a pilot on the 4th of July 1916, and shot down his first German aeroplane on the 6th of September in the Ypres area.

He went down to the Somme as a de Havilland pilot with No. 29 Squadron. On the morning of the 9th of November, he flew, with two companions, into a formation of six of the new Albatros fighters. The fight which followed lasted twenty-five minutes and, although indecisive, was a brilliant one; McCudden's aeroplane came back with twenty-four bullet holes, a greater number of hits than he received in any of his subsequent fights.

Two officers, returning from a later patrol of the same squadron, attacked seven enemy aeroplanes near Arras. One of the de Havilland pilots, Second Lieutenant N. Brearley, had to withdraw from the fight owing to his gun jamming, but he was pursued and shot down, with a bullet in his chest, in front of the German trenches, where his machine collapsed. He was able to roll into a shell hole, where he stayed until darkness gave him the opportunity to crawl to the British lines. Here, however, he got caught up in the barbed wire whence he was rescued by the infantry. His companion meanwhile fought hard, but was eventually overwhelmed, shot down, and made prisoner. Other losses of the day from attacks by enemy airmen included the pilot of an artillery aeroplane brought back dead by his observer, a wounded observer brought back from an offensive patrol in a severely damaged machine, and a wounded pilot who was just able to land within our lines.

On odd days of fine weather, in October, observers of the III Brigade had seen that new trenches were being dug by the enemy far behind his present defences, notably to the north of Quéant. On the 9th of November a formation was sent out to report fully on this new digging. Eight F.E.2b's of No. 11 Squadron started off, and eight Nieuports of No. 60 Squadron were ordered to fly out to meet them over Bourlon, west of Cambrai. The Nieuport pilots had many fights on the way out and got split up; only one of them picked up the reconnaissance formation which, however, got back safely with a report revealing a new and continuous line stretching from west of Bourlon Wood, past Quéant, rounding Bullecourt, crossing the Sensée River, and passing south of Héninel to join the German third line south-east of Arras. The trenches thus early discovered were to form part of a line, identified with the name of the German commander, which was later to become famous.

The retreat to the Hindenburg Line in the following year was to be a delayed but definite effect of the fighting on the Somme in 1916. Two other series of new defences, nearer the front, which from the time they were begun were continuously reconnoitred and photographed from the air, were grouped, firstly, in front of Bapaume, continuing towards Ablainzevelle, to the north-west, and to Rocquigny to the southeast and, secondly, a system, branching off from this line, south of Achiet-le-Grand, which arched round to the Bapaume-Cambrai road west of Beugny, and continued beyond the eastern outskirts of the village of Ytres.

After dark on November the 9th bomb raids were made on the station at Vitry and the aerodromes at Douai, Buissy, Vélu, and Villers, and, on the following morning, at Valenciennes, where forty-four 20-lb. bombs, dropped by No. 27 Squadron, fell among five aeroplanes standing on the aerodrome, and on hangars and sheds alongside. Throughout the 10th there was a notable decrease in the offensive spirit of the enemy pilots, only one British aeroplane being lost, as compared with three German aeroplanes destroyed, and three sent down damaged. Pilots of the Naval Air Service squadron had many fights. They had, on the previous day, reported that in three enemy two-seater aeroplanes which they attacked at close range, the observers had collapsed, apparently hit, and on the 10th they drove down two further enemy aeroplanes, one of them out of control.

The aerodrome of No. 18 Squadron at Lavieville had been bombed during the night of the 9th/10th November, but no damage was done. One of the enemy pilots turned his machine-gun on mechanics who were placing landing flares. In retaliation, during the following night, four pilots of the squadron went out on roving commissions to drop bombs on lighted aerodromes or other suitable targets. No lighted aerodromes were seen. One pilot got as far over as Valenciennes where he found the station lit up. He dropped six bombs, which burst on trains in the station and started a fire. Two other pilots dropped their bombs on Vélu, and one of them attacked transport on the Bapaume road with machine-gun fire. The fourth pilot dropped three of his bombs on balloon sheds, and the remaining five, a little later, on a moving train east of St. Léger.

These bombs were released when the F.E.2b was only 150 feet above the trucks and their explosions buffeted the machine. The pilot then flew alongside the train to give his observer an opportunity to use his machine-gun, a performance which he repeated against another moving train on the journey home. The front of this train, against which Buckingham bullets were used, caught fire. Three pilots of No. 19 Squadron during the same night dropped twenty-four bombs on the headquarters in Havrincourt Château, and a pilot of No. 13 Squadron made two attacks on the aerodrome at Douai where his phosphorus bombs set fire to sheds. The enemy also did night bombing, Amiens being his main objective. During the two nights bombs fell on the station and various parts of the town, killing sixteen and wounding forty-five. In the second of these raids, on the 10th/11th, an enemy bombing machine landed with engine trouble, and its pilot and observer were made prisoners.

Although the weather was misty, it was now dry and cold, and preparations were pushed on for the attack on both sides of the Ancre to be made by the Fifth Army. (On the 30th of October the Reserve Army had become known as the Fifth Army). The special bombardment began at five in the crisp morning of November the 11th, and went on with bursts of great intensity until a quarter to six on the morning of the 13th, when it changed to a barrage covering the forward move of the infantry. The assault was made through a dense white fog which, although it entirely eliminated air support, blinded also the eyes of the defence. North of the Ancre, Beaumont-Hamel was taken and the outskirts of Beaucourt reached, whilst, south of the river, a brilliant success took the advance beyond St. Pierre Divion to a maximum depth of about 1,600 yards.

This attack was so rapidly and efficiently made that the number of prisoners captured was actually greater than the attacking force. Owing to the complete lack of air observation during the day, it was often extremely difficult for the Army commander to ascertain the positions which his troops had reached, but, on the following morning, when the attack was renewed north of the river the mist had gone, and contact observers of Nos. 4 and 15 Squadrons cleared up the situation and reported the flare-marked progress of the new attack. They told of the taking of the whole of Beaucourt and of the extension of our line to the north-west. Artillery observers sent down to the guns the positions of 157 German batteries which were firing, and helped to silence many of them. German infantry, too, who were incautious enough to expose themselves, paid the penalty. Three hundred men were seen by an observer of No. 15 Squadron in a ravine north of Beaucourt and reported by area call. The corps *War Diary* says:

<blockquote>Heavy artillery dealt with them.</blockquote>

Another observer of this squadron who was correcting the fire of a siege battery, saw about 250 men congested in two bits of trench. His wireless call brought forth immediate fire, and the pilot helped in the destruction with fire from his own machine-guns. Eight companies of infantry on the road north of Achiet-le-Petit were also reported by the same squadron and suffered the fate of their comrades nearer the front.

During the night of November the 14th/15th ten pilots of No. 18 Squadron, which had come under the orders of the V Brigade on the 10th, went out with bombs on roving flights about the enemy back areas. Many of them were out for two hours or more. They made low attacks on stations, moving trains, and transport, not only with their bombs but with their machine-guns. A German aeroplane followed two of the aeroplanes home, and when the aerodrome had been lighted up in answer to their signal, dropped four bombs which made large holes on the landing ground, but missed the sheds. To distract the attention of enemy airmen, flares were lighted on a dummy aerodrome in a field where bombs would fall harmlessly. This ruse served its purpose later in the night by diverting an aeroplane machine-gun attack, bullets intended for the aerodrome buildings losing themselves in the mud.

During the next four days the Fifth Army extended its gains eastwards and northwards up the Beaumont Hamel spur. The 16th and 17th were good flying days, and a hard frost on the ground greatly helped the advancing troops. The 16th was notable for the success of the artillery co-operation. Area calls of Nos. 4, 7, and 15 Squadrons brought devastating fire on to trenches which were seen to be heavily manned and offering vigorous resistance; a party working in a dump at Miraumont was dispersed with heavy casualties; a six-gun battery was destroyed, four of the pits catching fire and blowing up; seven other gun pits were demolished and nineteen damaged, several by the explosion of their ammunition: and of the fifty-seven active batteries reported by area call many were silenced by artillery fire. Contact patrol observers had no difficulty in reporting the movements of the infantry. A contact aeroplane of No. 7 Squadron was shot down into the German lines behind Beaucourt, and two observers in artillery machines came back wounded, one by a bullet from the trenches, and one from an attack by a hostile aeroplane.

There was a notable bombing raid by No. 27 Squadron in the morning on the big railway junction at Hirson, distant nearly ninety miles from the squadron's aerodrome. Six Martinsydes took part in the raid, two as escort, and were led by Captain P. C. Sherren. Eight 112-lb. bombs were dropped on the station from about 1,000 feet; six coaches were blown off the track, rolling-stock in the sidings was destroyed, and two station buildings were seen to collapse. All the pilots returned safely after a four and a half hour flight. Other successful raids were made by the III Brigade on the dumps at Courcelles and on hutments and ammunition dumps in Logeast Wood.

The fighting by the offensive and defensive patrols was again fierce. Six de Havillands of No. 24 Squadron fought three enemy pilots who, it was known later, had left their aerodrome near Cambrai with orders to attack our artillery machines. The first of the hostile formation to be engaged had its engine put out of action and fell apparently out of control; the second was shot down and fell behind Delville Wood, the two occupants being captured; the third was shot down to crash near the front line trenches. Another enemy aeroplane, a new Albatros fighter, was captured almost intact, its successful opponent being a lumbering B.E.2d. This machine (pilot. Captain G. A. Parker, observer, Second Lieutenant H. E. Hervey), of No. 8 Squadron, was on artillery patrol when the Albatros crossed the lines nearby.

The B.E. pilot turned to follow, and a long duel between the two was fought backwards and forwards over the lines. Eventually the Albatros landed with the British aeroplane alongside it. The pilot was taken unhurt and his machine was found to have suffered nothing more than a slightly damaged engine. To these enemy losses must be added four other aeroplanes shot down out of control by our offensive patrols at a cost of two machines to ourselves.

Throughout the night bomb and machine-gun attacks were kept up on the enemy's railheads and dumps, and on the aerodrome west of Flesquières. The enemy airmen, in turn, were highly successful in a raid against the French aerodrome at Cachy where they put twenty-one aeroplanes out of action. The French authorities, in consequence of their loss, asked if the Royal Flying Corps would, for the next two days, send out patrols to protect their front as far as the Amiens-Roye road. This was readily agreed to, but on the 17th our extended patrols met few enemy airmen and there was little fighting, and on the next day the execrable weather kept the German air service on the ground.

On the 17th, there was an unfortunate loss of two de Havillands of No. 29 Squadron which, in diving to attack an enemy formation, collided and fell in enemy territory, whilst another de Havilland, of No. 24 Squadron, was lost in a fight with a large German formation.

The naval squadron, which had claimed two of the successes on the previous day, again fought well, shooting down two aeroplanes, one of which hit a fence and fell to pieces. A third enemy aeroplane was destroyed by a pilot of No. 32 Squadron.

In the last attack of the Somme battles, made on November the 18th, when the western outskirts of Grandcourt were reached, the elements played their final part. A thaw set in changing the battlefield once again into a sea of mud, and mixed rain and snowstorms shrouded the movements of the infantry from the eyes of the observers who were flying low over them. So, ended the greatest continuous battle which the world had yet seen. It was a battle of limited objectives against intricate defences, and required time for its full development.

An autumn of average wetness must have seen the campaign develop according to plan. Had luck been with the Allied commanders, offering them what is not uncommon in Picardy, an autumnal summer, the whole course of the war in the west must have been different. But apart from what might have happened, which is of no more than academic interest, the great struggle achieved the three main objects for which it had been waged. It not only removed the tension at Verdun, but it also enabled General Nivelle to turn on the enemy and, before the year had ended, to sweep the German armies back almost to the positions from which, in February, they had sprung with such advertised confidence. It kept the main German forces pinned to the Western front at a time when our Allies were all fighting hard. Finally, it dealt a blow at the morale of the enemy troops from which they never recovered.

In the air the victory had been more complete. From beginning to last of the battle the air war was fought out over enemy territory. Even when the hostile aeroplanes increased to the point when they were nearly equal in numbers and often superior in performance to those of the Royal Flying Corps, the German air policy remained, on the whole, a defensive one. As the enemy air service multiplied, so did our casualties grow, but it must be admitted that they were not heavy in view of the great volume of work that was done day after day to further the task of the army. It was still possible on the 4th of November for a German First Army Order to point out, in a strangely pleading sentence, that:

> The airman must always remember that if he attacks *in front* of our lines, he interferes seriously with the enemy's fire direction

and may perhaps make it altogether impossible, thus bringing help and affording protection to his own infantry and artillery.

This bonus of goodwill which was offered to the airmen who foraged over the British lines will make curious reading for the members of the Royal Flying Corps, who looked out on the German front line as their starting-off point. All the enemy accounts of the battle make reference to the overwhelming superiority of the Allied artillery. General Ludendorff says in *My War Memories:*

> ...The enemy's powerful artillery, assisted by excellent aeroplane observation and fed with enormous supplies of ammunition, had kept down our own fire and destroyed our artillery.

Sir Henry Rawlinson, in a letter dated the 29th of October 1916, quotes some interesting figures of the help given by the air to the artillery of the Fourth Army. He states that between the 23rd of June and the 20th of October 1,721 shoots were observed from the air on to enemy batteries, bringing destruction or damage to 521 of them, and silencing 307 others, and that, in addition, 281 observations were made of bombardments of enemy trench systems. These figures, he points out, do not include many shoots based on aeroplane reports, nor shoots directed against troops in movement, he says further:

> The reports on attack days, on the relative positions of our own troops and of hostile troops, furnished by aeroplane observers during the operations, have been remarkably accurate.

His experiences in the battle had brought home to him, he said, the enormous importance of aeroplane and artillery co-operation, and pointed to the necessity for a great future development in this branch of flying work.

The very completeness of the early successes of the Flying Corps made General Trenchard anxious for the future. He knew, long before the battle ended, that the situation could not last, and, on the 22nd of September 1916, in an important memorandum, (*Future Policy in the Air,* Appendix 9), he considered what would be the effects of a change of German air policy from defence to offence under some drastic reformer. He thus anticipated the appointment of General von Hoeppner and foreshadowed his influence on the future air war. In his memorandum he expressed the view that the only effective way to counter a more aggressive enemy was for the Royal Flying Corps to undertake a still more vigorous offensive policy.

During the earlier part of the Somme struggle, although the corps pilots and observers went about their work in the air ceaselessly from dawn to dusk, intermittent offensive patrols had sufficed to keep the enemy airmen away from the front, but after the formation of the new pursuit squadrons, it was found that to achieve the same result, fighting squadrons had to be in the air, in strength, through the whole day. Many new fighting squadrons would be required to maintain the offensive under these changed conditions.

Accordingly, on the initiative of General Trenchard, Sir Douglas Haig sent a letter to the War Office on the 16th of November, asking for twenty fighting squadrons extra to what he had already estimated would be necessary to sustain the offensive in the early spring of 1917. This number would give a proportion of two fighting squadrons to one artillery squadron. So, opened a new era in the air war with wide new problems of design, supply, tactics, and training.

The Work of the I and II Brigades during the battle
(See map)

In the five strenuous months during which the centre of interest was over the Somme uplands, the role of the flying squadrons to the north, although a secondary one, was important. Whilst the armies for which these squadrons flew were concerned with keeping the enemy alert and their front secure, the airmen themselves carried the offensive far into enemy territory. The air knows no barriers, and this offensive was an extension of the activity over the main battles, on which it had a direct bearing. It kept on the German aerodromes in the north aeroplanes which might have been withdrawn to the Somme, and it had a moral and dislocating effect on troops in course of transfer to reinforce the south.

Working with the Second Army in the Ypres area was the II Brigade, commanded by Brigadier-General T. I. Webb-Bowen, and with the First Army, which joined up with the Third Army on the northern end of Vimy Ridge, the I Brigade under Brigadier-General D. le G. Pitcher. The brigades co-operated with their armies in the incessant minor attacks which went on along their fronts. The most important of these was made near Armentieres on the 19th of July, and the air work in cooperation with it was done by corps squadrons Nos. 2, 10, and 16, and army squadrons Nos. 32 and 25. The corps squadrons photographed and reconnoitred the battle front before and during the attack, and constantly patrolled in search of enemy batteries.

The army squadrons denied to the enemy any view of the infantry movements preliminary to the action, especially in the area of Lieutenant-General R. Haking's XI Corps, which made the main assault and bit deeply into the enemy lines. On the day of the attack the patrols of Nos. 25 and 32 Squadrons foraged as far over as Lille, and had many fights, in the course of which two Fokkers were destroyed. Second Lieutenant J. Godlee who shot one of the Fokkers to pieces in the air was himself mortally hit in the head during the combat, but piloted his de Havilland back to the British lines before he lost consciousness and crashed. General Haking, in a report on the air work for his corps said:

> The observation on the hostile batteries, the photographic work and the reconnaissance were excellent. I am particularly pleased with the manner in which our fighting machines kept back the enemy's aeroplanes, prevented them from crossing our lines, and from gaining information as to the number of reserves we had available. The bombing raids were also most useful and disturbed the enemy at a critical time.

The bombing of the enemy communications and centres in the north during the whole time that the Somme battles were being fought, was done by both brigades, but was most intense on the front of the I Brigade, particularly on junctions, billets, and dumps along the great railways radiating from Lille southwards to Lens, Douai, Cambrai, and Valenciennes. Frequent air reconnaissances of these systems, which enabled headquarters to follow the transfer of enemy units to the south, also indicated the centres where bombing would have the greatest effect. One of the most successful raids by the I Brigade in July, although only a few bombs were dropped, was made in the afternoon of the 30th, on the railway sidings at Ascq, four miles east of Lille. Fourteen 20 lb. bombs, dropped by No. 25 Squadron, hit sheds on the side of the line. A terrific explosion followed, which was clearly heard and felt by the bombing pilots nine thousand feet above, and volumes of smoke and flame shrouded the whole village as the aeroplanes turned for home.

Bombing by the squadrons of this brigade went on steadily day and night until the middle of September when it was intensified, following the brilliant jump forward on the Somme, to hamper the transference of reinforcements. Twice in the morning of the 16th of September Douai station was attacked by Nos. 2 and 25 Squadrons, and again after midnight by three pilots of the latter unit. These raids were forerunners of a big attack on the morning of the 17th, when twelve aeroplanes of No. 25 Squadron, in company with seven each from Nos. 10 and 16 Squadrons, dropped twenty-two 112-lb. and seventy-five 20-lb. bombs, and destroyed sheds and trucks, set fire to the station buildings, and blew up parts of the railway line.

Six German pilots made vain efforts to interfere with the bombing and two of them were driven down. On the next big railway raid, made on the morning of September the 22nd, great damage was inflicted on the junction at Somain, midway between Douai and Valenciennes. Seventy 20-lb. and twenty-five 112-lb. bombs were dropped by Nos. 25, 16, and 10 Squadrons, which flew over in two formations at half an hour's interval. Two trains in the station caught fire and blew to pieces in a succession of explosions, and the station buildings and other rolling-stock were left burning. The trains which exploded had been hit from 1,500 feet by three pilots of No. 25 Squadron, one of whom, apparently hit by an anti-aircraft shell, was compelled to land.

Four German aeroplanes attacked the raiders: one of them was shot down and crashed, and the others withdrew after two of them were damaged. Thirty-three small bombs distributed on dumps and billets in front of the First Army during the day, brought the total number of bombs dropped by squadrons of the I Brigade, since the opening of the Somme battle, to five thousand. On the morning of the 23rd St. Sauveur station at Lille was the objective of Nos. 25, 10, and 16 Squadrons. Fifty-two bombs were dropped (twelve of them 112-lb.) scoring hits on sidings and station buildings. Next day it was the turn of Seclin, south of Lille, on the main Douai line. Nos. 25 and 10 Squadrons again supplied the bombers who met with no resistance. Their sixteen 112-lb. and thirty-six 20-lb. bombs set fire to the station and blew up a road bridge over the railway.

But the most interesting raid made in the period by this brigade took place on the 25th of September, in an attempt to intercept traffic on the same line at the station of Libercourt, nearer Douai. First of all, the three German aerodromes at Provin, Tourmignies, and Phalempin were attacked to distract the attention of the enemy airmen. Three aeroplanes (two F.E.2b's of No. 25 Squadron escorted by an F.E.8 of No. 40 Squadron) visited each aerodrome and dropped phosphorus bombs at intervals which kept the landing grounds shrouded in smoke. To inform the enemy, whom they thus robbed of their vision, of their continued presence over them, the British pilots dropped, from time to time, a further 20-lb. high explosive bomb.

The aerodrome bombing took place between 1.20 p.m. and 2.0 p.m., and besides keeping the enemy on the ground, destroyed a hangar at Provin and caused a fire at Phalempin which spread over the northern part of the village and burnt all day. During the time that the aerodrome bombing was going on, a similar formation of three went up to make the first attack on trains on the line near Libercourt. At 1.40 p.m. a train was seen leaving the station southwards, and another a little further south was approaching the main line from Henin-Liètard. One F.E.2b dived on to each train. The main line train was attacked from 800 feet by Captain R. Chadwick with six 20-lb. bombs. The engine was hit and derailed and the two front coaches telescoped.

Troops who crowded on to the line from the train were attacked by Chadwick and his observer with their machine-guns, and chased towards Ostricourt village, many falling on the way. The main line was now blocked near the junction, and the second train was compelled to halt, thus offering an easy target to Second Lieutenant C. H. C. Woollven flying the second F.E. Again, the engine and carriages were hit, and again the troops were scattered with machine-gun fire.

Whilst these attacks on the trains were in progress, the main raiding party was approaching Libercourt station on to which their first bombs began to fall at 1.50 p.m. This formation was made up of seven B.E.'s of No. 16 Squadron, and six F.E.2b's of No. 25 Squadron, accompanied by an escort of F.E.8's of No. 40 Squadron. In all, fourteen 112-lb. and thirty-four 20-lb. bombs struck the station buildings, sidings, and rollingstock and set fire to a station dump. That the preliminary attack on the aerodromes in the neighbourhood of the bombing achieved its purpose is evident from the fact that only one German pilot made an appearance whilst the bombs were dropping and he made off rapidly as soon as he was attacked.

The I Brigade continued to bomb aerodromes, billets, and stations whenever the weather brought the opportunity. On the 17th of October the raiders got as far over as St. Amand, north of Valenciennes, where their forty-nine bombs derailed a moving train, hit the station buildings, and caused an explosion in a factory nearby. Whilst the attack was in progress on St. Amand, a second formation raided Denain junction, south-west of Valenciennes, where once again direct hits were reported, with some of the thirty-six bombs, on the station and on a moving train. On the way home, the bombers met five German aeroplanes. One of these was pursued and, although no shot was fired at it, the enemy pilot got into a steep dive and crashed into a lake near Douai.

Up to the middle of October the raiders of the brigade did their work without being much bothered by German airmen, but their attacks were having such effect that in the latter part of the month they began to be stoutly resisted. (From the middle of October 1916 German air units were gradually withdrawn from the Somme front to reinforce other sectors). On the 20th of October, whilst Nos. 10 and 25 Squadrons were dropping eighty-five bombs on billets and camps at Petit Hantay, they were attacked by nine aeroplanes, two of which they destroyed without loss to themselves.

On the next day a raid on Haubourdin station, south-west of Lille, was again fiercely opposed. Fifty-two bombs were dropped with good effect on the station by Nos. 16 and 25 Squadrons whilst the escort of No. 40 Squadron engaged the enemy airmen. There were nine separate fights during which three German aeroplanes went down hit. All our machines again returned safely. On the morning of October, the 22nd Seclin station was visited once more by Nos. 10 and 25 Squadrons who dropped fourteen 112-lb. and thirty-six 20-lb. bombs, hitting a train that was steaming into the station, and damaging station buildings. Of six Roland scouts which unsuccessfully attacked the bombers, three were shot down, two being seen to crash.

In November Henin-Liétard, Don, and Somain stations were the chief objectives of the I Brigade. Two attempts on Somain failed because of bad weather, but on a third attempt, on the 16th, sixteen 112-lb. and forty small bombs made direct hits on the station and trains and started a blaze. Twelve German pilots attacked the raiders on the way home and severely wounded an observer in a machine of No. 25 Squadron. The last raid by the I Brigade before the Somme battle ended was made on November the 17th on Carvin junction where forty-six bombs demolished buildings and started fires.

Although the bombing of the II Brigade had not the same direct bearing on the main battle as the railway bombing of the I Brigade, it had the effect of extending the air offensive and of keeping the enemy airmen busy along its front, quite apart from the material damage that the bombs inflicted. In July Comines, Menin, and Courtrai stations were the more important objectives. The Courtrai raid was made on the 29th, when twenty-nine 112-lb. bombs dropped by Nos. 6, 16, and 5 Squadrons set fire to an oil store in the station.

In August, in addition to widespread minor bombing, there was the raid on the airship sheds near Brussels to which reference has already been made, and big raids on the stations at Ledeghem, Courtrai, Roulers, and the billeting villages of Tenbrielen, Houthem, and Vijfwegen. In September the bombing increased, and special attention was paid to the German aerodromes, particularly on the 7th, when, as part of a general offensive along the whole line, two attacks were made on six aerodromes grouped in pairs near Roulers, Menin, and Roubaix.

The railway stations at Mouscron, Courtrai, Ledeghem, Comines, Wervicq, Quesnoy, Lille, and Langemarck all suffered extensive raids. The station and dumps at Quesnoy, midway on the line between Comines and Lille, were attacked three times in the month, the first raid, on the 6th, being the most effective, when twenty-eight 112-lb. bombs, dropped by Nos. 5, 6, and 42 Squadrons, blew up what seemed to be an ammunition dump near the station. One of the bombing aeroplanes of No. 42 Squadron was shot down on the way home. On the 15th eighteen 112-lb. and, on the 25th, twenty bombs of the same weight were dropped on the village again and large fires resulted. Fires were started, too, in the goods yard east of Lille which was also attacked on the 25th.

Nor were the billeting villages nearer the front neglected; they were raided by night as well as by day. In October and November, the weather brought some measure of rest to the enemy, but every break in the rain saw the bombers in the air, although their raids were restricted to villages and dumps nearer the front. Night and day raids were made in November on the two aerodromes near Menin.

Enemy airmen on both the I and II Brigade fronts made many attempts to cross the lines from time to time, and succeeded occasionally in bombing such places as St. Omer, Calais, Dunkirk, and Boulogne. It was in a successful attack on a bombing formation that Major L. W. B. Rees gained his Victoria Cross. About ten raiders crossed the British lines in the early morning of the 1st of July near Festubert. Second Lieutenant J. C. Simpson of No. 32 Squadron gallantly attacked them single-handed, but was quickly shot down and killed. Rees, who had seen the formation from a distance, headed towards them under the impression that they were British bombers returning from a raid, and he came up with them ignorant of the fact that they had already killed an officer of his own squadron.

As soon as he identified their nationality he flew straight in to attack. The first aeroplane, into which he got a burst from close range, dived away home, and the second, after receiving some thirty rounds, went straight down and landed in the German lines. The bombing formation now broke up, but the leader and two others still headed into the British area. Major Rees followed but was wounded in the leg and partly lost control of his rudder. He persisted in his attack, however, and kept up his fire until he was within ten yards of the rear machine whence he could see the German observer, apparently wounded, firing wildly upwards.

The enemy leader now abandoned the raid and turned for home, but he could not shake off Major Rees who did not leave the fight until he had finished all his ammunition. He had, single-handed, frustrated the raid and scattered the bombers back home. The efficacy of his attack impressed the enemy whose attempts at daylight raiding afterwards were few. One such attempt in the early morning of the 8th of August met a similar fate. Six Roland biplanes, loaded with bombs, were met over Bethune by three F.E.'s of No. 25 Squadron, which fought them back over their lines, forcing them to drop their bombs in their own territory where, too, one of the Rolands was shot down on to its nose.

Spasmodic night raids, however, mostly on villages near the front, were kept up by the enemy, and one, which was more ambitious in conception, was crowned with an outstanding success. It was made between 1 and 2 o'clock in the morning of the 21st of July on the ammunition dump at Audruicq, half-way along the Calais-St. Omer railway. The dump had been located on air photographs taken by the German 6th Squadron, and the attack on it was made by four aeroplanes of the German 40th Squadron. One shed was set on fire by a direct hit. Fire parties worked feverishly to save the dump, but the boxed ammunition began to go up, the fire spread in all directions, and an explosive chaos followed.

Trucks filled with ammunition on the lines about the dump were soon ablaze and carried the destruction to distant sheds. In all twenty-three sheds and some eight thousand tons of ammunition were totally destroyed, a mile of railway track torn up, six men killed, and two officers and twenty-one men injured. Few houses in the villages for miles around the dump escaped damage, but the civilian casualties were few. The destruction at the dump reached its height long after the enemy airmen had gone home. They could have seen no more than that their bombs started a fire. The later history of the fire offers a commentary on some of the reports of the British bombing which have already been quoted.

The blowing up of Audruicq dump was a success of the first importance, but other enemy raids did little damage. On the whole the offensive patrols which were maintained on these fronts, as on the Somme, more than held their own, although they had wide areas to cover and could not prevent a certain amount of artillery and photographic work being done by the enemy. The fighters which the offensive patrols met were mostly Fokkers and Rolands, which had not the advantage over our fighters that the new German single-seaters had in the Somme area. Consequently, the enemy airmen on the fronts of the First and Second Armies often avoided combat, so that much of the fighting was indecisive. Nevertheless, many enemy aeroplanes and a few balloons were destroyed on these fronts mainly by pilots of Nos. 20, 25, 29, 1, and 40 Squadrons.

The last word of this flying story of the great Somme struggle must be with the squadrons. Pilots and observers flew without rest and fought a type of warfare new to the world with the age-old spirit of their race. But if they fought with an old courage they gave it a new meaning, bringing to it something of the buoyancy and something, too, of the restlessness of the air itself. They were above the primeval conditions which, in spite of scientific ingenuity, must in the end always characterize the fighting of the infantry.

From the air they saw the battlefield robbed of its hideous intimacy. Water-filled craters and trenches and shell-churned communications, stark realities to the man on the ground, added only a different shade of colour to the patchwork view outspread below the aeroplane. When the flying officers returned from their part in the battle, they dropped down on to aerodromes in the comparatively peaceful serenity of the French countryside. They were not a melancholy company. Fighting to them was a sport, a grim one, but still a sport, and they relived their adventures in the mess with a zest that borrowed something from a playing-field dressing-room.

They did not belittle their risks. Rather, they accepted them as the price to be paid for the joy of the new life that was theirs. They met in the air an enemy who lived under similar conditions, and their combats were clean rapid contests in which brain and artistry were exalted above mere muscle. Many of the squadrons suffered grievous losses, but they came from the battle strong in the knowledge that they had been called upon to play a big part and that they had not failed. (Statistics of the work and casualties of the Royal Flying Corps during the Somme Battles are given as Appendix 8).

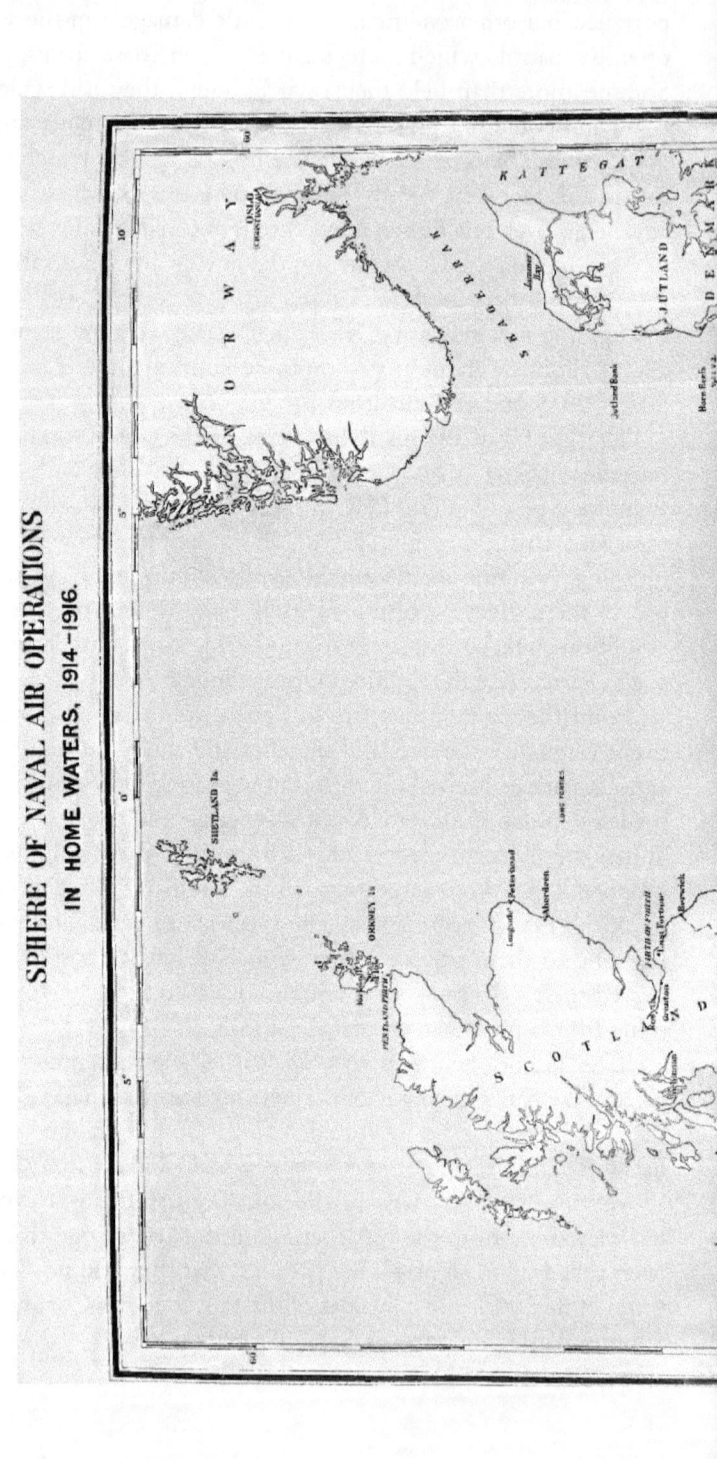

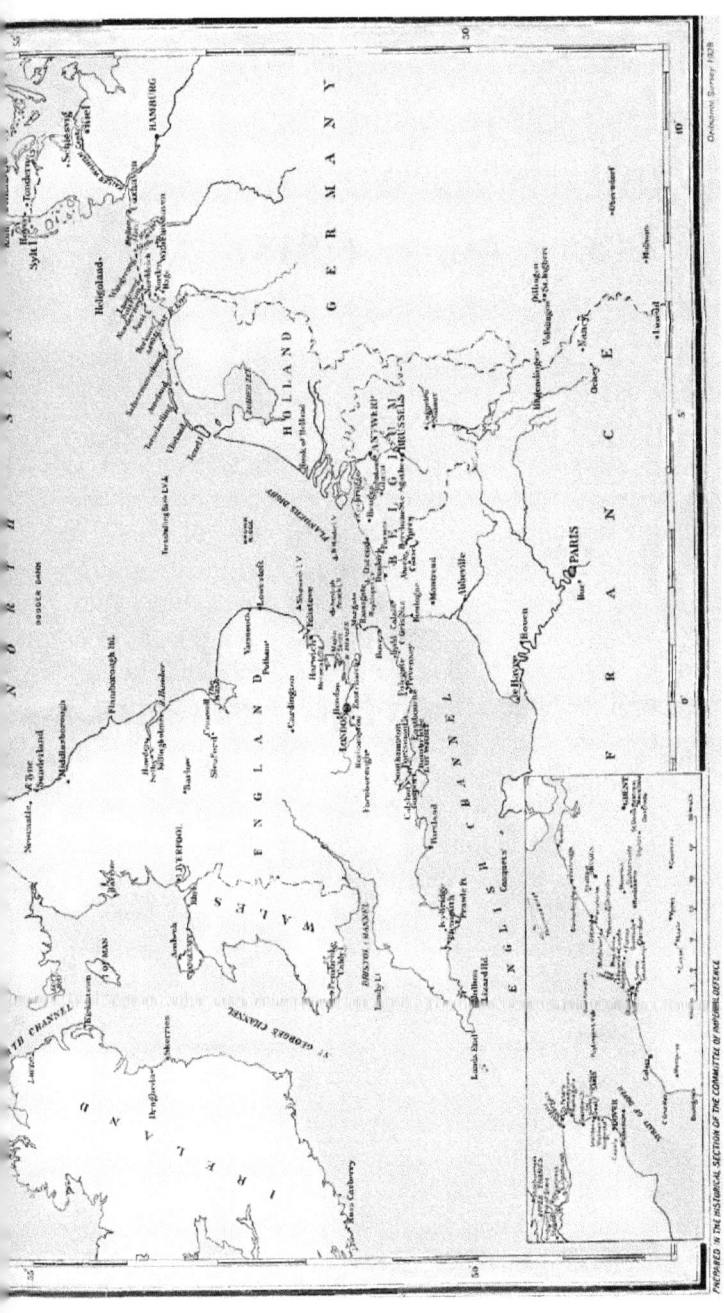

CHAPTER 6

The Royal Naval Air Service in Home Waters (1915)

The essential difference between the naval and military air services is in the element over which they normally work. The sailor is always at war with the sea as the airman is at war with the air, but the naval airman has to reckon with both. Aeroplanes, operating from a shore base, can of course work over the sea within their radius of action, but they suffer the disadvantage that a forced landing on the water must almost certainly spell disaster. The ideal sea-going aircraft must be seaworthy as well as airworthy. In theory the aeroplane can be made seaworthy by the substitution of floats for wheels, and in practice this would be so but for the all-important fact that the sea is never still.

The seaplane, before it can get into the air, must be strong enough to overcome the irregular resistance of the changing surface, or, in other words, must compromise with the sea by a sacrifice of some part of its efficiency in the air. The adjustment of this compromise is governed by engine power. The concession to the sea is always given grudgingly. The risk of damage, in confused waters, to the float seaplane has never been overcome, but as the aero engine increased in power, seaworthiness could be taken more and more into account and the boat seaplane, or flying boat, which can ride the waves for long periods, was developed. The flying boat, however, since it had to wait upon the progress of engine design, has little early history in the war.

The great forward step towards the solution of the naval air problem, the provision of efficient aircraft carriers, in effect self-contained sea-going aerodromes, was slow in coming. The director of the Admiralty Air Department did not cease to urge the need for specially constructed carriers, but the demands for cruisers, destroyers, and other recognised classes of warships and the difficulties connected with the evolution of a satisfactory type of vessel for a service as yet in its infancy, prevented any definite programme of construction being embarked upon. The policy which was adopted, the conversion of merchant vessels (usually passenger steamers), had the disadvantage that the adapters had to work within the limitations imposed by the design of the existing ships. And here, again, there was the old difficulty that most of the vessels, suitable for conversion as carriers, were already taken up for other services which were given precedence.

When war came the opposing armies searched at once for contact, and never lost touch until the end. The military aeroplane, from the very beginning, had the endurance to fly over that vital area where all the enemy movements of attack or defence must culminate. All the multifarious activities of the Royal Flying Corps grew naturally from that fact. Intense and alive as the development of the military air service was, it was certain to be more concentrated and, in a special sense, more restricted, than the development of the Naval Air Service. The General Officer Commanding the Royal Flying Corps in France was living in the centre of things. He was never far away from the commander-in-chief, and the aeroplane gave him a rapid means of visiting any or all of his units for inspection and discussion, even as it enabled his subordinate commanders to keep in close touch with him.

The chain of liaison, parallel between the flying units and the military formations with which they directly worked, and lateral, back to the Royal Flying Corps headquarters and so to the commander-in-chief, was tight-knit. The continuous interchange of demands and ideas was subject to searching criticism and discussion from every angle. The flying officers were never tired of talking 'shop' because it was the most alive topic of conversation, and from the discussions the hundred and one improvements in technique and tactics crystallised.

There was, and could be, no parallel position between the Naval Air Service and the navy. The conditions were wholly different. The naval air stations were scattered, some of them in remote places, and the personnel were, perforce, more detached from one another and from the forces with which they co-operated than were the military airmen. There were, of course, exceptions, but, on the whole, it is true to say that the naval airman stands out as a more solitary figure than his army comrade, having something of the loneliness of the element over which he flew. The Commander-in-Chief of the Grand Fleet, from his flagship, was not, and could not be, in the same close touch with his aircraft commanders as the military Commander-in-Chief in France.

The naval problems, too, were more diverse and complex. The whole expanse of the North Sea lay between us and the enemy. Air reconnaissance of the North German fleet bases and bombing attacks against the naval airship sheds necessitated the carrying of aircraft for two hundred miles or more across the sea, to enemy waters, before they could be launched against their objectives. Further, the supporting ships, whilst waiting in the jaws of the enemy for the return of the aircraft, must face many risks. It may be doubted whether any form of strategical air reconnaissance of the German harbours, however continuous and however useful, could have kept the Admiralty completely informed of the enemy's fleet movements. Happily, the need was not there, so amazing was the efficiency of the naval intelligence system. Cross bearings taken by the direction finding stations whenever the German fleet used its wireless—especially active when important movements were beginning—and information acquired from British submarine outposts and from other intelligence sources, usually gave the Admiralty ample warning of impending enemy activity.

But the need and importance of tactical reconnaissance remained. Contact between the opposing fleets, if it ever came, must be comparatively brief and might be decisive. The tremendous responsibility of the naval commander is, at the last, concentrated in an intense few hours. Whilst it might be a matter for argument how far the destruction of the German fleet would have made for immediate peace, there can be no question that the destruction or crippling of the British fleet would have swept away, at a blow, the base on which rested the whole superstructure of the Allied effort.

What the British admiral wanted from his air service was simple to define but enormously difficult of accomplishment. Once contact was joined, aircraft might give help by noting the changes of course of the enemy or even by reporting the effects of our gunfire, but these matters were of minor importance compared with information as to the enemy's presence, disposition, and direction of movement, before the action began. The large airship, the only type of aircraft capable of extended cruises, was, on the outbreak of war and for long afterwards, the prerogative of the enemy. The immediate alternative was to carry seaplanes in a ship which had the speed of the Grand Fleet, but the commander-in-chief had no such ship at his disposal until the war was already eight months old.

★★★★★★

A proposal for a specially constructed ship to carry seaplanes had been submitted by Messrs. William Beardmore and Co., after consultation with the Admiralty Air Department, in December 1912. The proposal, however, was ultimately rejected by the Board, who stated that the general question should be deferred until experience had been gained from experiments with *Hermes*.

★★★★★★

And even then, the carrier had drawbacks which severely limited her usefulness. The open waters of the North Sea were usually too disturbed for the seaplanes to get away and, under the best conditions, the carrier must stop to hoist her aircraft, and, to that extent, be something of a hindrance to the fleet, as well as leaving herself open to submarine attack. The obvious development was the flying of the aircraft directly off the ship, but the pathway to this accomplishment was long and tedious.

Had the provision of suitable aircraft to ensure scouting work for the fleet been the sole, or even the main, concern of the Admiralty Air Department, there is small doubt that ships' aircraft would have been more rapidly developed than they were. Two other factors, however, dominated the early expansion of the Naval Air Service. These were the submarine war and the airship raids against England. The first led to the building and equipping of stations around the British coasts for small-type patrolling airships, the second to the production of offensive rather than reconnaissance aircraft.

The Admiralty were called upon to assume responsibility for the defence of this country against air raids in September 1914, and they did not relinquish it to the War Office until February 1916. It was evident from the first that an aeroplane or fighting seaplane of high performance would be the only effective means of bringing the enemy to combat in the air, and the Admiralty therefore encouraged private makers to develop these types. Furthermore, their policy, whereby the Zeppelins were to be continuously attacked in their inland sheds, and the submarines in their bases, especially in Belgium, was responsible for the development not only of heavy naval bombing aeroplanes but also of fighting and reconnaissance aeroplanes. The building up of an aeroplane organisation inside the Naval Air Service absorbed personnel and equipment which might otherwise have been available for the development of air co-operation with the fleet.

The Submarine Campaign and the Belgian Coast

The occupation by the German armies of the Belgian Coast in October 1914 brought about a complete change in the strategic position of these islands. The great ports of Zeebrugge and Ostend, which had fallen to the enemy almost intact, offered shelter to submarines and destroyers on the flank of the continuous cross-Channel traffic and of the ships which passed through the Straits carrying food and stores to London. The coastal ports were connected by waterway with the inland port of Bruges, exhaustively equipped and ideally situated out of range of bombardment from the sea to form a base for the assembling and housing of submarines and for the general repair of all the craft operating from Belgium. But that was not all. Zeppelins, from which the enemy hoped so much, could now be based within easy reach of London, the nerve-centre of our whole war effort.

Dover and Dunkirk took on a new importance. On the 11th of October 1914, the Straits were made a separate command under Rear Admiral the Honourable H. L. A. Hood, a command which was to become widely known as the Dover Patrol. (*The Dover Patrol* by J. J. Bennett, the Royal Navy, the English Channel and the Zeebrugge Raid during the First World War by an eyewitness is also published by Leonaur). At Dunkirk, the nearest harbour to the enemy bases, a great naval air station gradually grew up. Established with the idea of denying to the Germans the use of territory within a hundred miles of Dunkirk for Zeppelin bases, it came to be the centre for the whole naval air effort against the enemy in Belgium.

Towards the end of October 1914 news was reaching the Admiralty that submarines, in sections, were arriving by rail at Bruges and were there being put together for canal transport to the coast ports. Commander Samson was instructed to watch for and to bomb any accumulations of trains in the town. This was done, with the help of the seaplane unit at Dunkirk, on the 2nd, 3rd, and 4th of November, after which the weather made further bombing impossible.

It is now known that the first German submarine to enter the Mole at Zeebrugge was the U.12 from Heligoland which went in on November the 9th. Her commander lost no time in getting to work. Two days later he destroyed the old torpedo-gunboat, *Niger*, off Deal Pier. The Admiralty was unaware at the time that the submarine had come from Flanders. For some days after the sinking of the gunboat, snowstorms swept the Channel and made air reconnaissance of the Belgian Coast impossible until the 20th, and then it was revealed that there were no submarines at Zeebrugge. As a result of the sinking of the *Niger*, a seaplane base was opened at Dover on the 21st of November, for work in co-operation with a destroyer patrol, but the patrol could do little to prevent submarines passing through submerged by day or on the surface by night.

That the new attempt to bar the Straits was of small value was shown on the 23rd, when the S.S. *Malachite*, bound from Liverpool with a cargo of general goods, was leisurely shelled for thirty minutes by a submarine off Le Havre, a proceeding which was repeated, three days later, in the same area against the collier *Primo*. The insecurity of the Channel was emphasized in the opening hours of the new year of 1915 by the sinking of the battleship *Formidable* off the Isle of Wight with a loss of 547 lives. This disaster had followed close on a torpedo attack on the new French dreadnought, *Jean Bart*, by an Austrian submarine in the Straits of Otranto.

The French battleship, damaged, got into port, but to those mindful of the history of the great raider whose name the dreadnought commemorated the incident had added significance. Jean Bart, operating from Dunkirk in the last quarter of the seventeenth century, had stirred up the waters of the Channel and of the North Sea and had inflicted continuous loss on Dutch and English shipping. No odds were too great for his courage nor any situation too difficult for his genius. Had his statue in Dunkirk been given the sudden gift of life his mind must have ranged along the coast to the Belgian ports and his lips have formulated a hope that the daring and success that were his might be denied to the raiders of the new enemy of his country, so well placed and so subtly equipped for their task.

Before the year 1915 was many weeks old the submarine war had been placed on a new footing. In the afternoon of the 29th of January, Hersing, the brilliant commander of the U.21, appeared off Barrow-in-Furness and, after making an unhindered reconnaissance of the coast, opened ineffective fire on the airship shed. Next day he destroyed a collier and coasting vessels off the Liverpool bar. Now it had been shown that submarines could get to the west coast of England, a press notice was issued from the Admiralty in Berlin, on the 4th of February, declaring that the waters round the British Isles, including the whole of the English Channel, were a war zone in which all enemy ships would be destroyed, and neutrals would navigate at their peril. This order came into force on the 18th of February 1915.

The German announcement of the submarine blockade led to an

immediate concentration of naval aircraft for the bombing of the Belgian bases. Aeroplanes and seaplanes from Hendon, Eastchurch, and the carrier *Empress* were sent to reinforce those at Dover and Dunkirk for a series of raids timed to begin on the 11th of February. Two Curtiss flying boats from Felixstowe were also ordered to co-operate. Snow and fog did not prevent the attempt being made on the morning of the 11th, but only one aeroplane got past the storm to Zeebrugge and Ostend and dropped three 20-lb. bombs on the harbour works in each town. Two other pilots dropped their bombs on gun positions along the coast.

The flying boats from Felixstowe failed to reach Zeebrugge, but their attempt was not without value. Visibility was restricted to a circular patch of about a mile radius from the boats and the sea was never in sight from above 300 feet, but Squadron Commander J. C. Porte navigated with such precision that, after a 150-mile round trip, he sighted Felixstowe dead ahead on his return. An attack carried out next day was more successful. Twelve aeroplanes and one seaplane took part in the raid, and hits were claimed on the harbour station and docks at Ostend, the Mole and power station at Zeebrugge, and on gun positions along the coast.

On the 16th of February the success was repeated by seventeen aeroplanes and seven seaplanes. Thirty-seven 20-lb. bombs were dropped about the harbour and station at Ostend, and two bombs of the same weight hit the Mole and lock at Zeebrugge. (A memorial tablet let into the wall of the German Marine Artillery living quarters recorded that seven members of that corps were killed by a bomb dropped during this raid). Hits with 100-lb. and 20-lb. bombs were made on important gun positions and on shipping. Three seaplanes and one aeroplane never came back. One seaplane pilot, whose craft was brought down by shrapnel off Zeebrugge, was interned in Holland, but what happened to his comrades was never known. Eight French military aeroplanes co-operated with the raid by bombing the German aerodrome at Ghistelles to keep the enemy airmen busy away from the British objectives.

In view of the limited number of aircraft at the disposal of the Admiralty the bombing of the Belgian bases could be little more than a demonstration. The Dardanelles Campaign was beginning to draw off some of the naval air strength. At the end of February Commander Samson's unit was withdrawn from Dunkirk to Dover and was soon on its way to the eastern Mediterranean. The formation of two naval aeroplane squadrons had been sanctioned by the Government in August 1914 to be organised on the same basis as the military squadrons. The idea at the time was that they could be used, if necessary, to reinforce the Royal Flying Corps. They were formed in the middle of October 1914, No. 1 at Fort Grange under Squadron Commander A. M. Longmore, and No. 2 at Eastchurch under Squadron Commander E. L. Gerrard. When Commander Samson's unit was withdrawn from Dunkirk, its place was taken by No. 1 Squadron. (The equipment of the squadron was five 80 H.P. Avros, one 80 H.P. Bristol, and one 100 H.P. Vickers).

Meanwhile, the Flanders submarine bases were being rapidly developed, and a special small type of U-boat, known as the U.B. class, was being built. The first submarines of this class, which were about ninety feet long and specially suitable for operating in confined waters, were put together in the dockyards at Antwerp. Presently, too, there was developed, also at the Belgian bases, a special minelaying submarine, the U.C. class—a complete innovation.

It was not long before the fact that the enemy was assembling submarines at Antwerp became known to the Admiralty and Squadron Commander Longmore was ordered to bomb the dockyards. Bombing attacks were made on the 24th of March and the 1st of April. Five aeroplane pilots started off in the morning mist for the first attack: one with engine trouble came down in Holland, two were driven back by the weather conditions, one of them having dropped his bombs on Ostend, and the remaining two made a daring attack on the dockyard.

The first pilot. Squadron Commander I. T. Courtney, took the defences by surprise: he dropped his four 20-lb. bombs across the yard from a height of 350 feet and was not fired at until he turned to leave, when he was met with a stream of small green rockets fired rapidly. Flight-Lieutenant H. Rosher, who followed a few minutes behind the first pilot, came in for the full effect of the antiaircraft defences as he dived downwind across the yards. He tells of the raid in a letter home:

> .... The excitement of the moment was terrific. I have never travelled so fast before in my life. My chief impressions were the great speed, the flaming bullets streaking by, the incessant rattle of the machine-gun and rifle fire, and one or two shells bursting close by, knocking my machine all sideways, and pretty nearly deafening me. On my return I found my machine was only hit twice—rather wonderful; one bullet hole through the

tail and a piece of shrapnel buried in the main spar of one wing. I have now got it out. I found myself across the yards, and felt a mild sort of surprise. My eyes must have been sticking out of my head like a shrimp's! I know I was gasping for breath and crouching down in the fuselage.

I was, however, by no means clear, for shrapnel was still bursting around me. I jammed the rudder first one way and then the other. I banked first on to one wing tip, and then on to the other, now slipping outwards and now up and now down. I was literally hedged in by forts (and only 1,000 feet up); and had to run the gauntlet before getting away. I was under rifle fire right up to the frontier, and even then, the Dutch potted me . . . —*In the Royal Naval Air Service*. (Flight Lieutenant H. Rosher was killed when testing an aeroplane at Dover on February 27th 1916; *With the Flying Squadron* by Harold Rosher, letters of the pilot of the R. N.A.S. during the First World War is published by Leonaur).

The raid on the 1st of April was made by one aeroplane, piloted by Flight Sub-Lieutenant F. G. Andreae, who dropped four 20-lb. bombs across the shipyard. It was quickly realised, however, that sporadic bombing at long range, which had to be done at this time with light-weight bombs, was of little value. The attacks on Antwerp were therefore given up, and bombing was confined chiefly to the nearer and important targets of Bruges, Ostend, and Zeebrugge.

Towards the end of April, the enemy caused some consternation when he began a long-range shelling of Dunkirk with a gun of heavy calibre. In the evening of the 30th of April, the third occasion on which the gun fired, six aeroplanes were sent up to note all gun-flashes from Nieuport to south of Dixmude, along a line which formed the arc of a circle that had Dunkirk for its centre. Each observer, before leaving, synchronised his watch with the aerodrome clock, and when over the enemy lines noted the times and positions of every gun-flash. These times, on the return of the aeroplanes, were compared with the times of the fall of the shells in the town.

After allowance was made for the duration of the flight of each shell, there was no doubt that a gun discovered at Clercken, south-east of Dixmude, by Flight Lieutenant D. C. S. Evill, was responsible. Now that the gun was found it could be dealt with. It was intermittently bombed by the Naval Air Service, and naval air observers gave help, as they could, in spotting on to the gun for French heavy batteries. The Clercken gun was finally put out of action by two French naval guns on the 9th of August. Dunkirk was now to enjoy freedom from long-range shelling for nearly two years.

THE SUBMARINE SCOUT AIRSHIP.

Whilst the Dunkirk unit was playing its part in the watching and bombing of the Belgian submarine bases, the problem of providing a continuous air patrol for the searching of home waters was receiving anxious attention. Its solution showed a touch of genius. On the 28th of February Lord Fisher, the First Sea Lord, sent for several airship officers and told them he wanted some small fairly fast airships to hunt submarines, and that he wanted them at once. The story of how, within three weeks, the body of a B.E.2c aeroplane was slung under the envelope of a Willows airship to produce the first of the famous Submarine Scouts has already been told in volume 1. As soon as the new airship had been tried, and the value of its principles demonstrated, the design was considerably improved in detail to withstand service conditions.

※※※※※※

The first experimental airship—S.S.1—was travelling near the ground at fifty miles an hour on the 8th of May 1915 when she struck the telegraph wires on the Dover-Folkestone road, caught fire, and was rapidly consumed. The occupants of the airship, who fell to the ground from fifteen feet or so, escaped with bruises and scorching.

※※※※※※

The design was governed by the resources immediately available for the building of the ships. The greatest difficulty was offered by the envelope and rigging. The firms best able to make the envelopes were waterproof garment manufacturers, whose workers, used as they were to patterns, could at first make little of drawings. For the making of the cars, too, firms of no airship experience had, with few exceptions, to be called upon. Indeed, a majority of the cars were made to Kingsnorth drawings by a firm whose previous experience had been confined to the fitting out of shops. The early 'S.S.' type had a normal endurance at full speed (40-50 miles per hour) of eight hours. Two private firms were invited to submit their own designs of airships to fulfil the requirements which had called forth the first Submarine Scout.

The S.S.2, built by Airships, Limited, did not come up to Admiralty requirements, and was struck off the active list, but the S.S.27, the car for which was designed for the standard envelope by Messrs. Armstrong-Whitworth, proved satisfactory. The car was similar in appearance to the B.E.2c, but on test gave the airship a full speed endurance of twelve hours. (Four of these Armstrong airships were built for the Naval Air Service and four for the Italian Government in 1916).

Messrs. Airships, undaunted by their early failure, designed a new car which resembled the Maurice Farman 'pusher' type. This car could be rigged to the standard envelope. Although these pusher airships were slightly slower than the B.E.2c type, they were more comfortable and generally better fitted for airship purposes. (Twelve of them had been taken into service by the end of 1916).

The areas which called most urgently for airship patrol were the Dover Straits and the northern and southern entrances to the Irish Sea. The first airship bases were therefore opened at Capel (Folkestone) on the 8th of May 1915, and at Polegate, near Eastbourne, on the 6th of July. A portable shed was also set up at Marquise, in France, at the end of June. By the end of the year Capel had five airships working and four more building, Polegate had three in service, and Marquise one. This latter station was handed over to the French Government on the 1st of January 1916, together with a new S.S. airship which had been built to the order of the French naval authorities.

The first west coast station was opened at Luce Bay for the patrol of the North Channel area on the 15th of July 1915, with accommodation for four airships, three of which were in commission before the end of the year. A portable shed for emergency landings was also set up on the Irish coast at Larne, facing Luce Bay. Anglesey was commissioned in the middle of September and the first flight was made on the 26th of that month. The station had its full complement of four ships by the end of December.

The reader will properly appreciate the value of the airship patrols only if he has some knowledge of their limitations and of the difficulties of submarine hunting. The flying officer who patrols on the look-out for underwater craft must have the patience, watchfulness, and subtlety of the angler. Submarine hunting has been described by an officer who has done much of it as a serious sport in which the fish are not at all keen to rise to the fly. Information as to the habits and movements of enemy submarines, of their varying visibility in different waters, and of the tell-tale clues which they left in their wake, had to be built up, bit by bit, from observation, experience, and deduction.

The submarine commander, given fair weather conditions, starts off with the great advantage that if he is wide awake and cautious he need never be seen from an airship except in translucent waters. In clear weather he may pick up aircraft some time before his own craft is visible to the airmen. The ordinary periscope is two or three inches in diameter. If a submarine cruises slowly at, say, one or two knots with a foot or so of periscope showing, she leaves behind simply a faint, oil-like trace which can only be picked up from the air in calm waters if the watcher knows exactly where to look for it. The scales, however, are not always weighted in favour of the submarine. In clear waters, such as the Mediterranean or the Baltic, in favourable conditions of light, submarines have been detected as deep down as eighty feet, and even in the western approaches to the English Channel they have been picked out thirty feet below the surface. But the muddy waters up-Channel and off Harwich give up no secrets.

If the airman takes every advantage of the weather conditions he may surprise his enemy. Sea mist, clouds, the glare of the sun, skilfully used, help him to come unheralded upon the submarine. The idiosyncrasies of seagulls in different waters came to be known and used. Flocks of the birds seen from the air dipping swiftly to the attack of a shoal of fish, create the delusion that they are pursuing the 'feather' of a moving periscope. But it came to be known, chiefly on the evidence of our own submarine officers, that gulls in the North Sea, either from sophistication or surfeit, seldom bothered to investigate a moving periscope, whereas in the waters off the west coast of Ireland, for instance, they would follow in its wake with blind persistence for hours.

Only an airman who has searched the wastes of the sea through countless hours can be fully aware of the weird multitudinous objects that float derelict on the surface of the water. Everything must be examined, and the keenness and watchfulness of the crew must be maintained in face of constant disappointment. There is the vexed question of oil patches as an indication of the presence of a submarine. The sources of oil from a submarine are few. The exhausts are automatically sealed when the craft dives so that there should be no leakage when it is under water.

On the other hand, there is usually enough oil from the periscope, propeller, rudder, and hydroplane bearings to give a thin trace of the direction the submarine has taken. This requires keen vigilance to follow, but to an experienced air observer under good weather conditions it is a definite clue. Some types of submarine, away from their base for an extended cruise, use their oil tanks for ballast, taking in salt water when a certain amount of heavy oil is used up. Oil and water do not mix. As the craft dives oil will be carried out by the exuded air and help further in the tracking of the submarine.

Slight damage, caused by bumping into wreckage, or by an attack, may set up a small leakage of which the crew are ignorant. An adventure of a British submarine will illustrate this fact. She grounded when about to attack a ship and received a strain which, unknown to her commander, caused a leakage of oil. For most of a whole long day the craft, although moving from eighty to one hundred feet below the surface of the sea, was dogged and bombed by a Zeppelin.

The development of the scouting airship was but a small contribution to the problem of defeating the strangle-hold of the submarine. It was an essential and valuable contribution. The air patrols imposed caution on the submarine commanders and considerably hampered their freedom of action. In the more important shipping lanes they made it hazardous for a submarine to break surface by day. By keeping them submerged, too, the patrols restricted their effective radius of action.

✶✶✶✶✶✶

On the surface the submarines used Diesel engines, but when submerged had to rely on electrical power which was limited by the charging of their batteries. A typical surface speed was 15 knots, but a useful cruising submerged speed might be little more than knots. At the latter speed the submarine could proceed no more than about 70 nautical miles before coming to the surface to recharge her batteries.

✶✶✶✶✶✶

Much of the work of the airships may appear negative in value, but their mere presence averted many attacks on merchant vessels. When all is said, however, the whole wide network of the anti-submarine organisation, absorbing an enormous amount of material and energy, could, for long, do little more than blunt the edge of the submarine weapon.

Zeppelin Bases in Belgium: destruction of L.Z.37 and L.Z.38.

No sooner had the new submarine war opened, with the anxieties which it brought in its train, than news reached the Admiralty of the rapid progress made in the building of sheds in Belgium for the housing of military raiding Zeppelins. Towards the end of April, it was known that the first of the new military Zeppelins, L.Z.37, arrived. Two others, the sister ships L.Z.38 and L.Z.39, quickly followed. They lost no time in carrying the air war to London. After a few skirmishing raids on various English towns, L.Z.38, on the 31st of May, dropped the first bombs to fall on the metropolis.

How the naval air unit at Dunkirk overcame the new and formidable menace, and pointed the way to the ultimate defeat of the Zeppelin as a raiding weapon, form some of the most striking pages of its history. Seven days after the first bombs had fallen in the east end of London, the naval pilots had destroyed two of the Zeppelins which had descended on Belgium with such high hopes, had damaged the third, and had made the Belgian sheds untenable as permanent bases.

They got in their first blow in the early hours of the 17th of May. At 3.15 a.m. the L.Z.39, which had set out with her two sister ships for a raid along the French and British Channel towns, was seen off Dunkirk going slowly east. A warning that the airships were out had been received some time before from England, and two of the Dunkirk aeroplanes were already patrolling in the air. Seven others went up at once when the Zeppelin was sighted. Three pilots got to grips with their enemy. Squadron Commander Spenser D. A. Grey and Flight Sub-Lieutenant R. A. J. Warneford were first to attack with machine-gun and rifle fire from below.

The Zeppelin, however, put her nose up and outclimbed them. Flight Commander A. W. Bigsworth, on an Avro, climbed steadily after the ship as she moved off in the direction of Ostend. At ten thousand feet over the town he was two hundred feet above her. As he flew along her back he dropped his load of four 20-lb. bombs. Smoke came from near the tail of the airship as Bigsworth turned back, but he was chagrined to see her move off, apparently little the worse, towards the shed at Evere. It was known afterwards that the ship made a rough but safe landing. A dead officer and some wounded men were taken from one of the gondolas, and an inspection of the airship revealed five damaged gasbags and the loss of the starboard after propeller.

Her two companion ships got back untouched, but their respite was to be brief. In the opening minutes of the 7th of June four pilots were on their aerodrome at Dunkirk, ready to start out to bomb the sheds at Evere and Berchem Ste. Agathe. It so happened that there was activity at the same hour at the airship bases. A raid on England by naval Zeppelins from the North German sheds and by the three military ships from Belgium had been ordered. The latter duly got away with their load of bombs. One of them, L.Z.38, had trouble in the air, landed again, and was put back into her shed at Evere. The other two ran into thick mist, lost their way, cruised bewildered for some time, and then began to pick their way home again. It is not known that they dropped any bombs. The position, then, as the aeroplane pilots move across Belgium to the attack is that L.Z.38 is shut up in her shed at Evere, and that her two sister ships are on their way home from their abortive flight to England.

Let us first follow the raid on Evere, made by Flight Lieutenant J. P. Wilson and Flight Sub-Lieutenant J. S. Mills on Henri Farman biplanes. Wilson got away at 12.40 a.m. and, flying on a compass course through the mist, reached Evere at 2.5 a.m. A searchlight from near the landing base began to signal a series of long flashes into the air. Wilson promptly replied with short flashes on his pocket lamp, which seemed to satisfy the searchlight party and earned him immunity from anti-aircraft fire for the fifteen minutes he spent circling over his target waiting until the faint light of early dawn should outline the shed.

At 2.20 a.m. the shed was just visible and Wilson, from 2,000 feet, let fall his three 65-lb. bombs, one of which appeared to hit the centre of the target and sent up dense smoke but no flames. Ten minutes later. Flight Sub-Lieutenant Mills arrived over the shed and was met with such accurate fire as he dived that he had to swerve clear of his target and go off to gain height. He returned at 5,000 feet and dropped his four 20-lb. bombs. The light on the ground as the bombs fell was still faint and the buildings were vague and shadowy. Suddenly the whole countryside was brilliantly illuminated as the bombs got home and L.Z.38, the first of the London raiders, went up in flames.

The aeroplane pilot turned back and was soon in a thick white fog. For two hours he steered by compass. When he judged that he was near home and dived low in search of somewhere to land, he came unexpectedly on the sea and saved a crash by a few feet. He turned south and landed on the beach between Calais and Dunkirk at a quarter to five. Flight Lieutenant Wilson, who was also in trouble in the fog, did not land until half an hour later in a field near Montreuil.

At the time when the attack on Evere was being made, Flight Sub-Lieutenant R. A. J. Warneford was having a thrilling duel at close quarters with the L.Z.37. He had set out with a companion aeroplane to bomb Berchem Ste. Agathe. At one o'clock, within a few minutes of starting, Warneford had picked up, far off towards Ostend, the faintly pencilled outline of an airship. At once he began the pursuit. His companion, meanwhile, was out of luck. The lights over his instruments failed, he got lost in the darkness, and landed in a field near Cassel where his aeroplane turned turtle. The pilot escaped injury.

At ten minutes to two, Warneford, who was flying a Morane, had caught up with his Zeppelin over Bruges, and came at once under vigorous machine-gun fire from the gondolas. He realised that he must force his bomb-loaded Morane still higher and retreated to do so. The Zeppelin commander, with supreme confidence, turned after him and for some time was able to keep the Morane under fire. Gradually Warneford outclimbed his giant enemy and, when he had reached 11,000 feet, was well above the airship. He turned back on her, switched off his engine, dived, and released his six 20-lb. bombs as he passed from one end of the ship to the other at a height of 150 feet above the envelope.

As the last bomb fell, a terrific explosion rent the Zeppelin and tossed the Morane high into the air and turned it upside down. Victor and victim went fluttering to earth. The Morane got into a nose-dive and Warneford was then able to regain control. He searched at once for his adversary, and as he looked saw that:

> The Zeppelin was on the ground in flames and also that there were pieces of something burning in the air all the way down.

It is stated that one member of the airship crew miraculously survived. He fell with the wreckage through the roof of a nunnery. Two nuns in the room into which he was precipitated were killed, but the airman, little the worse for his ordeal, went back to his service to fly again.

Warneford's adventure was not ended when he got control of his aeroplane once more. He found that a joint in his petrol pipe had been broken by the violence of the explosion and he was forced at once to land. He chose a field close by a wood and prepared to destroy his aeroplane. When all was ready for the firing of the petrol, he listened intently. Not a sound came to suggest that he had been seen. Constantly vigilant, he worked at the repair of the broken joint. At last it was done. After many abortive attempts he was able to start his engine and scramble into the Morane as it moved off. He flew away west after an involuntary sojourn inside the enemy lines of thirty-five minutes.

In the fog he flew on, ignorant of his position, and landed eventually to learn that he was at Cape Gris-Nez. For his achievement, the first victory over the Zeppelin in the air, Warneford was awarded the Victoria Cross. He did not long survive to enjoy the honour which had come to him. By one of those unhappy chances, not uncommon in his service, he lost his life ten days later in a simple accident. A Henri Farman aeroplane, which he was testing at Buc, near Paris, broke up in the air and Warneford, with an American passenger, was killed in the crash which followed.

The survivor of the three new airships, L.Z.39, which had been fortunate to escape destruction in the encounter with Flight Commander Bigsworth on the 17th of May, was moved to the eastern front. There in her shed near Kovno she was destroyed by fire in November 1915. The Dunkirk aeroplane unit had brilliantly justified the policy which had led to the establishment of the base as a counter to the enemy airships. The sheds in Belgium were henceforth abandoned, except for emergency landings.

Reorganisation of the Royal Naval Air Service,

Meanwhile there had been political happenings at home of which one of the minor effects was to bring the policy and organisation of the whole Naval Air Service under review. On the 15th of May 1915 Lord Fisher, the First Sea Lord, resigned. Ten days later Mr. Asquith, the Prime Minister, formed his Coalition Ministry. Mr. Winston Churchill, the First Lord, resigned on the 26th, and was succeeded by Mr. Arthur Balfour with Sir Henry Jackson as First Sea Lord. Mr. Churchill had held his responsible position since October 1911. His eager mind, quick to illuminate what there was of promise in a novel weapon, had made him a firm believer in, and a warm friend of, the Naval Air Service. He had brought together in the Air Department, under Captain Murray Sueter, a band of experts whose enthusiasm was proof against disappointment and against the criticism of those who were impatient of the growing pains of the new arm.

Mr. Churchill's powerful backing of the Air Department through its difficult early days made smooth many a cumbered path. Under his aegis the Department had developed not only the air side of naval work, but many minor services which, useful as they were, had little to do with the air. There were fifteen armoured car squadrons, of which six were on active service, two at the Dardanelles, one in East Africa, and three in France. There were three armoured trains which had originated in the Antwerp operations and were now working along the railways in Flanders. There was, lastly, an anti-aircraft section numbering twenty-four officers and 1,500 men, which was part of the home ground defence against air raids. The time had come, it was decided, when all these semi-military ground services should be handed over to the army, leaving the Air Department free to confine its energies to the help of the navy, and one of Mr. Balfour's first acts was to arrange that the War Office take them over *en bloc*.

There remained the important problems of reorganisation and policy. Mr. Balfour held the view that the air stations should not be directly under the Air Department as hitherto, but under the control of the senior naval officers in the areas from which they worked, he said:

> It will be of the greatest possible importance to bring them into the regular routine of day-to-day naval work, and organise them for naval purposes as if they were destroyers or submarines.

Mr. Balfour had a long talk with Sir John Jellicoe who was in agreement with this proposal. The commander-in-chief, in a memorandum dated the 4th of June 1915, laid down what he considered to be the functions of a Naval Air Service as follows:

> (*a*) Observation duties from the coast generally, and from naval bases in particular.
> (*b*) The attack of enemy aircraft wherever met.
> (*c*) The aerial defence of all naval centres, such as dockyards, magazines, since the army who, properly speaking, should carry out this work, have apparently turned it over to the navy.
> (*d*) Scouting for enemy submarines and enemy minelayers, which properly comes under the heading of reconnaissance work.

In July the whole question was considered by the Board, and regulations for the reorganisation of the Naval Air Service were issued to take effect on the 1st of August 1915. The air stations were grouped under the senior naval officers with the immediate gain that the liaison between air and surface craft was made much closer. An air service officer was appointed to the staff of each senior naval officer as an adviser on air technical matters.

As soon as the reorganisation of the naval air stations was in hand, the question of remodelling and enlarging the Air Department at the Admiralty came up for settlement. It was considered that Commodore Murray Sueter should be free to give his undivided time to the development and supply of aircraft, and that he could best do this under a non-technical officer of flag rank who would be responsible for the service as a whole. The officer chosen for the new appointment was Rear-Admiral C. L. Vaughan-Lee who took over on the 8th of September, with Commodore Sueter as his superintendent of aircraft construction. A further step was the setting up of a design section. Mr. Balfour wrote:

> It is at least as important to have skilled technical experts concerning themselves with the development of aircraft as to have them in connexion with the development of sea-craft. There must, I submit, be a new department or sub-department corresponding with the D.N.C. (Director of Naval Construction).

The foremost of the design questions at the moment were those connected with the new programme of rigid airships, (see chapter 7, 'Airship Development'), and in October it was decided that the responsibility for their design and building should be transferred to the Director of Naval Construction, and for their engines and propelling machines to the Engineer-in-Chief. The organisation provided that the main principles of design should be worked out at the Admiralty, as was done for ships, and the detailed design at the naval air station at Kingsnorth or at the contractor's works. The design and construction of non-rigid airships, aeroplanes, and seaplanes was to remain for the time being under the Air Department, which was itself drastically reorganised and enlarged. (The design and construction of non-rigids and their engines was nominally taken over by the Director of Naval Construction and by the Engineer-in-Chief in July 1916).

Seaplane operations against the German Coast.

The new Board of Admiralty could draw comfort from the blow which in June the naval airmen at Dunkirk had inflicted on the military Zeppelins, but those Zeppelins, although they might in emergency be used for sea reconnaissance, were not strictly a naval problem. The Admiralty was, at this time, responsible for the defence of the country against air raids, and the Belgian successes heartened our own people as much as they depressed the enemy. That was all to the good. So far as home air defence was concerned, the situation was easier. But the Zeppelin as a reconnaissance auxiliary of the German Fleet was a naval problem pure and simple and one which was far more difficult of solution.

The naval Zeppelins, housed in the distant sheds on the coast of North Germany, gave the Admiral of the High Sea Fleet a great advantage over Sir John Jellicoe. The Commander of the Grand Fleet had to face the possibility that every movement which he made at sea in the daylight hours would be promptly reported to his invisible enemy. He might be compelled to fight an action, without air support, against an enemy whose airships were cruising over him in undisputed supremacy.

Without air support. A whole story of failure and disappointment is in that phrase. The *Mayfly* disaster in September 1911 had brought about the immediate cessation of naval airship experiments. 'It is the work of a lunatic,' a distinguished admiral said as he viewed the wreckage of the ill-fated *Mayfly*. But the development of the airship was a lunacy in which the Germans persisted, and when, in the early summer of 1912, Captain Murray Sueter and Mr. Mervyn O'Gorman had visited Germany on behalf of the Committee of Imperial Defence, their report revealed progress too disquieting to be ignored. A memorandum of the technical subcommittee of the Committee of Imperial Defence says:

> The report shows that German airships have, by repeated voyages, proved their ability to reconnoitre the whole of the German coastline on the North Sea. In any future war with Germany, except in foggy or stormy weather, it is probable that no British war vessels or torpedo craft will be able to approach within many miles of the German coast without their presence being discovered and reported to the enemy. . . . In favourable weather the German airships can already be employed for reconnaissance over vast areas of the North Sea, and one airship, owing to the extended view from high altitudes under favourable weather conditions, is able to accomplish the work of a large number of scouting cruisers. It is difficult to exaggerate the value of this advantage to Germany. . . .

The situation called for immediate action, and the Admiralty responded by the reconstitution, in September 1912, of the airship section which had been disbanded after the *Mayfly* setback, and by ordering airships from various sources. (Volume 1). In July 1913 the construction of two rigid and six non-rigid airships was approved. In August 1914 the construction of the first of the rigids had only just been begun by Messrs. Vickers, and it was not long before the work on her had to be abandoned owing to urgent shipbuilding demands.

When war came therefore the Admiralty turned to heavier-than-air craft. On the 14th of August 1914 Captain Murray Sueter suggested the fitting out of a large liner to carry eight to twelve seaplanes and capable of keeping station with the Grand Fleet. The Commander-in-Chief welcomed the suggestion, and in October the purchase of the *Campania* was approved. This old Cunarder of some 20,000 tons had been built in 1893 for the American service. Her full sea speed had been twenty-two knots, and she was one of the few vessels available at the time which offered the necessary speed and space.

She was reconstructed by Messrs. Cammell, Laird to take ten or eleven seaplanes, and was fitted with a 120-foot flying deck above the forecastle. On the 17th of April 1915 she was ready and commissioned for service with the Battle Fleet under Captain O. Swann, R.N. We may leave the *Campania* to her experimental work at Scapa Flow for a survey of the doings of the smaller carriers.

It has already been told how, on the outbreak of war, the cross-Channel steamers *Empress*, *Engadine*, and *Riviera* were taken over and fitted out as seaplane-carriers in Chatham Dockyard, and how they made a raid on Cuxhaven on Christmas Day of 1914. A second air raid against the north German coast was planned for March 1915. On the 20th of the month the *Empress*, escorted by the Harwich force of light cruisers and destroyers, set out for a raid on the wireless station at Norddeich and a reconnaissance of Norden to locate reported Zeppelin sheds. But the raid was unsuccessful, a lumpy sea and a strong wind making it impossible to get the Short seaplanes away.

A further attempt on the 23rd, in which the light cruisers *Arethusa* and *Aurora* each carried a seaplane to supplement those in the *Empress*, was foiled by thick fog off the enemy coast. On the 20th of April the *Empress*, whose temporary canvas protection had proved unsatisfactory, was sent to Liverpool to be refitted with weatherproof hangars, and her place was taken by the *Ben-my-Chree*. (The *Engadine* and *Riviera* had already been similarly refitted). On the 3rd of May the operation against Norddeich was tried again, this time with three carriers, *Ben-my-Chree*, *Engadine*, and *Riviera*, but once more a choppy sea made the launching of the seaplanes impossible, and the expedition came back empty-handed. One of the accompanying British submarines had come under attack, near Texel, from a Zeppelin which dropped ten bombs in her vicinity without, however, causing any damage. Three days later there was another attempt again made abortive by fog.

Undaunted by failure, the squadron set out once more on the 11th of May. As the force approached the German coast a Zeppelin was sighted in the far distance. An attempt was made to fly a Sopwith Schneider Cup seaplane, fitted with wheels, off the dismountable forward platform of *Ben-my-Chree*, but the engine backfired and wrecked the starting gear. At the same time three seaplanes were hoisted out from the *Engadine* and quickly got away. The pilots, however, were soon enveloped in thick fog and compelled to turn back.

Only one returned safely to his ship before the fog closed over the whole flotilla. The other two met with disaster: one, for some reason unknown, spun into the sea and its pilot was not seen again; the other, through engine trouble, crashed on alighting on the water, the pilot being rescued and the wreckage salved. After this raid, the seaplane carriers based at Harwich were dispersed. The *Ben-my-Chree* went to the Mediterranean, the *Riviera* to Dover, and the *Engadine* to the Firth of Forth for work with the Battle Cruiser Fleet.

Meanwhile, to continue the offensive against the Zeppelins which were habitually dogging the normal North Sea patrols sent out from Harwich, Sopwith Schneider Cup seaplanes from Felixstowe were put on board some of the light cruisers. The *Arethusa*, so equipped, was out on the 2nd of June when a Zeppelin came into view. The seaplane got away safely and, at 1,800 feet, was climbing well when the pilot mistook the smoke made by the accompanying destroyers for the smokescreen recall signal and returned to his ship, thus missing a good opportunity to test the fighting power of the seaplane against the airship.

In spite of the continued failure of the seaplane operations, there was no choice but to go on. The Sopwith pilots had not yet had a real chance to show what they could do, and it was important that the offensive against the reconnoitring airships should not be abandoned. Furthermore, reports had come into the Intelligence Department at the Admiralty that transports were being collected in the Ems river, and it was desirable that the truth of these reports should be tested. Another combined operation was therefore planned with the double object of bringing the Zeppelins to action and of reconnoitring the Ems River and the neighbourhood of Borkum.

The force arrived off the island of Ameland as dawn broke on the 4th of July with the promise of a perfect morning. The carriers *Engadine* and *Riviera*, which had come from Rosyth and Dover, respectively, specially for the raid, stopped to hoist out their Short seaplanes whilst the destroyers circled in protection around them. The *Riviera* carried four and the *Engadine* one; all five were quickly on the water, and the four from the *Riviera* went away at ten minutes to three. The *Engadine's* Short, as it was taking off, got into the wash of a destroyer, split its propeller, and had to be hoisted in again. Two of the pilots who got away were compelled, by unsatisfactory engine performance, to return before they reached Borkum. One of the others, after reconnoitring the islands of Juist and Borkum, ran into clouds on the way back and failed to locate the squadron. At 7.0 a.m. when his petrol had run out, he landed near a Dutch trawler and was taken on board. The trawler, at the pilot's request, ran down and destroyed the seaplane, and then took him into Holland, whence he was released on the plea that he was a shipwrecked mariner.

The fourth pilot. Flight Lieutenant H. Stewart, made a careful reconnaissance of the islands and of the Ems River and was able to say that there were no transports in the area. He dropped two small bombs on a battery and two others on torpedo boats lying in Randzel Gat. A German seaplane pilot, from a station on Borkum, climbed after him and followed him part of the way back to his ship, but did not attack. He was guided to the *Riviera* by the presence of four Zeppelins which, he rightly judged, would be watching the movements of our ships, lost to his sight below the clouds.

The immunity of these Zeppelins had resulted from accidents to the three Sopwith Schneider Cup seaplanes which the *Engadine* had carried specially to fight them. The weather conditions were as good as they could well be, and the four Zeppelins were plentiful targets. The seaplanes were new machines fresh from the makers. The floats on all three broke up on the water: two sank, but the third was salved, and all three pilots were rescued. An exceptional opportunity had been lost. Much had been risked to give the seaplanes their chance. Their repeated failures created a distrust of the Naval Air Service among many responsible naval commanders. Not until January of 1916 were any further combined operations against the German coast attempted.

Unhappily, the experience of the commander-in-chief with the seaplanes in the *Campania* was not of a kind to allay this distrust. Exercises had been carried out for the first time in June 1915. There had been great initial trouble in hoisting out the seaplanes on a rolling sea, and then when they were out their floats broke up. One pilot had got into the air successfully and had made a careful reconnaissance of the whole fleet, but he could send down no information owing to the complete failure of his wireless transmission.

Aircraft Experiments in Gunnery Spotting.

Meanwhile the success of kite balloon observation at the Dardanelles had pointed to a possible alternative to the seaplane, and experiments in the control of fire by aeroplanes, carried out in co-operation with the old battleship *Revenge*, had shown considerable promise. These experiments had begun at Dover in February 1915. It was first proved, beyond dispute, that owing to the long range of fire, wireless was the only effective method of signalling from the aircraft to the ship.

Signals in the opposite direction were made at first by the ship's searchlight. In suitable weather this proved fairly satisfactory, although it was difficult to keep the searchlight accurately trained, and the task of reading its messages imposed a tedious watchfulness on the observer in the air. These drawbacks, together with the need for some all-weather and long-distant means of communication, pointed to the necessity of equipping the aircraft for wireless reception. Experimental receiving sets were therefore fitted in a few seaplanes and aeroplanes, and tests again carried out with the battleship showed that, once jamming had been overcome, the ideal means of intercommunication had been found.

The *Revenge* was then ordered to Shoeburyness to carry out actual firing trials in co-operation with aeroplanes from Eastchurch and seaplanes from the *Empress* and the Isle of Grain. These trials, which took place in the first days of April 1915, put the problem of fleet spotting on a new basis.

Before the firing began, test flights had revealed weakness in the sending set on the battleship, the note not being pitched high enough to be heard clearly in the aircraft above the roar of the engine. A Rouzet set from the aerodrome at Eastchurch was thereupon installed in the battleship and was heard distinctly when tested. On the 7th of April *Revenge* went to her firing ground off the Maplin Sands and began the trials. Four consecutive seaplane flights could not get into touch with the ship owing to wireless failure. Whilst the fourth seaplane was still in the air, exasperatingly silent. *Revenge* got into communication with an aeroplane from the Eastchurch aerodrome, and directed the observer to get on with the spotting.

The aeroplane was never seen from the ship, but the order to fire soon came down on the wireless, and *Revenge* opened at 11,000 yards with single shots. The fall of each was reported, and the target was quickly being hit. In the light of later developments, it is, perhaps, difficult to recapture the thrill of this day's work. For the first time in the history of the British Navy a battleship commander had held communication with, and had had his fire controlled with uncanny precision by, an invisible air-observer. The feat was the more noteworthy in that the observer, Flight Lieutenant B. Binyon, the wireless officer from Eastchurch, had had no experience in the art of spotting.

The trials were continued next day; once again the seaplanes failed, but once again Flight Lieutenant Binyon in an aeroplane was successful, and got the battleship on the target with the second shot. To test the observation, the captain of *Revenge* deliberately shifted his sights, but each time the message from the aeroplane giving the fall of the shots was so exact that it seemed like an eerie reading of the captain's mind.

These wireless spotting successes aroused great interest at the Admiralty. Mr. Winston Churchill and Lord Fisher were both enthusiastic. A naval gunnery officer, Commander E. Altham, was appointed to investigate the whole problem of spotting for the fleet. He made a wide study of the subject, including the development of artillery control in the Flying Corps, and the work of the kite balloon ship at the Dardanelles. His report, a model of clear statement, urged the immediate formation of a school at the seaplane base at Calshot for the training of observers in fire-control. The suggestion was readily adopted and firing practice, in co-operation with the guns of the fort at Calshot Castle, began on the 21st of June. He also suggested that the reports of the *Revenge* experiments be sent to the Commander-in-Chief of the Grand Fleet with a view to similar trials being made with the aircraft in *Campania*.

The papers were forwarded to Sir John Jellicoe on the 23rd of July. In reply he agreed that the value of air spotting was proven, but stated that from his experience with *Campania*, apart altogether from the failure of the wireless communication, there could be few occasions when seaplanes would be able to work from the open sea. The only solution was a light seaplane which could rise from the deck of the carrier, but no seaplane had yet succeeded in flying off *Campania*. The really important point brought to notice by the correspondence, he said, was that air spotting could, and unquestionably would, be used to great advantage by the German High Sea Fleet in a naval action, he goes on:

We, on the other hand, will not only be powerless to carry out aerial spotting, but I am afraid we shall also be unable to prevent the Germans doing so by means of their Zeppelins since our seaplanes are incapable of engaging the Zeppelins owing to their insufficient lifting power, and our aerial guns will not be able to reach them. In view of the remarkable accuracy with which aerial spotting can be carried out, this matter is one of the most serious import to which I invite Their Lordships' earnest attention. I regret that I am unable to propose any means of meeting this menace, unless it be by the use of aeroplanes, rising from the deck of *Campania*, capable of climbing above the Zeppelins, and able to land on the water and be supported sufficiently long by air bags to allow of the rescue of the pilots.

Within a week of the writing of this letter, that is to say on the 6th of August 1915, a Sopwith Schneider Cup seaplane (pilot. Flight Lieutenant W. L. Welsh) was flown off the deck of *Campania* when the carrier was steaming at seventeen knots into the wind. Wheels, fitted under the floats of the seaplane, were dropped into the sea as soon as the machine was in the air. The marks of the wheels along the deck showed that the seaplane had run for 113 feet, under its own power, before taking off. It was thus clear enough that small craft, whether light seaplanes or fighting aeroplanes, capable of attacking reconnoitring Zeppelins, could be got away without exposing the carrier to the danger from submarines which stopping to hoist out entailed.

The problem, however, of how to get away the heavier machines equipped for fleet reconnaissance work, remained. So dubious were the authorities about the value of *Campania* to the Grand Fleet that, in October, her withdrawal was seriously debated. In the end it was resolved that she should be reconstructed to give a longer deck to allow of the flying off of two-seater reconnaissance aircraft. At the end of November 1915, therefore, she went back to Messrs. Cammell Laird at Liverpool. Whilst the *Campania* was in dock, her seaplanes, from the shore base at Scapa, continued their anti-submarine patrols in the area of the fleet anchorage.

Kite Balloons at Sea.

Before the carrier had left Scapa Flow, for refit, the fact that the kite balloon could be used at sea by the Grand Fleet had been demonstrated. The suggestion that a balloon ship be fitted out for fleet work had been put before Sir John Jellicoe by the Admiralty at the end of May 1915, with reports of the doings of the *Manica* at Gallipoli. On the information which was laid before him, the commander-in-chief held that the fitting out of a fast balloon-carrying ship was hardly warranted. Instead, he recommended the setting up of a balloon station at Scapa Flow from which tests could be made on board *Campania*.

Whilst the matter was under the consideration of the Board of Admiralty, there came news of the success of a notable balloon experiment carried out under the direction of Rear-Admiral R. H. S. Bacon, who had succeeded Rear-Admiral the Hon. H. L. A. Hood in the command of the Dover Patrol on the 13th of April 1915. The *Hector*, the second of the balloon ships to be fitted, had gone to the Dardanelles where she arrived, as has been told, on the 9th of July 1915. The third ship, the *Menelaus* (4,672 tons), taken over from the Ocean Steamship Company, was ready on the 8th of July, and was put under the orders of Admiral Bacon for air spotting of bombardments of the Belgian coast to be made by the new 12-inch monitors.

The *Menelaus* differed from the first two ships in that she carried her balloon already inflated. To be of any great use it was obvious that the balloon would have to be let up close to the enemy coast, but there was the difficulty that *Menelaus* was too big a target to survive for long under the eyes of the German gunners. It was the balloon and not the parent ship that was wanted close in. Admiral Bacon therefore ordered that experiments should be made to see if *Menelaus* could pass her balloon, complete with observers, to the trawler *Peary*.

The first trial took place on the 7th of August. The balloon ship was laid stern to wind at a slow speed; the *Peary* came up alongside on a parallel course and caught a heaving line, to which she at once secured her own balloon cable. The line was hauled back to *Menelaus* and the trawler's cable was attached to the balloon. The *Peary* then hauled in her cable until she was taking the strain of the balloon, the slip wire from *Menelaus* was let go and taken in by the trawler, and the control of the balloon by *Peary* was thus completed. The trawler went off for a fifteen-minute trip before passing her lofty cargo back to *Menelaus*. During the transfer the balloon plunged badly and the observers in the basket had an uncomfortable time.

Their disability, however, was ephemeral. The important thing was that the practicability of handing over the balloon at sea, ready for work, had been demonstrated. In this first trial the telephonic communication between the balloon and the trawler failed, but in further trials on the 13th and 17th of August, this failure was rectified. On the 7th of September the *Peary*, with the balloon from *Menelaus*, spotted experimentally for the *Redoubtable*—as the old *Revenge* had been renamed—in a shelling of Westende subsidiary to a main bombardment of Ostend. The balloon was transferred to the trawler at 9.0 a.m. and was ready at 10.0 a.m., when the battleship opened fire.

Mist over the land made the observation from the basket of the balloon uncertain at first, but later, when the mist cleared, the observer kept up a running report, by telephone to the trawler, of the fall of the shots and the positions of enemy guns which were firing. The observations, as they came down, were signalled from *Peary* to the firing ship. When firing ceased, the balloon was passed back from the trawler to *Menelaus*, which then returned to Dover. In the meantime, Vice-Admiral Sir David Beatty, commanding the Battle Cruiser Fleet, had been attracted to the value of balloons for the Grand Fleet. He said in a memorandum dated August the 20th:

> They could often be sent up in weather where it would not be possible to launch a seaplane; probably in weather that would be prohibitive for Zeppelins.

Sir John Jellicoe was informed, when he submitted this memorandum to the Board of Admiralty, that a new balloon ship, *City of Oxford*, would be put at his disposal for trials as soon as her refitting was completed.

******

The *City of Oxford*, a cargo vessel of 4,019 tons, had been purchased by the Admiralty in October 1914. Her upper works were reconstructed to give her the appearance of a battleship, and she did a spell of service as a phantom dreadnought. She was not converted into a kite balloon ship until early in 1916, and was then attached to the Dover Patrol in March, relieving the *Menelaus* for Grand Fleet experiments.

******

Until experiments had proved the value of the balloon to the fleet, the fitting out of a special high speed balloon-ship, they held, was not justified. They further pointed out that the urgent needs of the army for balloons were being met from naval sources.

Sir David Beatty returned to the subject in a letter on the 23rd of September 1915, when he again urged the need of a suitable balloon vessel for scouting work before a fleet action. In the result a naval kite balloon section—No. 9—was put at his disposal for experimental work at Rosyth. The experiments were conducted under the keen supervision of Rear-Admiral the Hon. H. L. A. Hood, now commanding the Third Battle Cruiser Squadron. The seaplane carrier *Engadine*, which had been based at Granton since the middle of July, was the most suitable vessel at hand from which to make the trials, and she was accordingly transferred to Rosyth on the 24th of October. Three days later the balloon was walked down to the dock and embarked on the carrier, where it was bagged down on the top of the seaplane hangar.

When the *Engadine* had got out beyond the Forth Bridge, the balloon was let up with two observers in the basket. It soared away at heights up to 2,000 feet, wholly unaffected by the speed of the ship, which was worked up to eighteen and a half knots. The basket remained steady throughout the trial, telephonic communication between the observers and the ship was uninterrupted, and the balloon smoothly followed each change of course of the ship, no matter how drastic.

On the 29th of October a more severe test was planned, and since the behaviour of the balloon was unpredictable, ballast was substituted for observers. The precaution was needless. The speed of the carrier was increased to twenty-two knots in a heavy sea, but the balloon rode the air smoothly, apparently but lightly affected by the pitching and rolling of the towing ship. The balloon was hauled down and let up again at will, and a maximum height of 3,000 feet was reached. A close examination of the rigging and fabric after the experiment was ended revealed no damage of any kind. The trial, indeed, had been successful beyond all that had been hoped for.

Rear-Admiral Hood, who witnessed the trials from *Engadine*, submitted a detailed report to Vice-Admiral Beatty, pointing out that the matter was of the most vital importance to the British Fleet in view of the remoteness of the chance that seaplanes or aeroplanes would, at that time, be able to give timely and detailed information of the disposition of the enemy fleet before an action, he said:

> I hope that a proper ship may be fitted without delay and if possible one that may have the speed to accompany the Battle Cruiser Fleet ... I think I have proved the value of the kite balloon for reconnaissance purposes; in a suitable vessel the strategic and tactical value will be very great; at 3,000 feet there will be a radius of vision of 60 miles and the communication will not be of the sketchy kind in use from aeroplanes, but will be conversation by telephone from a skilled observer sitting com-

fortably in a basket, to a responsible officer in the balloon ship, who with efficient W/T and all signal books and codes at hand, will rapidly signal by the most efficient method the information that may well win or lose the Dominion of the World....

Vice-Admiral Beatty, in forwarding the report on the experiments to the Admiralty at the end of October, stated that:

> The advantage that the enemy has hitherto possessed by the aid of his Zeppelins in obtaining early information of the position, composition, disposition, and course and speed of our Fleet will by the use of the kite balloons be in a great measure nullified.

He pointed out that whilst the balloon suffered from lack of speed as compared with the Zeppelin, it had advantages in that it could not be driven off by gun-fire, was more mobile, and could be hauled down and taken to any position in the teeth of a strong wind, and hoisted again. He advocated the use of balloons in the *Campania* in place of some of her heavier-than-air craft.

Admiral Jellicoe would now have preferred that a special ship be fitted as a balloon carrier; but the urgent demands for large fast merchant ships for other war purposes had first to be met, and the Admiralty decided, in the end, that the plans for the reconstruction of *Campania* should be modified to enable the carrier to take an inflated balloon aft. In the discussion which preceded the decision, Rear-Admiral F. C. T. Tudor, the Third Sea Lord, suggested that some of the existing balloon ships, whose speed was insufficient to enable them to work with the fleet, might be used as sheds from which the balloons could be transferred to the light cruisers. This suggestion, which recognised that the real function of the balloon at this time was to extend the range of vision of the scouting screen of the fleet, was not taken up: many tides were to wash against Heligoland before it was finally adopted. (See the account of the sortie of the German Fleet on August the 18th/19th, 1916, in chapter 7).

END OF THE FIRST SUBMARINE CAMPAIGN

The first submarine campaign reached its climax in August 1915. The losses included the unarmed White Star Liner *Arabic*, torpedoed without warning on the 19th of August. The sinking of the *Lusitania* off the south coast of Ireland with a loss of 1,198 men, women, and children, on the 7th of May, had strained relations between America and Germany. The Arabic episode, with a further toll of American lives, brought the two countries to the brink of war. A storm of controversy blew up anew in Germany. Admiral Tirpitz urged that unrestricted submarine warfare was the only means of winning the war for Germany.

The Chancellor, faced by a collection of sharp diplomatic notes from America, was anxious that attacks on passenger ships should be abandoned. In the end the Chancellor prevailed upon the Emperor to issue orders, on the 27th of August, that submarine commanders were not to sink passenger steamers, in the prohibited zone, without warning and before the removal of the passengers and crew. In view of the effectiveness of the rapidly extending defensive measures, submarine warfare in British waters, under the new conditions, would be a risky business. Furthermore, an Austro-German offensive was about to begin in the Balkans, so that the waters of the Mediterranean would offer important hunting grounds for the submarines. Consequently, on the 18th of September 1915, enemy submarines were ordered to withdraw from the Channel and from our west coast. The first submarine campaign against commerce thus came to an end, even as it reached its climax, giving us breathing space in which to get on with our counter measures.

The Flanders submarines, however, did not cease their depredations, particularly off the East Coast, where the Lowestoft fishing fleets suffered heavily. Rear-Admiral Bacon had for long been preparing an attack on the submarine bases in Belgium. He had had a special range constructed in the Thames Estuary where the salient features of the coast about Zeebrugge were exactly reproduced, and here the whole operation was rehearsed, with seaplanes from the *Riviera* co-operating. Although the air-spotting results were reasonably successful, the inability of the seaplanes to get off any but fairly smooth water precluded reliance being placed on them for the actual bombardment. Admiral Bacon had been at pains, therefore, to devise an alternative means of getting forward observation. By fixing a tall iron tripod to a raft he had built what were, in effect, tiny portable islands which could be planted, with an observation party, in shallow waters.

Destruction of the Naval Zeppelin L.12.

Whilst these preparations for the bombardment of the Belgian coast were being pushed forward, important changes in the organisation of the air units of the Dover Patrol were being made. Of all the naval commands in home waters, this was, perhaps, the one most affected by the new Admiralty air policy, whereby senior naval officers were given control of the operations of aircraft in their command.

On the 1st of August Admiral Bacon became responsible for the aeroplane and seaplane bases at Dover and Dunkirk, together with the 'S.S.' airship stations at Capel and Polegate. To advise him on air matters Wing Commander C. L. Lambe was appointed to the Admiral's Staff on the 5th of August, an appointment which put him at the head of the Dover-Dunkirk group of air bases, and marked the beginning of a rapid development of their work and importance. When Wing Commander Lambe took over, the air unit at Dunkirk was No. 2 Wing under Wing Commander E. L. Gerrard, which had relieved No. 1 Wing on the 2nd of August. (Admiralty orders, in June, had changed the nomenclature of the aeroplane units. They were now called wings, the word squadron being reserved for a group of six aeroplanes or seaplanes). No. 2 Wing were not at Dunkirk long, but during their brief stay they had the satisfaction of helping to complete the destruction of an airship.

Five naval Zeppelins had set out from the North German sheds on the 9th of August for a raid on British east coast towns. One of them, L.12, appeared over Westgate, in misty weather, a little before 11.0 p.m. and moved on, over Ramsgate, towards Dover, where she appeared soon after midnight and began to bomb. Her commander was hopelessly confused in his reckoning, and was under the impression that he was attacking Harwich. He dropped about a dozen bombs. Three incendiaries fell on the Admiralty Pier: two of them burnt themselves out on the parapet, and the third set fire to the platform without doing much damage. The remaining bombs fell in the harbour. One which burst under the bows of the trawler *Equinox* wounded one man severely and two more slightly, but none of the others caused any damage or casualties.

The airship was hit, almost as soon as she appeared over Dover, by an anti-aircraft shell, but was still able to put her nose up and outclimb two aeroplanes which went up in pursuit. She was not, however, to get away so easily. The damage done by the shell soon began to make itself felt, and L.12, losing gas rapidly, was compelled to descend to the surface of the water off Ostend. A message that the Zeppelin was coming down was received at Dunkirk soon after 8.0 a.m. There was a thick mist along the whole coast, but bombing attacks were ordered at once.

Flight Commander J. R. W. Smyth-Pigott went away first at 8.25 a.m. About three miles off Ostend he found the airship about his own level (2,000 feet) and turned away to gain more height. He lost the ship for a few minutes, and when he again saw her she had four torpedo-boats in attendance and was apparently being hauled down. He made two attacks, first with 20-lb. bombs and then with grenades, and, although he could not observe any direct hits, he saw, as he left, that the back of the airship was broken. The next officer who set out to attack the Zeppelin was shot down and killed. A third aeroplane delivered its attack at a quarter to ten as the airship was being towed between the two harbour piers at Ostend.

There were two more attacks before midday, and four in the afternoon, which scattered parties of workmen who were trying to haul the Zeppelin on to the quay. Owing to the heavy fire which met the aeroplanes over the target, none of the pilots observed the effect of the bombs close enough to say whether they secured any direct hits, but the fact remains that during the afternoon the rear half of the airship slipped back into the water and further attempts to salve her were given up. The L.12 was broken up on the spot and the materials sent back to Germany by rail. Within a few days of this attack on the Zeppelin, No. 2 Wing were withdrawn from Dunkirk and sent to the Dardanelles, No. 1 Wing returning on August 15th to their old aerodrome in time to provide protective air patrols for Admiral Bacon's long-planned bombardment of Zeebrugge, which began at 5.30 in the morning of the 23rd of August.

Bombardments of the Belgian Coast.

The objectives of the bombardment were the locks and caissons of the canal connecting the seaport with Bruges, and the factory where it was believed the enemy submarines were assembled. The *Riviera* accompanied the bombarding fleet. Although there was a heavy sea, three Short seaplanes were got away from the carrier, but not one of them flew lower than 2,500 feet, from which height nothing could be seen of the cloud-patched coast. The fighting patrols of No. 1 Wing were also handicapped by the weather, but one pilot (Flight Sub-Lieutenant R. H. Mulock) had a brief encounter with a German seaplane at a thousand feet off Zeebrugge and forced it back to its base. Incidentally he reported that from this height the coast was visible up to a distance of three miles.

For the observation of his fire Admiral Bacon was compelled to rely on two of his island tripods, which had been run in close to the coast before the firing began and which, within their limits, gave fair observation: aircraft, alone, however, could offer a direct view so essential to accurate reporting of the fire, and the Admiral expressed the opinion that had the pilots had discretion to fly below a thousand feet they must have given him valuable help. Optimistic reports from agents put the damage caused by the bombardment high, but air reconnaissances, two days later, revealed no damage to the lock gates and only slight damage to the Solway works power station.

Ostend was chosen for the next attack, which took place on the 7th of September. As the main force approached the coast the sun came over the horizon with the pink tinge of a London sun in November, bringing with it a threat of fog. Three Shorts from *Riviera* were flying over the monitors ready to observe the fire, but before this could be opened, a light mist had descended between the ships and their targets. Admiral Bacon, thus denied any datum mark without which indirect fire was impossible, decided to postpone the bombardment until the mist should clear again, since it was highly important not to endanger civilian life and property in the town of our Ally. Although the targets were invisible to the ships, they were clearly outlined to the airmen who circled round, mystified by the delay.

At 7.0 a.m. a signal was made by one of the pilots that the weather was clear for spotting, but the order was flashed back that the seaplane remain near the flagship. The three seaplanes flew until their petrol was running low, when they returned—two to the *Riviera*, and the other direct to Dover. Meanwhile there was no attempt to arrest the arrangements made for the co-operation of the wing at Dunkirk, and one spotting and two fighting aeroplanes remained near the fleet until lack of petrol compelled them to return. Further, a bomb raid on the store hangars south-west of Ostend, planned to be a diversion during the bombardment, was carried out according to programme. Seventeen French and six British aeroplanes made the attack and claimed many hits.

The fleet was still waiting off Ostend at about a quarter to one when three German aeroplanes suddenly appeared and began to bomb. One bomb, dropped from a height of 8,000 feet, hit the light cruiser *Attentive*, killing two men, wounding seven others, and putting a gun out of action. Admiral Bacon at once ordered the ships to separate. In the afternoon the squadron returned and found that the whole sea front was now white and clear in the sun. The bombardment opened at half past three, at a range of 18,000 to 19,000 yards. Admiral Bacon did not go closer at first, as he had seen a kite balloon over Ostend obviously ready to observe for the shore batteries of whose effective range he had as yet no exact knowledge. He was not long to remain in doubt.

Barely had the flagship (*Lord Clive*) opened fire when the first shots from the coastal battery fell within a hundred yards of the monitor. Before the ships had got into position to bombard two seaplanes had gone up from the *Riviera*. One flew into Dunkirk and sent down a message to Wing Commander Longmore informing him that the operation was about to begin. The seaplane then went on to the monitors and was shortly followed by one spotting and four fighting aeroplanes from Dunkirk. The three spotting aircraft, although bothered by patches of mist below them, were able to report the main effect of the monitors' fire. They were witnesses, too, of the amazing accuracy of the shore guns.

Two shells went singing past the aeroplane when it was flying at 7,000 feet. Their downward course was anxiously watched by the pilot and observer, who were relieved to see them burst, one just ahead and one just astern of the flagship. Shortly afterwards they saw *Lord Clive* receive a hit on the port quarter. Admiral Bacon had turned sixteen points to open the range, but the enemy shells followed and straddled the flagship with twenty rounds in as many minutes, four of them damaging the ship, and the remainder being grouped within a radius of fifty yards. The effectiveness and range of the new shore guns came as something of a shock. (They were the four 28 cm. guns of the famous Tirpitz Battery, T. 4, which had an effective range of 35,000 yards). Admiral Bacon quickly realised that he was hopelessly outranged, and decided to break off the action and not to try again until the guns had been definitely located and the 15-inch monitors were ready to deal with them.

The exact positions of the guns were pin-pointed by the officers in the aeroplane before they returned. The Tirpitz battery thus makes its first appearance in the Dunkirk naval air records. It runs through them continuously afterwards. Repeatedly photographed and reconnoitred, bombed from the air, bombarded from the sea and from the land with the help of air observation, it remains to the end, not indeed untouched, but with its powerful efficiency unshaken.

On the 13th of September the new 15-inch monitor, *Marshal Ney*, arrived at Dover, and two days later was part of the fleet which again set out to bombard the Belgian Coast. The ships were off Zuidcoote Pass at dawn, but the weather proved too poor for effective firing, and the fleet was compelled to lie in waiting in Dunkirk Harbour and

Roads until the 19th. Aeroplanes from Dunkirk kept up protective patrols over the ships whilst they were at anchor, and when *Lord Clive* and *Marshal Ney* made a brief bombardment of the enemy coastal batteries on the 19th, two Henri Farmans helped to direct their fire.

Admiral Bacon had discussed with Sir John French how the Dover Patrol might co-operate with the military offensive at Loos planned to begin on the 25th of September. It was decided that the ships should bombard the extreme ends of the Belgian coast to lead the enemy to believe that a landing at Knocke or an advance from Nieuport might be intended. To give colour to the landing idea, thirty motor lighters on their way to Devonport were diverted to Dover and the news of their arrival was allowed to reach Germany.

The army had also asked for the co-operation of eight naval aeroplanes for daily bombing of the railway between Courtrai and Deynze, and that the request might be acceded to, Admiral Bacon asked on September the 20th for aeroplane reinforcements for Dunkirk: next day nine aeroplanes from Eastchurch were flown across. (The Eastchurch reinforcements remained at Dunkirk until the end of November, after which they were gradually withdrawn, the last pilot leaving on the 6th of January 1916).

On the 25th and the two following days, and again on the 30th and the 3rd of October, the bombardment of the coast went forward according to programme. As the bombardment was general and not against specific targets there was no call for detailed aircraft spotting, and the main task of the aeroplanes was to avert enemy bombing attacks on the fleet. This they effectively did. There was an attempt, too, on the 25th to bomb the Tirpitz battery. Eight aeroplanes took part in the raid, and dropped twenty-two 20-lb. and six 65-lb. bombs. Visibility was poor over the battery and some pilots bombed the dockyard instead. Only one bomb was seen to burst on the earthworks of the battery. During the time the ships were exposed off the enemy coast there were anti-submarine patrols, by seaplanes from the recently reopened station at Dunkirk, on the seaward side of the fleet.

DUNKIRK: ATTACKS ON SUBMARINES AND AIRCRAFT.

The Dunkirk pilots who flew on various duties along the Belgian coast took every opportunity to attack submarines whenever they were seen. On the 26th of August 1915, Squadron Commander A. W. Bigsworth, flying a Henri Farman to bomb Zeebrugge, surprised a submarine on the surface about six miles north-west of Ostend. He spiralled down to within 500 feet of the sea and got into a good attacking position over the submarine which, to avoid him, was now zigzagging. Two of his 65-lb. bombs appeared to make direct hits. For a moment the aeroplane was thrown partly out of control by the concussion, but when it was righted the pilot saw the U-boat disappear tail first.

Again, on the morning of the 6th of September, Flight Sub-Lieutenant Mulock with Second Lieutenant J. H. D'Albiac as observer, on a coastal reconnaissance, sighted a submarine seven miles north of Ostend. He went home to Dunkirk at once for bombs and was fortunate in once more finding the U-boat awash. Diving to 400 feet he let go his five 20-lb. bombs as he passed over the target and saw the last two explode either on the deck or in the wash above the deck as she was in the act of submerging.

The same pilot on reconnaissance on the morning of the 26th, during the fleet bombardment, found a submarine moving west four miles north of Zeebrugge. He returned to make his report, and Flight Sub-Lieutenant G. H. Beard went off immediately in a Henri Farman, and after a long search saw a submarine on the surface off Ostend. This he attacked from a height of 700 feet, his bombs falling close alongside. The submarine remained stationary on the surface. The pilot flew back and signalled, with his pocket handkerchief, to the monitors. The *Sir John Moore* read the word 'submarine' waved out in Morse, but the remainder of the message giving her position could not be taken in as the aeroplane was repeatedly masked by funnel smoke.

The bombarding ships, as a defensive measure, increased to full speed. When the pilot returned to Dunkirk five aeroplanes were sent off to continue the attack. Two of them found the submarine still on the surface, but after she was bombed, without direct hits, she submerged. During October and November submarines were often attacked by Dunkirk aircraft. On the 28th of the latter month Flight Sub-Lieutenant T. E. Viney (observer, Lieutenant Comte de Sincay, a French flying officer attached for interpreting duties who flew voluntarily as an observer), on a Henri Farman aeroplane, attacked a stationary submarine off Westende with two 65-lb. bombs, one of which seemed to get a direct hit.

It appeared to the airmen that the U-boat broke in two as she sank, but it is now known that no German submarine was lost on this day. Although it cannot be claimed that any underwater craft were definitely destroyed as a result of these various air attacks, it is, at least, certain that some were damaged, and there is evidence, too, that the attacks were not without effect on the morale of the crews. The German U-boat historian, Gayer, says:

> At the end of September in Flanders, air attacks of greater severity were begun on the incoming and outgoing boats; U.B.6 and U.C.1 suffered some damage through them. (*Die deutschen U-Boote in ihrer Kriegsführung, 1914-1918, Vol. II*).

There were few encounters with German aircraft along the Belgian coast throughout the year. The enemy had not yet developed his fighting aircraft, relying rather on his increasingly efficient anti-aircraft guns. Only two decisive combats are recorded by the Dunkirk wing. The first took place on the 28th of November. Flight Sub-Lieutenant J. B. P. Ferrand with Air Mechanic G. T. Oldfield was on submarine patrol in an F.B.A. (Franco-British Aviation Company) flying boat when he came upon a German destroyer, with an escort of four seaplanes, north of Westende. The flying boat attacked the seaplanes. Three of them made off towards Ostend, but the fourth accepted combat and was quickly shot down by the observer, disappearing nose-first in the sea. The flying boat pilot then turned on the destroyer, but his bombs failed to hit.

The second notable fight occurred on the 14th of December. A merchant vessel had stranded on the sandbank near the Whistle Buoy on the 12th, and could not be towed off for some time on account of the stormy weather. News came into Dunkirk that two enemy aeroplanes had attempted to bomb the steamer. Continuous air patrols were thereafter maintained in her vicinity. In the afternoon of the 14th they were rewarded. Flight Sub-Lieutenant C. W. Graham with Sub-Lieutenant A. S. Ince as observer, was patrolling on a Nieuport aeroplane when he intercepted a large two-seater seaplane directly over the stranded vessel. Three times the Nieuport pilot dived to give his observer a good firing position immediately beneath the seaplane.

At the third attempt the enemy fell, a flaming mass, into the sea, where the bombs, which had been meant for the merchant ship, exploded and hurled the wreckage of the German seaplane back into the air. The Nieuport, in which the petrol tank had been holed and emptied during the fight, was forced to land near the paddle minesweeper *Balmoral*. The aeroplane turned turtle on striking the water and took the pilot under, strapped in his seat. He freed himself with difficulty and, with his observer, was rescued by the mine-sweeper.

CHAPTER 7

The Royal Naval Air Service in Home Waters (1916)

When the year 1915 drew to a close the foundations for a wide expansion of the Naval Air Service had been laid. Early in the new year the service was relieved of two serious responsibilities. The final evacuation of the Gallipoli peninsula, in January, and the taking over by the War Office, in February, of the burden of protecting this country against air raids, released considerable aircraft and personnel. A notable effect of this was a strengthening of the air base at Dunkirk and an intensifying of the air offensive against the enemy bases in Belgium. A secondary effect was the initiation of bombing raids into Germany, the genesis of the Independent Air Force.

Airship Development

But perhaps the most remarkable development in 1916 took place in the airship service. To understand this expansion, it is necessary to go back to the summer of the previous year. Mr. Balfour, soon after he succeeded Mr. Churchill as First Lord, called a conference to debate the whole airship building policy. The position when the conference met on the 19th of June 1915, was that fifty of the 'S.S.' type airships were already on order. The naval air station at Kingsnorth, however, had just constructed a larger airship, called the Coastal or 'C' type. The original coastal was made up of an Astra-Torres envelope and a car obtained by joining two Avro fuselages end on after the tails had been cut off. (The later Coastals had specially constructed cars slightly larger than the Avro and of heavier design).

The 'S.S.' was useful chiefly for searching narrow channels such as the Dover Straits or the Irish Narrows. The Coastal was designed to undertake more protracted patrols. At full speed, about forty-five miles an hour, it had an endurance of eleven hours. It was decided, as a result of the conference, that the 'S.S.' programme of fifty ships should be completed, but that no more of this type were to be laid down. Instead thirty Coastals were to be ordered at once. The areas which called for patrol by the Coastals were off Pembroke and Land's End, off the mouths of the Humber and the Forth, and beyond the important stretches of coast off Norfolk and north of Aberdeen.

Sites for the stations were selected, and the intricate work of preparing them and of building sheds and huts to house the airships, workshops, stores, and personnel, was pushed forward as rapidly as possible. Contracts for the envelopes, fins, and cars for the Coastals were, as for the 'S.S.'s, placed with private makers. The parts were delivered direct to Kingsnorth, where the airships were assembled and tested, this work beginning in September 1915, when the first supplies from the makers arrived.

The members of the conference did not confine their recommendations to the increased building of non-rigids. They urged, also, that work should be resumed at once on the rigid airship—No. 9—which had been stopped in February 1915, and that three further rigids should be built. These suggestions received the approval of the Board at the beginning of July, and gave us the nucleus of a rigid airship fleet.

Twenty-seven Coastal airships were built at Kingsnorth and delivered to various naval air stations in 1916. In addition, four were supplied to the Russian Government and one to the French. The first Coastal station to be opened was at Pembroke, commissioned early in January 1916, with personnel from the airship base at Marquise, now handed over to the French Government. The initial flight from the station, however, was made by the S.S.15, which had been refitted at Wormwood Scrubs after its spell of duty at Marquise.

The first Coastal flight did not take place until the 9th of June. By the end of the year the station had received two other S.S. airships and a second Coastal. The latter, on the 30th of July, set up the year's endurance record for this type of ship when she remained out for eighteen hours thirty-five minutes, covering 475 miles. One of the airships from Pembroke—S.S. 42—was wrecked on the 15th of September, after a remarkable flight. The ship, piloted by Flight Lieutenant E. F. Monk, went away at about 7.45 a.m. in search of a submarine reported to be near Lundy Island. When the airship came near the island she ran into squalls, and, as the weather conditions threatened to get worse, the pilot decided to return. He made his station at 10.45 a.m., but as the airship touched the landing ground she was lifted thirty feet in the air by a violent gust of wind and then dashed down again. The impact carried away most of the port suspensions to the car which turned nearly upside down; at the same instant the trail rope broke and the airship began to rise.

This process was helped, says the pilot in his report, by the wireless operator falling out when about twenty feet from the ground. As the rapidly rising airship drifted out over the Bristol Channel the pilot clambered to the top of the upturned car, whence he realised that all controls had gone and that there was nothing to do but keep his precarious seat and trust to luck. He caught a fleeting glimpse of Caldy Island from 3,000 feet before he was whirled into the clouds. The next land he saw was Lundy Island which the airship skirted at a height of 7,000 feet. About this time, and without warning, the forward starboard suspensions, which had been supporting the main weight of the engine, snapped, and the car fell into a vertical position, engine down.

The pilot, as he was pitched forward, contrived to keep a hold and to scramble to a position on the axle of the undercarriage. At 2.0 p.m., that is to say three hours after she broke away, the airship, now at over 8,000 feet, began to fall. She dropped slowly at first but at an increasing speed, and spinning, as she came out of a cloudbank over the fields of Devonshire. She crashed near Ivybridge. Flight Lieutenant Monk, who let go his hold just before the airship met the ground, escaped with injuries to the back. The wreckage of the ship was rebuilt at Wormwood Scrubs as the S.S.42A which was sent back to Pembroke. The pilot, when he had recovered from his injuries, returned to his station to take command of the newly conditioned airship.

******

On the 12th of September 1917, this ill-fated vessel, piloted by another officer, was making a night landing at Pembroke when she crashed into a farm building and was seriously damaged; she drifted out to sea where the crew were seen to fire distress signals. Destroyers and motor launches followed the airship but failed to locate her until daylight next morning, when they found that the pilot and wireless operator had disappeared from the wreckage.

******

Pulham, the second Coastal station, was commissioned at the end of February 1916. It received its first ship on August the 31st, another in November, and a third in December. The usual routine patrols were made from the station which was also the headquarters of the parachute experimental staff.

Howden, north of the Humber, was opened on the 15th of March. Its first Coastal arrived from Kingsnorth on the 26th of June, another a few days later and two more in September. At the end of December, the old Parseval, No. 4, which had made history by her patrols over the Channel during the passage of the original Expeditionary Force, was sent to Howden from Barrow to be used, with two other of the Parsevals (Nos. 6 and 7) yet to be completed by Messrs. Vickers, as training ships for rigid airship personnel.

******

The construction of these two ships formed part of the airship programme approved by Mr. Winston Churchill, the First Lord, in July 1913. No. 6 carried out her trials in May 1917, and No. 7 in December 1917. No. 5 also underwent her trials in November 1917. This ship had a Parseval envelope made by Messrs. Vickers. The car was of modified Coastal pattern. No. 5 went to the East Fortune air station early in 1918.

******

Longside, west of Peterhead, was opened on the 15th of March. The first flight was made on the 16th of June, by which time two Coastals had been delivered. Another arrived at the end of August and a fourth in November.

The Mullion station, near the Lizard, which, situated as it was on the flank of the important western approaches, was destined to become one of the most active anti-submarine patrol centres, was commissioned in June. The first Coastal airship, sent to Mullion from Kingsnorth on the 8th of June, was lost in the Channel on the way through some undiscovered cause. The pilot and two of the crew were drowned; the wireless operator was saved. Two other airships were sent at once, by rail, and the first flight took place on the 1st of July. A third airship was on the strength of the station in October.

One of the few airship and submarine encounters of the year took place off the Lizard on the 9th of September. The airship C.10, whilst on patrol in co-operation with the destroyer *Foyle*, sighted two burning sailing ships and flew on to investigate. She carried one 65-lb. and four 16-lb. bombs. As the pilot neared the ships he saw a submarine on the far side of them, but when he was still a few hundred yards away the U-boat submerged. The pilot searched the area, but a strong wind was breaking the surface of the water and all trace of the submarine was lost. The *Foyle*, in response to a wireless signal from the airship, had rushed to the spot and now took up the search.

After a short time, the U-boat again came to the surface but dived immediately the destroyer opened fire. The *Foyle* after a further abortive search returned and picked up the survivors from the burning vessels. A point brought out by this episode is the disability under which the airship attacks. She can be seen from a long distance and gives an alert commander, under favourable conditions, plenty of time to get under. The two sailing vessels were French: they had been first attacked by gun-fire, after which the submarine crew compelled the French sailors, at the point of the revolver, to transfer to them food and instruments. They forced the Frenchmen, also, to carry and put on board the incendiary bombs which were to fire their vessels. The work was proceeding steadily when the airship was sighted.

Her arrival on the scene, said the Frenchmen, came as a surprise. It seemed to be a new experience for the submarine crew, who abandoned a quantity of gear already assembled for transfer, and got under without any loss of time. The articles which the enemy took from their victims make curious reading: the list includes coffee, condensed milk, tinned crab, carrots, the captain's panama hat, and a collection of old boots.

East Fortune, first established as an aeroplane station, received two Coastals, by air from Kingsnorth, in August 1916. One of these, wrecked at sea, without loss of life, soon after she arrived, was replaced on the 22nd of September. Two others arrived by rail in December. One of the Coastals from this station, the C20, made an encouraging flight in co-operation with the Battle Cruiser Fleet on the 30th of September. The pilot kept station in accordance with visual signals from the flagship, on the look-out for enemy submarines. Vice-Admiral Sir David Beatty, in his report of these exercises said:

> It is recommended that every opportunity should be taken for the Coastal type of airship to work with the fleet. Although they are themselves of limited value, the preliminary stages of training in fleet work will have already been gone through by the time that the North Sea and rigid types make their appearance. When these join up, it would appear that they will take over under certain conditions a large number of the duties now performed by light cruisers.

Reference has been made to the building and testing of the Coastal airships at Kingsnorth. When the navy took over the lighter-than-air service of the country, in January 1914, the Admiralty arranged with the War Office that the Naval Air Service should have the use of the military airship station at Farnborough, until their own station at Kingsnorth should be ready. The transfer from Farnborough to Kingsnorth took place in March 1915. (Kingsnorth had been opened with the nucleus of an airship staff in April 1914).

From that time expansion was rapid and Kingsnorth became a great airship dockyard and the centre of invention and experiment. The first and all the earlier 'S.S.' type airships were constructed and tested there. In September 1915 the work of assembling the S.S. ships was decentralised to Barrow, Folkestone, and Wormwood Scrubs, so that Kingsnorth might be free to concentrate on the building of the new Coastals. (The airship shed at Wormwood Scrubs had been built by the London *Daily Mail* in 1909 to house the *Clement Bayard* purchased by the newspaper to foster public interest in airships).

Two modified types of airship were designed and completed to the trial stage at Kingsnorth during the year. The first, or North Sea type, was designed to give an endurance of twenty-one hours at a speed of forty-eight knots. The construction of six of this class was approved in January 1916. The first ship was put in hand at the beginning of February, but was not ready for twelve months. The second, or improved S.S. 'Pusher' (S.S.P.) type, was built to give seventeen hours endurance at forty-three knots. Six of these were ordered, the first undergoing her preliminary trials in January 1917.

One early experiment conducted at Kingsnorth may be quoted, not only for its historical interest, but also because it typifies the vision and courage which the personnel brought to their work. The science of aeronautics was young. Ideas which seemed to work out in theory had always to stand the ultimate practical test in the air. The risk in this, the supreme test of the inventor's faith in his machine, had to be accepted, not in the excitement of battle, but in cold blood. Commander N. F. Usborne, whose tenacious ability had done much to sweep aside the difficulties and prejudices that dogged the early development of the small airship, and Lieutenant-Commander de Courcy W. P. Ireland, a pre-war naval aeroplane pilot, were convinced that the special qualities of the airship and of the aeroplane could be combined to produce an effective weapon against raiding Zeppelins.

The airship had endurance and cruising powers and might form a lofty carrier from which an aeroplane could be launched for immediate attack. They worked out plans whereby a complete B.E.2c aeroplane could be rigged to an 'S.S.' type airship envelope in such a way that the aeroplane could be released in the air and flown away at the will of the pilot. The original idea allowed for the pilot to open the valve of the airship, before the aeroplane was slipped, so that the envelope might make its own way slowly to earth. The first trials, to test the flying capabilities of the composite craft, were made in August 1915, by Flight Commander W. C. Hicks, and revealed weaknesses in the controlling gear.

These were remedied and the airship-plane, as it was called, was finally ready for a launching trial on the 21st of February 1916, when it was taken up by Commander Usborne and Lieutenant-Commander Ireland. It was anxiously watched away by a group of officers on the station who saw it ascend, in a series of circles, to a height of about four thousand feet when suddenly the aeroplane was seen to drop. It fell away from the envelope in a side slip and then turned on its back, throwing out one of the occupants. It crashed, out of control, into the goods yard at Strood station, where Commander Usborne was found dead, strapped in his seat. The body of Lieutenant-Commander Ireland fell in the river and was brought ashore by a lighterman.

An investigation into the accident showed that a loss of pressure in the envelope resulting from the fact that the airship-plane had exceeded its equilibrium height had caused a premature release of the forward suspension. The weight of the engine had caused the aeroplane to drop nose forward, and the ensuing strain was so great that the remaining suspension wires parted. It is possible, also, that some of the controls on the aeroplane were damaged as it fell clear. The Admiralty decided, as a result of this disastrous ending to the experiment, that further launching trials should not take place until one of the new rigid airships should be available.

In addition to all its design, construction, and experimental work, Kingsnorth at first had the task of training officers and men in the handling and navigation of airships. (After a preliminary training at the Naval Air Station at Roehampton or Wormwood Scrubs). Thirty-six airship pilots were trained at the station in 1915 and fifty-six in 1916. By the end of the latter year, however, the Naval Air Service training establishment at Cranwell was in a position to take over this responsibility.

The first lighter-than-air shed, built to house a kite balloon, was completed at Cranwell in March 1916. From this modest beginning a great airship training centre sprang up. Free balloons were transferred to Cranwell from the Wormwood Scrubs training station in May, and thirty-eight men qualified during the year as free balloon pilots. An S.S. airship, on her way from Wormwood Scrubs to the Cranwell station in November, was wrecked near Sleaford: the wreckage was salved and the ship was rebuilt. Another S.S. ship arrived from Kingsnorth in December. By this time, too, a shed was completed to house a Coastal, ready at Kingsnorth to fly up when the weather should prove favourable. During this first year of its existence the school trained 139 ratings as airship riggers.

Only one other airship station was opened in 1916. This was an S.S. station at Caldale (afterwards called Kirkwall), in the Orkney Islands, commissioned in July with two S.S. ships to form a base from which patrols could be made in co-operation with the Grand Fleet based at Scapa Flow, and in search of enemy submarines.

By the end of 1916, the fifty ships of the 'S.S.' programme had been completed. (This number includes the S.S. *Zero* built at Capel, Folkestone). Of these, four were supplied to the French and four to the Italian Governments. Four more, ordered by the Italian Government direct from Messrs. Vickers, are not included in the total of fifty.

A new and greatly improved type of S.S. ship, known as the *Zero*, had been designed and built, under the encouragement of Vice-Admiral Bacon, and the direction of Flight Lieutenant A. D. Cunningham, at the air station at Capel, Folkestone, in June 1916. What was wanted was an airship which could be towed by ships of the Belgian Coast patrol, and by the monitors, to assist in gunnery spotting.

If this could be done successfully, the Vice-Admiral at Dover stated, the airship could take the place of a kite balloon ship. The first essential in the design was a stream-lined car strong enough to withstand all the stresses imposed by towing. The pusher-type car, designed and built by the staff at Capel, eliminated many of the inconvenient features inherent in the various models of aeroplane bodies hitherto used. It was shaped like a boat and gave comfortable seating to a pilot, a wireless rating, and an engineer. The ship, when ready and tried, proved a great success: she was agreeably stable and showed greater endurance and speed than any others of her class.

The first S.S. *Zero* was flown across to St. Pol, near Dunkirk, on the 21st of September, where a portable shed from Folkestone had been erected to receive her. Towing trials with the monitor *Sir John Moore* had been made off Capel on the 7th of September, and they were repeated, off Dunkirk, on the 23rd. Although the trials, so far as the towing was concerned, were successful, it was soon realised that the slow speed of the airship, when released from the monitor near the enemy coast, would make her use, in action, impracticable. She would not long survive enemy gunfire and aircraft attacks.

Nevertheless, although the *Zero* gave promise of little future in the sphere which had prompted her design, she proved such a general advance on all other 'S.S.' ships, that she was at once adopted as a standard design. By July 1917, sixteen of the *Zero* craft had been delivered to the various naval air stations.

The trial of the *Zero* ship from the *Sir John Moore* did not represent the first attempt by surface craft to tow an airship. The problem was one which had exercised the minds of a few airship and naval officers from the outbreak of war. Trials with the *Astra Torres* airship (No. 3), and the steamship *Princess Victoria*, had been made so early as November the 2nd 1914, when, in a fifteen-mile-an-hour wind, the airship dropped a tow rope from 300 feet on the quarter-deck of the steamer. The rope was caught and made fast, and the airship was towed with great ease, against and with the wind, whilst the steamer was making her full speed of twenty-one knots. The pilot had the airship under complete control throughout the trial, and formed the opinion that there would have been no difficulty about hauling the ship down low enough to change the crew or replenish the fuel.

No further experiments seem to have been made until March 1916, when the question was taken up again at Kingsnorth. A part of the landing ground was marked out to represent the after-part of the upper deck of a destroyer, and a trail rope from one of the newly built Coastals was dropped on this marking and made fast exactly as if it were dropped on a surface vessel. The preliminary trials were entirely satisfactory, and a report was sent to the Admiralty with the suggestion that they should be repeated at sea.

The suggestion was adopted and, on the 12th of May, further trials, in the harbour at Harwich, were made with the co-operation of the light cruiser *Carysfort*, which took the airship, C.1, in tow with great ease. In a second experiment on the 16th of May, the light cruiser was moving at twenty knots, but again there was no difficulty about taking over the airship. Commodore R.Y. Tyrwhitt, under whose directions the trials were made, reported:

'It was not possible to try refuelling as the airship was not fitted with a traveller with which it is proposed to hoist the petrol tins. I am of opinion that refuelling is perfectly feasible and should be tried as soon as convenient ... I am very much impressed with the handiness of these machines and the skill of the pilots who have perfect control of their ships and appear to be able to do what they please.'

Tests in refuelling and in the changing of crew were made at Kingsnorth and repeated at sea off the Thames Estuary with the light cruiser *Canterbury* on the 6th of September. The C.1 was taken in tow and manoeuvred without strain up to twenty-six knots. The *Canterbury* then slowed down to twelve knots, the airship was hauled down to the quarter-deck, and the places of three members of the crew in the car were taken by three of the airship personnel in the light cruiser. As only under ideal weather conditions would it be possible to ensure the safe landing of the airship on deck, an alternative method, more suitable for usual North Sea weather, was tried. The airship was let up to about 100 feet, and the crew were then again changed, being hauled up and down, one by one, in a boatswain's chair.

From this height, too, refuelling was carried out. The contents of a sixty-gallon tank on the deck of the cruiser were forced by compressed air through a hose in eight minutes to tanks on the airship. Thus, the fact that both the S.S. *Zero* and the Coastal type airships could be towed safely, even at high speeds, had been amply proved. It increased their possible radius of action either for anti-submarine patrol or reconnaissance work with the fleet at sea.

In view of its limited offensive qualities the chief function of the airship, at this time, let it be emphasized, was the detection rather than the attempted destruction of enemy submarines. Bombs were carried, but the airship commander could seldom hope, owing to the bulk and lack of speed of his craft, to get up with a submarine before it submerged, nor was there much chance, in the turbid home waters, of his having any sight of the craft once the sea had closed over it.

The whole value, therefore, of information acquired on the routine patrols from the stations round the coast depended on the efficiency of the communication between the airship observer and the local senior naval officer responsible for the work of the destroyers, sloops, and auxiliary patrol vessels. The essential was that immediately on the receipt of an air report of a submarine being sighted the attacking vessels should know where to concentrate for the hunt. An airship commander who had been, perhaps, long on patrol and out of sight of land, could not always be relied upon to give the exact latitude and longitude of any spot on the sea over which he was flying.

What was wanted were shore stations equipped with wireless direction-finding apparatus which could systematically plot the movements of each patrolling airship, and so pass on to the senior naval officer the exact location of the airship at any moment when a sighting message came through. A scheme for a chain of these stations to be built by the Marconi company had been approved in August 1915, and their erection was pushed forward so that they should be ready as the new coastal airship bases were commissioned.

✶✶✶✶✶✶

For the patrol area off the east and north-east coast these special wireless stations were situated at Peterhead, Berwick, Flamborough Head, and Lowestoft; for the Dover Straits, at Sandwich, Lydd, and Pevensey; for the Irish Channel, at Kirkistown, Larne, Skerries (Drogheda), on the Irish Coast, and at Rhyl and Amlwch (Anglesey); for the St. George's Channel, at Ross Carberry, and Pembroke; and, lastly, for the south-western approaches to the English Channel, at the Lizard and Prawle Point.

✶✶✶✶✶✶

The directional wireless stations were of two kinds—those which could receive only, and those which could, in addition, transmit up to a distance of 150 miles. It was laid down as a general rule that the airship commander should, when on patrol, make his call sign every hour to enable two or more stations to get regular cross-bearings, and so follow the course of the ship. These calls were answered by the transmitting stations which would also, when asked, tell the airship commander where he was.

The lover of romance may be disappointed with the early work of the airships specially designed to hunt for submarines. It is true that, up to the end of 1916, there were few encounters, and none that were decisive, with enemy underwater craft. In part this was due to a slackening of the submarine war in home waters until September 1916. In part, also, it was due to the fact that not until the end of the year were all the stations in commission in a position to carry out flying duties. The thoughtful reader, however, who looks below the surface of things, cannot fail to find romance of a remarkable kind in this setting up of an airship network around these islands.

At a time when the resources of the country were being taxed to their utmost to put forth the great effort which culminated in the long battles of the Somme, when other fronts were expanding and demanding every type of war material, when the air and submarine threats to this country were using up, in defence, an incalculable store of energy, means were found to build, equip, and staff, what were, in effect, self-contained schools, and to improvise and put into practice a method of intensive instruction. Every station played its part in the training of pilots and airship personnel.

Many of the officers and men were enlisted into the service from school or from civilian life, often with no qualifications other than their intelligence, good health, and youthful enthusiasm. They had to be fitted for the highly technical work of navigating airships over the sea, of recognising and co-operating with all types of surface craft, of bombing, and of keeping their airships and equipment in repair. Little wonder, then, that whilst the organisation was being set up, the airship patrols from the various stations were of a disjointed nature. The people of this country in the days before the war had shown little interest in the airship. The *Mayfly* setback in 1911 had been too readily accepted in condemnation of lighter-than-air craft.

Happily, not everyone was sceptical. There was, inside and outside the service, a small band of enthusiasts to whom disaster and disappointment were the salt of endeavour, and it was on the technical knowledge and experience of these pioneers that the country had to rely, when the need came, for the rapid building up, under duress, of what was to prove an essential part of the defence against the submarine, one of the most subtle and powerful weapons that the country was called upon to meet.

The building up of the rigid fleet was, necessarily, a much slower affair. It was not to be expected that our designers could, in a few short months, accomplish what had taken the German airship builders long years to do. Before ever the building stage was arrived at, the designs for the new ships had to be got out, and the construction and equipping of gigantic sheds, to serve as workshops, had to be completed. When the Admiralty decided, in July 1915, to lay down the nucleus of a rigid fleet, the only private shed in existence in this country big enough to serve as a constructional workshop was the one housing the incomplete No. 9 at Messrs. Vickers station at Barrow. (There were two service sheds at Kingsnorth big enough to house rigids, but these sheds were being used for the erection of the nonrigid airships).

The government, as they ordered new airships, made themselves responsible for first building the sheds for the makers. It will be recalled that the decision of July 1915 envisaged three rigids in addition to No. 9. Orders for these three ships were placed in October 1915. In design the new ships—to be known as the '23' Class—followed the leading features of No. 9, but the hull was slightly longer, and the gas capacity greater with a consequent greater disposable lift. (Under specified conditions—68 lb. per 1,000 cubic feet capacity—5.7 tons in the '23' Class as compared with 3.8 tons for No. 9 Airship).

The three ships were numbered 23 to 25. Messrs. Vickers built No. 23 at Barrow, Messrs. William Beardmore No. 24 at Inchinnan, Renfrewshire, and Messrs. Sir W. G. Armstrong-Whitworth constructed No. 25 at Barlow, near Selby, in Yorkshire. (The three ships made their trial flights in September and October 1917).

In January 1916, five additional airships of the '23' Class (Nos. 26 to 30) were ordered. Of these, however. No. 26, built by Messrs. Vickers at Barrow, was the only one completed which followed the general design of the '23' Class. (No. 26 was not ready for flight until March 1918). The design of the remaining ships was improved in the early summer to constitute the '23X' Class. The building of the ships was entrusted to Messrs. Beardmore (Nos. 27 and 28), and to Messrs. Armstrong (Nos. 29 and 30).

An event which was to have an important influence on the airship-building programme of this country occurred in the early hours of the 24th of September 1916. The Zeppelin L.33, damaged by anti-aircraft fire over the East End of London, was forced eventually to land at Little Wigborough, north of Mersea Island. The ship took fire, following a slight explosion on landing, but as she had lost most of her gas, the fire burnt out without doing much damage to the structure, and complete drawings of the Zeppelin were carefully made.

We were now in a position to build replicas of the L.33, the performance of which was a long way ahead of the '23X' Class. The government at once decided not to proceed with the construction of two of these (Nos. 28 and 30) which, although approved, had not yet been begun, but to build, instead, five replicas of the Zeppelin. It so happened that the latest ships ordered (in February 1916) of a modified wooden Schütte-Lanz type, undertaken by Messrs. Short Brothers at Cardington, were numbered 31 and 32. The first of the British rigids of Zeppelin design therefore had the same number as her German prototype. None of the '33' Class was completed before the war ended. It was, however, the second ship of this class, the R.34, built by Messrs. Beardmore, which flew from England to America and back in July 1919.

Meanwhile the first rigid to be completed, No. 9, made her trial flight—the first ever made by a British rigid airship—on the 27th of November 1916. (A Rigid Airship Trial Flight had been formed at Barrow-in-Furness, under Wing Commander E. A. D. Masterman, in March 1916, to prepare the rigids for flight, to put them through their trials, and to instruct their crews). It was found that the disposable lift was lower by nearly a ton than that specified in the contract, and the ship was handed back to the makers. Several alterations were made of which the chief was the substitution of a single 250 horse-power Maybach engine, recovered from the wrecked L.33 Zeppelin, driving a single propeller aft, in place of the original two engines in the after-car driving wing propellers.

The alterations were successful, and the disposable lift, when the airship was flown again, was shown to be increased by 1.7 tons. The airship went to her station at Howden on the 4th of April 1917. (For the housing of the rigids, sheds were completed at the air stations at Howden, December 1916; Pulham, February 1917; Longside, March 1917; East Fortune, April 1917; and Cranwell, June 1917).

Such, in outline, is the story of the early war development of the airship service in this country. But the reader will have remarked that the first of the rigids, which of all the airships were the only ones capable of fleet reconnaissance work comparable with what could be done by the naval Zeppelins for the German fleet, was not finally delivered to the Naval Air Service until the spring of 1917. The smaller non-rigids, which had been designed solely for anti-submarine patrol, had not only done all that was expected of them, but some of them had also, as has been seen, come triumphantly through experiments which proved that, in fair weather, they could be taken to sea in tow of the fleet as a practical reconnaissance alternative to the rigid airships. But, even so, it was not until September 1916, when the refuelling experiments proved successful, that the commander-in-chief could take the airship into his calculations for distant fleet work. What he had to rely upon, up to that time, were his aircraft carriers.

Aircraft Carriers in the North Sea

It will be remembered that, towards the end of November 1915, the *Campania* had left the Grand Fleet and had gone to Liverpool for structural alterations, so that reconnaissance seaplanes might be flown from the forward deck, and so that an inflated kite balloon might be carried aft. The *Campania* was back with the Grand Fleet at Scapa

Flow on the 12th of April 1916.

Meanwhile, for North Sea work, a further aircraft carrier had been commissioned in September 1915. She was the Isle of Man passenger steamer *Viking* (2,900 tons), of a speed of twenty-two knots. The vessel was renamed *Vindex*, and was converted by the Cunard Company at Liverpool to take four large and one small seaplane aft, and two single-seater fighting aeroplanes forward. Electric cranes were installed for the hoisting in and out of the seaplanes, but a special flying-off deck and hangar was built forward for the aeroplanes. As space was restricted the aeroplanes were carried dismantled in their hangar, but they could be quickly assembled. The *Vindex* was the first of the smaller carriers to be fitted with a forward flying deck, an arrangement which marked a considerable advance for this type of vessel. The first successful flight off the deck of the *Vindex* was made by Flight Lieutenant H. F. Towler, in a Bristol Scout aeroplane, on the 3rd of November 1915.

The *Vindex*, escorted by the Harwich force, attempted her first raid against the German coast on the 18th of January 1916. The intention was to bomb the Zeppelin sheds at Hage, but the squadron ran into heavy fog and the raid had to be given up. Eleven days later, a second attempt was prevented by a determined enemy submarine attack delivered as the squadron approached the enemy coast. (*The Harwich Naval Forces*, their part in the Great War, 1914-1918 by E. F. Knight is also published by Leonaur).

More intense airship-bombing raids on this country were to be expected in the better weather which spring would bring. Commodore Tyrwhitt, undaunted by continuous disappointment, did not lose hope that the seaplanes, operating from the carriers, would deal a blow at the Zeppelins where they were most vulnerable, that is, in their sheds. He therefore planned an ambitious raid against the airship base believed to be at Hoyer, on the Schleswig coast. The raid took place on the 25th of March. The bombing force of three Short and two Sopwith 'Baby' seaplanes, carried in *Vindex*, was supported by the whole of the available Harwich force, in turn supported by the Battle Cruiser Fleet from Rosyth.

This reopening of activity against the German coast coincided with a more offensive spirit in the enemy fleet consequent on the appointment of a new commander-in-chief. Admiral R. Scheer had succeeded Admiral von Pohl on the 18th of January 1916. As Admiral Commanding the Second Squadron, Scheer had vigorously advocated a more enterprising role for the German fleet, and his new appointment gave scope to his enterprise. the German official naval historian says:

> From the beginning of the year 1916, onwards, one central idea underlay all operations of the German High Sea Forces—namely, the definite desire to bring about a naval action. (*Der Krieg zur See, 1914-1918.* By Captain O. Groos, Volume V).

The March raid gave Admiral Scheer the opportunity, as he says, to test his preparations. Commodore Tyrwhitt left Harwich as day broke on the 24th and made his way through snow squalls across the North Sea. At half past four next morning he was well inside the Vyl light vessel. The *Vindex*, with supporting destroyers, went farther in and got her seaplanes away at half past five. She then awaited the return of her bombers. At seven o'clock two of them could be heard and then dimly seen through the falling snow, on their way back. They were hoisted inboard and the pilots made their reports. They had found, they said, no sheds at Hoyer.

One of them had dropped his bombs on a large factory at this place and stated that he had left the building in flames; the other had reconnoitred inland before attempting to bomb, and had made the discovery that the airship base was at Tondern. There he attempted to attack the sheds from a low height, but his bombs jammed in the carrier and he had no alternative but to take them back as he had brought them. In vain did *Vindex* wait for the return of the other three seaplanes. Commodore Tyrwhitt ordered his destroyers to sweep eastwards in search of them, but they were never seen. It was known later that both the Shorts and the Sopwith, with their three pilots and two observers, had fallen into the enemy's hands. The engine trouble which brought them down was due in each case to defective magnetos.

A report was afterwards received from Flight Lieutenant G. H. Reid, one of the Short pilots, telling of his adventures. He steered a compass course through the clouds, came out low over snow-covered country, and dropped one of his three 65-lb. bombs on an unknown building. He turned back and picked up and followed the coast line to Hoyer. Finding no sheds there he flew inland towards Tondern, but was forced to turn back after eight minutes: the storm increased as he got inland and snow which clogged the wires in the guide tubes made his controls difficult. As he was passing over Hoyer once more, his observer, Chief Petty Officer Richard Mullins, called his attention to a waving figure in a Sopwith seaplane on the water close to the shore.

Flight Lieutenant Reid went down on to the sea, jumped from his seaplane into the shallows, and waded across to the Sopwith. He learned that the pilot, Flight Lieutenant J. F. Hay, had been struggling vainly for fifteen minutes to restart his engine and after further abortive efforts invited him to return on the Short. German soldiers were seen making their way towards a group of curious civilians on the shore who had from time to time shouted unintelligible encouragement across to the seaplane pilot. Time was pressing. The two officers returned to the Short. Flight Lieutenant Hay climbed on one of the wings and held on to the strut as the seaplane took the air again.

Their departure was speeded by the German spectators who, innocent of any idea that aircraft from England could idle in their waters on such a morning, waved a cheery farewell, a courtesy which was reciprocated. The Short pilot had reached the island of Sylt when the port side of the engine suddenly cut out. Chief Petty Officer Mullins, with much difficulty against the pressure of wind, climbed across to the engine, opened up the casing, and tried to put the trouble right. He could do nothing. The reduced engine-power being insufficient to keep the seaplane in the air, the pilot had to turn hurriedly to reach the water on the inside of the island. Here the observer tried again to repair the engine, but soon discovered the cause to be a broken magneto which was irreparable. With the starboard side still working, however, the pilot could 'taxi' at about four knots and he therefore headed round the island for the open sea.

On the way the seaplane grounded on many sandbanks and the occupants had to jump out to push it off again. They came thus laboriously to the far side of Sylt, but by this time the craft had been over three hours on the sea, in addition to its time in the air, and the petrol was nearly finished. The position was beginning to appear somewhat hopeless when a desperate chance was offered. A small German sailing-boat, fitted with an oil-engine, was seen ahead. If the seaplane could catch up with her the officers might, with the aid of surprise and their machine-gun, capture the vessel and use her for the journey back to their parent ship. The pilot gave chase, but the seaplane became almost unsteerable in the more choppy open sea, and the sailing vessel gradually drew away.

The seaplane was still following when a motor-boat filled with soldiers appeared suddenly ahead to cut it off, at the same time as two German seaplanes landed on the water immediately behind. The occupants of the Short just had time to smash most of their instruments, destroy their confidential maps, and throw the machine-gun overboard before they were taken. It was impossible to set fire to the seaplane: the petrol was almost finished and everything about the aircraft and its crew was saturated with water.

Meanwhile, the destroyers which had been sweeping in search of the missing aircraft had found and sunk two armed trawlers off Röm Island. The flotilla was reforming after the encounter when *Laverock*, manoeuvring to pick up enemy survivors, came into collision with *Medusa*, which had to be taken in tow. Shortly afterwards German seaplanes came over and dropped bombs close to the ships, but without doing any damage. When it became clear that it was useless to wait further for the missing seaplanes, Commodore Tyrwhitt ordered *Vindex* and her escorting destroyers to return to Harwich.

The Admiralty now discovered that the High Sea Fleet was on the move, and an order was sent to Commodore Tyrwhitt to withdraw without delay. He was warned to expect destroyer attacks during the night. As the squadron moved home the violence of the gale increased. At half past five the Commodore learned that strong enemy forces were sweeping west and north-west, in other words making straight for him. Meanwhile, Vice-Admiral Sir David Beatty had moved down from his patrol station off Horn Reefs to cover the Harwich squadron. Soon after nightfall the *Medusa* had to be abandoned owing to the heavy seas, but the Harwich squadron was not long to move unhampered.

The captain of the light cruiser *Cleopatra* suddenly became aware, by the glare from their funnels, of two German destroyers steaming across his bows. He turned and cut one clean in two, but the manoeuvre brought him into collision with *Undaunted* whose bows were stove in—damage which reduced her speed to six knots. An Admiralty message at 11.0 p.m. told the commodore that the German commander had recalled everything for the night, but he was warned that the enemy cruiser force would come out again in the morning.

At 1.0 a.m. the Admiralty learned, through an intercepted message from the commodore to Sir David Beatty, of the plight of *Undaunted*, and of its consequent crippling effect on the commodore's movements, and they immediately ordered Admiral Jellicoe to put to sea and to concentrate all sections of the Grand Fleet. At 5.0 a.m. the Admiralty, learning that part of the German fleet was out again, ordered Commodore Tyrwhitt to retire on the Battle Cruiser Fleet. An action of some magnitude seemed inevitable. For a few hours, as the forces converged, the tension was at the extreme, but soon after 9.30 a.m. it was suddenly snapped when it became known in Whitehall that the enemy had given up and was returning to port.

So, ended these great fleet movements set in motion by a small seaplane raid on the German coast. As a bombing raid it was a failure, but it appeared to show that the enemy fleet could be induced, by the threat of an air raid against his coast, to put to sea. Commodore Tyrwhitt, in his report, submitted that another air raid on the newly discovered base at Tondern be attempted with the primary object of enticing the enemy fleet to action. The proposal, approved by the Admiralty, was put before the commander-in-chief, was ultimately adopted, and elaborate plans, which envisaged the possibility of a decisive battle, were worked out.

Whilst the plans were being prepared a new diplomatic storm blew up on the subject of submarine warfare, which was to issue in a decision affecting the strategical position in the North Sea. It will be remembered that the American protests, arising from the sinking of the *Arabic* in August 1915, led to a lull in the submarine war around Great Britain during the winter months. Soon after Admiral Scheer, a strong advocate of ruthless submarine warfare, took up his new appointment, activity against merchant shipping in home waters reopened.

On the 24th of March 1916 the cross-Channel steamer *Sussex* was torpedoed without warning, with a heavy loss of civilian life including a number of Americans. An American note to the German Government in April threatening to break off diplomatic relations led, after fierce internal controversy, to the temporary abandonment by the German Government, on April the 24th, of the idea of unrestricted submarine warfare. Admiral Scheer, deciding that submarine attacks conducted under prize regulations of visit and search would be disproportionately risky, recalled all submarines from British waters. These submarines could now be used for purely military purposes in the North Sea fleet operations which he was planning.

Meanwhile, on the 25th of April, a group of German battle cruisers, with a scouting force of four Zeppelins, crossed the North Sea and bombarded Lowestoft and Yarmouth. On the approach of the enemy seaplanes and aeroplanes went up from the air stations at Yarmouth and Felixstowe to reconnoitre and bomb the ships, and to attack the Zeppelins. Bombs were dropped but with no apparent hits. One of the reconnaissance pilots was wounded and his machine badly damaged by anti-aircraft fire from the German battle cruisers. Commodore Tyrwhitt's force got into action for about fifteen minutes with the enemy fleet as it retreated, and two naval pilots followed one of the Zeppelins for sixty-five miles out to sea where they made an unsuccessful attack on her with bombs and Ranken darts.

******

Ranken darts are explosive cylindrical darts designed by Engineer Lieutenant Francis Ranken, R.N., in the middle of 1915. They were released, three at a time, from a container of 24. Four vanes on the tail of each dart spread, on release, to grip the envelope of the airship after the head had passed through, and so give time for the charge to detonate inside.

******

A week later the plans for the seaplane raid on Tondern were complete. Minefields and submarines were to be placed across the enemy's probable lines of advance, and Admiral Jellicoe was to take the Battle Fleet to the southern approaches to the Skagerrak, with Vice-Admiral Beatty in advance south of him, to be ready for the hoped for sortie of the enemy. The air raid was to be made by the seaplanes of *Vindex* and *Engadine*, which were to operate off Sylt under the direction of the commodore commanding the First Light Cruiser Squadron.

Early on the 3rd of May our squadrons moved. Next morning the minefields had been laid and the Grand Fleet was in position. Soon after 3.0 a.m. *Vindex* and *Engadine* were hoisting out their seaplanes off the island of Sylt. But the pilots were once again to taste the bitterness of failure. Eight of the eleven Sopwith 'Baby' seaplanes which had been got out failed to leave the water; four of them broke their propellers, three suffered engine failure, and one capsized in the wash of the destroyers.

Of the three pilots who got off, one fouled the wireless aerial of the destroyer *Goshawk* and disappeared in the sea with the wreckage of his seaplane; the second had to return with engine trouble after a brief flight; the third alone reached Tondern. There he found the Zeppelin sheds shrouded in mist: he dropped his two 65-lb. bombs but scored no hit. From a material point of view the air raid had been a failure. Bombs had, however, been dropped and, so far as the enemy was aware, other bombs might be on their way. If an air attack was likely to induce the enemy fleet to come out, the two bombs might be as effective in bringing this about as two dozen.

Until half-past nine no enemy movement was seen. At that time, however, the light cruisers *Galatea* and *Phaeton* sighted a Zeppelin to the south and engaged her at long range. After a few shots the airship, L.7, which had, in fact, hurriedly left her shed at Tondern to reconnoitre the British forces, was hit and was forced to alight on the water. There she was found almost at once by the British submarine E.31, which promptly opened fire with her 12-pounder gun and destroyed the Zeppelin in flames. The submarine picked up the seven survivors of the airship crew of twenty.

******

The E. 31, with her prisoners, eventually reached Harwich. Her homeward journey was made exciting by a night attack from a German cruiser. The submarine only escaped being rammed by brilliant handling, and a shell from the cruiser which went through the casing fortunately failed to explode.

******

Admiral Jellicoe kept his vigil until two in the afternoon when he decided that it was useless to wait longer, and turned for home. The big sea battle had not eventuated, but it was not to be long delayed. Admiral Scheer's preparations were not, in fact, yet completed. According to his plans all forces of the High Sea Fleet were to be fully ready by the 17th of May. His numerous submarines were to go out two days before to take up positions off the bases of the Grand Fleet. The idea was that the High Sea Fleet should advance, that the Battle Cruiser Fleet from Rosyth should be drawn across the line of the submarines, following a preliminary bombardment of Sunderland by the enemy battle cruisers, and that such as survived submarine attack should be enticed towards the main enemy battle fleet.

The Battle of Jutland.

This scheme, which seemed to ignore the existence of directional wireless, relied upon adequate airship reconnaissance of the Grand Fleet movements from Scapa to guard against any possibility of a periodical sweep by Sir John Jellicoe taking the High Sea Fleet by surprise. Weather favourable for Zeppelin reconnaissance was therefore essential to the carrying out of the enterprise. The weather in the latter part of May showed no signs of playing its assigned part in the operation. There was another fact making for delay. The battle-cruiser *Seydlitz*, which had struck a mine on her way out on the 24th of April to take part in the Lowestoft bombardment, was unexpectedly not ready for sea again until so late as the 28th of May. As Admiral Scheer was not prepared to do without this ship, the 29th became the earliest date for the projected operations.

But the weather was still impossible for airship reconnaissance. Nor could the German commander-in-chief wait upon the weather much longer if he was to have the help of his submarines. These had gone out, according to plan, in the middle of May, and were under orders to return from their stations at sea on the 1st of June. Throughout the 29th the German Fleet, cleared for action, was waiting with steam raised for the order to move. On the 30th the German naval airship commander reported that no air reconnaissance could be counted upon for the next two days. The scheme involving the bombardment of Sunderland was therefore abandoned, and an alternative plan for an advance into the Skagerrak was adopted.

Late in the afternoon a wireless message was sent out to all units of the High Sea Fleet that this operation would take place next day, the 31st of May. For the alternative operation airship reconnaissance was not of the same decisive importance, since the Jutland coast would afford a certain amount of protection against surprise from the eastern flank, and the greater distance from the British bases would lessen the risk that Admiral Scheer might be forced into action against his will. Early in the morning of the 31st of May, Vice-Admiral Hipper, commanding the Scouting Forces, which were to act as an enticement to the British fleet, left the Jade with orders to show himself off the Norwegian coast before dark, so that news of the undertaking might be reported to the British Admiralty.

This was a superfluous precaution. The departure of the enemy submarines in the middle of May had been detected and had aroused attention. By May the 28th, it became clear to the Admiralty that some considerable movement was afoot, and, at noon on the 30th, a message was sent to Sir John Jellicoe that there were indications of the German Fleet coming out. Harwich destroyers and mine-sweeping sloops on the East Coast were recalled and all submarines ordered to be ready for sea. At 5.40 p.m. on the 30th of May the Admiralty sent a message to Admiral Jellicoe and to Vice-Admiral Beatty, ordering them to concentrate their forces, ready for eventualities, eastward of Long Forties, (about sixty miles east of the Scottish coast). At 7.37 p.m. the commander-in-chief sent a telegram to Vice-Admiral Beatty informing him that he would proceed to a stated rendezvous, about 240 miles from Scapa. By 11.30 p.m. the Grand Fleet and the Battle Cruiser Fleet were at sea.

But the *Campania* did not take her allotted place under Sir John Jellicoe. After rejoining the Grand Fleet on the 12th of April, the aircraft in the carrier had made many encouraging flights. Seaplanes had been successfully hoisted out and re-embarked whilst the ship was under way, and, on the 29th of May, five pilots had made flights off the deck in the Sopwith 'Baby' seaplanes whilst the carrier was steaming at nineteen to twenty knots. The balloon which *Campania* now carried was the first of the improved streamline type, originated by Captain Caquot of the French Army.

This balloon could be flown in higher winds and was more stable than the Drachen type hitherto in use. On the morning of the 30th of May *Campania* had gone out of harbour on one of her routine co-operation exercises, and her aircraft had made successful spotting flights throughout the day for ships carrying out firing practice. The balloon had been let up to 1,200 feet and four officers had been given the opportunity to observe during the firing. The carrier finished her spotting exercises at 3.30 p.m. and got back to her anchorage in Scapa Bay at 5.15 p.m.

Four fighting seaplanes from the shore station at Scapa were flown to the carrier when she got back to harbour, bringing the total number of serviceable aircraft on board the *Campania* to three Shorts, three Sopwith 'Baby', and four Sopwith Schneider Cup seaplanes. At 5.35 p.m. the carrier received the preparatory signal sent out to all ships of the Grand Fleet to leave Scapa and, at 7.0 p.m., she received a further signal to raise steam to full speed; by 9.30 p.m. she was ready to proceed. Her stationing and timing signal was sent at 10.54 p.m., but she did not receive it. It is stated that neither the ships of the fleet nor their lights could be seen from the anchorage of *Campania*, and it was only when the carrier was asked by the officer in charge of the gate if she was leaving that night, that her commanding officer (Captain O. Swann, R.N.) realised that the fleet had sailed. He weighed at once and went out, passing the outer boom at 1.15 a.m., some two and a quarter hours behind *Iron Duke*.

For some time, Sir John Jellicoe was unaware that *Campania* had not sailed as ordered. About midnight he received a signal from the light cruiser *Blanche* that there were no signs of her. It was not, indeed, until about 2.0 a.m. that he learned she had left harbour. In view of the presence of enemy submarines and of the fact that the *Campania* had no destroyer escort, the commander-in-chief ordered the carrier, at 4.37 a.m., to return to port. He was reinforced in this decision by the opinion that *Campania* was so far behind that there was no possibility that she could overtake the Grand Fleet. The carrier got back safely at 9.15 a.m.

Whilst Sir John Jellicoe's reasons for sending his only means of air reconnaissance back to harbour were, of course, adequate at the time, examined in the fuller light of all the later facts they are seen not to be conclusive. The carrier, responding to the strenuous efforts of the engine-room staff, was gaining on the Grand Fleet at the rate of at least three miles an hour and, on this calculation and subject to no mishap, would have caught up some hours before the battle began. But it was not to be and the personnel of the *Campania*, keen and confident as they were, were denied any part in the action.

With the Battle Cruiser Fleet from Rosyth went the *Engadine* (Lieutenant-Commander C. G. Robinson), carrying two Shorts and two 'Baby' Sopwiths. Sir David Beatty had orders that if he did not sight the enemy by 2.0 p.m. on the 31st he was to stand towards the commander-in-chief who would steer for Horn Reefs. Two minutes before the appointed time nothing was in sight and the signal was made for the Battle Cruiser Fleet to alter to north by east at 2.15 p.m. The light cruisers were taking up their new line of direction when, at 2.20 p.m. *Galatea* made the historic signal 'Enemy in sight.' At 2.32 p.m. the Battle Cruiser Fleet altered course to cut off the German force from Horn Reefs. The *Galatea* from her forward position continued for some time to report the directions of the enemy's movements.

Meanwhile, at 2.40 p.m., Sir David Beatty ordered *Engadine* to send a seaplane away to scout to the north-north-east in which direction Galatea had reported a large amount of smoke. The seaplanes in the carrier were housed, wings folded and secured for sea, in their hangar. To get a machine on the water when the ship was rolling in a swell was no easy matter. The unwieldy doors of the hangar had to be opened, the seaplane drawn out, the wings spread, and the engine run up, before the machine was hoisted. (This procedure even in harbour, when the carrier was steady, had never been accomplished under twenty minutes).

Within twenty-eight minutes of Sir David Beatty's signal one of the Shorts with Flight Lieutenant F. J. Rutland as pilot and Assistant Paymaster G. S. Trewin as observer, was in the air. Wireless messages from the seaplane were received in *Engadine* as follows:

3.30 p.m. Three enemy cruisers and five destroyers, distance from me 10 miles bearing 90°, steering course to the N.W.

3.33 p.m. Enemy's course is south.

3.45 p.m. Three enemy cruisers and 10 destroyers steering south.

These observations were important. The first knowledge that Admiral Hipper had of the presence of the Battle Cruiser Fleet had come suddenly at 3.20 p.m., when he sighted two columns of large ships steering rapidly towards him. At once he realised that the pre-arranged plan whereby he was to go on towards the Norwegian coast must be abandoned. He must endeavour now to fall back on Admiral Scheer, and accordingly he recalled the 2nd Scouting Group to the north and himself swung to starboard. It was the turn about of the 2nd Scouting Group which was reported by the seaplane observer.

The clouds were at 900 feet and visibility, generally, was poor, and that his observer might count the numbers and plot the disposition of the enemy, the pilot was compelled to fly low and close to the 2nd Scouting Group which kept the seaplane under fire. At 3.48 p.m. the observer was sending out a message that he could now see four cruisers, when a petrol pipe broke and Flight Lieutenant Rutland was forced to go down on the water. He made good the defect with a piece of rubber tubing and then reported to *Engadine* that he was ready to go on again. He was, however, told to go alongside and, at 4.0 p.m. he was hoisted in.

There is no record that the signals from the seaplane, telling of the turn of the enemy scouting forces, reached Sir David Beatty. The *Engadine* endeavoured to pass them on by searchlight as they came down, but was unable to get into touch with the *Lion*. As it happened, this failure to communicate the information was discounted by the fact that *Galatea*, from her forward position, reported the change of course at 3.44 p.m. A minute later Sir David Beatty ordered the Battle Cruiser Fleet to alter course to conform. The *Engadine* took no further part in the action. She kept about four miles on the disengaged side of the battle cruisers and followed their movements.

The one seaplane flight was the only attempt at air co-operation in the Battle of Jutland. According to the German plans, five Zeppelins were to go out, if the weather permitted, on the 31st of May, to reconnoitre certain specified areas.

★★★★★★

One was to carry out a long distance reconnaissance over the Skagerrak; another over the Hoofden; and the remainder over a sector between north and west from 280 to 200 miles from Heligoland. The airships for the northern area were to leave at 2.0 a.m., and those for the southern at 6.0 a.m. and 8.0 a.m. See Groos, *Der Krieg in der Nordsee*, Vol. V.

✶✶✶✶✶✶

The weather kept them in their sheds, however, most of the morning, and it was not until 11.30 a.m. that the five airships left. The result was that at the opening of the battle no airship had crossed the line Terschelling-Horn Reefs. Wireless messages, however, which were repeated to the airships, gave their commanders news of the action being fought by the 2nd Scouting Group and the positions and courses of the German and British Battle Cruisers. The three Zeppelins, L.14, L.21, and L.23, which were flying towards the High Sea Fleet, were the victims of the poor visibility, and saw and heard nothing of the battle.

All the airships were recalled, owing to the uncertainty of the weather, between 4.0 p.m. and 6.0 p.m. The westerly ones, L.9 (with a broken propeller shaft), and L.16, landed between 6.0 p.m. and 7.0 p.m. The L.23 and L.21 got back to their sheds at 1.30 a.m. and 1.0 a.m. respectively, on the 1st of June, and the L.14 at 4.0 a.m. The latter ship, according to her track chart, was eleven miles to the north of the British flagship when she turned, and although her course back was across the scene of the battle, no ship was sighted from the Zeppelin, nor was any gunfire heard.

We left the Battle Cruiser Fleet moving to cut off Admiral Hipper's cruisers. The opposing forces closed rapidly and, at 3.49 p.m., *Lützow*, the admiral's flagship, fired the first gun, and, shortly afterwards. *Lion* opened fire in reply. Up to 4.40 p.m. a running action between the battle cruisers ensued. At that hour the enemy battle fleet came into sight. Five minutes later *Lion* turned with the object of drawing the enemy back to the Grand Fleet. There was further fighting up to ten minutes past five, after which came a lull for half an hour, whilst the ships were drawing nearer and nearer to the Grand Fleet. Then, at 5.40 p.m., Admiral Beatty's force renewed the action when Hipper's scouting force was picked up again in the mist.

We must turn now to the Grand Fleet. Sir John Jellicoe had received a message from the *Lion* at 4.45 p.m. which was, unhappily, incorrectly taken in, and gave the impression that the enemy battle fleet was steering southeast. Other messages came from the Commodore Commanding the Second Light Cruiser Squadron on board *Southampton*. From these signals Admiral Jellicoe learned, at 4.48 p.m., that the German battle cruisers had closed on the German battle fleet, and that the latter were steering north. The later alterations of course to N.N.W. and back to north were also received from the *Southampton*. Between 5.0 p.m. and 5.30 p.m. the commander-in-chief received no further messages. The Battle Fleet was ready to deploy: every man was waiting at his station. It is reasonable to assume that sometime during this period, if not before, the commander-in-chief would have ordered air reconnaissances.

Between 5.35 p.m. and 6.14 p.m. a series of signals came in to *Iron Duke* which were deemed to be too confusing and too contradictory to give any reliable information of the enemy's position. At 6.0 p.m. *Lion* could be seen from *Iron Duke* about five miles off to the southwest steering east. At 6.14 p.m. Admiral Jellicoe got news that *Barham* and *Lion* were both in sight of Admiral Scheer's battleships. Their two reports indicated that the position of the German fleet was such that a deployment of the Grand Fleet on the starboard wing column would involve it in action with the enemy fleet before the movement could be completed, and expose the British Battle Fleet to destroyer attack. Admiral Jellicoe therefore decided to deploy to port on a south-east by east course, and the order was made at fifteen minutes past six.

To what extent the seaplanes of *Campania* might have clarified the confusing situation in the phase which preceded the decision of the commander-in-chief as to the time and mode of his deployment, can never be known. As it happened the enemy fleet was denied the help of its airships. In view of the lowness of the clouds and the limited visibility it seems doubtful that, even had the wind abated early enough to allow the Zeppelins to start off at their appointed times, they would have been of much use. The height at which they would have been compelled to fly to observe in any detail would have made them large and vulnerable targets.

On the other hand, the conditions were such that seaplanes must have proved a much better reconnaissance medium than the Zeppelins. They would also have flown entirely unchallenged by enemy aircraft. In the anxious period before the deployment, reliable and speedy air reconnaissance would have been of inestimable value to Sir John Jellicoe. Whether the information would have been obtained, and what course the battle might have taken had it been reported in time to be of use, are matters which may offer fruitful speculation to the student.

The *Engadine* remained on the fringe of the action. Had any further reconnaissances been ordered, there is little likelihood that her seaplanes could have got off the tumultuous waters stirred up by the swiftly moving ships. About 6.40 p.m. the *Engadine* fell in with the cruiser *Warrior* making her way out of the battle in a severely damaged condition. The carrier stood by *Warrior* for about an hour when her captain ordered *Engadine* to take her in tow. For a hundred miles she struggled along with her charge in the direction of the Scottish coast. At about seven next morning it became clear that the bulkheads of the cruiser were giving way, and while there was yet time to save the ship's company, her captain ordered that she be abandoned.

Lieutenant-Commander Robinson brought *Engadine* alongside *Warrior* and began the task of taking on board her complement. This was a delicate operation. The two ships were riding close against one another, and the violent motion between them made the transfer, especially of the wounded, difficult. The difficulty was successfully overcome with one exception. A severely wounded rating was thrown from his stretcher into the water between the two ships. The captain of *Warrior* forbade two of his officers from jumping to the rescue of the wounded man, as to do so was courting almost certain death. Flight Lieutenant F. J. Rutland, from *Engadine*, however, had already gone overboard unobserved from the fore part of the carrier. He worked himself aft and put a bowline round the wounded man who was then hauled on board. There it was found that he was already dead from crushing between the two ships, the captain of *Warrior* reported:

> A fate which Lieutenant Rutland must have escaped by a miracle. (Flight Lieutenant F. J. Rutland was awarded the Albert Medal, First Class).

When the transfer of the whole of the *Warrior's* company of 705 officers and men, including thirty wounded, was completed, the cruiser, her decks awash, was left to her fate some 160 miles eastward of Aberdeen. She was never seen again. The *Engadine*, with her load, arrived at Rosyth at 1.35 a.m. on the 2nd of June.

For the story of the battle, until night came on the 31st of May to the relief of the enemy fleet, and then the slipping away of Admiral Scheer in the dark hours to the shelter of Horn Reefs, the reader must turn to naval histories. Admiral Scheer reached the Reefs at about 3.30 a.m. and there, in the knowledge that his airships were patrolling to seaward to protect him against surprise, he waited. Five airships which had been held in reserve had gone out—four soon after midnight, and one at 2.30 a.m.—in accordance with the instructions for scouting and screening the fleet originally laid down for the 31st of May.

At 3.19 a.m. on the 1st of June a report from the L.24 was received by Admiral Scheer that numerous hostile vessels, including twelve large ships, were in Jammer Bay, on the north-west coast of Denmark, at 3.0 a.m. Heavy clouds made it impossible for the airship commander to keep touch with this fleet. Whatever this reported force may have been, it was certainly no part of the British Fleet. Admiral Scheer was convinced, however, that it was the British Battle Fleet. At 3.30 a.m. a more accurate report was received by the Admiral from L.11, which had sighted the British battle cruiser fleet about ninety miles north-west of Heligoland as it was making to close the commander-in-chief.

Shortly afterwards the L.24 reported that the force which it had discovered in Jammer Bay was now steering south at high speed. Scheer, convinced as he was that this force was the fleet with which he had been in action the night before, explained away the L.11 report by assuming that this was a new force, perhaps the Harwich Force, which had come out after the battle had begun. The L.11, meanwhile, had continued her reconnaissance, under fierce fire from time to time, and had come upon and reported the rear of our battle fleet, and, a little later, on Vice-Admiral Sir C. Burney's division. But Admiral Scheer, weakened as his fleet was, had already given up any idea of further operations, and had given the order for his ships to return to harbour.

So, ended the greatest sea battle of the war and, by virtue of the size of the fleets engaged, of all times. Its interest to the student of air power lies, not in what aircraft did, but in what opportunities of perhaps vital importance were open for their use.

After Jutland there was a lull in the activity in the North Sea. Some little time must elapse before the German fleet could be made ready for sea again. It might be expected that the naval Zeppelins, relieved of some of their fleet reconnaissance duties, would at once resume their raids on English towns. The short light nights of summer, however, made this too hazardous until the beginning of August.

Commodore Tyrwhitt, warned by the Admiralty that raiding was to begin again, ordered *Vindex*, on the 29th of July, to be ready to put to sea at one hour's notice during the dark hours, with the object of sending up aircraft to attack returning airships. On receipt of news that a raid was expected, the *Vindex*, with the light cruiser *Conquest* and a destroyer escort, put out from Harwich in the afternoon of the 2nd of August. Just before 7 p.m., Flight Lieutenant C.T. Freeman flew a Bristol Scout aeroplane off the deck of the carrier in pursuit of a Zeppelin which had been sighted some time before. Whilst searching for her he saw two others, one ten miles and the other twenty miles away. He flew towards the nearest and attacked, down sun, with a container of Ranken darts dropped from 500 feet above the envelope.

The darts missed and the pilot turned and dropped another half container, but the Zeppelin commander manoeuvred his ship skilfully to avoid them. Flight Lieutenant Freeman was not to be shaken off and, when he had once more got into a favourable position, attacked a third time, and was rewarded with a hit, followed by a puff of smoke from the airship which dropped about 3,000 feet with the aeroplane diving in pursuit. The Zeppelin then turned back and the aeroplane pilot, having expended all his ammunition, steered for his parent ship. Throughout his attacks he had come under machine-gun fire from the fore part of the upper surface of the Zeppelin. He found, as he turned for home, that his engine would not pick up, and he was forced eventually to alight on the sea near the North Hinder lightvessel. The air-bags kept the aeroplane afloat, but the engine began to settle slowly into the water.

Darkness was closing in, and unless help came quickly the prospects of a rescue were small. The only means the pilot had of calling for help was by some sort of light signal. The bump on landing had jammed his Very pistol, but he had some cartridges and these he cut open and burned. Through ninety minutes nothing came to break the stillness of the sea, and Flight Lieutenant Freeman sat high on the tail of his aeroplane as its nose settled gently down. Suddenly a steamship came in sight. Lighting all the letters he had in his pocket and firing his revolver, he succeeded at last in attracting attention.

The steamer—a Belgian ship bound for the Hook of Holland—lowered a boat and rescued the officer and his engine. After a few days internment in Holland, Flight Lieutenant Freeman was released as a shipwrecked mariner. His exploit had shown the value of the aeroplane, flown from a carrier, as an offensive weapon against the Zeppelin. The aeroplane carried no machine-gun. Had it been so armed there would have been small doubt that, given a suitable incendiary bullet, the Zeppelin would have been brought down. As a result of this encounter machine-guns were at once fitted on all the aircraft carried by the *Vindex*. There was another airship attack on England on the night of the 8th and 9th of August, and then the Zeppelins were temporarily withdrawn from raiding for work once more with the High Sea Fleet.

The August Sortie of the High Sea Fleet

The offensive spirit of Admiral Scheer seems not to have been impaired by his experiences in the Battle of Jutland, and he was completing plans for a sweep across the North Sea for a bombardment of Sunderland. Owing to the failure of his intelligence, particularly of his airship reconnaissances, on the 31st of May he had run into the British battle fleet with no preliminary warning. In any advance against the British coast it was essential that he should not be surprised or cut off, and he therefore organised his reconnaissance forces, including airships and submarines, into outpost lines, which, he calculated, would protect both flanks of his advance. What he wanted was early knowledge of the location and direction of advance of Admiral Jellicoe's squadrons.

The submarines he placed in two lines near the English coast, and in two other lines to cover the approaches from the Flanders Bight. The airships at his disposal numbered eight. Four of these he ordered to watch an area which extended between Norway and Peterhead, another was to watch the Flanders Bight, whilst the remaining three cruised off the Firth of Forth, Sunderland, and the Humber-Wash area, respectively. So long as no collision with the British fleet occurred, and so long as the airship reports gave no disquieting news of the possibility of the German fleet being cut off, Scheer intended, he says, to push on so as to be off Sunderland at sunset on August the 19th.

The German Admiral left harbour about 8.0 p.m. on the 18th. The Grand Fleet had forestalled him by a few hours. The result of this early departure was that our main squadrons passed unseen in the darkness across the area patrolled by the northern line of Zeppelins.

The *Engadine* put to sea with the Battle Cruiser Fleet, but once again, as at Jutland, the *Campania* did not go out. She had developed defects in her machinery. This was the more unfortunate since she was now in a position to send two-seater reconnaissance seaplanes, as well as the small single-seaters, directly from her deck. Since Jutland the two-seaters had been successfully flown off the deck by several pilots, the first occasion being on the 3rd of June. Her balloon, however, had that morning been transferred, with a staff of officers and men, to the battleship *Hercules*, for endurance trials at sea, and went out, aloft, with the battleship. (This balloon was the first of the new 'M' type which incorporated the latest improvements designed by Captain Caquot. It had a triple air-inflated tail which gave it remarkable stability. It became the standard type for all future kite balloons, ashore and afloat).

The British battle fleet rendezvous was fixed for five in the morning of the 19th, about a hundred miles east-north-east of the Firth of Forth, with the battle cruisers about thirty miles to the south. As Scheer's object was obscure the British intention was to turn south from the rendezvous towards the southern part of the North Sea.

Meanwhile there was a movement of the Harwich Force which was destined later to change the whole course of the operation. Commodore Tyrwhitt with his light cruisers and destroyers had left harbour at 10.30 p.m. on the 18th, and was off his patrol area, along the Brown Ridge, at 3.0 a.m. next morning. There about three hours later he was sighted by the Flanders Bight Zeppelin, L.13, which reported to Scheer that two destroyer flotillas with a cruiser squadron behind were moving at full speed on a south-westerly course. The Zeppelin then seems to have lost touch with the Harwich Force, but picked it up again on a north-easterly course soon after 8.0 a.m. The report of the composition of the squadron, on this second observation, differed from the first one, and, as the course also was wholly different (Commodore Tyrwhitt had turned to keep his patrolling station), Scheer might have been led to conclude that we had two separate forces in the Flanders Bight.

At about this time, too, he got fragmentary information from a submarine and, a little later, from a Zeppelin, that there were forces in the north steaming away from him. This is explained by the fact that Admiral Jellicoe had, at 7.0 a.m. turned the whole of his fleet to the north, a course which he held for two hours before resuming his southerly movement once again.

The picture which Scheer formed in his mind from the somewhat baffling reports led him to believe that there was no danger in adhering to his intention to bombard Sunderland, and he therefore kept to his course. Soon after midday his whole conception of the British dispositions was suddenly altered by a further report from the Flanders Bight Zeppelin, L.13. She had sighted Commodore Tyrwhitt, once more, at about noon, and reported to Scheer at 12.20 p.m. that a force, about thirty units strong, was moving towards him. Ten minutes later the 'thirty units' were reported to include battleships. Here was Scheer's opportunity to bring his overwhelming force to the defeat of a detachment of the British battlefleet. He at once abandoned the Sunderland enterprise and turned south-east to meet the newly reported fleet. He was badly misled.

Commodore Tyrwhitt had no battleships with him, and his greater speed would have enabled him to out-distance the High Sea Fleet at his will. Indeed, the commodore had turned south soon after Scheer, and was already drawing rapidly away from him. The commander of the L. 13 had lost sight of the Harwich Force soon after making his incorrect report of its composition and, since the airship failed to pick it up again, Scheer was left to hug his delusion. At 2.35 p.m. he decided that there was no further prospect of coming up with the enemy in the south and as it was too late to think about bombarding Sunderland, he altered course for home.

We must turn to the Grand Fleet. Scheer says (*Germany's High Sea Fleet in the World War*):

> There was a possibility that we might have joined battle with the enemy fleet at 2.0 p.m., if the report of L.13 had not induced me to turn south with a view of attacking the ships sighted in that direction.

This is true. When Scheer turned, the advanced screen of our battle cruisers was no more than thirty miles away from his scouting forces, and the rival flagships little more than twice that distance. But for his turning, an action, under conditions overwhelmingly favourable to the British fleet, could hardly have been avoided.

All the same it is difficult to understand Scheer's lack of information as to the composition and movements of the Grand Fleet. The *Galatea* had sighted a Zeppelin at 8.24 a.m., and from that time onwards airships were frequently in view and were indeed engaged with gunfire from both the battle cruiser fleet and the battle fleet. He had got, as already indicated, an airship report before ten o'clock which spoke of 'hostile craft on a north-easterly course' but he seems to have heard nothing further about the movements in the north until after he altered course for his fruitless pursuit of Commodore Tyrwhitt. He says(*ibid*):

> The visibility in the locality of the Fleet, justified the assumption that our airships commanded a clear view over the whole sea area.

It was after he had turned, he says, that he got reports from two airships and a submarine which told of strong enemy forces in such a position that he calculated the opposing fleets would have met had the original course of the High Sea Fleet been maintained.

From the air point of view the possibilities at the moment when Scheer turned are interesting. Had the balloon been flown in one of our advanced cruisers it seems fairly certain, in view of the splendid visibility, that the German Fleet would have been sighted. Had this happened, Admiral Beatty then had the seaplanes in the *Engadine* at his disposal for more exact reconnaissance.

In fact, however, Admiral Jellicoe had little information on which to base his movements. It was not until about 2.0 p.m. that he knew what Scheer's location had been at half past twelve and then, as there was no indication that the German fleet had turned away, he concluded that the two fleets must now be so near one another that an action was imminent. He did indeed order complete readiness for battle. Soon after this, however, Admiral Jellicoe learned that the German fleet had been turning to starboard at half past twelve, and at about a quarter to four he knew that Scheer was on his way home. So, slipped away a possibly great chance. There was nothing left but for the Grand Fleet to return, dogged by submarine attacks, to harbour.

The failure to derive any benefit from the taking to sea of the balloon is worth examination. It would have been of little use for reconnaissance purposes since it was so far back that its range of vision could hardly have outdistanced the observation from the forward cruisers. Actually, no observers were allowed to ascend, and the balloon was kept aloft, tenantless, for a period altogether of twenty-eight hours, when it was hauled down and deflated 'in order to prevent its indicating the position of our fleet to the enemy'.

The only air work attempted by the *Engadine* was the sending away of a seaplane to attack a Zeppelin at 2.0 p.m. The Zeppelin had long been in sight, but the sea was running too high for the Sopwith Baby seaplanes. After the Zeppelin had cruised at a low height for some time, however, the flying personnel on the carrier could no longer tolerate their enforced inactivity. Flight Lieutenant Rutland was successfully hoisted out, but when he attempted to take off, the propeller of the seaplane was smashed in the crest of a wave and the machine had, with great difficulty, to be hoisted inboard again. By this time the airship had sheered off and no further flight was tried.

Vice-Admiral Beatty, in his report of the proceedings of the Battle

Cruiser Fleet, stated—

> I would submit that the balloon should be flown from a ship in the advanced cruiser screen in order to increase the range of vision ahead of the Fleet. Had the kite balloon been well forward during the operations, I am of opinion that the enemy might possibly have been sighted.

******

Note:—After the Battle of Jutland, and in view of the proved value of kite balloons towed from ships, Admiral Jellicoe had asked, early in June, for eleven balloons, one for each battle squadron and battle cruiser flagship, and two for use in the light cruiser squadrons. On the 30th of September he increased his demands to twelve balloons of the latest 'M' type, complete with spares. The proposal received Admiralty approval on the 13th of October, and shore bases to house the balloons and to supply them to the ships, inflated, as they were wanted, were begun at Scapa and at North Queensferry, Rosyth. The stations were completed early in 1917.

******

AIR RECONNAISSANCE OF THE SCHILLIG ROADS,

About this time an ingenious plan to attack the German fleet at its anchorage in the Schillig roads, with highspeed torpedo-carrying motorboats, was being developed. The boats, which had a draught of only three and a half feet, were to be carried across the North Sea in the supporting light cruisers and placed on the water near their objective, for a dawn assault, at high tide, across the Mellum and its neighbouring flats. Preliminary air reconnaissance to make sure there were no booms across these flats—obstacles which would make the enterprise impracticable—and to plot the disposition of the enemy fleet, was necessary.

The plans for this reconnaissance were unusual. It was arranged that a flying boat should go out direct from Harwich, come down beside a specified ship of Commodore Tyrwhitt's force off the German coast, refuel, make the reconnaissance which was expected to take three or four hours, be refuelled again on the way back, and so fly home.

The Harwich force left harbour on the night of the 28th of September. An 'America' flying boat with a crew of four went away in doubtful weather at 6.15 next morning. It was in charge of Flight

Lieutenant A. Q. Cooper, and the observer was Lieutenant Erskine Childers, whose knowledge of the Schillig roads, acquired both from the sea and from the air, was unique in the Naval Air Service. Not long after the flying boat had left. Commodore Tyrwhitt decided that the weather, which was getting increasingly squally, was against the success of the operation, and therefore ordered part of his force to return along the proposed line of flight of the aircraft to turn it back.

He himself remained near the pre-arranged refuelling position in case the flying boat got through unwarned. Flight Lieutenant Cooper, through patches of fog, made a praiseworthy flight, came upon Commodore Tyrwhitt's light cruisers at 10.15 a.m. and read a searchlight signal that he was to return. This he could not do without refuelling, and he therefore landed in a heavy sea near the *Landrail*, one of the refuelling destroyers. The water was too rough for the flying boat to get off again, and it was taken in tow in the hope that smoother water would be encountered. Whilst the fuel hose was being passed, the destroyer swung off the wind with the result that a wing extension of the seaplane fouled the ship and was broken. The crew of the seaplane, which was now unflyable, were taken off by the destroyer and the aircraft taken in tow. It rode the heavy sea splendidly almost to the British coast when it suddenly collapsed and sank.

The reconnaissance was tried again, this time with more success, on the 22nd of October. The flying was now entrusted to two Short seaplanes from the *Vindex*. The force was off the enemy coast before dawn, and the seaplanes got away without a hitch and were well on their way at a quarter to six, before it was yet light. The *Vindex*, in accordance with the pre-arranged plan, left for home immediately the seaplanes had been launched, as the light cruisers were to hoist in the aircraft, when they came back, at their boats' davits.

At 6.40 a.m. a Zeppelin was seen from the cruisers, flying low, but she seems not to have noticed either the seaplanes or the British ships. At 9.10 a.m. one of the seaplanes (pilot, Flight Commander H. F. Towner; observer, Chief Petty Officer A. Blackwell) returned, followed by the second (pilot, Flight Lieutenant F. N. Halstead; observer. Lieutenant Erskine Childers) fifteen minutes later. They were both safely hoisted in by the cruisers and the force then returned. Both pilots, who had flown independently, had been chagrined to find that a thick fog shrouded their main objective.

Although they came down to within fifty feet of the sea, they could distinguish nothing after passing the island of Wangeroog. Flight

Commander Towler landed on the sea near Heligoland to consult with his observer, and they decided to make a final effort. They saw some minor trawler and destroyer movements but nothing of the fog-enveloped German fleet. Lieutenant Erskine Childers, in the second seaplane, baulked of his main reconnaissance, took photographs of the islands of Heligoland, Langeoog, Baltrum, and Norderney, and of a group of fast-moving enemy destroyers. Two groups of these, totalling seventeen, were sighted. The whole reconnaissance, which had been made exactly to programme, deserved better luck. There had been no indication from the sea of the possibility of fog over the Schillig roads. There was no further reconnaissance in connexion with the motor-boat enterprise, which did not, in fact, take place until August 1918, and then only in a much modified form.

Effects of the Renewed Submarine Campaign

Although there was no means of knowing it at the time, the destroyer movements off Heligoland were significant. In the early part of October, a new and formidable submarine campaign against commerce had been begun. This meant that no longer were the Ems and Flanders submarine flotillas at Scheer's disposal for outpost work in protection of his sweeps into the North Sea. He did, indeed, try a sweep without them on October the 19th, but nothing came of it, and he seems to have realised that without the submarine help it was too dangerous to persist in his sorties. He therefore detached two of his destroyer flotillas from Heligoland to Zeebrugge to make attacks on the guardships in the Dover Straits, to help the Flanders submarines to get through more easily for their new campaign against commerce. It was probably preliminary movements of these destroyers which were seen from the seaplanes near Heligoland on the 22nd, since the flotillas arrived at Zeebrugge before dawn on the 24th of October.

Although the normal daily air patrols from Dunkirk of the Belgian bases could not be made either on the 24th or 25th owing to bad weather, the Admiralty had become aware, on the morning of the 24th, that a number of destroyers had, in fact, reached Zeebrugge. On the 26th, the haze was still thick enough to prevent more than spasmodic observation from the air, but some unusual activity was reported. Additional destroyers were seen in Ostend, and a number of armed barges were stated to be moored in the canals towards Bruges.

Admiral Bacon made preparations for a possible sortie by the enemy. The force under his command, although reinforced from Harwich, was small, and he therefore disposed it to protect the Belgian coast area and the all important massed food ships in the Downs. He could attempt no defence of the Dover Straits. When the enemy destroyers, therefore, aided by a clear starlit night, made their sortie on the 26th, they inflicted severe damage on the unarmed drifters which were patrolling the net line between the Goodwins and Ruytingen Buoy.

One British destroyer, six drifters, and an empty transport were sunk, and two destroyers, three drifters, and one trawler were damaged. One German destroyer suffered damage in a collision with a rudderless, burning drifter. The enemy did not repeat this success against the straits. Admiral Bacon was further reinforced, and this fact, together with the threat of air attacks, made Admiral Scheer decide to send one of the destroyer flotillas back to Wilhelmshaven. (See 'The Luxeuil Bombing Wing' section in this chapter.)

The submarine campaign of which the Flanders destroyer activity was a subsidiary feature, was causing considerable anxiety. The attacks on shipping were spreading steadily westwards down the English Channel to the open waters at the outer end. Already in September there had been serious losses off the Isle of Wight and off Portland Bill. So disquieting was the position that Admiral Sir S. C. Colville, the Commander-in-Chief at Portsmouth, asked, on September the 16th, that seaplanes be stationed at Portland to supplement the patrols made from Calshot. Before a decision was come to the value of these patrols was forcibly brought home.

Flight Lieutenant E. J. Cooper was flying off the Casquets on September the 24th when he saw a submarine on the surface making ready to sink the steamer *Borgundi-i* of Christiania. The Norwegian crew were already in their boats pulling towards the submarine. As soon as the enemy commander sighted the seaplane, he got ready to dive, but kept the open boats alongside to shelter him from any possible bombing, since he rightly judged that the British pilot would not accept the risk of blowing up the merchant crew. The pilot dropped his bombs when the submarine had got under, but they were of light weight and had no effect. He then landed on the water, and after a talk with the captain flew off to report the presence of the submarine to three trawlers which he had seen some distance away. The merchant vessel, saved from destruction by the mere appearance of a seaplane, resumed her interrupted journey.

The Admiralty, as a first measure, approved of the establishment of a mid-Channel patrol flight of four seaplanes on the 28th of September. For convenience of upkeep, the flight was placed under the Calshot station, whether it worked from Calshot or from Portland. The admiral had also asked for two airship stations to be set up, one on the Isle of Wight and one at Portland, but, after consideration, it was decided in November to augment instead the temporary seaplane base at Bembridge on the Isle of Wight, which worked as a sub-station of Calshot. Four Short seaplanes were therefore sent to Bembridge to institute a patrol up to sixty miles from that centre.

At the end of November there was a good example of how the new patrol organisation worked. A report of a submarine off the Casquets was received in Portland, and Flight Sub-Lieutenant J. R. Ross (with Air-Mechanic J. Redman) went off at once on a Short. Within half an hour he sighted the steamer *Ibex*, asked her on his Morse lamp if she had seen the submarine, and, in reply, learned the direction in which she last appeared. He went off in search and came upon a tank steamer and another steamer flying the Norwegian flag. About half a mile north of the latter, he picked up a thin tell-tale oil track, and following the track to its source found oil still coming up, a certain indication that the submarine was under him.

At once he went across to the Norwegian and tried to tell her, with his flash lamp, where the submarine was: his message was apparently not understood since the vessel held to her course. He then flew off to warn the tank steamer, and had gone three miles in her direction when he looked back and saw the submarine on the surface again, lying in wait for the Norwegian. The pilot turned at once and went straight for the submarine, which went under again before a 65-lb. bomb burst near her. The tank steamer was drawing close and was signalled from the seaplane.

Her reply, however, could not be read as her flags were blurred against her upper works, so the pilot landed alongside to talk to her captain; he was asked to direct the steamer over the position of the submarine. Unhappily the seaplane stalled, soon after it got off again, and crashed into the sea. The tank steamer which was, in fact, a decoy ship, H.M.S. Q.7. had rescued the airmen, and was about to hoist in the seaplane when the submarine suddenly appeared on the surface and began to shell the ship. The seaplane was at once cut adrift, and the submarine (U.B.19) was eventually sunk by Q.7 at close range.

******

The special service Q-boats, ostensibly innocent merchantmen, had their armament well hidden. When a submarine was sighted every pretence of escape was made, and if the submarine opened fire the Q-boat commander would, if necessary, simulate the panic that might be expected from a more or less undisciplined crew, stop and abandon his ship, leaving only the essential engine-room staff and gun crews on board. Every encouragement would be given to the submarine commander to approach as close as he wished, until, at the most favourable moment, the white ensign would be hoisted and the hidden guns would be suddenly unmasked and brought into action.

******

Gratifying as these isolated successes were, all the antisubmarine measures, of which the air patrols formed a small part, were no more than palliatives. The losses of merchant ships rose steadily. The outlook was so threatening that it compelled a drastic revision of naval policy. There followed important changes in the composition of the Board of Admiralty. Admiral Jellicoe, on November the 22nd, was offered, and accepted, the post of First Sea Lord, and Sir David Beatty took command of the Grand Fleet. A new phase in the naval war had begun.

AIR OPERATIONS FROM DUNKIRK.

The reorganisation which enabled the Dunkirk air command to respond to the many calls made upon it during 1916 was put in hand by Wing Commander Lambe, after full discussion with the Admiralty Air Department, within a few days of his appointment in August 1915. His first step was to obtain approval for the amalgamation of the aeroplane units at Dover and Dunkirk into one wing. What he aimed at was to bring the strength of this wing (No. 1) up to eight squadrons of six aeroplanes each. Two of these were to be stationed at Dover for reconnaissance and patrol work in the Straits area, but were to be drawn upon to relieve those at Dunkirk from time to time. Owing to the demands still being made from the Dardanelles, however, there was an acute shortage of aeroplanes and pilots, and it took some time before Wing Commander Lambe's aim could be approached.

But, by November 1915, he could look forward to considerable reinforcements. Many officers and men, including those from the disbanded armoured car units, were under training in England, and new types of aeroplanes which were being built to Admiralty orders would be ready when flying conditions improved at the end of the winter. He suggested, therefore, in the middle of November 1915, that it should be possible for the Dunkirk command to undertake a wider offensive policy in the spring of 1916, and he sought approval for the organisation of a special bombing force. He pointed out that bombing attacks, to be effective, must not only be made in force, but must also be sustained.

The essential routine work of reconnaissance, fleet co-operation and photography, would, he estimated, fully occupy the energies of No. 1 Wing at St. Pol, and he urged that the employment of two additional offensive wings should be sanctioned and that the construction of new aerodromes to accommodate them should be begun at once. His proposal was based on the assumption that No. 4 Wing from Eastchurch, consisting of four squadrons of six pilots each, could be transferred to one of the new aerodromes, and that it would be possible to make up the other wing (No. 5) by detaching four squadrons from No. 1 Wing. On this basis all three wings would consist of four squadrons.

In addition, there was to be a squadron at Dover for local defence and training duties. These suggestions were approved, and the work on sites chosen at Coudekerque and Petite Synthe was put in hand. The Admiralty made it clear that the new wings were to be available for military duties when not required for naval air work. To cope with the increase in supply and repair which the new units would entail, the existing repair organisation at St. Pol. was detached from No. 1 Wing, was enlarged and re-equipped, and given a separate identity as the Central Repair Depot.

It will have been observed that the existing Naval Air Service squadron consisted only of six aeroplanes. There were, however, officers graded as Flight Commanders and Squadron Commanders. These officers were scarce, and it had been found necessary in No.1 Wing to group the squadrons for purposes of command. Wing Commander Lambe, on the 6th of December 1915, proposed a revision of nomenclature whereby a unit of six pilots should be known as a Flight, and two or three Flights should form a squadron. Each wing could be composed of a varying number of squadrons. These proposals would bring the Naval Air Service aeroplane organisation more into line with that of the Royal Flying Corps.

Once again, the scheme was approved. Not only did it sweep away the confusion arising from the use of the same names to signify totally different formations in the two air services but, what was more important, it economized the use of officers who combined the technical abilities of a pilot with the rarer qualities of leadership.

It will be remembered that in September 1915 the formidable Tirpitz battery had been revealed for the first time, and had so effectively out-ranged the monitors that Admiral Bacon was forced to give up further bombardment of the submarine bases until he should have some effective counter to the Tirpitz guns; in other words, until he got his new 15-inch monitors, *Erebus* and *Terror*. The old monitors, however, were kept at Dover ready to meet any calls that might come for assistance in connexion with land operations on the Belgian coast. One such call came from General Foch, in January 1916, for bombardment of gun positions near Westende.

The firing took place on the 26th of January 1916, and is interesting as being the first occasion on which one aeroplane observer registered the guns of five monitors firing systematically. To make this possible it had been necessary to meet and overcome two great difficulties. The first, which had been brought out during the experiments made with *Revenge* in the previous year, was the need for wireless reception in the aircraft, and the second was the need for some practical method whereby the shots from each separate ship of a number bombarding the same target could be reliably identified. The first difficulty was overcome largely through the enthusiastic work of Lieutenant C. W. Nutting and his brother officers in the *Riviera*.

The second disappeared before a simple suggestion made by Flight Lieutenant H. Stewart, also of the *Riviera*. This was that the air observer should buzz on his wireless at the precise moment when he saw the shell explode and then follow this signal with his spotting correction. In the ship the procedure was as follows. The control officer noted the time when his gun fired and, since he knew the time of flight, noted also when the shell might be expected to burst. When the buzz from the aeroplane was heard in the ships, each control officer compared the time it was received with his expected time of burst and, if they coincided, knew at once that the spotting correction which followed referred to his gun. To obviate the confusion which would result if two or more ships fired at the same moment, a slight time interval between the fire from each gun was essential. Twenty seconds proved sufficient and was normally adopted.

From a technical point of view spotting was now on a sound basis, but the bombardment of the 26th of January revealed an interesting personal problem. It so happened that fairly good ground observation had been obtained from fixed stations in the Nieuport lines, and there was an appreciable discrepancy between the estimates of the fall of the shells made by the two methods of observation. There seemed little doubt that the air observers were at fault. A test was arranged. Plans of three targets well known to the airmen were made to three different scales corresponding to varying heights of observation. Spots were marked on the plans, and the air observers were invited to give their impressions of the actual distances of the spots from the target. They gave widely different estimates.

Admiral Bacon thereupon decided that since the targets for the fleet on the Belgian coast were few, each observer could easily learn by heart the distances of all salient points in the neighbourhood of the more important objectives. Thus, a shell pitching near any of these numerous points could be accurately signalled without loss of time. A further device to help the observer was the introduction of transparent grids, scaled into 100 yard squares, which could be placed over the target on the chart. The human error arose partly from inadequate training and partly from a tendency personal to each observer. An airman may under-estimate or over-estimate distances, but since he is likely to be consistent—a fact which was demonstrated during the tests—he will register the target although he may require more rounds to do so than if his observations were dead accurate. Every opportunity was given to observers to get practice in the art of spotting for the ships, but there were no further bombardments for the remainder of the winter.

Meanwhile, German aircraft operating from the Belgian aerodromes and from the Zeebrugge seaplane station were making a number of raids on the Kentish coast. About one in the moonlit morning of the 23rd of January nine bombs were dropped on Dover. The malthouse of a brewery and the Red Lion Hotel were wrecked, one man was killed and six people were injured. Soon after midday the alarm was raised again; this time five bombs were aimed at the airship sheds at Capel, but failed to do any damage. On the 1st of February a ship—a coaster at anchor—was sunk by a bomb off the Kentish Knocke.

On the 9th an aeroplane bombed a school at Broadstairs, and on the 20th seaplanes attacked the Kentish coast and Lowestoft. The only casualty was a boy killed on the Beach Road at Walmer, and the material damage on land was slight, but a ship was sunk off Deal. It was a difficult matter to deal with guerrilla raids of this nature. Very little warning preceded the dropping of the bombs, and before our aircraft could climb high enough the raiders had usually disappeared. The most effective answer appeared to be a bombing offensive against the aerodromes from which the activity emanated.

The bombing force being organised at Dunkirk was soon to be in a position to undertake this. No. 5 Wing, formed at Dover under Squadron Commander Spenser D. A. Grey, began to take up its quarters on the new aerodrome at Coudekerque at the beginning of March 1916. Before the wing was completely installed it was called upon to take part in a combined Allied raid on the aerodrome at Houttave, between Ostend and Bruges, and on the seaplane base at Zeebrugge. The attack was arranged for the morning of the 20th of March.

The timing was appropriate since, in the quiet afternoon of Sunday the 19th, there was another daring daylight attack on the Kentish coast. Five enemy seaplanes took part. Twenty-four bombs dropped on Dover killed seven persons, of whom four were soldiers, and injured eighteen others (eleven soldiers), and did damage to a hundred houses; one of fourteen bombs on Ramsgate fell on a motorcar, blew the driver to pieces, killed a woman, and killed five and wounded eight of a party of children on their way to Sunday School. Nine other bombs on Deal and one on Margate did little damage.

This time the raiders did not all escape. A Royal Flying Corps officer, Lieutenant R. Collis, who was flying from Folkestone to France, met one of the enemy seaplanes on its way back from Dover and shot it down in flames. Toll was exacted too for the victims of the Ramsgate raid. Flight Commander R. J. Bone, from the Westgate naval air station, chased one of the seaplanes on his Nieuport Scout and shot it down into the mine-field off the Goodwins.

On the day this raid was made, a Dunkirk pilot, from over Houttave, had carefully sketched the lay-out of the aerodrome to facilitate the next day's attack. This was made at dawn by eight British bombers and four fighters, ten French bombers and nine fighters, and eleven Belgian bombers and five fighters. The British dropped twenty-five 65-lb. bombs and the French and Belgians eighty-six of various weights. The attack on the seaplane base, with twenty-eight 65-lb. bombs, was made by seven seaplanes from the *Riviera* and *Vindex* and by two from Dunkirk. Many hits on the objectives on both raids were reported. The division of the 9th Flotilla which escorted the carriers engaged in a sharp little action with three German destroyers, during which the British destroyer *Lance* suffered somewhat severely.

There were no further bombing raids until late in April. By this time No. 5 Wing at Coudekerque was up to full strength. It had one flight of the new Sopwith two-seater aeroplanes (1½ Strutters), but was otherwise equipped with the French Breguet and twin-engine Caudron bombers. The advance party of No. 4 Wing, too, under Squadron Commander C. L. Courtney, was opening up the new aerodrome at Petite Synthe, where it had arrived from Eastchurch on the 11th of April.

Towards the end of April mining operations off the Belgian coast, to catch the mine-laying submarines of the Flanders flotilla, were undertaken. The idea was to close the passage between the Thornton Ridge shoal and the Belgian coast by a double line of deep mines across the exit from Zeebrugge and by a mine-net barrage on the same line and at North Hinder. By 7.30 a.m. on April the 24th the double line of mines had been laid, and the net-barrage was in position over a stretch of thirteen miles. The air command at Dunkirk co-operated by bombing attacks on the new coast aerodrome at Mariakerke, west of Ostend, by protective fighting patrols over the ships, and by seaplane anti-submarine patrols. The first raid on Mariakerke was made at dawn on the 23rd by eight bombers of No. 5 Wing.

Next morning, whilst the mines were being laid, twelve bombers from Nos. 4 and 5 Wings attacked Mariakerke again with thirty-two 65-lb. and twenty-four 16-lb. bombs. Soon after the mines were in position seaplanes from Zeebrugge attempted to bomb the drifters and supporting ships which remained behind to watch the nets. They were driven off.

Flight Sub-Lieutenant H. R. Simms (observer, Sub-Lieutenant H. A. Furniss), on a Nieuport, fought one of the seaplanes near its base. After a fifteen-minute duel the German pilot fell forward on his controls, and the seaplane dived into the water where it was blown up by its own bombs. The air command at Dunkirk now had to meet many calls for protective flights over the ships which made daily patrols of the barrage line. Seaplanes, too, were employed over the patrol area from the Outer Ratel to the Thornton Ridge. A routine flight was made by one seaplane at dawn, ahead of the ships, to prevent them being surprised by enemy forces, and other flights throughout the day ensured a strict watch on the patrol area.

One of the Short seaplane pilots, on the 4th of May, came upon an enemy submarine off Thornton Ridge. As he was getting into position to drop his bombs the seaplane was hit and damaged by gun-fire. The nearest bomb fell ten yards short of the submarine, which had turned back towards Zeebrugge. The pilot (Flight Sub-Lieutenant T. G. M. Stephens) had great difficulty in getting his damaged seaplane back to his base.

The bombing of aerodromes went ahead. In the dark hours of the 5th of May nineteen aeroplanes of Nos. 4 and 5 Wings dropped fifty 65-lb. bombs on Mariakerke. One pilot failed to return. The raiders were escorted by Nieuport fighters, an early instance of night operations by this type of aircraft. On the 19th of May the aerodrome at Ghistelles, south of Ostend, was attacked with twenty-three 65-lb. and eighteen 16-lb. bombs. Two days later Mariakerke was revisited, but the visibility was poor and the bombing was too indiscriminate to be of military value.

Then came retaliation. With the exception of an afternoon attack on Deal by one aeroplane on the 3rd of May, the Kentish coast had, so far as heavier-than-aircraft are concerned, enjoyed a period of quiet following the raid of the 19th of March. This quiet was broken in the early hours of the 20th of May, when five machines dropped fifty small bombs on Dover, St. Peter's, Sholden, and Ringwold. The damage done was surprisingly small: the casualties were one soldier killed and a sailor and a woman wounded. Once again payment was exacted for the raid. Flight Sub-Lieutenant R. S. Dallas, who was patrolling at 12,000 feet in his Nieuport Scout off Blankenberghe, saw, at 7.0 a.m., one of the raiders, a seaplane, far below him, on its way back to its base. He dived steeply and fired half a tray of ammunition from his Lewis gun at close range. The seaplane side-slipped into the water, floundered for a bit, and then sank.

The most severe retaliation, however, was against Dunkirk, which was bombed by day and night from the 19th to the 22nd of May. In all 372 bombs fell in the town and killed thirty-two people and wounded eighty-nine. During one of these raids, made in the afternoon of the 2 1 St, the Nieuport pilots from St. Pol had many fights, and two of the enemy aeroplanes were destroyed by Flight Commander R. H. Mulock and Flight Sub-Lieutenant Dallas. This strong enemy retaliation gave food for thought. It emphasized the disparity of the conditions under which attacks by the opposing air services were made. Indiscriminate bombing of French towns by the enemy, although possibly of no military value, was a serious threat to the lives and property of the civilian population. To it we had no effective answer. It was out of the question that we should indulge in the promiscuous bombing of Belgian towns.

A discussion took place between the French and British air commanders, and it was arranged that defensive patrols to protect Dunkirk against enemy aircraft should be shared by the French squadron located at Furnes, and the Naval Air Service at Dunkirk. These patrols had barely been begun when the French squadron was called away to the Verdun sector, and the Naval Air Service assumed sole responsibility for the air defence of the Dunkirk area. The French offered the use of their aerodrome at Furnes together with all tents and huts.

This offer was gladly accepted, and on the 10th of June, a unit known as 'A' Squadron, consisting of two flights of Nieuport Scouts under Squadron Commander F. K. Haskins, was detached from No. 1 Wing at St. Pol. and sent to Furnes. The occupation of the new advanced ground, situated as it was ten miles nearer the lines than St. Pol, greatly facilitated the air offensive work along the Belgian coast. Aeroplanes could get away rapidly to protect ships of the Dover Patrol against air attack, could do much to hinder enemy air observers from spotting for batteries along the Nieuport sector, and stood a better chance of intercepting aircraft which set out to bomb Dunkirk. The squadron at Furnes was, indeed, the first homogeneous fighting unit of the Royal Naval Air Service.

The most important effect of the bombing of Dunkirk was a revision of our own bombing policy. In a memorandum to Admiral Bacon, Wing Captain Lambe wrote on the 1st of June:

> Although at present there appears to be no means for successfully combating night bombing attacks by enemy aircraft, the lesson learnt during the past two months is that it is inadvisable to carry out offensive operations unless you have sufficient pilots and machines to continue it by day and night, and also a sufficiency of fast fighting machines to prevent retaliation by day.

In his reply on the 6th of June, Admiral Bacon stated:

> The chief lesson learned by our airmen in Flanders during the last two months, I hope, is one which the Military have known for some time, namely, that indiscriminate bombing is useless. The point they will eventually appreciate is not only that it is useless, but absolutely harmful to well thought out military operations . . . I intend to limit day bombing to such occasions of general attack or a general advance or to the attack of submarines and other vessels at sea. Night bombing may be use-

ful against vessels in a harbour *when present in sufficient numbers* to make success probable, but otherwise bomb-dropping leads merely to the strengthening of anti-aircraft defences without adequate compensation.

All organised bombing by the Dunkirk command was therefore stopped until the beginning of August, when it was resumed, in an attempt to divert air activity from the Somme front. Admiral Bacon, in his memorandum, went on to point out that the most urgent necessity was for fighting aircraft, and that every aeroplane which could possibly be used as a fighter should be equipped for that duty, not only to protect Dunkirk and the aerodromes, but also to drive off enemy aircraft:

> I shall soon want, on a certain day, every machine I can get to drive off hostile craft from north, south, east and west, and the success of the operation I have in view will depend on this.

The operation referred to was an attempt to get at the Tirpitz battery by means of a naval 12-inch gun, known as the Dominion battery, which was being specially mounted near Adinkerke, that is at a range of 27,000 yards. The firing first began on the 8th of July.

Meanwhile the enemy made no attempt to repeat the bombing raids against Dunkirk. The main concern of the British fighting pilots was the attack of German spotting aircraft which appeared anywhere near the Nieuport lines. This proved difficult as they were content to retreat at the first sight of a naval aeroplane, and there were few encounters at close quarters. On the 1st of June Flight Sub-Lieutenant L de B. Daly of No. 4 Wing, flying a Nieuport, was almost within range of two spotting aeroplanes above Dixmude, when the enemy saw him and dispersed. One dived steeply and landed, and the other flew off towards Ypres.

The Nieuport pilot followed, and was rapidly overhauling his enemy when an Albatros aeroplane came up unseen from behind and wounded Daly twice in the right arm. As he swung round to meet the attack his port gun was shot out of action and his starboard gun misfired. His right arm being useless, he was unable to recock the gun and was forced to retreat. He was now losing blood rapidly. To stem the flow, he gripped his right arm with his left hand, took the control lever between his knees, and so piloted his Nieuport safely to the Royal Flying Corps aerodrome at Abeele.

The seaplane patrols became of double importance about this time. Early in June the Admiralty knew that an additional destroyer flotilla had been sent to Zeebrugge, and they suspected that this reinforcement foreshadowed attempts to raid our sea communications to Holland and our shipping in the Downs. On the 4th of June a seaplane pilot, on early morning patrol, came under fire from three German destroyers north of Zeebrugge. His observer advised the nearest British destroyers of their presence and a brief action followed. Four days later Flight Sub-Lieutenant R. Graham (observer, Petty Officer E. A. Boyd) was on the look-out ahead of the patrol, when just before 5.0 a.m. he saw three destroyers off Zeebrugge which opened heavy fire on the seaplane. Graham turned back, with the destroyers in pursuit, to inform the ships of the patrol, but the wireless broke down.

The observer made a temporary connexion with a piece of wire and got a message through to the fleet, although his hands had been badly burned by sparks during the repair. The pilot then landed near the destroyer *Leven* and semaphored his report. The seaplane was damaged by the heavy sea and had to be towed back to harbour. The three destroyers which had been sighted were the herald of a movement towards Dunkirk, and the *Lord Clive* and the patrolling destroyers were quickly in action with twelve of the enemy, but the engagement was not prolonged, the German ships turning back before the Harwich flotilla could get up. The movements of the hostile destroyers during the remainder of the morning were reported by the successive seaplane patrols.

About this time, too, there were some dramatic incidents off the Belgian coast in which pigeons, released from damaged French aircraft, got back to their lofts at Dunkirk with calls for help. On the 8th of June a severely wounded pigeon arrived at St. Pol with a message that a French seaplane was down between Ostend and Zeebrugge. A French destroyer went off to the rescue, and came upon the scene just as a German torpedo-boat had got the seaplane in tow. The enemy ship fled as soon as it was attacked but the seaplane was sunk. The Dunkirk air unit were impressed with the work of the French pigeon-service, and asked our Ally for a few trained with which to begin a service of their own. (Pigeons had been used by some of the home naval air stations since the early days of the war). These were willingly provided and soon proved their worth.

On the 10th of June pigeons were released from two patrolling seaplanes from a height of 4,000 feet near Zeebrugge, and got back to the station at Dunkirk with reports that the patrolled area was clear of the enemy. Ten days later news of a seaplane which was down on the water and unable to get off again was received by pigeon, and on the 24th of June another seaplane was rescued through the same agency. These were the beginnings. The pigeon organisation in the Naval Air Service rapidly expanded. The birds will often make their appearance in this history, for they flew in time and again, when all other communication was cut off, to initiate help for stranded aircraft.

Although the enemy destroyer activity abated after the attempted raid of the 8th of June, our patrolling ships had to face increased aircraft attacks by seaplanes operating from Zeebrugge. It was difficult to ensure them protection since the fighting aeroplanes were of limited endurance, and the keeping up of continuous patrol over the fleet strained the available fighting strength to the utmost. The aeroplanes had the further disadvantage that they could not long survive if they were forced down, by engine failure or other cause, on the sea.

The strain on the fighting aeroplanes was eased on the 24th of June when four Sopwith 'Baby' seaplanes were transferred to Dunkirk from the *Vindex*. They had been asked for by Wing Captain Lambe early in the month, as being admirably suited for offensive work in co-operation with the patrolling ships. They could be refuelled at sea, if necessary, and hoisted in or out. They were welcomed, too, as an addition to the fighters which were to hold off enemy aircraft during the impending attempt on the Tirpitz battery.

There had been reinforcements, also, of fighting aeroplanes. They were only two in number, but each had a performance which was remarkable for the period. They were the Sopwith Pup (80 horse-power Le Rhone engine) and the Sopwith Triplane (110 horse-power Clerget). The first Pup arrived at the end of May and the Triplane in the middle of June, and both were sent to the fighting squadron at Furnes where they caused something of a sensation. They could climb faster and higher than any aeroplane hitherto seen, were faster on the level, gave a splendid view and could be thrown about in the air with great ease and rapidity.

★★★★★★

The Triplane had the better performance. When tested, it climbed to 10,000 feet in thirteen minutes, at which height its air speed was 106 miles an hour. The 'Pup' took a minute more to reach the same height, where its speed was 104½ miles an hour. The ceiling of the 'Pup' was 17,500 feet, whereas the Triplane, in September, reached the extraordinary height of a little over 22,000 feet. The Triplane, however, had the disadvantage that even a slight crash necessitated a disproportionate amount of repair work. The original Sopwith 'Pup' and Triplane both survived the war.

******

All was in readiness for the firing on the Tirpitz battery at the beginning of July, but not until the 8th was the visibility along the coast good enough for reliable air observation. Every precaution had been taken to keep knowledge of the mounting of the 12-inch gun at Adinkerke from the enemy. The emplacement was near a farm, and a barn-like building with a removable roof had been erected over the gun. The French were to co-operate with two 9.2 guns on railway sidings near Coxyde. The air arrangements were elaborate. A carefully co-ordinated time-table was drawn up for the firing of the British and French guns, and another time-table for the sending of wireless messages both from the air and from the ground so that there should be no mutual interference between the French and British wireless.

Seven spotting aeroplanes from Dunkirk were over the Tirpitz battery on the 8th, in relays, at heights ranging between 11,000 and 16,000 feet from 2.0 p.m. to 8.0 p.m. They could receive as well as send wireless messages, and were informed by a buzz each time the gun was fired. Immediately the air observer saw a burst he made a long dash before giving his spotting correction. This enabled the control officer of the Dominion battery to distinguish his shells from those fired by the French guns. The arrangements worked without a hitch and the wireless communication was perfect. A balloon section (No. 11) working on land from a position near Coxyde also assisted in the spotting. The balloon observers reported a few rounds, but on the whole, they got but fleeting views of the distant target, which was obscured by the smoke of the bursting shells and by haze.

The aeroplanes, however, from over the Tirpitz battery got the gun on the target on the seventh round fired and third round spotted. Wide and continuous fighting patrols protected the spotting aeroplanes and kept enemy aircraft from getting any view of the Dominion battery. To provide these patrols all the available fighting aeroplanes from the three wings at Dunkirk, as well as from Dover, and also seaplanes from the Dunkirk base were called upon. Very few enemy aircraft appeared, and there were but two brief engagements, both indecisive. To delude the enemy into the belief that the bombardment was coming from the sea, monitors, accompanied by the *City of Oxford* balloon ship and by the balloon barge *Arctic*, operated off the coast.

******

The *Arctic*, a steel, non-propelled barge, was requisitioned for kite-balloon work in January 1916. Her reconstruction was completed in May, when she was attached for service with the Dover Patrol. She was towed at sea behind the monitors.

******

On the following day, July the 9th, the firing was continued. Aeroplane observers, in rotation, kept watch on the Tirpitz battery from 10.50 a.m. to 7.0 p.m. A feature of the shooting on this day was the work of the Coxyde balloon which provided unbroken observation for nine hours. From the basket, at a height of about 2,000 feet, the observers had a remarkable view. The coastal area lay clear in the sunshine up to a point several miles beyond Ostend. The movements of shipping in Ostend harbour could be plainly followed. Of the hundred and nine rounds fired by the British and French guns during the day only eleven were not spotted from the balloon. The result of the exceptional observation, both from the aeroplanes and from the balloon, was that the target was found on the third round fired.

Enemy airmen were active throughout the day and there were a number of fights in the afternoon; one German aeroplane was shot down into the sea off Westende and another to land, apparently in trouble, just behind the enemy lines at Ypres. There were no British losses by enemy action. One pilot, however, whilst escorting a spotting aeroplane home, had total engine failure and was forced to alight on the sea off La Panne. His Nieuport sank in a few minutes and he was compelled to strike out for the shore, a distance of over a mile. He landed safely.

Twice in the day the Tirpitz battery was photographed, and on each occasion the photographic aeroplane, although flying at 13,000 feet, was hit by anti-aircraft fire. The plates, exposed in the afternoon, showed, when they were developed, the effect of the fire very clearly. The concrete emplacements of all four guns had been hit, but not the guns themselves, although two of them had possibly been put temporarily out of action. The Tirpitz battery did not submit quietly to the fire. With the help of balloon observation, it got the range of the two French guns and dropped 104 shells in their vicinity, forcing them eventually to withdraw.

There was quiet, owing to unfavourable weather, until July the 20th, when firing was resumed. But low clouds made observation difficult, and a variable wind made regular shooting impossible so that firing was stopped after eleven rounds had been sent over. Tirpitz this time got the range of the naval gun, but a smoke screen was put up and his shots did no damage. This device was also used to advantage by the Tirpitz battery next day, when a smoke screen so obscured the guns that firing had to be abandoned.

Photographs were again procured of the battery on the 19th and 20th of July. Those obtained on the former day from a height of 14,000 feet excited considerable interest. They had been taken in spite of a mist which made visual observation of the results of the fire difficult, and showed in detail all the damage that had been done. The guns, it was seen, were still apparently intact although the emplacements had been well battered. The photographs had been taken with a new camera. The excellent enemy anti-aircraft fire along the Belgian coast had compelled pilots to fly higher and still higher, and minor improvements made from time to time in the design of the camera were more or less negatived by the increased heights from which the plates had to be exposed.

Up to the early summer of 1916 the French and Belgians, however, were getting better results than the Naval Air Service at Dunkirk. Admiral Bacon, therefore, anticipating Admiralty approval, gave the officer in charge of the photographic section a blank cheque on his private account, and sent him to London to buy the best lens he could find. From the second of two visits he returned with two 8-inch lenses of about 37-inch focal length. The designing and building of an apparatus to use the lenses began at the Central Repair Depot at the beginning of June, and the new camera was first used over the Tirpitz battery on the morning of the 9th of July.

As a result of this first exposure it was found that although the photographs were excellent, the area of ground covered by each plate was so small in comparison with that covered by previous cameras that the actual guns of the battery were missed. Hasty alterations were made. A gunsight type of viewfinder was fitted to enable the observer to take accurate sighting, and the camera was suspended in such a way that it could be controlled independently of the aeroplane and sighted on any object within a considerable radius under the machine. (Admiral Sir Reginald Bacon, *The Dover Patrol, 1915-1917*). The result, on July the 29th, was that from a height of 14,000 feet, a picture of the Tirpitz battery was procured in which the guns and shell holes showed up clearly and twice as large as in any photograph previously obtained.

By this time the 12-inch gun was getting badly worn. Cloudy weather, too, now came along to make observation uncertain. Furthermore, an attempt to fire the gun on the 3rd of August was completely nullified by the efficiency of the smoke-screen put up by the enemy. Admiral Bacon decided that the best course was to mount more guns and keep them in reserve for use in conjunction with a possible advance along the coast which, it was hoped, might result from the military operations on the Somme.

In July and August, the enemy showed more inclination to dispute our seaplane patrolling off the Belgian coast. His destroyers always gave the aircraft a lively reception, but now his submarines began to show a willingness to stay on the surface when they sighted a seaplane and to use their guns to protect themselves. On the 24th of July a patrolling seaplane pilot, Flight Sub-Lieutenant F. J. Bailey (observer, Sub-Lieutenant F. W. Mardock) made to attack a submarine twelve miles off Zeebrugge when his engine was shot out of action at the range of a mile by a shell from the U-boat. He got on the water safely and began to taxi laboriously towards Holland, but was overtaken and captured by a German torpedo-boat.

Fighting seaplanes from Zeebrugge, too, were more determined in their attacks, and it became necessary, in August, to send out a Sopwith Baby seaplane as escort to the less wieldy reconnaissance machines.

It will be remembered that organised bombing by the Dunkirk wings had been stopped at the end of May 1916. In August it was resumed, in co-operation with the Royal Flying Corps, in an attempt to divert air activity from the Somme front. General Trenchard, on the 1st of August, asked that the Naval Air Service should bomb the aerodrome at St. Denis Westrem, south-west of Ghent, where numbers of new aeroplanes had been reported, and also the great ammunition dump at Meirelbeke a few miles beyond.

The raid took place on August the 2nd, and was co-ordinated with an attack by aeroplanes of the II Brigade, Royal Flying Corps. When the ten twin-engine Caudrons and one Maurice Henri Farman of Nos. 4 and 5 Wings, escorted by five Sopwith two-seaters, arrived over St. Denis Westrem about 1.30 p.m., eight aeroplanes were standing on the landing ground. Forty 65-lb. and four small bombs were dropped amongst these and about the aerodrome sheds and buildings.

The raid marks an interesting step in the progress of air tactics as applied to bombing. The eleven bombers flew in wedge formation until they neared their target when they altered to line ahead to drop their bombs in succession. They then reformed. The signals for the manoeuvres in the air were given by Very lights, fired by the pilot of a Sopwith two-seater, who flew independently of the bombing formation. At Meirelbeke, where three Sopwiths of No. 5 Wing dropped thirty-one le Pecq bombs, the ammunition dump and railway trucks in the sidings received direct hits, but there were, apparently, no consequent explosions. Twenty single-seater fighters, in four formations, patrolled to protect the returning bombers, but the only opposition was fierce anti-aircraft fire, and one of the fighters, from a height of about 12,000 feet, was shot down by a direct hit of an anti-aircraft shell.

After this raid a wider programme of bombing, whereby the Naval Air Service could further help the Flying Corps operations, was agreed on between Wing Captain Lambe and General Trenchard. In addition to enemy aerodromes and ammunition dumps in the northern area, the Hoboken shipyards and Zeppelin bases in Belgium were included in the objectives. For three months there had been no attempted airship raids on England. This quiescent interlude was due, in the main, to the fact that the nights of early summer were not long or dark enough to allow the airships to attack without considerable risk. In the early hours of the 29th of July, the raids were resumed. The attacking Zeppelins came from the naval sheds in North Germany, but preparations had recently been reported at the airship bases near Brussels and at Cognelée, near Namur, and it was evident that raiding attempts by military Zeppelins would not long be delayed.

Before these began, however, a well-executed bomb attack by two Dunkirk pilots gave warning of the determination of the Naval Air Service to make the use of the Belgian bases highly dangerous. The raid was made in the early morning of the 9th of August by Flight Sub-Lieutenants R. H. Collet and D. E. Harkness, flying Sopwith 1½ Strutters without observers. Collet flew over the sea and crossed the coast east of Zeebrugge. He was soon above Berchem Ste. Agathe, but he had seen through the open door of the shed as he glided down to bomb that there was no airship inside, and he therefore went on to Evere where, from little more than 150 feet above, he scored eight direct hits with le Pecq bombs on the large airship hangar.

The second pilot arrived over Evere in time to see the results of the first attack. He dropped eight further le Pecq bombs, some of which were seen to hit the shed, and went on to drop four more on the hangar at Berchem Ste. Agathe. Both pilots got back safely to their aerodrome. It seems that there were no airships in the sheds at the time the bombs were dropped, but so accurate was the aiming that the attack must have aroused considerable disquiet in the minds of the military airship commanders. The next raid was made by four Sopwiths on the Lichtervelde ammunition dump, south of Thourout, in the afternoon of the 18th. Part of the dump was seen burning as the bombers left.

On the 25th two Sopwith pilots, after a good piece of navigation in thick weather, bombed the Zeppelin sheds at Cognelée, a distance of some 120 miles from their aerodrome. The target had been attacked by No. 27 Squadron of the Royal Flying Corps three weeks earlier, and the two naval aeroplanes received a warm reception, the anti-aircraft fire being reported as extremely accurate. No direct hits on the sheds were made. One of the pilots on the return journey made a small miscalculation of his course and found himself over Bruges with not enough petrol left to reach the lines. He was forced to land in Holland. Owing to the load of bombs which had to be carried, it was impossible to allow much margin of petrol above what was required for the long double journey.

The Hoboken shipyards were attacked by three Sopwith pilots of No. 5 Wing in a hailstorm on the afternoon of the 2nd of September. The results were unobserved. Next morning, in conjunction with the renewed bombing offensive against enemy aerodromes opened by the Royal Flying Corps, eighty-two 65 -lb. bombs were dropped on the Ghistelles aerodrome by seventeen bombers of Nos. 4 and 5 Wings. On the 7th the same wings, again in cooperation with the Flying Corps, attacked St. Denis Westrem with eighteen aeroplanes. One Caudron pilot failed to return. This raid, which is reported to have done much damage, brought retaliation.

Soon after 10.0 p.m. on the 8th three or four aeroplanes bombed St. Pol, Furnes, and Petite Synthe but did no damage. Next night a more determined attack was made on Furnes. Thirty bombs fell from a low height on the hangars of No. I Belgian Squadron. The Dunkirk wings continued their bombing of the enemy aerodromes. They attacked St. Denis Westrem on the 17th and 21st, Ghistelles on the 9th and 23rd, and the aerodrome at Handzaeme on the 9th and 24th. Other bombing targets in September were the Lichtervelde ammunition dump, the Tirpitz and Hindenburg batteries, the airship sheds outside Brussels, and, for the seaplanes, the seaplane station at the Zeebrugge Mole.

The enemy weakly retaliated again in the afternoon of the 24th when a few bombs were dropped on Dunkirk, killing three people and wounding fourteen. The raiders were pursued back to their aerodrome, and one of them, an L.V.G. two-seater, was shot down in flames near Ghistelles by Flight Sub-Lieutenant S. J. Goble who, on his Sopwith Pup, had left his aerodrome two minutes after the bombs had fallen on Dunkirk.

Photographs of the Zeebrugge Mole, taken in the latter part of September, seemed to reveal an increasing number of seaplanes. Wing Captain Lambe in a letter to Admiral Bacon on the effect of the aerodrome bombing policy stated:

> It appears probable that the recent attacks on the enemy's aerodromes—which were undertaken with the object of forcing the enemy to withdraw machines from the battle-front—have so far failed, in so much, that little activity has been noticed as regards their land machines. It appears probable, however, that the enemy are concentrating a large force of seaplanes with the idea of retaliation, since that type of machine could be better spared, and during the next spell of fine weather bomb attacks may be expected on the S.E. coast of England, on the monitors on patrol, and possibly also on Dunkirk.

A further attempt by the Dover Patrol to help the Somme operations in the middle of September took the form of a demonstration against the Belgian coast. This had been suggested by Sir Douglas Haig, and it was staged by Admiral Bacon with characteristic thoroughness. A multitude of trawlers were anchored between Dunkirk and La Panne within sight of the enemy; troops and field guns were embarked in monitors at Dunkirk, and there were many other devices to induce the enemy to believe that a landing on the coast was contemplated. Between the 8th and 15th of September the coast was bombarded between Middelkerke and Westende.

Before the firing opened the eyes of the Tirpitz battery were put out. Flight Sub-Lieutenant C. R. Mackenzie, on a Nieuport, on the 7th of September shot down the Tirpitz balloon in flames. Some night spotting was attempted with moderate success on the 8th of September, but thence afterwards, until the 15th, the weather was too bad for air work and the monitors fired without air observation. The bombardment ended on September the 15th, the day the attack was renewed on the Somme.

On September the 24th the *Terror* bombarded Zeebrugge. Seaplanes from the *Riviera* attempted to observe for the monitor, but the visibility was too poor for useful spotting. A patrol of fighting seaplanes from Dunkirk was maintained over the ships throughout the day. After this bombardment the patrol of the mine-net barrage was abandoned owing to the impossibility of keeping the nets in order in the heavy winter seas.

As foreshadowed in Wing Captain Lambe's letter to Admiral Bacon most of the air encounters over the Belgian Coast were with enemy seaplanes from the end of September. Of the eight enemy aircraft destroyed in this area by Dunkirk pilots between the 24th of September and the 23rd of October, six were seaplanes, which did not, in any case, put up much of a fight against the Sopwith Pups or Nieuport Scouts which were responsible for their destruction. One of these seaplanes, shot down in the afternoon of the 22nd of October off Blankenberghe by Flight Sub-Lieutenant D. M. B. Galbraith, was probably the same machine as had reconnoitred the Thames Estuary earlier in the afternoon.

As an instance of the handiness of the small fighting aeroplane as compared with the heavy seaplane, a combat on the 20th of October may be quoted. Flight Lieutenant G. V. Leather, on a Nieuport, was flying off Ostend at 14,000 feet, when he saw a few thousand feet below a twin-engine enemy seaplane. He dived and shot before the enemy observer could effectively reply. The seaplane pilot then made for Ostend, dropping steeply, but Flight Lieutenant Leather had no difficulty in keeping close up until he was in position to attack the pilot. A short burst killed or wounded the pilot, and the seaplane then side-slipped sharply into the sea leaving only wreckage on the surface. The Nieuport received no hits.

On the morning of this encounter the Dominion gun again fired a few rounds, with air observation, at the Tirpitz battery, and this induced the German battery commander to send up his balloon. This could be plainly discerned on the sky-line from the advanced aerodrome at Furnes, and Flight Lieutenant E. W. Norton, on a Nieuport, armed with Le Prieur rockets, left to attack it. Fifty minutes later those who were watching the distant balloon from the aerodrome saw it suddenly burst into flames and fall to earth. The Nieuport pilot returned safely.

It was at this time that the fighting strength of the Dunkirk wings was drawn upon to equip a squadron of eighteen aeroplanes for duty with the Royal Flying Corps on the Somme. The Squadron—known as No. 8 Naval—was made up of some of the most experienced fighting pilots in the Naval Air Service, and placed under Squadron Commander G. R. Bromet who had been in charge of the air station at Dover. One complete flight of Sopwith 'Pups' was supplied by No.1 Wing, one of Nieuport fighters by No. 4 Wing, and one of Sopwith two-seaters by No. 5 Wing. The squadron went to Vert Galand aerodrome to take up its new duties at the end of October.

There it was soon to prove that the 'Pup' was equal in performance to the best of the new German fighters. So outstanding, indeed, were the fighting qualities of the 'Pups' that it was agreed between General Trenchard and Wing Captain Lambe that they should replace the Sopwith two-seaters. This was done on the 16th of November. Gradually, also, they replaced the Nieuports, and by the end of the year the squadron was completely equipped with 'Pups.'

******

To get the 'Pups' Wing Captain Lambe had to undertake to supply the 80 horse-power Le Rhone engines. This he did by taking them out of crashed Nieuports. A few he begged from the French naval air service. The engines, after being thoroughly overhauled in the Dunkirk depot, were taken across to Dover where they were fitted in the 'Pups'.

******

It was kept up to strength in pilots and material through the Naval Air Service at Dunkirk. The squadron had a remarkable record over the Somme area; down to the end of December 1916 it destroyed twenty-four enemy aeroplanes, of which twenty fell to the 'Pups' and four to the Nieuport fighters. Its own loss was two pilots killed.

We have already seen how, on the 24th of October, Admiral Scheer sent destroyer reinforcements to Zeebrugge to make raids in the Dover Straits area in connexion with the reopened submarine campaign. For some days the weather along the coast was unfavourable for reconnaissance. On the 1st of November, however, the clouds lifted, and observers saw destroyers moored at Ostend and a collection of barges at various points along the canals as well as in Ostend and Zeebrugge harbours. The weather continued unsettled, but in fair intervals up to the 9th it was seen that the destroyers were still active at Ostend.

Wing Captain Lambe had got permission to reopen the bombing offensive on the 9th of November when the moon would be favourable for night flying. Six Short seaplanes were sent out at intervals from 6.42 p.m. on the 9th to bomb Ostend and Zeebrugge. One failed to return, and the pilot was later reported a prisoner. Another pilot with engine trouble landed near Nieuport. He was adrift on the sea for eight hours, and as soon as it was light on the morning of the loth was repeatedly attacked by an enemy seaplane. The craft was many times hit, but the pilot was untouched. The seaplane was towed back to Dunkirk by a French patrol boat. The remaining four Shorts dropped one 500-lb. and nine 65-lb. bombs in the neighbourhood of the docks at Ostend, and eighteen 65-lb. bombs about the Zeebrugge Mole.

Before dawn on the 10th the aeroplanes took up the attack. Nineteen bombers of Nos. 4 and 5 Wings dropped seventy-five le Pecq, thirty-nine 65-lb. and thirty-four 16-lb. bombs on Ostend. In the afternoon of Sunday, the 12th, the docks at Ostend were raided again by ten bombers of No. 5 Wing. A fog drifted in from the sea after the aeroplanes had started and the pilots had to search for their target from 150 feet above. Forty-four 16-lb. and thirty-one le Pecq bombs were dropped, with apparently good effect, on the Ateliers de la Marine dockyard. All the pilots got back safely, including one who was forced to land on the sea off Calais: his aeroplane was brought in undamaged by a French trawler.

The next raid, made on the 15th, took place in ideal weather conditions. The attack was opened by two Short seaplanes which bombed Ostend and Zeebrugge before daylight, and was followed by a raid of twenty-two aeroplanes of Nos. 4 and 5 Wings on Ostend. The objectives were the Ateliers de la Marine and the Slyken Electric Power Station, at which eighty le Pecq, sixty-nine 65-lb. and fifty-three 16-lb. bombs were aimed. A fire caused by one of the bombs is reported to have lighted up the whole town, and direct hits were claimed on the Ateliers de la Marine, but none on the power station. On this raid four bombing aeroplanes of a new type were used for the first time. They were Shorts (250 horsepower Rolls Royce engines) which had been designed to carry bombs to a total weight of about 900 lbs. In the raid of the 15th each Short, however, carried eight 65-lb. bombs, twice the weight carried by the Caudrons on the same raid.

During a seaplane patrol along the buoyed line off the coast on the morning of the 16th of November, Flight Sub-Lieutenant R. Graham was forced by engine trouble to alight on the sea at 8.30 a.m. One of the floats, damaged by a heavy wave on landing, sprung a leak, and the Sopwith seaplane turned upside down. The pilot released his pigeon which had been nearly drowned, but it did not reach its loft. A search patrol went out at 11.0 a.m. to look for the missing seaplane, and, at 12.45 p.m., Flight Sub-Lieutenant J. H. Woolner found it with only the bottoms of the main floats above water: on one of these the pilot was sitting. He had indeed been washed off his precarious seat many times.

Flight Sub-Lieutenant Woolner landed, on his Short, and made many attempts, all unsuccessful, to take the marooned pilot off. At last Graham tried to swim across to the Short, but the sea was turbulent and he could not reach it. Furthermore, the Short pilot completely lost sight of him in the broken water and was compelled to get into the air again to make a search. He sighted Graham once more and landed near enough to pick him up. By this time, he was utterly exhausted, having been awash in the icy winter sea for nearly five hours. The Short pilot, with his extra load, found he could not again get off the choppy water. At 2.15 p.m. he released a pigeon with a message which read:

Have picked G. up and am now 12 miles N.E. of Nieuport taxying N.W.

The pigeon flew into Dunkirk an hour later. A French torpedo-boat went to the rescue and brought the Short seaplane back to harbour.

One effect of the renewed bombing offensive was a further increase in the volume and accuracy of the antiaircraft fire, and the next attack, made before dawn on the 17th of November, once again in perfect weather, was met by heavier gunfire than any hitherto encountered. Twenty aeroplanes took part and dropped eighty-one le Pecq, twenty-four 100-lb., eighteen 65-lb. and forty-eight 16-lb. bombs on the same objectives as were attacked on the 15th. Once again, many hits were reported on the Ateliers de la Marine, but again the power station escaped. A bomb which fell in one of the workshops at the former objective started a fire which lighted up the windows and gaping roof for some time afterwards. Two of the Short bombers, picked out by searchlights, were hit by antiaircraft fire, but were both safely landed on the beach near the lines.

Two final raids, before the bombing offensive ceased on the 29th of November, were made, by day, on Zeebrugge. Three Sopwith pilots on the 22nd dropped thirty-four le Pecq bombs, some of which hit sheds on the Mole and a ship alongside. The last raid, made on the 28th, was hampered by thick clouds, and only two of the four Sopwith pilots reached Zeebrugge where they dropped twenty-three le Pecq bombs. So far as can be stated with certainty, the material damage inflicted by these day and night attacks on Ostend and Zeebrugge was of no great importance. Nevertheless, it would be wrong to conclude from this that they were of little military value. The fear of air attack had a cramping effect on the operations of the destroyers which had been sent to Zeebrugge specially to raid our sea communications. Admiral Scheer says, (*Germany's High Sea Fleet in the World War*):

> One difficulty connected with the sending out of large numbers of torpedo-boats from Zeebrugge was, that in order not to expose them to aerial bombardment, they were not allowed to lie by the Mole, but sent up to Bruges. This entailed very considerable delay, on account of the lock, for it took 2½ hours to get four torpedo-boats through.

THE LUXEUIL BOMBING WING.

The operations from France in 1916 carried out by the Royal Naval Air Service were not confined to the Dunkirk area. The question of long distance bombing raids against naval and military centres in German territory had been constantly before the Admiralty from the outbreak of the war. It was not, however, until the spring of 1916, with the production of the Sopwith 1½ Strutter and the Short Bomber aeroplanes, that steps could be taken to put the policy of systematic raiding into Germany into effect. It was anticipated that enough aeroplanes and trained personnel would be ready for the bombing to begin in the early summer, and it was arranged with the French authorities that the bombers should work from an aerodrome at Luxeuil in the Nancy area, whence many great German munition and industrial centres were accessible.

Captain W. L. Elder, R.N., was sent to France at the beginning of May to make arrangements for the reception of the new bombing unit, to be known as No. 3 Wing; it was hoped that by the 1st of July the wing would be equipped with thirty-five bombing aeroplanes (twenty Sopwith Strutters and fifteen 250 horse-power Shorts) and also with twenty Sopwith Strutter Fighters. (The original No. 3 Wing had been disbanded towards the end of the Dardanelles Campaign in December 1915). It was further intended that the strength of the wing should be gradually increased to a maximum of one hundred aeroplanes.

The preparations were well in hand when an urgent plea came

from General Trenchard. Owing in part to the failure of the French manufacturers to fulfil their engine contracts, and in part, also, to difficulties of supply at home, the Royal Flying Corps at the front had to face a serious deficiency. They were in fact short, by no less than twelve squadrons, of the number estimated to be necessary to maintain effective co-operation with the army in the forthcoming operations on the Somme. General Henderson viewed the situation with some anxiety. He considered that a minimum reinforcement of four fighting squadrons or seventy-two aeroplanes was essential.

Only twelve aeroplanes of adequate performance could be detached from all the Flying Corps units at home, and help was therefore sought from naval air resources. The Admiralty could only respond at the expense of their new bombing wing. Anxious as they were to strike a blow at German munition centres, they realised the urgency of the Flying Corps demands and agreed to hand over at once a number of Sopwith two-seaters: by the middle of September 1916 they had transferred no less than sixty-two of this type.

In the result No. 3 Wing was not equipped with a sufficient number of aeroplanes to make bombing on a large scale possible until October, and thence down to the end of the year the weather seriously curtailed operations. (The number of aeroplanes in the wing ready for service was twenty-two at the end of August; by the end of December the number had increased to forty-seven). There had been a raid on the 30th of July on the Benzine stores at Mülheim in which three of the naval aeroplanes from Luxeuil co-operated with six French aeroplanes, but the first big raid did not take place until the 12th of October when the Mauser factory at Oberndorf came under attack. Fifteen naval bombers and six fighters and sixteen French bombers and numerous fighters took part. The formations were attacked by enemy fighters out and home, and six French and three British aeroplanes were lost: the enemy disclaims any casualties to his own fighters.

On the 23rd of October the Thyssen Works at Hagendingen were visited by thirteen naval bombers escorted by seven fighters: direct hits on the blast furnaces were reported. On the 10th of November the steel works at Volklingen were raided by nine bombers, and on the following day by fourteen bombers. The escorts reported considerable fighting on both occasions, but there were no British losses. On the 12th of November the blast furnaces at St. Ingbert were attacked. The last two raids of the year were made on the iron works at Dillingen on the 24th of November and the 27th of December; nine bombers reached the target on each raid and reported many direct hits. In a fight during the first attack one German biplane was shot to pieces in the air. All our own aeroplanes returned undamaged.

Something of the diversity of the work of the Royal Naval Air Service has been told. When war came a limited patrol of the important areas off the East Coast, and of the Straits of Dover for the safeguarding of the passage of the expeditionary force, had sufficed to use up the available resources of the service. The reader has seen how, during the next two and a half years, the navy developed airships, balloons, balloon ships, aeroplanes, seaplanes, aircraft carriers, armoured cars, and armoured trains, each bringing its own problems of design, supply, and organisation.

The early doings of these services in the Dardanelles, in home waters, and in France have been told. Much is yet to tell. Wherever on the wide seas ships of the navy operated came calls for the help of aircraft. Over the Turkish and Bulgarian seaboards, the desert fringes of the Red Sea and of the Persian Gulf, the swamps of the Rufiji delta, and over the beleaguered garrison of Kut-el-Amara, naval aircraft played their part. As the submarine war spread through the Mediterranean, the demands for aircraft to keep watch over the vital sections of our long lines of communication became almost insatiable.

Overshadowing all these responsibilities was the menace of the air attacks against Great Britain, which, until February 1916, the Admiralty had to meet. These happenings must be related later in this history. It was inevitable that whilst the vast organisation was being built up, there should at times be failures. These have been no less frankly stated than the successes. Those who are minded to draw conclusions from what has already been written should remember that the tale is not yet told.

Appendix 1

ORDER OF BATTLE OF THE ROYAL FLYING CORPS

General Officer Commanding: Major-Genera

St. Omer (Advanced Headqua

First Wing.
(Lieut.-Col. H. M. Trenchard, C.B., D.S.O.).
Aire (Advanced Headquarters: Merville).

No. 2 Squadron.	No. 3 Squadron.	No. 16 Squadron.
(Major T. I. Webb-Bowen).	(Major J. M. Salmond, D.S.O.).	(Major F. V. Holt, D.S.O.).
Merville.	Chocques.	La Gorgue.
7 B.E. 2.	9 Morane Parasol.	2 Voisin.
5 B.E. 2c.	3 Blériot.	1 Vickers Fighter.
2 Maurice Farman.	1 Avro.	1 Blériot.
	1 S.E. 2.	4 B.E. 2c.

Special First Wing Grouping for the Battle.

Group.	Landing Ground.	Aeroplanes.	Working With.
A (Capt. H. C. T. Dowding)	Merville.	4 (Wireless)	'N' Group Artillery.
C (Capt. R. B. Martyn)	Merville.	8 (6 Lamp Artillery) (2 Tactical)	IV Corps.
D (Major F. V. Holt, D.S.O.)	Merville.	4 (Tactical)	First Army H.Q.
B (Capt. D. S. Lewis, D.S.O.)	Hinges and Chocques.	4 (Wireless)	'S' Group Artillery.
E (Major J. M. Salmond, D.S.O.)	Chocques.	10 (4 Lamp Artillery) (4 Tactical) (2 Reserve)	I Corps and Indian Corps.
F (Capt. A. B. Burdett)	Aire.	6 (Reserve)	Bombing duties.

Total Strength: 7 Squadrons and 1 Flight of
85 Aeroplanes (additional at A

THE 10th MARCH 1915 (NEUVE CHAPELLE)

D. Henderson, K.C.B., D.S.O.

rs : HAZEBROUCK).

Second Wing.
t.-Col. C. J. Burke, D.S.O.).
HAZEBROUCK.

Third Wing.
(Lieut.-Col. H. R. M. Brooke-Popham).
ST. OMER.

Squadron.	No. 6 Squadron.	No. 1 Squadron.	No. 4 Squadron.
A. C. H. Lean).	(Major G. S. Shephard).	(Major W. G. H. Salmond).	(Major C. A. H. Longcroft).
LEUL.	POPERINGHE.	ST. OMER.	ST. OMER.
ot.	7 B.E. 2.	4 B.E. 8.	*(less flight attached to Second Wing).*
tinsyde	4 B.E. 2c.	8 Avro.	
ut.			
i Farman.			6 B.E. 2.
arily			1 Martinsyde Scout.
d from			
Ving).			
at of			
quadron			
Voisin.			

No. 9 *Squadron.*
(*Hq. and 'C' Flight only*).
(Capt. H. C. T. Dowding).
ST. OMER.
5 Maurice Farman
(2 working with First Wing 'A'
Group).

The Aircraft Park (Major W. D. Beatty).
Advanced Echelon : ST. OMER. *Port Echelon* : ROUEN.

9 Squadron.
ft Park, 18, including unserviceable).

Appendix 2

ORDER OF BATTLE OF THE ROYAL FLYING
General Officer Commanding: Major-G
St. Omer (Advanced H

First Wing.				Secon
(Lieut.-Col. H. M. Trenchard, C.B., D.S.O.).				(Lieut.-Col. C
Aire (Advanced Headquarters: Merville).				Steenvoorde (Adv
				Pope

No. 2 Sqdn.	No. 3 Sqdn.	No. 16 Sqdn.	No. 5 Sqdn.	No. 6 S
(Major T. I. Webb-Bowen).	(Major D. S. Lewis, D.S.O.).	(Major F. V. Holt, D.S.O.).	(Major A. G. Board).	(Major Shepha
Merville.	Choсques.	La Gorgue. (less Flt. at Aire).	Abeele.	Abeel
3 B.E. 2a.	1 Blériot.	1 B.E. 2a.	6 Avro.	5 B.E
4 B.E. 2b.	13 Morane	3 B.E. 2c.	5 Vickers	5 B.E
5 B.E. 2c.	Parasol.	3 Voisin.	Fighter.	1 Ma
		4 Maurice Farman.	1 Martinsyde Scout.	Sco

First Wing Allocation of Aeroplanes for the Battle.

Squadron.	Aeroplanes.	Working with.
2	2 Tactical	IV Corps.
	4 Wireless	Second Group H.A.R.
	4 Lamp	C.R.A. 7th and 8th Divisions.
	2 Reserve	
3	2 Tactical	I and Indian Corps.
	2 Wireless	I Corps.
	2 Lamp	Indian Corps.
	2 Wireless (plus one from No. 16 Sqdn.)	No. 1 Group H.A.R.
	2 Lamp	2nd Division.
	2 Tactical	Reserve.
16	3 Wireless (tactical)	First Army.
	4 (Not Wireless) Tactical	First Army.
	1 Wireless	Attached No. 3 Squadron.
	4 Bombing	As ordered.

Total Strength: 9 Squadrons.
103 Aeroplanes (addit
1 French Kite Balle
1 R.N.A.S. Balloon.

...RPS ON THE 9th MAY 1915 (AUBERS RIDGE)
...eral Sir D. Henderson, K.C.B., D.S.O.
...quarters: HAZEBROUCK).

...ing.
Burke, D.S.O.).
ed Headquarters:
RE).

Third Wing.
(Lieut.-Col. H. R. M. Brooke-Popham)—
(Major C. A. H. Longcroft temporarily in
Command 1.5.15–23.5.15).
ST. OMER.

No. 8 Sqdn.	No. 1 Sqdn.	No. 4 Sqdn.	No. 7 Sqdn.
(Major L. E. O. Charlton, D.S.O.).	(Maj. W. G. H. Salmond).	(Maj. C. A. H. Longcroft).	(Major C. G. Hoare).
ABEELE.	BAILLEUL.	BAILLEUL.	ST. OMER (less Flt. at BOULOGNE).
6 B.E. 2c.	2 B.E. 8.	6 B.E. 2.	7 R.E. 5.
	2 Avro.	2 B.E. 2c.	4 Voisin.
	3 Morane Parasol.	3 Voisin.	
	4 Caudron.	2 Caudron.	
	1 Martinsyde Scout.	1 Bristol Scout.	

Balloons: No. 2 Kite Balloon Section, R.N.A.S.
(Major Hon. C. M. P. Brabazon),
arrived from England 8th of May but
took no part in the battle.
Temporarily attached to I Corps, one
French Kite Balloon Section (40e Compagnie d'Aérostiers), with one Balloon.

1st *Aircraft Park* (Major H. R. P. Reynolds).
Advanced Echelon: ST. OMER. *Base Echelon:* ROUEN.

at Aircraft Park, 37, including unserviceable).
ttached.

Appendix 3

ORDER OF BATTLE OF THE ROYAL FLY[ING CORPS]
General Officer Commanding: Brigadier-Gen[eral ...]

St. O[mer]
No. 12 S[qdn.]
(Major C. L. [...])

St. [...]
11 B.E. 2c, 1 B.E. 2b, 1 Voisin, 1 [...]

First Wing.
(Lieut.-Col. E. B. Ashmore, M.V.O.)
AIRE (Advanced Headquarters: HINGES).

CASSEL (Ad[...])

No. 2 Sqdn. (Maj. J. H. W. Becke). HESDIGNEUL.	No. 3 Sqdn. (Maj. D. S. Lewis, D.S.O.). LOZINGHEM (AUCHEL).	No. 10 Sqdn. (Maj. U. J. D. Bourke). CHOCQUES). OBLINGHEM	No. 16 Sqdn. (Maj. H. C. T. Dowding). LA GORGUE.	No. 6 Kite Balloon Section. R.N.A.S. (Flt. Lt. Hon. A. S. Byng). South of LESTREM.	No. 8 Kite Balloon Section. R.N.A.S. (Flt. Lt. J. Ogilvie Davis). South-west of BETHUNE.	No. 1 Sqdn. (Maj. P. B. Joubert de la Ferté). BAILLEUL.	No. 5 Sqdn. (Maj. A. G. Board). ABEELE.
12 B.E. 2c. 1 Bristol Scout.	13 Morane Parasol. 1 Morane Scout.	12 B.E. 2c. 1 Bristol Scout.	6 Maurice Farman. 7 B.E. 2c. 1 B.E. 9. 1 Bristol Scout.			4 Avro. 8 Morane Parasol. 1 Caudron.	3 Avro. 4 Vickers Fighter. 5 B.E. 2c. 1 Bristol Scout.

Special Allocation of Duties for the Battle.

Squadron.	Duty.
No. 10 (1 Flight)	Strategical reconnaissance First Army Hqrs.
No. 10 (2 Flights)	Artillery co-operation with Indian Corps and part of No. 4 Group H.A.R.[1]
No. 16 (1 Flight)	Tactical reconnaissance Army front.[1]
No. 16 (2 Flights)	Artillery co-operation III Corps and with remainder No. 4 Group H.A.R.[1]
No. 2	Artillery co-operation IV Corps and part of No. 1 Group H.A.R.[1]
No. 3	Artillery co-operation I Corps (including No. 5 Group H.A.R.) and with remainder of No. 1 Group H.A.R.[1]

[[1] All co-operating aeroplanes fitted with wireless.]

No. 6 Kite Balloon Section 4 Group H.A.R. and Artillery of Indian Corps and III Corps.
No. 8 Kite Balloon Section 1 Group H.A.R. and Artillery of IV and I Corps.

Total Strength: 12 Squadrons.
161 Aeroplanes (additional wi[th...])
4 Kite Balloon Sections, R.N[...]
4 Balloons.

418

G CORPS ON 25th SEPTEMBER 1915 (LOOS)
l H. M. Trenchard, C.B., D.S.O., A.D.C.

ER.
adron
, Newall).

ER.
stol Scout, 1 Martinsyde Scout.

	Second Wing				Third Wing		
t.-Col. J. M. Salmond, D.S.O.).				(Lieut.-Col. W. S. Brancker).			
ced Headquarters: ABEELE, 25.9.15 only).				BEAUVAL (Advanced Headquarters: BLANGOUENE).			
No. 6 Sqdn.	No. 7 Sqdn.	No. 2 Kite Balloon Section. R.N.A.S. (Flt. Lt. W. F. Mac-Neece).	No. 4 Kite Balloon Section. R.N.A.S. (Flt. Lt. Hon. G. de St. C. Rollo).	No. 4 Sqdn. (Capt. H. Le M. Brock) (Acting). BATZEFUX.	No. 8 Sqdn. (Maj. A. C. H. MacLean). MARIEUX.	No. 11 Sqdn. (Maj. G. W. P. Dawes). VILLERS-BRETONNEUX.	
Maj. G. S. Shephard). ABEELE.	(Maj. C. G. Hoare). DROGLANDT.						
B.E. 2c. F.E. 2b. Bristol Scout.	8 B.E. 2c. 2 R.E. 5. 1 Bristol Scout.		STEENWERCK.	1 B.E. 2a. 2 B.E. 2b. 11 B.E. 2c. 1 Morane.	1 B.E. 2a. 1 B.E. 2b. 11 B.E. 2c. 2 Bristol Scout.	11 Vickers Fighter (less 1 Flight at Vert Galand providing protective patrols for First Wing).	

1st Aircraft Park: ST. OMER
(Major D. G. Conner).

3rd Aircraft Park: CANDAS
(Captain G. B. Hynes).

Base Echelon: PONT DE L'ARCHE, near ROUEN.

ircraft Parks, 40, of which 24 serviceable).
.S.

Appendix 4

ORDER OF BATTLE OF THE ROYAL FLYING CORPS ON 1st JULY 1916 (SOMME)

General Officer Commanding: Major-General H. M. Trenchard, C.B., D.S.O., A.D.C.

St. André-aux-Bois (Advanced Headquarters: Fienvillers).

Ninth (Hq.) Wing.
(Lt.-Col. H. C. T. Dowding).
Fienvillers.

- **No. 21 Squadron.** (Maj. J. R. Campbell-Heathcote).
  Fienvillers.
  14 R.E.7.
  4 B.E.2c.
  1 B.E.2e.

- **No. 27 Squadron.** (Maj. A. E. Borton, D.S.O.).
  Fienvillers.
  17 Martinsyde Scout.

- **No. 60 Squadron.** (Maj. F. F. Waldron).
  Vert Galand.
  4 Morane Biplane.
  9 Morane Scout.

- **No. 70 Squadron (two Flights).** (Maj. G. A. K. Lawrence, D.S.O.).
  Fienvillers.
  8 Sopwith two-seater.
  (4 of these did not arrive from the depot until 3rd July).

I BRIGADE.
(*Brigadier-General D. le G. Pitcher*).
Château Werppe, 1 m. N.E. of Chocques.

First (Corps) Wing.
(Lt.-Col. J. H. W. Becke).
Béthune.

- **No. 2 Squadron.** (Maj. R. A. Cooper).
  Hesdigneul.
  10 B.E.2c.
  8 B.E.2d.

- **No. 10 Squadron.** (Maj. W. G. S. Mitchell).
  Chocques.
  11 B.E.2c.
  1 B.E.2d.
  1 B.E.12.

- **No. 18 Squadron.** (Maj. G. I. Carmichael, D.S.O.).
  Bruay.
  12 F.E.2b.

- **No. 3 K.B. Squadron.** (Maj. P. K. Wise).
  Béthune.
  Nos. 8 and 10 K.B. Sections.

Tenth (Army) Wing.
(Lt.-Col. P. L. W. Herbert).
Norrent-Fontes.

- **No. 25 Squadron.** (Maj. R. G. Cherry).
  Lozinghem.
  17 F.E.2b.
  1 F.E.2c.

- **No. 32 Squadron.** (Maj. L. W. B. Rees).
  Treizennes.
  12 D.H.2.

First Army Aircraft Park (Maj. G. C. Ross-Munby)—Aire.

II BRIGADE.

(Brigadier-General T. I. Webb-Bowen).
OXELAERE.

Second (Corps) Wing.
(Lt.-Col. C. A. H. Longcroft).
ECKLE.

- **No. 1 Squadron.** (Maj. G. F. Pretyman, D.S.O.). BAILLEUL.
  - 8 Morane Parasol.
  - 5 Morane Biplane.
  - 2 Nieuport Scout.
  - 2 Nieuport 2-seater.
- **No. 5 Squadron.** (Maj. R. M. Vaughan). DROGLANDT.
  - 10 B.E.2c.
  - 2 B.E.2d.
- **No. 6 Squadron.** (Maj. R. P. Mills). ABEELE.
  - 11 B.E.2c.
  - 7 B.E.2d.
- **No. 7 Squadron.** (Maj. F. J. L. Cogan). BAILLEUL.
  - 8 B.E.2c.
  - 4 B.E.2d.
- **No. 16 Squadron.** (Maj. D. W. Powell). LA GORGUE.
  - 10 B.E.2c.
  - 2 B.E.2d.
- **No. 2 K.B. Squadron.** (Maj. W. F. MacNeece). MONT ROUGE.
  - Nos. 2 and 9 K.B. Sections.

Eleventh (Army) Wing.
(Lt.-Col. F. W. Richey).
NIEPPE.

- **No. 20 Squadron.** (Maj. G. J. Malcolm). CLAIRMARAIS.
  - 13 F.E.2d.
- **No. 29 Squadron.** (Maj. E. L. Conran). ABEELE.
  - 15 D.H.2.
  - 2 F.E.8.

Second Army Aircraft Park (Major D. G. Conner)—HAZEBROUCK.

III BRIGADE.

(Brigadier-General J. F. A. Higgins, D.S.O.).
CHÂTEAU DE SAINS.

Twelfth (Corps) Wing.
(Lt.-Col. G. S. Shephard).
AVESNES.

- **No. 8 Squadron.** (Maj. P. H. L. Playfair). BELLEVUE.
  - 14 B.E.2c.
  - 4 B.E.2d.
- **No. 12 Squadron.** (Maj. J. C. Halahan). AVESNES-LE-COMTE.
  - 14 B.E.2c.
- **No. 13 Squadron.** (Maj. E. W. Powell). SAVY.
  - 12 B.E.2c.
- **No. 4 K.B. Squadron.** (Maj. F. H. Cleaver). BARLY.
  - Nos. 5 and 7 K.B. Sections.

Thirteenth (Army) Wing.
(Lt.-Col. C. F. de S. Murphy).
FOUFFLIN-RICAMETZ.

- **No. 11 Squadron.** (Maj. T. O'B. Hubbard). SAVY.
  - 8 F.E.2b.
  - 4 Vickers Fighter.
  - 3 Bristol Scout.
  - 3 Nieuport Scout.
- **No. 23 Squadron.** (Maj. A. Ross-Hume). LE HAMEAU.
  - 14 F.E.2b.
  - 3 Martinsyde Scout.

Third Army Aircraft Park (Major F. H. Kirby, V.C.)—FRÉVENT.

IV BRIGADE.

(*Brigadier-General E. B. Ashmore, C.M.G., M.V.O.*)
Les Alençons.

Third (Corps) Wing.
(Lt.-Col. E. R. Ludlow-Hewitt, M.C.).
Bertangles.

Fourteenth (Army) Wing.
(Lt.-Col. C. G. Hoare).
Bertangles.

No. 3 Squadron.
(Maj. H. D. Harvey-Kelly, D.S.O.).
Lahoussoye.
12 Morane Parasol.
4 Morane Biplane.

No. 4 Squadron.
(Maj. T. W. C. Carthew, D.S.O.).
Baizieux.
17 B.E.2c.
1 B.E.2d.

No. 9 Squadron.
(Maj. A. B. Burdett).
Allonville.
18 B.E.2c.

No. 15 Squadron.
(Maj. H. le M. Brock, D.S.O.).
Marieux.
16 B.E.2c.

No. 1 K.B. Squadron.
(Maj. C. Bovill).
Contay.
Nos. 1, 3, 11, 12 & 14 K.B. Sections. Additional Balloon specially attached for tactical duty: 4, 6, and 13 K.B. Sections (Major H. R. Hunt).

No. 22 Squadron.
(Maj. R. B. Martyn).
Bertangles.
18 F.E.2b.

No. 24 Squadron.
(Maj. L. G. Hawker, V.C., D.S.O.).
Bertangles.
19 D.H.2.
3 Bristol Scout.[1]
2 Morane Scout.[1]

[1] Attached from the squadrons of Third (Corps) Wing.

Fourth Army Aircraft Park (Major A. Fletcher)—Beauval.

Engine Repair Shops (Maj. G. B. Hynes)—Pont de l'Arche, Rouen.

R.F.C. Port Depot (2nd Lieut. J. M. Patten)—Boulogne.

Strength: 27 Squadrons.
421 Aeroplanes.
(Additional 216 Aeroplanes at Aircraft Depots.)
4 Kite Balloon Squadrons.
14 Balloons.

No. 1 *Aircraft Depot* (Maj. A. Huggins)—St. Omer (127 aeroplanes, including unserviceable).

No. 2 *Aircraft Depot* (Maj. R. C. Donaldson-Hudson)—Candas (89 aeroplanes, including unserviceable).

Appendix 5

ARRIVAL OF AIR UNITS FROM ENGLAND DURING THE BATTLES OF THE SOMME, 1916

A. AEROPLANE SQUADRONS.

Squadron.	Aeroplanes.	Aerodrome.	Date of Arrival at Aerodrome.	Allotment.
No. 34 (Major J. A. Chamier)	18 B.E. 2e.	Allonville	15th July	3rd Wing (IV Brigade)
No. 19 (Major R. M. Rodwell)	18 B.E. 12.	Fienvillers	1st August	9th Wing
No. 40 (Major R. Loraine)	12 F.E. 8.	Treizennes	'A' Flt., 2nd August 'B' & 'C' Flts., 25th August	10th Wing (I Brigade)
No. 42 (Major J. L. Kinnear)	8 B.E. 2d. 10 B.E. 2e.	Bailleul	15th/16th August	2nd Wing (II Brigade)
No. 45 (Major W. R. Read)	12 Sopwith two-seater.	Fienvillers	15th October	9th Wing
No. 41 (Major J. H. A. Landon)	17 F.E. 8.	Abeele	21st October	11th Wing (II Brigade)
No. 46 (Major P. Babington)	12 Nieuport two-seater.	Droglandt	26th October	2nd Wing (II Brigade)
From Dunkirk: No. 8 (R.N.A.S.) Sqdn.-Commdr. G. R. Bromet.	6 Sopwith two-seater. 6 Sopwith single-seater. 6 Nieuport single-seater.	Vert Galand	26th October	22nd Wing (V Brigade)

B. KITE BALLOON SECTIONS.

Section.	Allotment.	Date of Allotment.
No. 14	III Brigade (No. 4 K.B. Squadron, 12th Wing)	12th July 1916
No. 15	II Brigade (No. 2 K.B. Squadron, 2nd Wing)	13th July 1916
No. 18	V Brigade (No. 5 K.B. Squadron, 15th Wing)	8th September 1916
No. 19	I Brigade (No. 3 K.B. Squadron, 1st Wing)	27th September 1916
No. 20	I Brigade (No. 3 K.B. Squadron, 1st Wing)	27th September 1916
No. 21	III Brigade (No. 4 K.B. Squadron, 12th Wing)	26th October 1916
No. 22	V Brigade (No. 5 K.B. Squadron, 15th Wing)	26th October 1916
No. 23	II Brigade (No. 2 K.B. Squadron, 2nd Wing)	26th October 1916

Appendix 6

SOME NOTES ON BOMBING ATTACKS (DECEMBER 1915)

Considerable experience has now been gained in the methods of carrying out bombing attacks. The experience so gained is insufficient to lay down any hard and fast rules as to the system to be adopted, and probably it is undesirable to do so.

The following notes are issued primarily with a view to circulating information of what has been done; and secondly, to obtaining suggestions which may be of assistance in shaping future policy.

METHODS OF ATTACK

1. The 'go-as-you-please' methods have been abandoned definitely, both by the French and by ourselves, in favour of attacks carried out by swarms of aeroplanes. It is now an accepted principle that attacks on all important objectives should be carried out by as many aeroplanes as possible, all the aeroplanes flying together and reaching the objective together.

This method is calculated to give A.A. guns the least possible chance of effect, and to render attack by hostile aircraft most difficult. Large intervals between aeroplanes are to be avoided as presenting a target to A.A. guns for a greater length of time.

Attacks on trains in motion appear to be the single exception to the swarm formation. Against this form of target, continuous bombardment by small detachments of aeroplanes is necessary. This practice was certainly most effective during the operations at the end of September.

The enemy's traffic was considerably disorganised, four or five trains were cut, and the line damaged in many places. Casualties to personnel in the trains is also reported by agents—in one instance a train being cut in half and forty soldiers killed.

Height

2. All machines flying in line ahead at the same height is a formation above all to be avoided, as being the most vulnerable against attack by A.A. guns.

The French fly at varying heights, and this undoubtedly increases the difficulties of the A.A. gunner. Varying heights of 6,000 feet and over have proved satisfactory. The chances of one aeroplane bombing another are so small as to be negligible.

Rendezvous

3. Alternative methods are:

(a) All the aeroplanes of all squadrons taking part are instructed to rendezvous over a given spot at a given hour.

(b) The aeroplanes of each squadron taking part are given a separate rendezvous equidistant from the objective, and are ordered to start at a given time.

The former method is adopted by the French. Both methods have been tried in the III Wing. In the attack on Hardily on the 14th December (b) method was tried. The squadrons reached the objective in rapid succession, not absolutely together as was intended. The system requires careful planning and synchronisation of watches.

The rendezvous must invariably be selected well behind the lines, out of view from the enemy.

Leadership

4. French method.—The Group Commander is the first to leave the ground, and he leads throughout the raid. His aeroplane is distinguished by the tricolour rosette on the sides and front of the nacelle and by metal pennants on the rear centre struts. The escadrille commanders also take part and usually follow the Group Commander. As soon as all aeroplanes have arrived at the rendezvous the Group Commander fires a succession of Very lights and leads off towards the objective well throttled down. The rest close in, keeping as close as is practicable.

For short-distance raids it would seem sufficient for the leader to give the signal for the start, on seeing which the aeroplanes move as fast as possible along a predetermined route on to the objective without further reference to the leader. The homogeneity of the aeroplanes would ensure their arrival over the objective approximately together.

For raids of longer duration, the leader should lead throughout, flying at the pace of the slowest machine, and displaying some easily seen distinguishing signal.

Aeroplanes should make the return journey in the same close formation. They must not disperse.

THE ATTACK

5. The French attack down wind. It is probably considered that any errors in estimating the direction of the wind have less effect when an aeroplane is flying down wind than when running into it.

A down wind attack has been tried only once—by the III Wing in their attack against Hervilly aerodrome on the 14th December. The majority of the bombs fell short, but this was probably due to the wind dropping between the time at which sights were set and the attack, two hours having elapsed.

It must be borne in mind that in attacking down wind any slight error in releasing the bombs is greatly magnified owing to the increased speed of the aeroplane. If, however, the practice of attacking down wind is to become general, constant practice by pilots over the camera obscura should obviate the difficulty.

A down wind attack has the advantage of reducing the time during which a target is presented to the A.A. guns.

6. The fact that fighting machines are cruising between the bombing machines and known hostile aerodromes gives confidence to the pilots. The area between the bombing machines and the lines will, as a rule, require careful patrolling.

The bombing machines must be adequately protected. It has been suggested that, if sufficient fighting machines are patrolling the area, and the objective is not more than 30 miles from the line, all the bombing machines should go single seater, and without further escort. For distances over 30 miles, two out of every ten aeroplanes should carry no bombs and be entrusted with escort duties only.

The French *avions de chasse*, when available, go out to meet returning bombing aeroplanes and protect possible stragglers. These latter must not be overlooked by escorting machines, and it would appear to be advisable for pilots in the bombing machines to occasionally look to stragglers.

When returning from a recent raid, one of the bombing machines, having fallen behind, was hard pressed by a German; the remaining pilots in the raid knew nothing of this till their return.

Armament

7. The general practice is for the pilot of a bombing machine to carry a machine-gun, a B.E.2c acting as escort, carrying two guns.

Bombs

8. The alternatives are two 112-lb. bombs or one 112-lb. bomb and six or eight 20-lb. bombs. Against every description of target the former appears to be the most effective.

Sights

9. The setting of sights before the aeroplanes leave the ground has been tried with success. The arrangement is for one aeroplane to fly over the camera obscura at the various heights at which it is proposed to drop the bombs. The ground speed can be read off with accuracy in the camera.

★★★★★★

(Author's note.)—A camera obscura was a light-excluded but with a convex lens of long focus mounted in the roof and directed vertically upwards. The aeroplane pilot flew in a straight line over the hut. An image of the sky was formed on a photographic plate at the focus of the lens. The plate was covered by a tray. This could be moved across the plate to keep the image of the aeroplane continuously over a small hole in the centre. The hole, in turn, was covered by a shutter opening electrically at regular time intervals. Thus, a series of photographs of the aeroplane in its path across the sky were obtained. From these could be calculated the course, height, and ground speed of the aeroplane as well as its horizontal distance from the camera at any moment. A later development projected the moving aeroplane across a sheet of paper fixed on a table in the hut. This enabled an immediate reading of its direction and ground speed to be made.

★★★★★★

The sight setting for any particular height is a function of the ground speed, and can be found by the following calculation:

Let t = the true time of fall *in vacuo* (not the corrected lag time), and let X = the ground speed in feet per second.

Then for a given height

$\dfrac{t \times 100}{X}$ is the setting on the sight.

$$t = \dfrac{h}{4} \text{ approximately.}$$

X should be found by taking, say, 10 second divisions on the paper of the camera obscura, measuring on the scale for height, and dividing by 10.

Camera obscura

10. The growing importance of bombing operations cannot be too fully impressed upon pilots. There are still pilots who belittle the importance. and utility of these operations. The results, both material and moral, of recent raids should be sufficient to convince all that well-conceived and thoroughly carried out bomb attacks may have far-reaching effects.

Skill in bomb-dropping can only be achieved by constant practice. Frequent use of the camera obscura should be made in order to ensure the attainment of that degree of skill which is essential to the success of the operation.

H.Q., R.F.C. (sgd) Evelyn B. Gordon, Major,
21st December, 1915. G.S.

Appendix 7

SOME NOTES ON THE GERMAN AIR SERVICE AT THE SOMME
(1916)
(Translated extracts from memoranda,
Archivrat im Reichsarchiv Potsdam).

1. ORGANISATION.

The organisation of the German Air Forces, as established in March 1915, continued practically unchanged until October 1916. Therefore, on 1st July 1916, a '*Feldflugchef*' (Chief of the Air Forces in the Field) was at the head of all the Field and Home Formations.

A. At the Front.

The units allocated to one Army (the number of units varied according to the prevailing tactical situation) were placed under the control, for discipline, &c., of the Staff Officer for Aviation of the Army concerned. He, for his part, was subordinate to the *Feldflugchef*. The Army Aviation Staff Officers were, therefore, liaison officers between the Supreme Command and the units at the front.

As regards tactical employment, some air units were under the direct control of Army H.Q., whilst others were at the disposal of Army Corps or Group H.Q.

Generally speaking, the employment of the units, which became more and more specialised, was as follows:

Immediately subordinate to the Army H.Q. were:

(1) A *Feldflieger-Abteilung* (Reconnaissance Flight).

(2) The *Kampfeinsitzer* (single-seater fighter) machines in the area of the Army.

(3) The *Kampfgeschwader* (bomber-fighter squadrons) detailed for bombing and for countering enemy aerial activity.

(4) An Army Aircraft Park, responsible for the supply of personnel and material to the air units of the whole Army.

In addition to dealing with all questions regarding reinforcements within the Army, the Aviation Staff Officer also arranged for the tactical employment of the air units immediately under the control of the Army according to the instructions of the Army Commander, to whom he acted merely as a tactical adviser.

As a rule, there were allocated to the Group, or Army Corps H.Q.:

(1) 1 *Feldflieger-Abteilung* (Reconnaissance Flight) for tactical reconnaissance within the limits of its sector.

(2) 1 *Artillerie-Flieger-Abteilung* (Artillery Flight).

The aviation units did not form part of the Army Corps or Division H.Q. establishments. A considerable number of the Reconnaissance Flights were 'permanent', that is to say, they always remained in the sector (on an average, one for each Corps or Group Sector and one for the Army Sector), being taken over by the relieving Corps in each case.

The distribution of units between the various Armies was arranged, according to the importance of the front held, by G.II.Q. through the *Feldflugchef*. Similarly, the air units in each Army were distributed by order of the Army Commander through his Aviation Staff Officer.

The above organisation underwent a change during the Battle of the Somme. Owing to the great number of air units that were gradually brought into the area, it became necessary to introduce an intermediate command between the Army Aviation Officer and the Flights. In the various Corps or Group areas, so-called *Fliegerleitungen* (Aviation Commands) were formed.

These were responsible for the employment of the air units attached to the Army Corps in consultation with the Corps Commander. These officers were subordinate to the Army Aviation Officer who, as tactical adviser to the Army Commander, continued to exercise a general influence on all questions of air warfare within the Army. Subsequently *Gruppenführer der Flieger* (Group Aviation Commanders) were substituted for the *Fliegerleitungen*.

The fundamental change in the distribution of the German Air Forces during the summer of 1916 was due to the fighting on the Somme. The prevailing principle on the Western Front after this battle was to concentrate as large an air strength as possible on every main battle front, even at the cost of leaving the lesser fronts denuded of aerial forces.

No extensive defensive measures were taken on the Somme to meet the attack that had been known to be in preparation for some time. It was only just before the commencement and during the early weeks of the Great Offensive that the concentration of powerful Air Force Units took place.

With the exception of the 'A' Army Detachment (Lorraine), which had only a small strength of air units, one or two *Flieger-Abteilungen* were withdrawn from all Armies on the Western Front during the period from 24th June to the middle of August. The 5th Army (Verdun), previous to this, had not had to give up any of these units to the German Armies on the Somme. It had, however, given up one complete *Kampfgeschwader* (six flights) and three *Kampfeinsitzer-Kommandos* (single-seater fighter H.Q.'s).

The greater part of the Air Force Units concentrated before Verdun at the beginning of the German offensive remained massed in this sector, in spite of the extremely difficult strategical situation that had arisen on the Somme, because it was the opinion at G.H.Q. that by continuing the offensive operations begun against Verdun, the German Armies on the Somme could most effectively and directly be relieved and supported.

On 29th August 1916 General von Falkenhayn retired from his position as Chief of the General Staff; his successor was General Field-Marshal von Hindenburg, who was assisted by General von Ludendorff, as Chief Quartermaster-General.

The new G.H.Q. ordered the immediate suspension of the Verdun offensive, and carried out a rigidly organised defensive on the Somme by concentrating all available forces. A vast reorganisation and expansion of the German Air Forces was begun; there was a relentless thinning of the air forces on all the lesser fronts, including the Verdun sector.

On 8th October 1916, by order of the new G.H.Q., a strictly centralized control of the German Air Force Units and of all aviation and antiaircraft material, at the front and at home, was established at the H.Q. of the General Commanding the Air Forces. General von Hoeppner was made responsible for the administration, and Colonel Thomsen, hitherto Chief of the Air Forces in the Field, was appointed Chief of Staff.

B. AT HOME.

At the head of the Home Units was an *Inspekteur der Fliegertruppen* (Inspector General of the Air Forces), who was immediately subordinate to the *Feldflugchef*.

The Inspector General had control of the *Flieger-Ersatz-Abteilungen* (Training Squadrons), which had to supply all material and personnel required at the front, and to organise the schools for flying personnel and other specialized branches, such as aerial photography and wireless.

All demands from Field and Home services were first dealt with by the Inspector General; they were then submitted for examination to the War Ministry and orders for their execution finally issued by the latter.

Training of different classes of personnel was carried out as follows:

(1) *Observers*, in observers' preparatory schools attached to the Training Squadrons, and observers' training schools which were immediately under the control of the Inspector.

(2) *Pilots*, in military and civil flying schools (the latter were attached to aircraft factories and were under military supervision).

In every training squadron final flying instruction was given to pupils who had passed out of the military or civil flying schools.

Aircraft, engines, and all spares, were supplied by private firms. Material and new types were tested by *Militär-Abnahme-Kommissionen* (Military Acceptance Commissions). There was no State Aircraft Factory.

C. BAVARIA.

Bavaria had a separate organisation: this State had its own 'Inspectorate of Military Aviation and Mechanical Transport' (*Inspektion des Militär-Luft- und Kraftfahrwesens*), to which the Bavarian *Flieger-Ersatz- und Ausbildungsformationen* (training and instruction units) were subordinate.

For tactical employment the Bavarian Field Units were subordinate to the *Feldflugchef*. Material was supplied partly by Prussia and partly by Bavaria. For discipline, the Field Units were subordinate only to the Bavarian Inspectorate. The system was extremely complicated. Consequently, as far as possible, the Bavarian aviation units were allocated to the Bavarian Armies.

2. Tactical Employment of Aircraft.
A. Co-operation with Infantry.

The severe defensive battles on the Somme in 1916 were of great importance in the further development of aerial tactics. The condition of aerial warfare on the Somme had shown that the principles of aerial tactics that had hitherto held good were no longer sufficient, and that the range of duties must be expanded.

Contact patrol had already been introduced by the Germans during the Verdun offensive; the results, however, had been by no means satisfactory. The German infantry, harassed by the enemy artillery fire, were unable adequately to signal changes in position of the front line by spreading white sheets. The necessary experience in the employment of this means of signalling and obtaining information was lacking both in the infantry and the Air Forces.

The Somme defence again demonstrated the great value of infantry contact work for troops and Commands. Already, at the commencement of the Somme battle, provisional instructions had been issued for the employment of contact machines. Towards the end of the battle these were consolidated in an order of the G.O.C. Air Forces.

The duties of the Infantry Contact Patrol airmen were:

(*a*) Identification of their own front line.
(*b*) Communication of information from the immediate fighting zone to the H.Q. Staffs in the rear.
(*c*) Continuous observation of the enemy zone of attack with the purpose of spotting at once any indications of an imminent hostile attack, and to communicate such information immediately to the artillery so that by means of concentrated annihilating fire the enemy preparations for attack might be destroyed in course of development.

It was stated in the G.O.C. Air Forces Order of 1st October 1916, that:

> The infantry contact airman is the most important means of obtaining and transmitting information (provided co-operation with the troops is good) during heavy fighting when, owing to increased enemy artillery activities, all communication between the Staff and the fighting units is cut off. Infantry, artillery and Commands will find the contact patrol to be an almost decisive factor for victory.

Development of the training of infantry airmen was expressly demanded by the Chief of the General Staff—contact patrols having soon gained the full recognition of the hard-pressed troops by their fearless co-operation.

Aeroplane observers were thoroughly trained in contact patrol duties at the home observers' schools, at the Army Aircraft Parks, and in the Reconnaissance Flights; infantry units in rest were systematically trained by means of practices and manoeuvres in co-operation with Air Force Units in offensive and defensive actions.

The results of this energetic training and instruction of the troops and Air Forces were seen during the defensive operations of 1917. Special units were not formed for infantry work. This duty was given to the ordinary Reconnaissance Flights.

During the battle of the Somme attempts were made with a special flashing apparatus (signalling lamp). In the majority of cases, however, the Morse signals made from the front line during an action were not carried out with sufficient care for the airmen to be able to understand them accurately. It was difficult also to sight the fast moving aeroplane. Finally, the troops in the front line were strongly against smoke and light signals because they attracted enemy artillery fire.

Experiments with light-signalling apparatus were therefore discontinued, and the use of signalling sheets was resumed.

The troops were also gradually better trained in this work, so that this method of communication between infantry and airmen proved generally satisfactory, particularly in the 1917 Flanders operations.

B. Artillery Co-operation.

The Battle of the Somme also showed the necessity of assisting the artillery by means of aerial observation more than had hitherto been done. In this respect the enemy had gained an unquestionable superiority, to which the success of his infantry at the beginning of the Somme battle was due. It was essential that when the next defensive action came this superiority should no longer be apparent. Special attention was therefore devoted to the training of the artillery airmen.

The G.O.C. Air Forces laid special stress upon the fact that ranging for the guns firing on targets lying beyond the possible ranges of observation from the ground and balloons was distinctly a duty for artillery airmen, as was also observation of barrage and destruction fire.

Wireless was the means of communication between the ground and the aircraft. Up to the battle of the Somme reception in aircraft had proved impossible, the firing battery communicating with the airmen by laying out sheets on the ground according to a code.

The experience gained on the Somme caused experiments with W/T reception in aeroplanes to be pursued with increasing energy. In October 1916 the G.O.C. Air Forces was able to state that the experiments to find a means of receiving, as well as transmitting, W/T signals from and to the ground, and also from and to other aeroplanes, had proved that the aircraft sets were perfectly suitable for service use. In the winter of 1916-17 the artillery aeroplanes were equipped with W/T sets for transmission and reception, whereby the efficiency of these units was very considerably increased.

C. FIGHTING.

The Germans first formed special squadrons for the purpose of bombing, the so-called *Brieftauben-Abteilungen* (carrier-pigeon detachments), namely 'O' (Ostend) in the late autumn of 1914, and Detachment 'M' (Metz) in the spring of 1915. The latter, however, was not intended solely for bombing; it was already realised that the activities might usefully be extended to include aerial combat. A particular reason for the formation was the necessity of warding off enemy bombing raids carried out against undefended South Germany by the enemy Air Forces concentrated in the Nancy-Luneville area in the spring of 1915.

Although the aeroplanes of that period were not of a type technically suitable for the purpose, this detachment was required to repulse enemy aeroplanes. As this could not be carried out by an offensive it had to be of a defensive character, that is, the machines were used for so-called *Sperrefliegen* (barrage-flights) to prevent the enemy from flying over the German lines.

More such squadrons were formed towards the end of 1915, the name being then changed to *Kampfgeschwader* (a *Kampfgeschwader* consisted of the squadron H.Q. and six Flights). Thus, theirs was a double duty, namely bombing and fighting, the second of which they were unable to carry out in the way hoped for.

It was thus soon recognised that for aerial fighting a light, fast, manoeuvrable aeroplane with good climb was essential, Fokker solved this problem in June 1915 by means of his well-known monoplane.

From the tactical point of view the question of air fighting remained obscure for some considerable time, since the Fokker machines were attached to the various units in small numbers only. Hence during the year 1915 individual fighting was the rule. It was only when the single-seater fighters were combined into the so-called *Kommandos* under Böelcke's leadership in the spring of 1916 that aerial combats were carried out in echelons or small groups.

The experience gained on the Somme also led to further improvements in the organisation and development of the *Kampfgeschwader*. These squadrons could not be effectively employed at the beginning of the Battle of the Somme, owing to the extremely difficult tactical situation in the air. The squadrons brought up to the Somme for the relief of the hard-worked reconnaissance and artillery flights, with their heavy two-seater C machines, were not suitable to attack the lighter and more manoeuvrable enemy aeroplanes. A rigid defensive, by means of patrols flying parallel to the front, had also proved ineffective, the patrol aeroplanes being unable to prevent the enemy squadrons from crossing the line. These squadrons thus were incapable of having much influence on the aerial war.

Further, the patrol and barrage duties of the *Kampf* squadrons prevented them from carrying out their proper duty of bombing. The importance of successful bombing was thoroughly recognised, but the conditions on the Somme made it necessary to desist from undertaking such attacks owing to the more pressing need for the protection of artillery aircraft. During the course of the battle, therefore, the *Kampf* squadrons were provisionally attached to the artillery flights for escort and protection. This provisional arrangement was subsequently confirmed, and four of the *Kampf* squadrons were split up into twenty-seven *Schutzstaffeln* (Protection Flights).

The G.O.C. Air Forces, however, opposed further efforts to dissolve the *Kampf* squadrons. In spite of the little opportunity for bombing offered to these squadrons in the battle of the Somme, the Germans remained firmly convinced of the great importance of methodical bombing.

A change in the air situation on the Somme was brought about by the introduction of *Jagdstaffeln* (Pursuit Squadrons). Hitherto there had been from one to four Fokker single-seater fighters allocated to the various reconnaissance flights in excess of their strength or, as at Verdun, these machines had been combined temporarily into special groups. This organisation, however, was not adequate to cope with the conditions prevailing on the Somme. A thorough reorganisation was undertaken; on the suggestion of the Chief of the Air Forces in the Field, Lieutenant-Colonel Thomsen, the existing single-seater fighters were grouped into *Jagdstaffeln* each consisting of fourteen aeroplanes. These new fighting units were formed as follows:

In August	*Jagdstaffeln*	1-7
In September	,,	8-15
In October	,,	16-24
In November	,,	25
In December	,,	26-33

The *Jagdstaffeln*, whose sole duty was fighting, were intended:

(1) To overcome the superiority of the enemy in the air on the Somme, and
(2) To make it possible at any time to counter-balance the constantly increasing numerical superiority of the enemy at least temporarily and on certain sectors of the front.

In G.O.C. the Air Forces Order of October 1916 the following statement is made:

The present system of aerial warfare has shown the inferiority of the isolated fighting aeroplane; dispersal of forces and a continuance of fights carried out when in a minority must be avoided by flying in large formations up to a whole *Jagdstaffel*. Fighting squadrons must be trained most carefully to operate in close formation as a single tactical unit, which is the manner in which they must carry out attacks. Each *Jagdstaffel* must have its own area and length of front.

As these fighting squadrons increased in number and their tactics developed their equipment in aeroplanes was also improved. The experiences gained on the Somme had taught that the Fokker monoplane E. type with rotary engines, which in the summer were still superior to those of the enemy, were now far inferior to the new enemy fighting aircraft, such as the single-seater Nieuport, F.E., and Sopwith biplanes, as regards speed and climb. The E. aeroplanes were therefore replaced from August 1916 by manoeuvrable machines with good climb—Halberstadt and Albatros D-types with 120 H.P. and subsequently 160 H.P. stationary engines. These D-aeroplanes were armed with two twin fixed machineguns, firing through the propeller.

The personnel of a *Jagdstaffel* was chosen with particular care. Only such pilots whose airmanship had already been proved reliable when with the reconnaissance flights could be recommended for training as fighter pilots. After a short course of practical training at the Grossenhain (Saxony) and Paderborn (Westphalia) single-seater fighter schools, these pilots passed for special training to the *Jagdstaffel* School near Valenciennes, which training was concluded in the *Jagdstaffeln* at the front.

Appendix 8

ROYAL FLYING CORPS STATISTICS FOR THE BATTLE OF THE SOMME [1]

1st July–17th November 1916.

Aeroplanes.

Serviceable on 1st July (of which 219 were artillery aeroplanes)	410 [2]
Serviceable on 17th November (of which 299 were artillery aeroplanes)	550
Struck off charge of squadrons	782
Missing	190
Completely rebuilt in depots	173
Returned to England in cases	178
Flown to England	57
Flown from England	867
Flown from Paris	139
Average rate of replacement in squadrons (per month)	10
Engines repaired at Pont de l'Arche	537

Pilots.

Available on 1st July	426
Available on 17th November	585
Killed, wounded, or missing	308
Struck off strength from all causes other than battle casualties	268

Observers.

Killed, wounded, or missing	191

Squadrons.

1st July	27
17th November	35

Balloons.

1st July	14
17th November	22

Wireless.

Ground stations at work	542
Operators on 1st July	689
Operators on 17th November	883
Casualties to operators	27
Aeroplanes fitted with	306

[1] These figures were compiled by Royal Flying Corps head-quarters immediately after the battle, and apply to all R.F.C. squadrons on the Western Front.

[2] The number actually on charge of the squadrons was 421.

Bombing.
  Raids with definite targets 298
  Number of bombs dropped 17,600
  Weight of bombs dropped . . . . 292 tons

Photography.
  Photographs taken 19,000
  Prints of photographs made 420,000

Artillery Co-operation.
  Targets registered with air observation . . . 8,612

Hostile aircraft.
  Destroyed 164
  Driven down damaged 205

Appendix 9

FUTURE POLICY IN THE AIR (SEPTEMBER 1916)

Since the beginning of the recent operations the fighting in the air has taken place over the enemy's line, and visits of hostile aeroplanes over our lines have been rare. It is to be hoped that this state of things may continue, but as one can never be certain of anything in war, it is perhaps an opportune moment to consider what policy should be adopted were this state of affairs to change, and were the enemy to become more enterprising and more aggressive.

It is sometimes argued that our aeroplanes should be able to prevent hostile aeroplanes from crossing the line, and this idea leads to a demand for defensive measures and a defensive policy. Now is the time to consider whether such a policy would be possible, desirable, and successful.

It is the deliberate opinion of all those most competent to judge that this is not the case, and that an aeroplane is an offensive and not a defensive weapon. Owing to the unlimited space in the air, the difficulty one machine has in seeing another, the accidents of wind and cloud, it is impossible for aeroplanes, however skilful and vigilant their pilots, however powerful their engines, however mobile their machines, and however numerous their formations, to prevent hostile aircraft from crossing the line if they have the initiative and determination to do so.

The aeroplane is not a defence against the aeroplane; but it is the opinion of those most competent to judge that the aeroplane, as a weapon of attack, cannot be too highly estimated.

A signal instance of this fact is offered to us by the operations which took place in the air at Verdun.

When the operations at Verdun began, the French had few machines on the spot. A rapid concentration was made, and a vigorous offensive policy was adopted. The result was that superiority in the air was obtained immediately, and the machines detailed for artillery co-operation and photography were enabled to carry out their work unmolested, but as new units were put into the line which had less experience of working with aeroplanes, a demand arose in some quarters for machines of protection, and these demands were for a time complied with. The result was that the enemy took the offensive, and the French machines were unable to prevent the hostile raids which the enemy, no longer being attacked, was now able to make.

The mistake was at once realised and promptly rectified. A policy of general offensive was once more resumed, and the enemy at once ceased to make hostile raids, all his time being taken up in fighting the machines which were attacking him. Superiority in the air was thus once more regained.

On the British front, during the operations which began with the Battle of the Somme, we know that, although the enemy had concentrated the greater part of his available forces in the air on this front, the work actually accomplished by their aeroplanes stands, compared with the work done by us, in the proportion of 4 to 100. From the accounts of prisoners, we gather that the enemy's aeroplanes have received orders not to cross the lines over the French or British front unless the day is cloudy and a surprise attack can be made, presumably in order to avoid unnecessary casualties.

On the other hand, British aviation has been guided by a policy of relentless and incessant offensive. Our machines have continually attacked the enemy on his side of the line, bombed his aerodromes, besides carrying out attacks on places of importance far behind the lines. It would seem probable that this has had the effect so far on the enemy of compelling him to keep back or to detail portions of his forces in the air for defensive purposes.

When Lille station was attacked from the air for the first time no hostile aeroplanes were encountered. The second time this place was attacked our machines encountered a squadron of Fokkers which were there for defensive purposes. This is only one instance among many.

The question which arises is this: Supposing the enemy, under the influence of some drastic reformer or some energetic leader, were now to change his policy and follow the example of the English and French, and were to cease using his aeroplanes as a weapon of defence and to start a vigorous offensive and attack as many places as far behind our lines as he could, what would be the sound policy to follow in such a case?

Should we abandon our offensive, bring back our squadrons behind the line to defend places like Boulogne, St. Omer, Amiens, and Abbeville, and protect our artillery and photographic machines with defensive escorts, or should we continue our offensive more vigorously than before Up to now the work done by the Germans compared with that done by our aeroplanes stands, as we have seen, in the proportion of 4 to 100; but let us suppose that the enemy initiated a partial offensive in the air, and that his work increased, compared with ours, to a proportion of 30 or 50 to 100, it is then quite certain that a demand for protective measures would arise for protective squadrons and machines for defensive patrols.

One of the causes of such demands is the moral effect produced by a hostile aeroplane, which is out of all proportion to the damage which it can inflict.

The mere presence of a hostile machine in the air inspires those on the ground with exaggerated forebodings with regard to what the machine is capable of doing. For instance, at one time on one part of the front, whenever a hostile machine, or what was thought to be a hostile machine, was reported, whistles were blown and men hid in the trenches. In such cases the machines were at far too great a height to observe the presence of men on the ground at all, and even if the presence of men was observed it would not lead to a catastrophe. Again, a machine which was reported in one place would certainly, since it was flying rapidly, be shortly afterwards observed in another part of the lines and reported again, but the result of these reports was often that for every time the machine was sighted a separate machine was reported, leading at the end of the day to a magnified and exaggerated total.

The sound policy then which should guide all warfare in the air would seem to be this: to exploit this moral effect of the aeroplane on the enemy, but not to let him exploit it on ourselves. Now this can only be done by attacking and by continuing to attack.

It has been our experience in the past that at a time when the Germans were doing only half the work done by our machines that their mere presence over our lines produced an insistent and continuous demand for protective and defensive measures.

If the Germans were once more to increase the degree of their activity even up to what constitutes half the degree of our activity, it is certain that such demands would be made again.

On the other hand, it is equally certain that, were such measures to be adopted, they would prove ineffectual. As long as a battle is being fought, any machine at the front has five times the value that the same machine would have far behind the lines.

If the enemy were aware of the presence of a defensive force in one particular spot he would leave that spot alone and attack another, and we should not have enough machines to protect all the places which could possibly be attacked behind our lines, and at the same time continue the indispensable work on the front.

But supposing we had enough machines both for offensive and defensive purposes. Supposing we had an unlimited number of machines for defensive purposes, it would still be impossible to prevent hostile machines from crossing the line if they were determined to do so, simply because the sky is too large to defend. At sea a number of destroyers will have difficulty in preventing a hostile destroyer, and still more a hostile submarine, from breaking the blockade. But in the air the difficulty of defence is still greater, because the area of possible escape is practically unlimited, and because the aeroplane is fighting in three dimensions.

The sound policy would seem to be that if the enemy changes his tactics and pursues a more vigorous offensive, to increase our offensive, to go farther afield, and to force the enemy to do what he would gladly have us do now. If, on the other hand, we were to adopt a purely defensive policy, or a partially offensive policy, we should be doing what the French have learnt by experience to be a failure, and what the rank and file of the enemy, by their own accounts, point to as being one of the main causes of their recent reverses.

Moreover, in adopting such a policy it appears probable that the Germans are guided by necessity rather than by choice, owing to the many fronts on which they now have to fight, and owing also to the quality and the quantity of machines they have to face on the Western Front alone. Nevertheless, one cannot repeat too often that in war nothing is certain, and that the Germans may, either owing to the pressure of public opinion, or the construction of new types of machines, or the rise of a new leader, change their policy at any moment for a more aggressive one.

Advanced Headquarters,
Royal Flying Corps,
22nd September 1916.

ALSO FROM LEONAUR
AVAILABLE IN SOFTCOVER OR HARDCOVER WITH DUST JACKET

THE 9TH—THE KING'S (LIVERPOOL REGIMENT) IN THE GREAT WAR 1914 - 1918 *by Enos H. G. Roberts*—Mersey to mud—war and Liverpool men.

THE GAMBARDIER *by Mark Severn*—The experiences of a battery of Heavy artillery on the Western Front during the First World War.

FROM MESSINES TO THIRD YPRES *by Thomas Floyd*—A personal account of the First World War on the Western front by a 2/5th Lancashire Fusilier.

THE IRISH GUARDS IN THE GREAT WAR - VOLUME 1 *by Rudyard Kipling*—Edited and Compiled from Their Diaries and Papers—The First Battalion.

THE IRISH GUARDS IN THE GREAT WAR - VOLUME 1 *by Rudyard Kipling*—Edited and Compiled from Their Diaries and Papers—The Second Battalion.

ARMOURED CARS IN EDEN *by K. Roosevelt*—An American President's son serving in Rolls Royce armoured cars with the British in Mesopatamia & with the American Artillery in France during the First World War.

CHASSEUR OF 1914 *by Marcel Dupont*—Experiences of the twilight of the French Light Cavalry by a young officer during the early battles of the great war in Europe.

TROOP HORSE & TRENCH *by R.A. Lloyd*—The experiences of a British Lifeguardsman of the household cavalry fighting on the western front during the First World War 1914-18.

THE EAST AFRICAN MOUNTED RIFLES *by C.J. Wilson*—Experiences of the campaign in the East African bush during the First World War.

THE LONG PATROL *by George Berrie*—A Novel of Light Horsemen from Gallipoli to the Palestine campaign of the First World War.

THE FIGHTING CAMELIERS *by Frank Reid*—The exploits of the Imperial Camel Corps in the desert and Palestine campaigns of the First World War.

STEEL CHARIOTS IN THE DESERT *by S. C. Rolls*—The first world war experiences of a Rolls Royce armoured car driver with the Duke of Westminster in Libya and in Arabia with T.E. Lawrence.

WITH THE IMPERIAL CAMEL CORPS IN THE GREAT WAR *by Geoffrey Inchbald*—The story of a serving officer with the British 2nd battalion against the Senussi and during the Palestine campaign.

AVAILABLE ONLINE AT **www.leonaur.com**
AND FROM ALL GOOD BOOK STORES

ALSO FROM LEONAUR
AVAILABLE IN SOFTCOVER OR HARDCOVER WITH DUST JACKET

ESCAPE FROM THE FRENCH *by Edward Boys*—A Young Royal Navy Midshipman's Adventures During the Napoleonic War.

THE VOYAGE OF H.M.S. PANDORA *by Edward Edwards R. N. & George Hamilton, edited by Basil Thomson*—In Pursuit of the Mutineers of the Bounty in the South Seas—1790-1791.

MEDUSA *by J. B. Henry Savigny and Alexander Correard and Charlotte-Adélaïde Dard*—Narrative of a Voyage to Senegal in 1816 & The Sufferings of the Picard Family After the Shipwreck of the Medusa.

THE SEA WAR OF 1812 VOLUME 1 *by A. T. Mahan*—A History of the Maritime Conflict.

THE SEA WAR OF 1812 VOLUME 2 *by A. T. Mahan*—A History of the Maritime Conflict.

WETHERELL OF H. M. S. HUSSAR *by John Wetherell*—The Recollections of an Ordinary Seaman of the Royal Navy During the Napoleonic Wars.

THE NAVAL BRIGADE IN NATAL *by C. R. N. Burne*—With the Guns of H. M. S. Terrible & H. M. S. Tartar during the Boer War 1899-1900.

THE VOYAGE OF H. M. S. BOUNTY *by William Bligh*—The True Story of an 18th Century Voyage of Exploration and Mutiny.

SHIPWRECK! *by William Gilly*—The Royal Navy's Disasters at Sea 1793-1849.

KING'S CUTTERS AND SMUGGLERS: 1700-1855 *by E. Keble Chatterton*—A unique period of maritime history-from the beginning of the eighteenth to the middle of the nineteenth century when British seamen risked all to smuggle valuable goods from wool to tea and spirits from and to the Continent.

CONFEDERATE BLOCKADE RUNNER *by John Wilkinson*—The Personal Recollections of an Officer of the Confederate Navy.

NAVAL BATTLES OF THE NAPOLEONIC WARS *by W. H. Fitchett*—Cape St. Vincent, the Nile, Cadiz, Copenhagen, Trafalgar & Others.

PRISONERS OF THE RED DESERT *by R. S. Gwatkin-Williams*—The Adventures of the Crew of the Tara During the First World War.

U-BOAT WAR 1914-1918 *by James B. Connolly/Karl von Schenk*—Two Contrasting Accounts from Both Sides of the Conflict at Sea During the Great War.

AVAILABLE ONLINE AT **www.leonaur.com**
AND FROM ALL GOOD BOOK STORES

www.ingramcontent.com/pod-product-compliance
Lightning Source LLC
Chambersburg PA
CBHW031306150426
43191CB00005B/105